Law and Anthropology

Blackwell Anthologies in Social and Cultural Anthropology

Series Editor: Parker Shipton, Boston University

Drawing from some of the most significant scholarly work of the nineteenth and twentieth centuries, the *Blackwell Anthologies in Social and Cultural Anthropology* series offers a comprehensive and unique perspective on the ever-changing field of anthropology. It represents both a collection of classic readers and an exciting challenge to the norms that have shaped this discipline over the past century.

Each edited volume is devoted to a traditional subdiscipline of the field such as the anthropology of religion, linguistic anthropology, or medical anthropology; and provides a foundation in the canonical readings of the selected area. Aware that such subdisciplinary definitions are still widely recognized and useful – but increasingly problematic – these volumes are crafted to include a rare and invaluable perspective on social and cultural anthropology at the onset of the twenty-first century. Each text provides a selection of classic readings together with contemporary works that underscore the artificiality of subdisciplinary definitions and point students, researchers, and general readers in the new directions in which anthropology is moving.

1 Linguistic Anthropology: A Reader *edited by Alessandro Duranti*
2 A Reader in the Anthropology of Religion *edited by Michael Lambek*
3 The Anthropology of Politics: A Reader in Ethnography, Theory, and Critique *edited by Joan Vincent*
4 Kinship and Family: An Anthropological Reader *edited by Robert Parkin and Linda Stone*
5 Law and Anthropology *edited by* Sally Falk Moore

Law and Anthropology

A Reader

Edited by

Sally Falk Moore

Blackwell Publishing

Editorial material and organization © 2005 by Blackwell Publishing Ltd

BLACKWELL PUBLISHING
350 Main Street, Malden, MA 02148-5020, USA
9600 Garsington Road, Oxford OX4 2DQ, UK
550 Swanston Street, Carlton, Victoria 3053, Australia

The right of Sally Falk Moore to be identified as the Author of the Editorial Material in this Work has been asserted in accordance with the UK Copyright, Designs, and Patents Act 1988.

First published 2005 by Blackwell Publishing Ltd

8 2011

Library of Congress Cataloging-in-Publication Data

Law and anthropology: a reader/edited by Sally Falk Moore.
    p. cm.
  Includes bibliographical references and index.
  ISBN 978-1-4051-0227-8 (alk. paper)–ISBN 978-1-4051-0228-5 (alk. paper)
  1. Law and anthropology. 2. Ethnological jurisprudence. I. Moore, Sally Falk, 1924-

  K487.A57L3815 2005
  340'. 115–dc22

                                                   2003026673
A catalogue record for this title is available from the British Library.

Typeset in Sabon on 10/12 pt
by Kolam Information Services Pvt. Ltd, Pondicherry, India

For further information on
Blackwell Publishing, visit our website:
http://www.blackwellpublishing.com

Contents

Acknowledgments

The editor and publishers wish to thank the following for permission to use copyright material:

Henkin, Louis, ed., 1981 *The International Bill of Rights*. New York: Columbia University Press.

Cowan, Jane K., Marie-Benedicte Dembour, and Richard Wilson eds., 2001 *Culture and Rights*. Cambridge: Cambridge University Press. Reproduced by permission of Cambridge University Press and the translators.

Montesquieu, Charles-Louis, 1989 [1748] *The Spirit of the Laws*. Ann M. Cohler, Basia Carolyn Miller, and Harold Samuel Stone, trans. Cambridge: Cambridge University Press. Reproduced by permission of Cambridge University Press and the translators.

Geertz, Clifford, 1983 *Local Knowledge*. New York: Basic Books.

Rouland, Norbert, 1994 *Legal Anthropology*. Philippe Plane, trans. Stanford: Stanford University Press. Translation copyright The Athlone Press 1994.

Morgan, Lewis Henry, 1963 [1877] *Ancient Society*. Eleanor Burke Leacock ed. Cleveland and New York: Meridian Books, The World Publishing Company.

Marx, Karl, 1956 *Selected Writings in Sociology and Social Philosophy*. T. B. Bottomore, trans. New York, Toronto, and London: Mcgraw-Hill Book Company. Reproduced by permission of The Mcgraw-Hill Book Company.

Newman, Katherine, 1983 *Law and Economic Organization*. Cambridge: Cambridge University Press. Reproduced by permission of Cambridge University Press and the author.

Durkheim, Emile 1933 *The Individual and Society, Collective Consciousness and Law*. New York: The Free Press of of Glencoe. Durkheim, Emile. Extracts reproduced and edited by permission of The Free Press, a Division of Simon and Schuster Adult Publishing Group from *The Division of Labor in Society* by Emile Durkheim, translated by George Simpson. Copyright © 1947, 1964 by The Free Press. All rights reserved.

Foucault, Michel, 1986 *Disciplinary Power and Subjection*. In *Power*. Steven Lukes, ed. New York: New York University Press. Reproduced by permission of New York University Press and Blackwell Publishing.

Galanter, Marc, 1989 *Law and Society in Modern India*. Delhi and Oxford: Oxford University Press. Reproduced by permission of Oxford University Press India, New Delhi.

Giddens, Anthony, 1991 *Modernity and Self-Identity*. Cambridge: Polity. Reproduced by permission of Polity Press and Stanford University Press www.sup.org.

Weber, Max, 1978 *Economy and Society*. Berkeley: University of California Press. Weber, extracts from *Economy and Society* translated/edited by Roth and Wittich, selection from pages 311–14, 316–17, 889–90, 1002–3. Copyright © 1978 The Regents of the University of California. Reproduced by permission of the University of California Press and Mohr Siebeck.

Habermas, Jürgen, 1984 *The Theory of Communicative Action*, vol. 1. Boston: Beacon Press. Habermas, Jürgen, extracts from *The Theory of Communicative Action, Volume 1: Reason and the Rationalization of Society*. Introduction and English translation copyright © 1984 by Beacon Press. German text: copyright © 1981 by Suhrkamp Verlag, Frankfurt am Main. Reprinted by permission of Beacon Press and Suhrkamp Verlag.

Lempert, Richard and Joseph Sanders, 1986 *Law and Social Science*. Philadelphia: University of Pennsylvania Press. Reproduced by permission of the University of Pennsylvania Press.

Rosen, Lawrence, 1980–81, Equity and Discretion in a Modern Islamic Legal System. *Law & Society Review*, 15(2).

Malinowski, Bronsiaw, 1926 *Crime and Custom in Savage Society* [S.I.]. Kegan Paul. Reproduced by permission of International Thomson Ltd.

Schapera, Isaac, 1955 *A Handbook of Tswana Law and Custom* London: Published for the International African Institute by the Oxford University Press. Reproduced by permission of the International African Institute.

Gluckman, Max, 1955 *The Judicial Process Among the Barotse of Northern Rhodesia*. Manchester: Manchester University Press on behalf of the Rhodes-Livingstone Institute, Northern Rhodesia. Reproduced by permission of the author's estate.

Bohannan, Paul, 1957 *Justice and Judgement Among the Tiv*. London: Oxford University Press for the International African Institute. Reproduced by permission of the International African Institute.

Pospisil, Leopold, 1971 *Kapauku Papuans and Their Law*. New Haven: Human Relations Area Files Press. Reproduced by permission of Human Relations Area Files Press.

Coombe, Rosemary, 1998 Objects of Property and Subjects of Politics. In *The Cultural Life of Intellectual Properties*. Rosemary Coombe, ed. Durham and London: Duke University Press. Copyright 1998 Duke University Press. All rights reserved. Used by permission of the publisher.

Cohen, Lawrence, 1999 Where it Hurts: Indian Material for an Ethics of Organ Transplantation. *Daedalus: The Journal of the American Academy of Arts and Sciences* 128(4). © 1999 by the American Academy of Arts and Sciences.

Ruffini, Julio L., 1978 Disputing over Livestock in Sardinia. *The Disputing Process: Law in Ten Societies*. Laura Nader and Harry F. Todd, eds. New York: Columbia University Press. Reproduced by permission of Columbia University Press.

Bowen, John R. 2000 Consensus and Suspicion: Judicial Reasoning and Social Change in and Indonesian Society 1960–1994. *Law and Society Review* 34(1).

Clifford, James 1988 Identity in Mashpee. In *The Predicament of Culture: Twentieth-Century Ethnography, Literature, and Art*. James Clifford, ed. Cambridge, MA and London: Harvard University Press. Clifford, James, Reprinted by permission of the publisher from "Identity in Mashpee" in *The Predicament of Culture: Twentieth-Century Ethnography, Literature, and Art* by James Clifford, pp. 277–343, Cambridge, MA: Harvard University Press, copyright © 1988, by the President and Fellows of Harvard College.

Darian-Smith, Eve, 1999 Locating a Reinvigorated Kentish Identity. In *Bridging Divides: The Channel Tunnel and the English Legal Identity in the New Europe*. Eve Darian-Smith. Berkeley and London: University of California Press. Reproduced by permission of The University of California Press.

Griffiths, Anne M. O., 1997 Academic Narratives: Models and Methods in the Search for Meanings. In *The Shadow of Marriage*. Anne M. O. Griffiths. Chicago and London: University of Chicago Press. Reproduced by permission of The University of Chicago Press and the author.

Wilson, Richard A., 2001 Human Rights and Nation Building. In *The Politics of Truth and Reconciliation in South Africa*. Richard A. Wilson. Cambridge, MA: Cambridge University Press. Reproduced by permission of Cambridge University Press and the author.

Merry, Sally Engle, 2001 Rights, Religion and Community: Approaches to Violence Against Women in the Context of Globalization. *Law and Society Review*, 35(1).

Winn, Jane Kaufman, 1994 Relational Practices and the Marginalization of Law: Informal Financial Practices of Small Businesses in Taiwan. *Law and Society Review*, 28(2).

Coutin, Susan Bibler, 1994 Enacting Law Through Social Practice: Sanctuary as a Form of Resistance. In *Contested States, Law Hegemony and Resistance*. Mindie

Lazarus-Black and Susan F. Hirsch, eds. New York and London: Routledge. "Enacting Law Through Social Practice: Sanctuary as a Form of Resistance" by Coutin, Susan Bibler, copyright ©1994 from *Contested States, Law Hegemony and Resistance* by Mindie Lazarus-Black and Susan F. Hirsch (eds). pp. 282–91, 299–303. Reproduced by permission of Routledge/Taylor & Francis Books Inc. and the author.

Gilboy, Janet A., 1991 Deciding Who Gets In: Decisionmaking by Immigration Inspectors. *Law and Society Review*, 25(3).

Eriksen, Thomas Hylland, 1997 Multiculturalism, Individualism and Human Rights: Romanticism: The Enlightenment and Lessons from Mauritius. *Human Rights, Culture and Context*. Richard A. Wilson, ed. London, Chicago, Illinois: Pluto Press. Reproduced by permission of Pluto Press.

Snyder, Francis, 1999 Governing Economic Globalization: Global Legal Pluralism and European Union Law. *European Law Journal* 5(3).

Nader, Laura, 1995 Civilization and Its Negotiations. *Understanding Disputes*. Pat Caplan, ed. Oxford and Providence Berg Publishers. Reproduced by permission of Berg Publishers.

Moore, Sally Falk, 2001 Certainties Undone: Fifty Turbulent Years of Legal Anthropology, 1949–1999. Huxley Memorial Lecture given by Sally Falk Moore. *Journal of the Royal Anthropological Institute* 7(1).

Every effort has been made to trace copyright holders and to obtain their permission for the use of copyright material. The authors and publishers will gladly receive any information enabling them to rectify any error or omission in subsequent editions.

General Introduction

What is an Anthropological Approach to Law?

An anthropological approach to law inquires into the context of enforceable norms: social, political, economic, and intellectual. This includes, but goes further than, what Western governments and courts define as law. In anthropology, while the "socio-legal" includes formal juridical institutions and their social surroundings, it also encompasses law-like activities and processes of establishing order in many other social domains, formal and informal, official and unofficial, in our own society and in others.

While the traditional project of anthropology has been the study of unfamiliar settings, today, that comparative perspective has informed new approaches to the familiar. Anthropologists now consider the socio-legal aspects of the modern state in two very different milieus: the unofficial but organized social sub-fields which exist within nation-states, and the transnational or global fields that criss-cross and transcend states, some of them official, some unofficial. What has been generally recognized is the fact that even in the West, formal, state-enforced law is by no means the only source of organized social order. Hence anthropologists have looked intensively at the contacts between state systems and the independently managed social fields within them. Inquiries are made into the way norms are generated, how mandatoriness is created, and how regularities are maintained.

On the large scale, anthropologists have looked at the networks of political and commercial transactions that transcend the ordinary jurisdictional range of the state. Attention is given to the legal and law-like orders involved in international, transnational, and global connections. These affect the affairs of states and their social fields, and vice versa. The most important characteristic of this plurality of normative loci, is that their locales and levels are interactive.

There have been many efforts to define "the legal" in some general, universally applicable way to encompass all of these variations. These definitions are continually being revised and re-imagined, but none are altogether satisfactory. For a learned critique of a recent, serious, try at this daunting, and perhaps unnecessary task by Brian Tamanaha, see William Twining 2003.

Legally oriented anthropologists have, on the whole, abandoned the definitional issue. Instead, anthropologists are likely to ask in some specific setting about power, control and justice: who makes the rules, who can undo them, how are they normalized and enforced, and how are they morally justified. In addition, they ask, what lies outside of the norm-governed domain and is open to individual or group improvisation? How does this optional domain of behavior intersect with the mandatory? How do people evade the norms and do they get away with it? In short, in social anthropology the domain of the normative is the point of entry into broad questions about regular and irregular social arrangements. It invites extensive and imaginative intellectual inquiries.

Anthropologists (and philosophers, and lawyers, and political theorists) have looked at different aspects of this intellectual problem in a great variety of places and times. This book is organized around the writings of three kinds of persons who have inquired into such questions. The first is a set of influential thinkers whose writings are part of the intellectual history of the West. Philosophers and lawyers, from Plato to Lewis Henry Morgan to Jürgen Habermas have written essays declaring with which matters law should occupy itself. They have supported their arguments with statements about how law has evolved.

In part I of this volume, interleaved with these writings are passages from the works of contemporary anthropologists that show that, though addressed differently, the same issues are still with us. The reader will soon perceive how speculative and generalizing the early commentaries are. Most are intensely concerned with what constitutes "good law," with ideas of morality in the abstract. They stand in contrast to the specific accounts of particular practices among particular peoples which anthropologists later provided.

Part II of this reader presents some instances of socio-legal practice observed by anthropologists in colonial settings. These observations were made in "the classical period" of ethnographic work. The anthropologists of that time were interested in constructing and reconstructing the pre-colonial system of "native law." They observed contemporary local affairs, discussed the past with their informants, and made conjectures about how the law-like aspects of the social system might once have worked before the time of colonial intervention. Their direct observations were often of disputes and the way conflicting claims were managed. They not only described indigenous practice, they sought to explain the logic of indigenous thought. They wanted to show that, if explained in their own terms, these law-like activities made practical and moral sense. On the whole, these ethnographic descriptions were non-judgmental, and did not much concern any abstract questions of justice.

The political context in which these ethnographies were produced affected their authors nonetheless. Some anthropologists were more, and some were less sympathetic to the colonial enterprise. European colonial governments felt empowered to alter local law to suit European ideas of rightness, the outlawing of slavery, and trials for witchcraft and the like, changes which they thought self-evidently appropriate. Colonial political domination was conceived as a civilizing mission. Not only the technical, but the moral and intellectual superiority of European civilization was assumed. This was congruent with an evolutionary conception of law in which the law of the industrial West was seen as the apogee of human achievement, to be emulated everywhere. Inevitably some of the interaction of the administration with anthropologists reflected the need for the colonial governments to know more about the people they were ruling. In British colonies the policy of indirect rule, and the establishment of formal courts under the aegis of the administration, required that the legal dimension be investigated. The relationship between colonial officials and anthropologists has been written about elsewhere (and hence will not be our concern here) but the fact of the relationship is one to bear in mind when reading the second part of this collection.

Part III, the largest part of this book, is a sampling of recent and present inquiries, and thus notes the powerful return of concerns with right and wrong. The anthropologists are seldom neutral observers of instances in which human rights are at issue, or gender discrimination is evident, or the exploitation of labor is apparent, let alone questions of corruption. Sometimes the political engagement of the observer is visible, sometimes the dilemmas of policy are apparent. The articles provide a glimpse of the wide range of topics currently touched on. From the cultural setting of the law of trademarks, to the sale of human organs for transplants, from the behavior of immigration inspectors to the many laws that impinge on the manufacture, assembling, and sale of Barbie dolls, from claims to Native American identity to the performance of reconciliation and revenge in post-apartheid South Africa, one begins to understand the vitality of the law and anthropology field today.

Political events and economic realities, not just normative rules, play a major part in the framing of the practices in these instances. What is clear is that the incapacities of the State are as apparent as the powers of the State. Local worlds are impinged on by global happenings. It does not go without saying that because something is the law, locally or internationally, it is obeyed.

Comparative questions emerge from inspecting the whole lot of these papers together, questions that many of the papers do not address directly: "Who is in control? Who is responsible for what? Could anyone take control? And to what end?" Anthropology is struggling to bring these profound issues to the surface by looking closely and specifically at attempts to define norms in different contexts.

Fieldwork: The Basic Technique

Today, anthropological fieldwork remains ideally the classical one of quite specific observation, inquiry, and interpretation, carried out either at a particular site or at multiple sites. The goal is to try to understand what is going on, and what it means to the actors, and to the collectivities in which they are embedded. The time and place can be anywhere: in industrialized society or in exotic islands, in the observed present or in the historically investigated past. It seems clear enough. But the reality is that many issues elude easy analysis. How much of the context must be established to fully understand any norm, legal or illegal, to say nothing of the intersection of many norms? Observing a moving, changing, social field, with multiple influences touching on it, and trying to make judgments about causality, about meanings, is a difficult affair. Nonetheless policy-makers and legislatures assume that they know what effects their actions will have. And formal law, a very self-conscious, self-defining field of activity, is chock full of explanations of itself. Anthropology asks, "How literally should such knowledge claims be taken?" This volume gives examples of the replies that anthropologists are currently offering, and the many and various sites where they look for answers.

REFERENCE

Twining, William, 2003 A Post-Westphalian Conception of Law. *Review of* Brian Tamanaha's *A General Jurisprudence of Law and Society*. A book review essay in *Law and Society Review* 37 (1). 199–257.

Part I
Early Themes That Reappear in New Forms

1

Plato, Augustine, Aquinas, and Others, Asking What Is Morally Right: Essays on Natural Law, Ideal Law, and Human Law

Introduction

In the history of the West debates about equality and liberty, about property and contract, about the individual and society, go back as far as the writings of Plato and Aristotle. It goes without saying that ideas about law were involved in those debates. Much of this literature concerns matters special to the period in which they were written. Nevertheless, what strikes the modern reader is the extent to which some of the ideas in the fourth century B.C. in ancient Greece have echoes in present philosophical thought.

Much of what Plato (427–327 B.C.) wrote was in dialogic form, ostensibly recording the views of his mentor, Socrates, as he posed questions to him. He sought answers about what is ideal, what is true and what is good. In *The Republic* he imagined a utopian commonwealth in which a philosopher-king of superior intellect would devote himself to discovering the ideal law, and then would impose it. The function of that law was to produce virtuous men. Plato was entirely aware of the profound distinction between the ideal and the actual world. However he thought that through reasoning he could discover the ideal, that major improvements could be made in society.

This theme continues in Aristotle (384–322 B.C.) who said, "Our purpose is to consider what form of political community is best of all for those who are most able to realize their ideal of life." And he asked "Should a well ordered state have all things, as far as may be, in common, or some only and not others?" (Aristotle, *Politics* 1943:80).

> Political Justice means justice as between free and . . . equal persons, living a common life for the purpose of satisfying their needs . . . we do not permit a man to rule, but the law, because a man rules in his own interest, and becomes a tyrant; but the function of a ruler is to be the guardian of

justice, and if of justice, then of equality...Political justice is of two kinds, one natural, the other conventional. A rule of justice is natural that has the same validity everywhere, and does not depend on our accepting it or not... Similarly the rules of justice ordained not by nature but by man are not the same in all places, since forms of government are not the same, though in all places there is only one form of government that is natural, namely, the best form. (Nichomachean *Ethics*, quoted in Morris 1971:21, 22).

Hundreds of years later, this dichotomy between the ideal law and actual practice came to have a Christian meaning. The ideal law was the Law of God. Saint Augustine (A.D. 354–430) contrasted the "city of God" with the "city of men." "The city of God is that mystical society of all those who, both now and in the hereafter, have accepted orthodox Christianity...On earth these societies are mixed, and it is only as a symbol that the church stands for the city of God" (Becker and Barnes 1961:243).

Saint Thomas Aquinas (A.D. 1225–1274) wrestled with the same thematic duality, but constructed more sophisticated categories in addressing it. "His social theories can best be approached through his doctrine of four-fold law: (1) *eternal law*, God's own will and purpose for the universe; (2) *natural law*, the progressive expression of this eternal law in reason; (3) *human law*, the application of natural law to human needs and the basis of the human social order, deriving its authority through conformity with natural law; and, (4) *divine law*, supplementing human reason and human law in regard to man's eternal destiny, salvation, as revealed in the sacred Scriptures" (Becker and Barnes, 1961:246). Harold J. Berman commented, "Law was seen as a way of fulfilling the mission of Western Christendom to begin to achieve the kingdom of God on earth" (Berman 1983:521).

By the time of Thomas Hobbes (1588–1679), the focus had shifted. Here the Law of Nature is, "a Precept, or generall Rule, found out by Reason" (Hobbes, *Leviathan* 1996:91). The condition of Man, "is a condition of Warre of every one against every one" and the Fundamental Law of Nature is to seek peace. The second Law is, "that a man be willing, when others are so too...to lay down this right to all things; and be contented with so much liberty against other men, as he would allow other men against himselfe" (Hobbes, *Leviathan* 1996: 92).

John Locke (1632–1704) also reasoned from the state of Nature in which men have perfect freedom to pursue their own interests, to the condition of Political Society where they have conceded that liberty to a collectivity. "Where-ever therefore any number of Men are so united into one Society, as to quit every one his Executive Power of the Law of Nature, and to resign it to the publick, there and there only is a *Political, or Civil Society*" (Locke 1996: 325).

Rousseau's (1712–1778) version of the same problem was to emphasize the consequence for individuals of the social contract, "by the social compact we have given the body politic existence and life: we have now by legislation to give it movement and will." He goes on to say, "All justice comes from God...but if we knew how to receive so high an inspiration, we should need neither government nor laws. Doubtless there is a universal justice emanating from reason alone; but this justice, to be admitted among us, must be mutual. Humanly speaking, in default of natural sanctions, the laws of justice are ineffective among men...Conventions and laws are therefore needed to join rights and duties and refer justice to its object ... In the state of society all rights are fixed by law ... Laws are, properly speaking, only the conditions of civil association" (quoted in Morris 1971:223, 224).

A compendium of selected quotations from some legal philosophers is no substitute for reading their works, but it gives us a glimpse of the background of current human rights arguments. The men quoted here are only a few of the many who have contributed to the development of Western thought on law and society. For an anthropologist, one of the more puzzling aspects of their reasoning is that Political Society is derived from a pre-existing, rather mythical, State of Nature. But this conjectural point of departure is not just a historical oddity. An analogous, abstract, theoretical proposition also can be found in John Rawls' "original position" (1971:12). Rawls allies himself to this tradition of reasoning and declares that, "In justice as in fairness the original position of equality corresponds to the state of nature in the traditional theory of the social contract. This original position is not, of course, thought of as an actual historical state of affairs, much less a primitive condition of culture. It is understood as a purely hypothetical situation characterized so as to lead to a certain conception of justice" (p. 12).

By contrast, anthropologists do not traffic in hypothetical original conditions. They do their fieldwork in existing living societies, observe local practices, and listen to explanations. The work of anthropology could not be further from this "original position" reasoning. Yet it is important to be aware of the resurgence of elements of this philosophical train of thought. Echoes can be heard in contemporary discussions of general legal principles, particularly those of universal application, as in discourse about human rights.

S.F.M

REFERENCES

Aristotle, 1943 *Politics*. Benjamin Jowett trans. New York: Modern Library Books.

Becker, Howard, and Harry Elmer Barnes, 1961 *Social Thought from Lore to Science*. 3rd edition. New York: Dover Books.

Berman, Harold, J., 1983 *Law and Revolution*. Cambridge, MA: Harvard University Press.

Hobbes, Thomas, (1651) 1996 *Leviathan*. Richard Tuck ed. Cambridge: University of Cambridge Press.

Locke, John, 1996 *Locke*. Peter Laslett ed. Cambridge: Cambridge University Press.

Morris, Clarence, ed., 1971 *The Great Legal Philosophers*. Philadelphia: University of Pensylvania Press.

Rawls, John, 1971 *A Theory of Justice*. Cambridge, MA: Harvard University Press.

Classic Themes in New Forms

The International Bill of Rights

Louis Henkin

Human rights is the idea of our time. It asserts that every human being, in every society, is entitled to have basic autonomy and freedoms respected and basic needs satisfied. These claims by every individual against his society are designated "rights," presumably in some moral order, perhaps under "natural law." The society has corresponding duties to give effect to these rights through domestic laws and institutions.

Today, the human rights idea is universal, accepted by virtually all states and societies regardless of historical, cultural, ideological, economic, or other differences. It is international, the subject of international diplomacy, law, and institutions. It is philosophically respectable, even to opposed philosophical persuasions.

From Louis Henkin (ed.) *The International Bill of Rights* (New York: Columbia University Press, 1981), p. 1.

Culture and Rights

Jane K. Cowan, Marie Benedicte Dembour, and Richard Wilson

RIGHTS AND CULTURE AS EMERGENT GLOBAL DISCOURSES

In the past few decades there has been a dramatic increase in negotiations between social groups of various kinds and political institutions, whether at the local, national or supra-national level, phrased in a language of 'rights'. Processes of globalization have led to rights discourses being adopted widely throughout the world, far from their original sites in the French and American revolutions. Just as importantly, they have framed new domains of political struggle, such as reproductive rights, animal rights and ecological rights. Constituting one historically specific way of conceptualizing the relations of entitlement and obligation, the model of rights is today hegemonic, and imbued with an emancipatory aura. Yet this model has had complex and contradictory implications for individuals and groups whose claims must be articulated within its terms.

However, despite the global spread of rights-based political values, the specificities of any particular struggle cannot be grasped empirically through a methodological focus on the local community alone. For in the process of seeking access to social goods (ranging from land, work and education to

From Jane K. Cowan, Marie Benedicte Dembour, and Richard Wilson (eds.) *Culture and Rights* (Cambridge: Cambridge University Press, 2001), pp. 1, 2, 20, 21, 22.

freedom of belief and recognition of a distinctive group identity) through a language of rights, claimants are increasingly becoming involved in legal and political processes that transcend nation-state boundaries. Our desire to explore the tensions between local and global formulations of rights leads us to consider in more detail the interplay between the languages and institutions at a multiple of levels, from the local through to the transnational.

A striking feature within the contemporary efflorescence of rights discourse is the increasing deployment of a rhetoric of 'culture'. We are particularly concerned with the implications of introducing 'culture' into rights talk. Although 'rights' and 'culture' have emerged as key-words of the late twentieth century, their relationship to each other, both historically and in the present, has been conceived in quite variable ways. Nancy Fraser (1997: 2) has identified the 'shift in the grammar of political claims-making' from claims of social equality to claims of group difference to be a defining feature of 'a post-socialist condition'. Yet this condition clearly draws on forms of activism and critique developed within civil society in the past four decades, particularly in North America and Europe.

CONCLUSION: TOWARDS BETTER THEORY AND PRACTICE

The cases in which rights and culture are mutually implicated have proliferated, emerging in the context of diverse local and national regimes and stymying the international community's efforts to deal with them coherently at the level of principle. It is therefore unlikely that any single model of the relationship between culture and rights, or between minority and majority rights, is going to be adequate for all cases, either normatively or analytically. Clearly, all of us, but especially those involved in advocating or adjudicating rights such as theorists, NGOs and legal and political institutions, need to become more sceptical about claims to culture, and to examine more closely the power relations and divisions they sometimes mask. At the same time, we need to be more cognizant of the role played by the law in essentializing categories and fixing identities, as a concomitant of its task of developing general principles to include, ideally, all possible cases. But the search for a single theory that would provide definitive guidance in all cases is quixotic, not only because of the existence of irreducible difference and contingency across contexts and situations, but also because it misconstrues what actually happens when universal principles are applied in the real world.

Finally, case studies such as those presented and analyzed here by anthropologists and sociologists enable a stronger grounding of the conversation between theory and practice. This is unquestionably a concern for theorists and activists alike. Claims around culture and rights show no sign of abating. To numberless activists and their communities, they provide a powerful, universally recognized language into which to translate – and validate – local struggles. There is a pressing need to develop approaches to such claims which are principled and theoretically informed, yet also sensitive to the contingencies and ambiguities that the world never ceases to offer up.

2

Charles-Louis Montesquieu: Law as an Expression of a Particular Cultural Complex

Introduction

The early importance of Natural Law thinking, and the universal implications it carried are evident. By no means have these ideas entirely disappeared. Today, both in religious contexts, and in secular talk about human rights, one can again identify universalist ideas.

The currency of this powerful conception serves to emphasize the importance of the work of a man who broke with the universalist tradition. We turn to Montesquieu's *The Spirit of the Laws* (A.D. 1748). Montesquieu (A.D. 1689–1755) had a radically different vision of law and government. He was wealthy, erudite and a major figure not only in Parisian society, but in Europe and in England where he lived for two years (1729–1731). His work was praised among others by David Hume, Adam Ferguson, and Adam Smith. He influenced the designers of the American Constitution. Not only did his work epitomize a pivotal change in thinking, a focus on law as man-made, but it also took into consideration the immense variety of legal systems generated in different parts of the world.

Many of his comparative pronouncements and reconstructions of history now seem fanciful, some of his remarks, quaint, some of them profoundly ill-informed. Some passages in which he expressed his opinion about the effect of climate on law are included below to illustrate aspects of his writings that are no longer taken seriously. But his way of thinking about legal diversity around the world, and his rejection of the idea of a universal natural law made an immense mark, and are the link between him and anthropology.

He developed a typology of political systems, distinguishing among monarchies, despotisms, and republics. And he made the case for democracy, for a free government of divided and balanced powers. In his view the goal of a modern government was political liberty. Considering that natural law and ecclesiastical thought were the background against which Montesquieu was writing, his achievement of an immense intellectual break with earlier work was remarkable, and was recognized as such. He emphasized the distinction between laws and "the spirit of the laws." Writing about the spirit of the laws was his project. That "spirit" was the composite product of many country-specific causes, from climate to demography, from what we might call "culture" to the purposes of the legislator.

S.F.M

Part 1, Book 1   *The Spirit of the Laws*
Charles-Louis Montesquieu

The object of war is victory; of victory, conquest; of conquest, preservation. All the laws that form the *right of nations* should derive from this principle and the preceding one.

All nations have a right of nations; and even the Iroquois, who eat their prisoners, have one. They send and receive embassies; they know rights of war and peace: the trouble is that their right of nations is not founded on true principles.

In addition to the right of nations, which concerns all societies, there is a *political right* for each one. A society could not continue to exist without a government. "*The union of all individual strengths,*" as Gravina aptly says, "forms what is called the POLITICAL STATE."[1]

The strength of the whole society may be put in the hands of *one alone* or in the hands of *many*.[2] Since nature has established paternal power, some have thought that government by one alone is most in conformity with nature. But the example of paternal power proves nothing. For, if the power of the father is related to government by one alone, then after the death of the father, the power of the brothers, or after the death of the brothers, the power of the first cousins, is related to government by many. Political power necessarily includes the union of many families.

It is better to say that the government most in conformity with nature is the one whose particular arrangement best relates to the disposition of the people for whom it is established.[3]

Individual strengths cannot be united unless all wills are united. *The union of these wills,* as Gravina again aptly says, *is what is called the* CIVIL STATE.[4]

Law in general is human reason insofar as it governs all the peoples of the earth; and the political and civil laws of each nation should be only the particular cases to which human reason is applied.

Laws should be so appropriate to the people for whom they are made that it is very unlikely that the laws of one nation can suit another.

Laws must relate to the nature and the principle of the government that is established or that one wants to establish, whether those laws form it as do political laws, or maintain it, as do civil laws.

From Charles-Louis de Secondat Montesquieu, *The Spirit of the Laws* [1748], tr. Ann M. Cohler, Basia Carolyn, Miller, and Harold Samuel Stone (Cambridge: Cambridge University Press, 1989), pp. xli, 8, 9, 231–3, 310, 311.

They should be related to the *physical aspect* of the country; to the climate, be it freezing, torrid, or temperate; to the properties of the terrain, its location and extent; to the way of life of the peoples, be they plowmen, hunters, or herdsmen; they should relate to the degree of liberty that the constitution can sustain, to the religion of the inhabitants, their inclinations, their wealth, their number, their commerce, their mores and their manners; finally, the laws are related to one another, to their origin, to the purpose of the legislator, and to the order of things on which they are established. They must be considered from all these points of view.

This is what I undertake to do in this work. I shall examine all these relations; together they form what is called THE SPIRIT OF THE LAWS.[5]

I have made no attempt to separate *political* from *civil* laws, for, as I do not treat laws but the spirit of the laws, and as this spirit consists in the various relations that laws may have with various things, I have had to follow the natural order of laws less than that of these relations and of these things.

I shall first examine the relations that laws have with the nature and the principle of each government, and, as this principle has a supreme influence on the laws, I shall apply myself to understanding it well; and if I can once establish it, the laws will be seen to flow from it as from their source. I shall then proceed to other relations that seem to be more particular.

NOTES

1   Giovanni Vincenzo Gravina, *Origine Romani juris* (1739), bk. 2, chap. 18, p. 160.
2   The eighteenth-century meaning of *plusieurs* was "many." The opposition is between "one" and "many," as between monarchies or despotisms and republics in Book 2.
3   *Il vaut mieux dire que le gouvernement le plus conforme à la nature est celui dont la disposition particulière se rapporte mieux à la disposition du peuple pour lequel il est établi.* No English word covers all the disparate topics Montesquieu joins with the word *disposition*.
4   Giovanni Vincenzo Gravina, *Origine Romani juris* (1739), bk. 3, chap. 7, footnote, p. 311.
5   Esprit des loix. Whenever possible, we translate *esprit* as "spirit," but "mind" and "wit" also appear.

Part 3, Book 14   On the Laws in their Relation to the Nature of the Climate

Chapter 1   The general idea

If it is true that the character[1] of the spirit and the passions of the heart are extremely different in the various climates, *laws* should be relative to the differences in these passions and to the differences in these characters.

Chapter 2   How much men differ in the various climates

Cold air[2] contracts the extremities of the body's surface fibers; this increases their spring and favors the return of blood from the extremities of the heart. It shortens these same fibers;[3] therefore, it increases their strength[4] in this way too. Hot air, by contrast, relaxes these extremities of the fibers and lengthens them; therefore, it decreases their strength and their spring.

Therefore, men are more vigorous in cold climates. The action of the heart and the reaction of the extremities of the fibers are in closer accord, the fluids are in a better equilibrium, the blood is pushed harder toward the heart and, reciprocally, the heart has more power. This greater strength should produce many effects: for example, more confidence in oneself, that is, more courage; better knowledge of one's superiority, that is, less desire for vengeance; a higher opinion of one's security, that is, more frankness and fewer suspicions, maneuvers, and tricks. Finally, it should make very different characters. Put a man in a hot, enclosed spot, and he will suffer, for the reasons just stated, a great slackening of heart. If, in the circumstance, one proposes a bold action to him, I believe one will find him little disposed toward it; his present weakness will induce discouragement in his soul; he will fear everything, because he will feel he can do nothing. The peoples in hot countries are timid like old men; those in cold countries are courageous like young men. If we turn our attention to the recent wars,[5] which are the ones we can best observe and in which we can better see certain slight effects that are imperceptible from a distance, we shall certainly feel that the actions of the northern peoples who were sent to southern countries[6] were not as fine as the actions of their compatriots who, fighting in their own climate, enjoyed the whole of their courage.

The strength of the fibers of the northern peoples causes them to draw the thickest juices from their food. Two things result from this first, that the parts of the chyle, or lymph,[7] being broad surfaced, are more apt to be applied to the fibers and to nourish them; and second, that, being coarse, they are less apt to give a certain subtlety to the nervous juice. Therefore, these people will have large bodies and little vivacity.

The nerves, which end in the tissue of our skin, are made of a sheaf of nerves. Ordinarily, it is not the whole nerve that moves, but an infinitely small part of it. In hot countries, where the tissue of the skin is relaxed, the ends of the nerves are open and exposed to the weakest action of the slightest objects. In cold countries, the tissue of the skin is contracted and the papillae compressed. The little bunches are in a way paralyzed; sensation hardly passes to the brain except when it is extremely strong and is of the entire nerve together. But imagination, taste, sensitivity, and vivacity depend on an infinite number of small sensations.

I have observed the place on the surface tissue of a sheep's tongue which appears to the naked eye to be covered with papillae. Through a microscope, I have seen the tiny hairs, or a kind of down, on these papillae; between these papillae were pyramids, forming something like little brushes at the ends. It is very likely that these pyramids are the principal organ of taste.

I had half of the tongue frozen; and, with the naked eye I found the papillae considerably diminished; some of the rows of papillae had even slipped inside their sheaths: I examined the tissue through a microscope; I could no longer see the pyramids. As the tongue thawed, the papillae appeared again to the naked eye, and, under the microscope, the little brushes began to reappear.

This observation confirms what I have said, that, in cold countries, the tufts of nerves are less open; they slip inside their sheaths, where they are protected from the action of external objects. Therefore, sensations are less vivid.

In cold countries, one will have little sensitivity to pleasures; one will have more of it in temperate countries; in hot countries, sensitivity will be extreme. As one distinguishes climates by degrees of latitude, one can also distinguish them by degrees of sensitivity, so to speak. I have seen operas in England and Italy; they are the same plays with the same actors: but the same music produces such different effects in the people of the two nations that it seems inconceivable, the one so calm and the other so transported.

It will be the same for pain; pain is aroused in us by the tearing of some fiber in our body. The author of nature has established that this pain is stronger as the disorder is greater; now it is evident that the large bodies and coarse fibers of the northern peoples are less capable of falling into disorder than the delicate fibers of the peoples of hot countries; therefore, the soul is less sensitive to pain. A Muscovite has to be flayed before he feels anything.

With that delicacy of organs found in hot countries, the soul is sovereignly moved by all that is related to the union of the two sexes; everything leads to this object.

In northern climates, the physical aspect of love has scarcely enough strength to make itself felt; in temperate climates, love, accompanied by a thousand accessories, is made pleasant by things that at first seem to be love but are still not love; in hotter climates, one lives for itself; if it is the sole cause of happiness; it is life.

Book 19, *Chapter 4   What the general spirit is*

Many things govern men: climate, religion, laws, the maxims of the government, examples of past things, mores, and manners; a general spirit is formed as a result.

To the extent that, in each nation, one of these causes acts more forcefully, the others yield to it. Nature and climate almost alone dominate savages; manners govern the Chinese; laws tyrannize Japan; in former times mores set the tone in Lacedaemonia; in Rome it was set by the maxims of government and the ancient mores.

Chapter 5   How careful one must be not to change the general spirit of a nation

If there were in the world a nation which had a sociable humor, an openness of heart; a joy in life, a taste, an ease in communicating its thoughts; which was lively, pleasant, playful, sometimes imprudent, often indiscreet; and which had with all that, courage, generosity, frankness, and a certain point of honor, one should avoid disturbing its manners by laws, in order not to disturb its virtues. If the character is generally good, what difference do a few faults make?

One could constrain its women, make laws to correct their mores, and limit their luxury, but who knows whether one would not lose a certain taste that would be the source of the nation's wealth and a politeness that attracts foreigners to it?

The legislator is to follow the spirit of the nation when doing so is not contrary to the principles of the government, for we do nothing better than what we do freely and by following our natural genius.

If one gives a pedantic spirit to a nation naturally full of gaiety, the state will gain nothing, either at home or abroad. Let it do frivolous things seriously and serious things gaily.

Chapter 6   *That one must not correct everything*

May we be left as we are, said a gentleman of a nation closely resembling the one of which we have just given an idea. Nature repairs everything. It has given us a vivacity capable of offending and one apt to make us inconsiderate; this same vivacity is corrected by the politeness it brings us, by inspiring us with a taste for the world and above all for commerce with women.

May we be left as we are. Our discretions joined to our harmlessness make unsuitable such laws as would curb our sociable humor.

Montesquieu's Foreword, p.xli

In order to understand the first four books of this work, one must note that what I call *virtue* in a republic is love of the homeland, that is, love of equality. It is not a moral virtue or a Christian virtue; it is *political* virtue, and this is the spring that makes republican government move, as *honor* is the spring that makes monarchy move. Therefore, I have called love of the homeland and of equality, *political virtue*.

NOTES

1 *Caractère* can mean mark or sign, trait, or a habitual way of acting and feeling. When Montesquieu uses *caractère*, he seems to mean a form or shape of the spirit, combining these meanings.
2 This is even visible: in the cold, one appears thinner.
3 It is known that it shortens iron.
4 We translate *force* as both "force" and "strength," as the context is more and less abstract.
5 The War of the Spanish Succession.
6 In Spain, for example.
7 In the eighteenth century these words referred to various body fluids, without the precise denotations they have in modern physiology.

Classic Themes in New Forms

Local Knowledge

Clifford Geertz

The realization that legal facts are made not born, are socially constructed, as an anthropologist would put it, by everything from evidence rules, courtroom etiquette, and law reporting traditions, to advocacy techniques, the rhetoric of judges, and the scholasticisms of law school education raises serious questions for a theory of administration of justice that views it as consisting, to quote a

From Clifford Geertz, *Local Knowledge* (New York: Basic Books, 1989), pp. 173, 214, 215, 216.

representative example, "of a series of matchings of fact-configurations and norms" in which either a "fact-situation can be matched with one of several norms" or "a particular norm can be...invoked by a choice of competing versions of what happened." If the "fact-configurations" are not merely things found lying about in the world and carried bodily into court, show-and-tell style, but close-edited diagrams of reality the matching process itself produces, the whole thing looks a bit like sleight-of-hand...the point here is that the "law" side of things is not a bounded set of norms, rules, principles, values, or whatever from which jural responses to distilled events can be drawn, but part of a distinctive manner of imagining the real. At base, it is not what happened, but what happens, that law sees; and if law differs, from this place to that, this time to that, this people to that, what it sees does as well.

[...]

The main approaches to comparative law – that which sees its task as one of contrasting rule structures one to the next and that which sees it as one of contrasting different processes of dispute resolution in different societies – both seem to me rather to miss this point: the first through an overautonomous view of law as a separate and self-contained "legal system" struggling to defend its analytic integrity in the face of the conceptual and moral sloppiness of ordinary life; the second through an overpolitical view of it as an undifferentiated, pragmatically ordered collection of social devices for advancing interests and managing power conflicts.[1] Whether the adjudicative styles that gather around the *Anschauungen* projected by *ḥaqq*, *dharma*, and *adat* are properly to be called "law" or not (the rule buffs will find them too informal, the dispute buffs too abstract) is of minor importance; though I, myself, would want to do so....They do not just regulate behavior, they construe it.

It is this imaginative, or constructive, or interpretive power, a power rooted in the collective resources of culture rather than in the separate capacities of individuals (which I would think in such matters to be, intrinsically anyway, about the same everywhere; I rather doubt there is a legal gene), upon which the comparative study of law, or justice, or forensics, or adjudication should, in my view, train its attention....Law, I have been saying, somewhat against the pretensions encoded in woolsack rhetoric, is local knowledge; local not just as to place, time, class, and variety of issue, but as to accent – vernacular characterizations of what happens connected to vernacular imaginings of what can. It is this complex of characterizations and imaginings, stories about events cast in imagery about principles, that I have been calling a legal sensibility. This is doubtless more than a little vague, but as Wittgenstein, the patron saint of what is going on here, remarked, a veridical picture of an indistinct object is not after all a clear one but an indistinct one. Better to paint the sea like Turner than attempt to make of it a Constable cow... Whatever the ultimate future holds – the universal reign of *gulag* justice or the final triumph of the market-mind – the proximate will be one not of a rising curve of legal uniformity, either across traditions or (something I have, so far, had rather to neglect here) within them, but their further particularization.

NOTE

1   For an excellent critical discussion of these two, as they call them, paradigms;
    which ends however by adopting a too little modified version of the second, see
    J. L. Comoroff and S. Roberts, *Rules and Processes: The Cultural Logic of Dispute
    in an African Context* (Chicago, 1981), pp. 5–21. For an example of the "rule
    centered" paradigm, see L. Pospisil, *Kapauku Papuans and their Laws* (New Haven,
    1958); for one of the "process centered," see Malinowski, *Crime and Custom in a
    Savage Society.*

3

Henry Maine: The Contrast between Archaic and Modern Law

Introduction

Scarcely more than a century after Montesquieu's *Spirit of the Laws* (1748), and only a few decades before the emergence of anthropology as a formal academic discipline, the Regius Professor of Law at Cambridge, Sir Henry Maine (1822–1888), wrote an enormously influential book, *Ancient Law* (1861). In it he attempted to lay out the difference between the legal conceptions found in "ancient communities" and those in "modern" society, i.e. in 19th-century England. He conceived of the difference in legal ideas as epitomizing an evolution from one social and intellectual condition to another. He later became the Legal Member of the Supreme Council of the Governor General in India, and Vice-Chancellor of the University of Calcutta. In 1869 he returned to England, and in 1871 published *Village Communities in the East and West*, in 1875, *Early History of Institutions*, and in 1883 *On Early Law and Custom*.

Like many 19th-century intellectuals, he was preoccupied with the difference between ancient and modern societies. For most of his examples he drew on classical and Roman law, not on any ethnographic data. He carried on important debates with other major writers, such as Lewis Henry Morgan and J. F. McLennan, particularly about his postulate that the initial stage of kinship organization must have been patrilineal. In support of his own patriarchal theory he also cited Darwin's *Descent of Man*.

Some of the historical sequences that he laid down had considerable influence, but that does not mean that they remain authoritative today. However, they give a picture of "archaic society" as he imagined it. He intended the major legal themes in *Ancient Law* to identify the characteristic movement of "progressive societies" from the archaic condition to the modern one. They are:

From Sentiment to Contract as the Basis of Social Cohesion

Maine contended that "True archaic communities are held together not by express rules, but by sentiment, or, we should perhaps say, by instinct" (1861, 1894:365). Kinship generated these sentiments naturally, the fiction of kinship induced them. Feudal societies were thus not truly archaic since they were bound together by contract.

From Family to Territory as the Basis of the Polity

All early societies, he said, thought of themselves as descended from a common ancestor. They thought of themselves as a kindred. Eventually the family was replaced by the principle of local contiguity (1861, 1894: 131, 132).

From Collective Family Property to Private Individual Property

"Far the most important passage in the history of private property is its gradual separation from the co-ownership of kinsmen" (1861, 1894:270).

From Tort to Crime

"Now the penal law of ancient communities is not the law of Crimes; it is the law of Wrongs, or, to use the English technical word, of Torts. The person injured proceeds against the wrong-doer by an ordinary civil action and recovers compensation in the shape of money damages if he succeeds" (1861, 1894:370).

From Status to Contract, from Kinship to the Individual as the Basis of Rights

"In the constitution of primitive society the individual creates for himself few or no duties" (1861, 1894:311). The rules he obeys stem from the station into which he was born and the commands of the chief of the household.

"The unit of an ancient society was the family, of a modern society, the individual" (1861, 1894:126).

"The movement of progressive societies has been uniform in one respect. Through all its course it has been distinguished by the gradual dissolution of family dependency, and the growth of individual obligation in its place" (1861, 1894:168). "Starting, as from one terminus of history, from a condition of society in which all the relations of Persons are summed up in the relations to Family, we seem to have steadily moved towards a phase of social order in which all these relations arise from the free agreement of individuals" (1861, 1894:169). "All the forms of Status taken notice of in the Law of Persons were derived from ... the powers and privileges anciently residing in the Family. If then we employ Status ... to signify these personal conditions only ... we may say that the movement of the progressive societies has hitherto been a movement from Status to Contract" (1861, 1894:170).

What is noteworthy about this very famous passage is that the phrase "status to contract" is seldom understood to mean what Maine intended. In archaic society one's legal situation was originally determined by place in the family, later, in modern society, negotiated by oneself. Status is often misunderstood to mean standing in the community, or some such thing. There are many other summary pronouncements in *Ancient Society*, too many to summarize here. The ones cited are sufficient to give a sense of the major outlines of Maine's thought on this subject. And these become important later on in anthropology because of the attention Gluckman gave to the project of reconstructing the law of "an archaic society" from fieldwork evidence gathered in Africa in the 1940s.

S.F.M.

REFERENCE

Maine, Sir Henry, 1894[1861] *Ancient Law*. London: John Murray

Classic Themes in New Forms

Criticism of Maine's Theory

Norbert Rouland

According to Henry Sumner Maine, contractual obligationships are characteristic of modern societies. In traditional societies it is the status of the individual within society and the groups which make up society which determine obligations, privileges and responsibilities – not the will of individuals....

Criticism of Maine's theory began in 1950 when it was called into question by the anthropologist Robert Redfield. Redfield took Maine to task for his reliance on Greek, Roman and Indian sources, and for having believed, following evolutionist thinking, that this data could be directly extrapolated to traditional societies which could still be observed. In 1964 Hoebel pursued this analysis. In common with Durkheim, he believed that status and contract were not mutually exclusive, but existed in different degrees.

In 1981 Leopold Pospisil went further in arguing, principally, that the classic evolutionist model should be stood on its head: contract could precede status. Pospisil used the Kapauku (New Guinea) as an example. In the pre-colonial era Kapauku society was characterized by the high degree of initiative and personal liberty accorded to its members. Colonization witnessed the transformation of this society towards the status model; a central power was put in place, which restricted individual liberty.

From Norbert Rouland, *Legal Anthropology*, tr. Philippe Planel (Stanford: Stanford University Press, 1994, pp. 228–9.

What, in conclusion, do we make of Maine's ideas and the subsequent criticism of them? In our view, three points emerge. On the one hand, historical and ethnographic observation demonstrates that it is impossible to find societies which conform exclusively to either the status or contract model: Durkheim and Hoebel were right in stressing that the two modes coexisted in all societies. However, it is also the case that in general each society is characterized by the dominance of one model over the other. This dominance, evolutionist thinking to the contrary, is not chronologically determined. As Pospisil has stated, status can follow contract. Our century offers many examples of such developments: on a number of occasions totalitarian or authoritarian regimes have succeeded democratic systems, determining the rights and duties of individuals principally on the basis of class. Social organization rather than historical inevitability determines the primacy of contract or status. The former is emphasized in politically conservative modern societies [*sociétés libérales*], where groups tend to be accorded less prominence than individuals. The latter enjoys a dominant position in two types of society: first, communal societies – this applies to traditional societies, particularly sub-Saharan African societies; second, collectivist societies – many modern dictatorships.

None the less, even in traditional societies, contractual obligations always exist in some form.

4

Lewis Henry Morgan: Evolutionist, Ethnographer, Lawyer

Introduction

Quite early in his life, Lewis Henry Morgan became committed to studying the Iroquois, a Native American people who, like Morgan, lived in northern New York State. When he was a young man, Morgan joined a fraternity, and, as he wanted its ceremonies to be modeled on Iroquoian rituals, he investigated them in detail. This preoccupation grew. The fraternity ultimately became a serious historical society one of whose aims was to record all the customs of the Iroquois before those disappeared.

In the course of collecting this ethnographic material, Morgan met Ely Parker, a remarkable member of the Seneca branch of the Iroquois. They became fast friends. Parker joined Morgan's fraternity, and helped him to gather information. Morgan's enthusiasm for the Iroquois eventually led to his representing them in an important legal case. A land company was trying to obtain a large piece of the Iroquois reservation by treaty. Morgan and Parker went to Washington together to try to prevent this. They put the Iroquois side of the issue before many senators. Their intervention was successful. They persuaded the senators not to ratify the treaty. Morgan's reward was to be adopted into an Iroquois clan in 1846. As time went on, Parker, too, had a remarkable career, and eventually became Grant's Commissioner of Indian Affairs.

Morgan, like many of his contemporaries, was interested in social evolution. He thought that in the Iroquois political structure he had discovered a remarkable and early form of democracy. He was also struck by the difference between the Iroquois method of designating kin and our own. He thought their classification represented an earlier stage of the social evolution of the family. He would explore this further.

Morgan traveled a good deal representing railroad interests. In the course of his travels he had contact with other Native American peoples. He noticed that the Chippewa, who spoke a different language from the Iroquois, classified their kinspersons the way the Iroquois did. He then wrote to all the Indian Agents in the US to find out if all Native American peoples classified their kin the same way. He met a missionary who had worked with the Tamils in southern India and found they had the same classification. Morgan then extended his researches, and with the help of the State Department, sent out questionnaires all over the world. He thought he had uncovered a major clue to the whole history of humankind.

By combining his information about kinship terminology with a theory of property, Morgan rationalized his data into a huge theoretical scheme that, for him, and many others whom he influenced, would explain the evolutionary path followed by human societies. His key idea was that there were two types of kinship terminology. One type (which included the Iroquois) grouped certain relatives together under the same term, the other type distinguished members of the same category of kin, and identified them by separate terms. These two types of kin namings he called classificatory kinship terms and descriptive kinship terms. He thought classificatory systems were earlier, descriptive systems more advanced. He inferred that the classificatory system was connected with communal property, the descriptive system with private property. Moreover, in his scheme the two kinship terminologies were associated with two forms of government, ancient society, which was kin-based, political society which was territorially based.

He published a number of books (including a study of *The American Beaver and His Works* (1868) whose industry he admired), several resulting from his work with the Iroquois, and a technical one on worldwide kinship terms. However, his magnum opus was published in 1877, and it was entitled *Ancient Society or Researches in the Lines of Human Progress from Savagery through Barbarism to Civilization*. Unlike Maine, he was convinced that matriarchal society was the original form. This book was the basis on which Friedrich Engels wrote *The Origin of the Family, Private Property and the State* (1884). Morgan was read by Karl Marx, and by many early anthropologists, and theorists of the evolution of society. Some of its information has proven to be inaccurate, and some of its logical constructs are deeply flawed, but the problems *Ancient Society* addressed inspired many intellectuals for a very long time, and the link between law and property that Morgan emphasized remains central.

S.F.M.

REFERENCES

Engels, Friedrich, 1942[1884] *The Origin of the Family, Private Property and the State*. New York: International Publishers.
Morgan, Lewis Henry, 1868 *The American Beaver and His Works*. Philadelphia: Lippincott.
—— 1964[1877] *Ancient Society*. Cambridge, MA: Belknap.

The Historical Place of Property

Lewis Henry Morgan

Independently of the movement which culminated in the patriarchal family of the Hebrew and Latin types property, as it increased in variety and amount, exercised a steady and constantly augmenting influence in the direction of monogamy. It is impossible to overestimate the influence of property in the civilization of mankind. It was the power that brought the Aryan and Semitic nations out of barbarism into civilization. The growth of the idea of property in the human mind commenced in feebleness and ended in becoming its master passion. Governments and laws are instituted with primary reference to its creation, protection and enjoyment. It introduced human slavery as an instrument in its production; and, after the experience of several thousand years, it caused the abolition of slavery upon the discovery that a freeman was a better property-making machine. The cruelty inherent in the heart of man, which civilization and Christianity have softened without eradicating, still betrays the savage origin of mankind, and in no way more pointedly than in the practice of human slavery, through all the centuries of recorded history. With the establishment of the inheritance of property in the children of its owner, came the first possibility of a strict monogamian family. Gradually, though slowly, this form of marriage, with an exclusive cohabitation, became the rule rather than the exception; but it was not until civilization had commenced that it became permanently established.

[...]

During the Later Period of barbarism a new element, that of aristocracy, had a marked development. The individuality of persons, and the increase of wealth now possessed by individuals in masses, were laying the foundation of personal influence. Slavery, also, by permanently degrading a portion of the people, tended to establish contrasts of condition unknown in the previous ethnical periods. This, with property and official position, gradually developed the sentiment of aristocracy, which has so deeply penetrated modern society, and antagonized the democratical principles created and fostered by the gentes. It soon disturbed the balance of society by introducing unequal privileges, and degrees of respect for individuals among people of the same nationality, and thus became the source of discord and strife...

Property and office were the foundations upon which aristocracy planted itself.

Whether this principle shall live or die has been one of the great problems with which modern society has been engaged through the intervening periods. As a question between equal rights and unequal rights, between equal laws and unequal laws, between the rights of wealth, of rank and of official position, and the power of justice and intelligence, there can be little doubt of the ultimate result. Although several thousand years have passed away without the overthrow of privileged classes, excepting in the United States, their burdensome character upon society has been demonstrated.

From Lewis Henry Morgan, *Ancient Society*, Eleanor Burke Leacock, ed. (Cleveland and New York: Meridian Books and The World Publishing Company (1877) 1963), pp. 511–12, 560, 561, 562.

Since the advent of civilization, the outgrowth of property has been so immense, its forms so diversified, its uses so expanding and its management so intelligent in the interests of its owners, that it has become, on the part of the people, an unmanageable power. The human mind stands bewildered in the presence of its own creation. The time will come, nevertheless, when human intelligence will rise to the mastery over property, and define the relations of the state to the property it protects, as well as the obligations and the limits of the rights of its owners. The interests of society are paramount to individual interests, and the two must be brought into just and harmonious relations. A mere property career is not the final destiny of mankind, if progress is to be the law of the future as it has been of the past ... Democracy in government, brotherhood in society, equality in rights and privileges, and universal education, foreshadow the next higher plane of society to which experience, intelligence and knowledge are steadily tending. It will be a revival, in a higher form, of the liberty, equality and fraternity of the ancient gentes ... A common principle of intelligence meets us in the savage, in the barbarian, and in civilized man. It was in virtue of this that mankind were able to produce in similar conditions the same implements and utensils, the same inventions, and to develop similar institutions from the same original germs of thought. There is something grandly impressive in a principle which has wrought out civilization by assiduous application from small beginnings; from the arrow head, which expresses the thought in the brain of a savage, to the smelting of iron ore, which represents the higher intelligence of the barbarian, and, finally, to the railway train in motion, which may be called the triumph of civilization.

5

Karl Marx: The Mode of Production at the Base – Law as Part of the Superstructure

Introduction

Marx's ideas are well known and much commented on. For him the economy was the basis of societal structure. The mode of production, the means of production, the social relations of production, were the core. He read Lewis Henry Morgan, and constructed his own sketchy version of a theory of the evolution of society which was not published in his lifetime (Hobsbawm, ed., 1964). His close associate, Friedrich Engels, worked out a more finished version of that "history" based on Morgan. Engels' *The Origin of the Family, Private Property and the State* (1884) was published after Marx's death. The book on *Law and Economic Organization* by Katherine Newman (1983) quoted here shows that some anthropologists have found many of these ideas fruitful and have produced their own revised versions of an evolutionary sequence.

A vast literature has formed around Marx's oeuvre. His ideas had considerable influence in anthropology where the spectacle of the colonial experience, even more than the dilemmas of the working class, stimulated sympathetic analysis. Marx's general theoretical approach certainly shaped the thinking of many of those interested in law. Marx's own words quoted here, more or less explain his position. He always saw law as being in the hands of those whose interests it expressed. But in his scheme of things, law was a secondary phenomenon, part of the superstructure, which in his view, claimed causal significance for itself that it did not have.

For recent anthropology, in addition to his economic ideas, Marx's most influential views were those about the social unconscious, the capacity of human beings to deny underlying economic realities and to become preoccupied with the surface representations of culture and practice. This theme was taken up by Pierre Bourdieu who wrote ethnography in a Marxist-influenced vocabulary, making much of cultural "misrecognition" and of "social capital" (1977). Bourdieu wrote on law using this approach to analyze "the sociology of the juridical field," (1987). What follows here are some key quotations from Marx himself that are pertinent to law.

Selected Writings

Karl Marx

I was led by my studies to the conclusion that legal relations as well as forms of State could neither be understood by themselves, nor explained by the so-called general progress of the human mind, but that they are rooted in the material conditions of life, which are summed up by Hegel after the fashion of the English and French writers of the eighteenth century under the name *civil society*, and that the anatomy of civil society is to be sought in political economy.

In the social production which men carry on they enter into definite relations that are indispensable and independent of their will; these relations of production correspond to a definite stage of development of their material powers of production. The totality of these relations of production constitutes the economic structure of society – the real foundation, on which legal and political superstructures arise and to which definite forms of social consciousness correspond. The mode of production of material life determines the general character of the social, political and spiritual processes of life. It is not the consciousness of men that determines their being, but, on the contrary, their social being determines their consciousness.

At a certain stage of their development, the material forces of production in society come in conflict with the existing relations of production, or – what is but a legal expression for the same thing – with the property relations within which they had been at work before. From forms of development of the forces of production these relations turn into their fetters. Then occurs a period of social revolution. With the change of the economic foundation the entire immense superstructure is more or less rapidly transformed. In considering such transformations the distinction should always be made between the material transformation of the economic conditions of production which can be determined with the precision of natural science, and the legal, political, religious, æsthetic or philosophical – in short ideological, forms in which men become conscious of this conflict and fight it out. Just as our opinion of an individual is not based on what he thinks of himself, so can we not judge of such a period of transformation by its own consciousness; on the contrary, this consciousness must rather be explained from the contradictions of material life, from the existing conflict between the social forces of production and the relations of production. . . .

From Karl Marx, *Selected Writings in Sociology and Social Philosophy*, tr. T. B. Bottomore (New York, Toronto, and London: McGraw-Hill Book Company, 1956), pp. 51–2, 78, 79, 147, 223, 225–7.

The ideas of the ruling class are, in every age, the ruling ideas: i.e. the class which is the dominant *material* force in society is at the same time its dominant *intellectual* force. The class which has the means of material production at its disposal, has control at the same time over the means of mental production, so that in consequence the ideas of those who lack the means of mental production are, in general, subject to it. The dominant ideas are nothing more than the ideal expression of the dominant material relationships, the dominant material relationships grasped as ideas, and thus of the relationships which make one class the ruling one; they are consequently the ideas of its dominance. The individuals composing the ruling class possess among other things consciousness, and therefore think. In so far, therefore, as they rule as a class and determine the whole extent of an epoch, it is self-evident that they do this in their whole range and thus, among other things, rule also as thinkers, as producers of ideas, and regulate the production and distribution of the ideas of their age. . . .

The social relations within which individuals produce, *the social relations of production, are altered, transformed, with the change and development of the material means of production, of the forces of production. The relations of production in their totality constitute what is called the social relations, society,* and, moreover, a society at a definite stage of historical development, a society with a unique and distinctive character. Ancient society, feudal society, bourgeois (or capitalist) society, are such totalities of relations of production, each of which denotes a particular stage of development in the history of mankind.

Capital also is a social relation of production. It is a *bourgeois relation of production*, a relation of production of bourgeois society. The means of subsistence, the instruments of labour, the raw materials, of which capital consists – have they not been produced and accumulated under given social conditions, within definite social relations? Are they not employed for new production, under given social conditions, within definite social relations? And does not just this definite social character stamp the products which serve for new production as *capital*?

Capital consists not only of means of subsistence, instruments of labour, and raw materials, not only of material products: it consists just as much of *exchange values*. All products of which it consists are *commodities*. Capital, consequently, is not only a sum of material products, it is a sum of commodities, of exchange values, of social magnitudes. . . .

Since the State is the form in which the individuals of a ruling class assert their common interests, and in which the whole civil society of an epoch is epitomized, it follows that the State acts as an intermediary for all community institutions, and that these institutions receive a political form. Hence the illusion that law is based on will, and indeed on will divorced from its real basis – on *free* will. Similarly, law is in its turn reduced to the actual laws.

Civil law develops concurrently with private property out of the disintegration of the natural community. Among the Romans the development of private property and civil law had no further industrial and commercial consequences because their whole mode of production remained unchanged. Among modern peoples, where the feudal community was disintegrated by industry and trade, a new phase began with the rise of private property and civil law, which was capable of further development . . .

It should not be forgotten that law has not, any more than religion, an independent history...

In historical fact the theorists who considered *force* as the basis of law were directly opposed to those who saw *will* as the basis of law.... If force is taken to be the basis of law, as by Hobbes, law and legislative enactments are only a symptom or expression of *other* conditions upon which the State power rests. The material life of individuals, which certainly does not depend on their mere "will," their mode of production and their form of intercourse, which reciprocally influence each other, are the real basis of the State. This material life is, at every stage in which the division of labour and private property are still necessary, quite independent of the *will* of individuals. These real conditions are not created by the State power; they are rather the power which creates it. The individuals who rule under these conditions, quite apart from the fact that their power has to constitute itself as a State, must give their will, as it is determined by these definite circumstances, a general expression as the will of the State, as law. The content of this expression is always determined by the situation of this class, as is most clearly revealed in the civil and criminal law. Just as the bodily weight of individuals does not depend upon their ideal will or caprice, so it does not depend on them whether they embody their own will in law, and at the same time, in accordance with individual caprice give everyone beneath them his independence. Their individual domination must at the same time form a general domination. Their individual power rests upon conditions of existence which develop as social conditions and whose continuance they must show to involve their own supremacy and yet be valid for all. Law is the expression of this will conditioned by their common interests. It is just the striving of independent individuals and their wills, which on this basis are necessarily egoistic in their behaviour to each other, which makes self denial through law and regulation essential, or rather self denial in exceptional cases and maintenance of their interest in general.... The same holds good for the subject classes, on whose will the existence of law and the State is equally little dependent.

Crime, i.e. the struggle of the single individual against the dominant conditions, is as little the product of simple caprice as law itself. It is rather conditioned in the same way as the latter. The same visionaries who see in law the rule of an independent and general will see in crime a simple breaking of the law. The State does not rest on a dominating will, but the State which arises out of the material mode of life of individuals has also the form of a dominating will. If this will loses its domination this means not only that the will has changed but also that the material existence and life of individuals has changed despite their will.

We have already seen how, through the activity of philosophers, a history of pure thought could arise by the separation of thought from the individuals and their actual relations which are its basis. In the present case, also, law can be separated from its real basis, and thereby we can arrive at a "ruling will" which in different periods has a different expression and which, in its creations, the laws, has its own independent history. By this means political and civil history is ideologically transformed into a history of the dominance of self-developing laws.

GI (1845–6)
MEGA I/5, pp. 307–9

Classic Themes in New Forms

Law and Economic Organization

Katherine Newman

KARL MARX AND FRIEDRICH ENGELS: LAW AND HISTORICAL MATERIALISM

There is a long and varied tradition of Marxist writings on law and legal development. Marx and Engels themselves never provided a complete theory of law, but rather expressed their views on law in the process of discussing larger philosophical and historical themes. As a result, writers in the Marxian tradition have been confronted with numerous fragmentary passages on law in Marx's and Engels's writings, which they have synthesized in an attempt to build a Marxist theory of law. However, since the fragments themselves are not entirely consistent, room has been left open for divergent interpretations, all of which may legitimately claim the imprimatur of Marx and Engels.

One of the more heated controversies to emerge from the recent literature concerns the extent to which Marx and Engels argued for a "determinist" view of law in relation to economic forces. This problematic has traditionally been addressed by quoting passages that stress the dependence of superstructural institutions upon the system of material production, as in the following well-known excerpt:

> The sum total of [the] relations of production constitutes the economic structure of society, the real foundation, on which rises a legal and political superstructure and to which correspond definite forms of social consciousness. (Marx in Tucker 1972:4)

An extreme determinist reading of this statement would suggest that the agenda, form, and content of law are directly derived from the economic relations of production, with no reciprocal causation admitted. The metaphor of "reflection" characterizes this position.

Although it seems reasonable to interpret Marx as believing that economic relations between classes determine the nature of property in any given society, and that this in turn defines the core areas of law, one can also find statements that indicate an understanding of the reciprocal effect, whereby law molds social development:

> According to the materialist conception of history, the *ultimately* determining factor in history is the production and reproduction of real life.... If somebody twists this into saying that the economic factor is the *only* determining one, he transforms that proposition into a meaningless, abstract, absurd phrase. The

From Katherine Newman, *Law and Economic Organization* (Cambridge: Cambridge University Press, 1983), pp. 17–25.

economic situation is the basis, but the various elements of the superstructure...
such as constitutions... juridical forms... political, legal, philosophical theories
... also exercise their influence... There is an interaction of all these elements in
which... the economic movement is finally bound to assert itself. (Engels to
Bloch, in Cain and Hunt 1979:56)

Whichever reading was actually intended by Marx and Engels, contemporary
Marxist scholars have advanced the view that superstructural institutions exist
in reciprocal interaction. Each has a certain causal influence on the others, but
retains a degree of independence.

The most influential proponent of this position is Louis Althusser (1969),
who identifies three levels of social structure (or "instances," as he terms
them): the *economic*, the *political*, and the *ideological*. In different modes of
production, different "instances" will be dominant, that is, will play the major
causal role. Nevertheless, each instance is "relatively autonomous." We take
this to mean that each develops its own idiom and institutional form. Similarly,
according to Althusser, each instance has its own history, that is, its own logic
of development.

Although Althusser admits that the economy is "determinant in the last
instance," he has clearly diverged from the more traditional reading of Marx
and Engels, which lays much greater emphasis on economic causation. The
Althusserian image seems to be one whereby each area of social structure *sets
limits* for the others, but the content and form of each remains at least partially
autonomous.

In discussing law, Althusserian or Structural Marxists argue that:

Law is always under the control of the ruling class in the broad sense but it does
not *always* originate in economic class conflict, function well for the ruling class,
reflect the full range of ruling class opinion, remain immune from the lawyers and
bureaucrats who administer it, or serve economic ends. (Sumner 1979:255)

The actors who shape the law are not necessarily economic classes, nor is the
agenda of law limited to the regulation of economic relations. However,
whatever the degree of relative autonomy between law and economy, it is
nevertheless clear that the Marxian paradigm as it was originally articulated
posits a strong relation between the two realms. These relations are perhaps
best understood in terms of the functions of law from the perspective of
historical materialism.

Marx and Engels discussed three principal functions of law: ideological,
political, and economic. These realms are always intertwined in the texts
themselves; I separate them here for the purposes of analytic clarity.

Ideologies are sets of concepts and beliefs that describe and explain the
world. Within the Marxian framework, ideologies are typically viewed as
representing the position of a particular class in society and as such tend to
be incomplete or biased systems of knowledge. Law may be seen as a form of
ideology that describes social relationships and expresses a social morality.
(See Sumner 1979 for a thorough treatment of this issue.)

As an ideological system, law performs in two ways. On the one hand, it legitimates the social order by presenting existing social relationships as normal, desirable, and just. On the other hand, according to Marx and Engels, law also fulfills an ideological function by obscuring and mystifying the true nature of social relations. Through doctrinal language, it presents an image of "legal man" detached from his foundations and stripped of his reality as "economic man." Law describes and guarantees a social realm of equality and liberty for all, which is *false* insofar as it ignores underlying socioeconomic inequalities. For example, the law regards an employment contract as an agreement freely concluded by two equal parties (employer and employee), whereas Marx argued that the propertyless laborer is *coerced* into selling his labor, given his inability to subsist any other way. The employer is *not* equal to the worker; in practice the former sets his own terms. Engels made a similar point with respect to the marriage contract: It obscures and disguises the subordination of wives. Law hides these realities behind the seemingly universal language of contract and as such is performing an ideological function.

Law is also ideological insofar as it represents people as isolated individuals – the citizen – rather than as members of classes. It is precisely one's inclusion in such groups that Marx argued determines one's social existence. Law therefore obscures relationships or conflicts between classes by presenting them as connections between individuals.

The second function of law in the Marxian tradition concerns its political role. Law is viewed as an instrument by which classes struggle to improve their lot vis-à-vis others. In most cases, the ruling classes will have the greatest access to law as a tool for furthering their interests. Marx described the Enclosure Acts, the Vagrancy Statutes, wage-reduction legislation, and the like as instances whereby property owners utilized the legal process to confiscate land, force the idle to work, and push down wages. Analyzing a series of statutes from the thirteenth century on, Marx showed that their cumulative effect was the creation of a landless proletariat (Marx 1970:672–93).

However, those in power are not the only actors seeking to use the law for their own ends. The role of law in the political arena is also seen in the struggle of nondominant classes to improve their living conditions by placing legal limitations on their opponents. Marx's discussion in *Capital* of the workers' struggle to enforce a maximum workday is an example of this latter type.

It is important to note that this "instrumentalist" reading of the political functions of law has been subject to considerable criticism by subsequent Marxist theorists, including Pashukanis (1978), Cain and Hunt (1979), and Sumner (1979). As Greenburg and Anderson (1981:295) put it, "instrumentalism exaggerates the extent of direct ruling class control over law." These objections are addressed to a position that overstates the influence of *one group* over the legal apparatus. However, most adherents to the Marxist tradition would agree that the law is an arena of struggle between groups and that particular laws can be read in many cases (though not all) as expressing the outcome of such conflicts. In this sense, law fulfills a political function.

Law also plays a crucial role or function in the economic realm. For Marx and Engels, social inequality flows from unequal access to basic resources, which are expressed in terms of property law. By defining and guaranteeing the rights of property owners, law regulates basic relationships between individuals. Another aspect of this involves the legal regulation of labor, either by contract or by traditional rules regarding pay, hours, and the mutual obligations obtaining between employers and employees.

All important economic relationships from the factory to the family find their expression in legal doctrine, which in turn guarantees a stable basis for economic production. As Engels put it:

> At a certain, very primitive stage of the development of society, the need arises to bring under a common rule the daily recurring acts of production, distribution and exchange of products, to see to it that the individual subordinates himself to the common conditions of production and exchange. This rule, which at first is custom, soon becomes *law*. (Quoted in Cain and Hunt 1979:55)

As this sketch indicates, Marx and Engels believed that law cross-cuts the ideological, political, and economic realms. Particular laws may address any or all three of these.

We will now turn to the theory of legal development they proposed. From their general perspective of historical materialism, Marx and Engels argued that in any given society legal change follows on the heels of developments in the economic mode of production. The best-known statement to this view is found in the preface to *A Contribution to the Critique of Political Economy*:

> At a certain stage of their development, the material productive forces of society come in conflict with the existing relations of production, or – what is but a legal expression of the same thing – with the property relations within which they have been at work hitherto . . . With the change of the economic foundation the entire immense superstructure is more or less rapidly transformed. (Marx in Tucker 1972:4)

As the forces of production develop, Marx and Engels suggested that the legal and political superstructure would eventually fetter the productive forces. Revolution would follow, which would overhaul the legal relations in society, once again bringing about a correspondence between the material foundation and the superstructure.

Marx and Engels did not elaborate this theory of legal change beyond this general formulation. It was left to later theorists, such as Karl Renner, to apply this framework. Renner was a Marxist scholar writing in the early 1900s. His book, *The Institutions of Private Law and Their Social Functions* (1949), is a classic work in the Marxist theory of legal development, although it is much criticized (cf. Sumner 1979:248–9; Cain and Hunt 1979:65). In it, Renner argued that an adequate understanding of the relationship between law and economy *cannot* be based on static studies of one historical period. Only by considering the connections between these two realms in the context of historical change can an adequate understanding be developed (Renner 1949:58). Renner's theory of legal evolution is based upon an examination of the transformations in law and society that took place between two important historical epochs: independent commodity production and early capitalism.

Renner's theory of legal change is explicitly analogous to one of the central tenets of Marx's theory of social change; namely, that the forces of production develop faster and therefore "out-distance" the social relations of production, finally coming into contradiction with them. Renner argued that:

> The historical development of the law, and the growth of individual laws and their decay, flow from the disparate development of the legal and economic institutions...The change in the social functions of legal institutions takes place in a sphere beyond the reach of the law and eventually necessitates a transformation of the norms of the law. (Renner 1949:52)

Renner presented a three-stage developmental model of legal change. The first stage consists of a point in time when law "matches" the social and economic circumstances from which it originates. During the second stage, transformations take place in the economic sphere (particularly in the organization of production), while the content of legal norms *does not* undergo any noticeable transformation. However, though the law itself has not altered, its social *functions* have undergone a drastic transformation: Preexisting legal doctrines combine to fulfill the social functions required by the new economic situation. The third stage of Renner's theory is the least explicated. He suggested that, over the long run, legal norms undergo a transformation in content such that they again correspond to the economic circumstances of their time.

Renner's discussion of transitions in property law provides an example of this thesis. In the age of simple commodity production, people owned their own means of production, sold their products directly to consumers, and were the owners of their homes and land. It was at this stage that the Roman law of *dominium* was adopted, which specified that individuals had the right "to free and unfettered control over tangible things." At the same time, a companion law emerged that allowed independent producers to purchase raw materials and sell finished products: the norm of free contract. Renner suggested that, at this point "the world of norms was...fully adapted to the substratum, the world of facts."

Gradually, however, simple commodity production gave way to classical capitalism. The independent producer became a wage laborer. He no longer owned the means of production: it owned him. He occupied his house as a tenant rather than as an owner. Despite these socioeconomic changes, the content of the law remained unchanged. How were these structural transformations dealt with by the law? Renner answered that the laws of property and contract were combined to accommodate the new arrangement. Workers themselves became "property" in the sense that the capitalists could now own their labor power.

> But what is control of property in law, becomes in fact man's control of human beings, of the wage laborers...We see that the right of ownership thus assumes a new social function. Without any change in the norm,...a *de facto* right is added

to the personal absolute domination over a corporeal thing. This right is not based upon a special legal provision. It is the power of control, the power to issue commands and to enforce them. (Renner 1949:107)

One reading of Marx would lead the researcher to look for transformations in the institutional structures or substantive content of law as one economic epoch gives way to the next. In contrast, Renner suggested that an analysis of changing *functions* of legal doctrines rather than institutional structures will provide a better understanding of the transformation of law.

The Marxist theories outlined in this section derived from studies of law under capitalism (or from the transition between feudalism and capitalism). Hobsbawm (1965:20) has pointed out that Marx's interest in preindustrial epochs was directed more toward understanding them as crucibles of emerging bourgeois society than analyzing them for their own sake. What light, if any, does the Marxist theory of legal development then shed on the evolution of legal institutions in precapitalist or preindustrial cultures? I would argue that by using the general approach of historical materialism, one can anticipate what a Marxist anthropology of law would look like. Marx and Engels argued that each mode of production contained within itself a distinctive set of superstructural institutions (including law), which were an integral part of the reproduction of that mode of production. Thus, if we examine the successive epochs of human history as distinct modes of production, we should expect to find particular forms of political and juridical systems associated with them. Although this observation is not made explicit in the two works that deal with precapitalist societies (*The Origin of the Family, Private Property, and the State* [Engels 1942] and *Pre-Capitalist Economic Formations* [Marx 1965]), shadows of the theory are visible therein.

In the Preface to the first edition of *The Origin of the Family*, Engels (1942:5) noted that the "materialistic conception" of history posits the production and reproduction of life's immediate essentials as the determining factor shaping social life in any given period. The production of food and clothing, dwellings, and tools constitutes one part of this, whereas the reproduction of human beings themselves composes the other. Thus the "stage of development of labor on the one hand and of the family on the other" determines "the social organization under which the people of a particular historical epoch live" (Engels 1942:5).

According to Engels, societies characterized by low levels of labor organization (i.e., hunters and gatherers) are able to produce nothing more than what they require for subsistence. Wealth distinctions are unknown, for accumulation of any kind is unknown. The social order of such societies is "dominated by kinship groups" (Engels 1942:6). Engels took Morgan's (1912) description of American Indians as a case in point: With an economy based on the sexual division of labor and hunting technology, individuals own their means of production and households are communally organized.

Blood revenge and war constitute the only means for settling conflict in these societies. There is "no place for ruler or ruled" (Engels 1942:144). Participation in public affairs is required of all. To modern ears, the equation of blood revenge with participatory democracy is curious. Nevertheless, Engel's larger point is that where individuals control their means of production, they also have equal access to juridical life, such as it is. They confront public life unmediated by separate, specialized institutions of law and government.

At a subsequent stage of social development, the productivity of labor increases and "private property and exchange, differences of wealth [and] the possibility of utilizing the labor power of others," follows. Engels (1942:6) traced this transformation through pastoral, horticultural, and agrarian forms of production. He connected the emergence of slavery to the increased demands for labor wrought by these new technologies and argued that classes begin to emerge as property rights to land and control over slave labor develop. Hereditary military leaders arise to defend the privileges of the rich from the demands of the poor, and their existence lays the foundation for a hereditary nobility and monarchy (Engels 1942:150).

Amid these class-based cleavages, the old society based on kinship dissolves and "in its place appears a new society, with its control centered in the State" (Engels 1942:6), organized on the basis of territoriality rather than blood ties. Taxation is instituted to support a "public force" that bolsters state power. Class antagonisms bring forth "armed men,... prisons and coercive institutions of all kinds" (Engels 1942:156). The state arises "in the thick of the fight between the classes," but it is dominated by the economically powerful, who cultivate political control through the exercise of state authority.

Although Engels refrained from discussing law per se within this framework, legal institutions are clearly meant to be associated with the emergence of the state. Equally clear, I would argue, is the thrust of his argument: Such superstructural institutions as law that stand between the disadvantaged many and the privileged few grow and become elaborated as a result of improvements in the productive capacity of a society, the consequent growth in economic surplus, and the resulting class antagonisms. The state, and the legal apparatus that supports it, is necessary to control these internal conflicts and to regulate property and labor relations.

The theory of legal development sketched in this section is far less elaborated than Marx and Engels's general theory of precapitalist society. Both theories are weakened by the poor quality of the data that formed the basis of their original arguments. However, an approach similar to theirs will be taken up with modern techniques and more reliable data sources in Chapter 3.

REFERENCES

Althusser, Louis. 1969. *For Marx*. Harmondsworth, England: Allen Lane.

Cain, Maureen, and Alan Hunt. 1979. *Marx and Engels on Law*. London: Academic Press.

Engels, Friedrich. 1942. *The Origin of the Family, Private Property and the State*. New York: International Publishers.

Greenberg, David, and Nancy Anderson. 1981. Recent Marxisant books on law: a review essay. *Contemporary Crises* 5:293–322.

Marx, Karl. 1965. *Pre-Capitalist Economic Formations*. New York: International Publishers.

Marx, Karl. 1970. *Capital*, vol. 1. London: Lawrence and Wishart.

Morgan, Lewis H. 1912. Ancient Society. Chicago: Charles H. Kerr and Co.

Pashukanis, Evgenii. 1978. *Law and Marxism: A General Theory*. London: Ink Links.

Renner, Karl. 1949. *The Institutions of Private Law and Their Social Functions*. London: Routledge & Kegan Paul.

Sumner, Colin. 1979. *Reading Ideologies: An Investigation into the Marxist Theory of Ideology and Law*. London: Academic Press.

Tucker, Robert, ed. 1972. *The Marx-Engels Reader*. New York: Norton.

Emile Durkheim: Collective Consciousness and Law

Introduction

Emile Durkheim (1848–1917), was one of the founders of modern sociological theory. While his views have been very much amended and revised by his successors, his vision of society remains a fundamental reference point for subsequent work. He wrote four major books: *The Division of Labor in Society* (1893), *The Rules of Sociological Method* (1895), *Suicide* (1897), and *The Elementary Forms of the Religious Life* (1912). His basic theoretical scheme involved a conception of the individual as largely a socially determined being. The most important commonality in a society was a form of *conscience collective* (collective consciousness), a set of common beliefs and sentiments and normative ideas which all members shared. Thus individuals were only partly unique beings. They were in a large part formed by the social values and ideas that they had internalized. These had moral authority for the individual who would feel guilty if he/she did not conform to them, but many of these values were also externally enforced. The *social facts* that composed this normative system were to be the object of sociological study.

In *The Division of Labor in Society* (1893) he generated an evolutionary theory of law and legal sanctions. He used no ethnographic data, but produced this purely as a theoretical construct. The ethnographic data would not have supported his evolutionary theory, which existed largely in his own imagination. Nevertheless, the theory is of interest because of the way he developed his argument, and the attention it received in the literature. The more viable parts of the argument raise an important question, namely to what extent the notion of the *conscience collective* can be sustained in complex societies in the face of the divisive implications of the division of labor.

Other modern considerations also imply that a common *conscience collective* is only pertinent to particular sub-groups in the contemporary world. In the attached readings this is obliquely remarked on by Galanter with respect to law in modern India, and by Giddens with regard to modern identities.

On Law

Emile Durkheim

Social solidarity is a completely moral phenomenon which, taken by itself, does not lend itself to exact observation nor indeed to measurement. To proceed to this classification and this comparison, we must substitute for this internal fact which escapes us an external index which symbolizes it and study the former in the light of the latter...

Indeed, social life, especially where it exists durably, tends inevitably to assume a definite form and to organize itself, and law is nothing else than this very organization in so far as it has greater stability and precision.[18] The general life of society cannot extend its sway without juridical life extending its sway at the same time and in direct relation. We can thus be certain of finding reflected in law all the essential varieties of social solidarity...

Our method has now been fully outlined. Since law reproduces the principal forms of social solidarity, we have only to classify the different types of law to find therefrom the different types of social solidarity which correspond to it. It is now probable that there is a type which symbolizes this special solidarity of which the division of labor is the cause. That found, it will suffice, in order to measure the part of the division of labor, to compare the number of juridical rules which express it with the total volume of law...

To proceed scientifically, we must find some characteristic which, while being essential to juridical phenomena, varies as they vary. Every precept of law can be defined as a rule of sanctioned conduct. Moreover, it is evident that sanctions change with the gravity attributed to precepts, the place they hold in the public conscience, the role they play in society. It is right, then, to classify juridical rules according to the different sanctions which are attached to them.

They are of two kinds. Some consist essentially in suffering, or at least a loss, inflicted on the agent. They make demands on his fortune, or on his honor, or on his life, or on his liberty, and deprive him of something he enjoys. We call them repressive. They constitute penal law. It is true that those which are attached to rules which are purely moral have the same character, only they are distributed in a diffuse manner, by everybody indiscriminately, whereas those in penal law are applied through the intermediary of a definite organ; they are organized. As for the other type, it does not necessarily imply suffering for the agent, but consists only of *the return of things as they were*, in the reestablishment of troubled relations to their normal state, whether the incriminated act is restored by force to the type whence it deviated, or is annulled, that is, deprived of all social value. We

From Emile Durkheim, *The Individual and Society: Collective Consciousness and Law* (New York: The Free Press of Glencor, 1933), pp. 64–5, 68–9, 109, 111, 129–31, 169–70, 181–2, 200, 226–8.

must then separate juridical rules into two great classes, accordingly as they have organized repressive sanctions or only restitutive sanctions. The first comprise all penal law; the second, civil law, commercial law, procedural law, administrative and constitutional law, after abstraction of the penal rules which may be found there...

There exists a social solidarity which comes from a certain number of states of conscience which are common to all the members of the same society...In determining what fraction of the juridical system penal law represents, we, at the same time, measure the relative importance of this solidarity...

The very nature of the restitutive sanction suffices to show that the social solidarity to which this type of law corresponds is of a totally different kind.

What distinguishes this sanction is that it is not expiatory, but consists of a simple *return in state*. Sufferance proportionate to the misdeed is not inflicted on the one who has violated the law or who disregards it; he is simply sentenced to comply with it. If certain things were done, the judge reinstates them as they would have been. He speaks of law; he says nothing of punishment. Damage-interests have no penal character; they are only a means of reviewing the past in order to reinstate it, as far as possible, to its normal form...

In the first, what we call society is a more or less organized totality of beliefs and sentiments common to all the members of the group: this is the collective type. On the other hand, the society in which we are solidary in the second instance is a system of different, special functions which definite relations unite...

The first can be strong only if the ideas and tendencies common to all the members of the society are greater in number and intensity than those which pertain personally to each member. It is as much stronger as the excess is more considerable. But what makes our personality is how much of our own individual qualities we have, what distinguishes us from others. This solidarity can grow only in inverse ratio to personality. There are in each of us, as we have said, two consciences: one which is common to our group in its entirety, which, consequently, is not ourself, but society living and acting within us; the other, on the contrary, represents that in us which is personal and distinct, that which makes us an individual...

The social molecules which can be coherent in this way can act together only in the measure that they have no actions of their own, as the molecules of inorganic bodies. That is why we propose to call this type of solidarity mechanical...

It is quite otherwise with the solidarity which the division of labor produces. Whereas the previous type implies that individuals resemble each other, this type presumes their difference. The first is possible only in so far as the individual personality is absorbed into the collective personality; the second is possible only if each one has a sphere of action which is peculiar to him; that is, a personality...

It is right, then, to classify juridical rules according to the different sanctions which are attached to them.

They are of two kinds. Some consist essentially in suffering, or at least a loss, inflicted on the agent. They make demands on his fortune, or on his honor, or on his life, or on his liberty, and deprive him of something he enjoys. We call them repressive. They constitute penal law. It is true that those which are attached to rules which are purely moral have the same character, only they are distributed in a diffuse manner, by everybody indiscriminately, whereas those in penal law are applied through the intermediary of a definite organ; they are organized. As for the other type, it does not necessarily imply suffering for the agent, but consists only of *the return of things as they were*, in the reestablishment of troubled relations to their normal state, whether the incriminated act is restored by force to the type whence it deviated, or is annulled, that is, deprived of all social value. We must then separate juridical rules into two great classes, accordingly as they have organized repressive sanctions or only restitutive sanctions.* The first comprise all penal law; the second, civil law, commercial law, procedural law, administrative and constitutional law, after abstraction of the penal rules which may be found there . . .

But, if there is one truth that history teaches us beyond doubt, it is that religion tends to embrace a smaller and smaller portion of social life. Originally, it pervades everything; everything social is religious; the two words are synonymous. Then, little by little, political, economic, scientific functions free themselves from the religious function, constitute themselves apart and take on a more and more acknowledged temporal character. God, who was at first present in all human relations, progressively withdraws from them; he abandons the world to men and their disputes. At least, if he continues to dominate it, it is from on high and at a distance, and the force which he exercises, becoming more general and more indeterminate, leaves more place to the free play of human forces. The individual really feels himself less *acted upon*; he becomes more a source of spontaneous activity. In short, not only does not the domain of religion grow at the same time and in the same measure as temporal life, but it contracts more and more. This regression did not begin at some certain moment of history, but we can follow its phases since the origins of social evolution. It is, thus, linked to the fundamental conditions of the development of societies, and it shows that there is a decreasing number of collective beliefs and sentiments which are both collective enough and strong enough to take on a religious character. That is to say, the average intensity of the common conscience progressively becomes enfeebled . . .

There is, then, a social structure of determined nature to which mechanical solidarity corresponds. What characterizes it is a system of segments homogeneous and similar to each other.

II

Quite different is the structure of societies where organic solidarity is preponderant.

They are constituted, not by a repetition of similar, homogeneous segments, but by a system of different organs each of which has a special role, and which are themselves formed of differentiated parts . . .

This social type rests on principles so different from the preceding that it can develop only in proportion to the effacement of that preceding type. In effect, individuals are here grouped, no longer according to their relations of lineage, but according to the particular nature of the social activity to which they consecrate themselves. Their natural milieu is no longer the natal milieu, but the occupational milieu . . .

It is true that in the industrial societies that Spencer speaks of; just as in organized societies, social harmony comes essentially from the division of labor. It is characterized by a co-operation which is automatically produced through the pursuit by each individual of his own interests. It suffices that each individual consecrate himself to a special function in order, by the force of events, to make himself solidary with others . . .

The following propositions sum up the first part of our work. Social life comes from a double source, the likeness of consciences and the division of social labor. The individual is socialized in the first case, because, not having any real individuality, he becomes, with those whom he resembles, part of the same collective type; in the second case, because, while having a physiognomy and a personal activity which distinguishes him from others, he depends upon them in the same measure that he is distiguished from them, and consequently upon the society which results from their union.

The similitude of consciences gives rise to juridical rules which, with the threat of repressive measures, impose uniform beliefs and practices upon all. The more pronounced this is, the more completely is social life confounded with religious life, and the nearer to communism are economic institutions.

The division of labor gives rise to juridical rules which determine the nature and the relations of divided functions, but whose violation calls forth only restitutive measures without any expiatory character.

Each of these bodies of juridical rules is, moreover, accompanied by a body of purely moral rules. Where penal law is very voluminous, common morality is very extensive; that is to say, there is a multitude of collective practices placed under the protection of public opinion. Where restitutive law is highly developed, there is an occupational morality for each profession . . .

Men cannot live together without acknowledging, and, consequently, making mutual sacrifices, without tying themselves to one another with strong, durable bonds. Every society is a moral society. In certain respects, this character is even more pronounced in organized societies. Because the individual is not sufficient unto himself, it is from society that he receives everything necessary to him, as it is for society that he works. Thus is formed a very strong sentiment of the state of dependence in which he finds himself. He becomes accustomed to estimating it at its just value, that is to say, in regarding himself as part of a whole, the organ of an organism. Such sentiments naturally inspire not only mundane sacrifices which assure the regular development of daily social life, but even, on occasion, acts of complete self-renunciation and whole sale abnegation. On its side, society learns to regard its members no longer as things over which it has rights, but as co-operators whom it cannot neglect and towards whom it owes duties. Thus, it is wrong to oppose a society which comes from a community of beliefs to one which has a co-operative basis, according only to the first a moral character, and seeing in the latter only an economic grouping. In reality, co-operation also has its intrinsic morality. There is, however, reason to believe, as we shall see later, that in contemporary societies this morality has not yet reached the high development which would now seem necessary to it.

Classic Themes in New Forms

Disciplinary Power and Subjection

Michel Foucault

When we say that sovereignty is the central problem of right in Western societies, what we mean basically is that the essential function of the discourse and techniques of right has been to efface the domination intrinsic to power in order to present the latter at the level of appearance under two different aspects: on the one hand, as the legitimate rights of sovereignty, and on the other, as the legal obligation to obey it. The system of right is centred entirely upon the King, and it is therefore designed to eliminate the fact of domination and its consequences.

My general project over the past few years has been, in essence, to reverse the mode of analysis followed by the entire discourse of right from the time of the Middle Ages. My aim, therefore, was to invert it, to give due weight, that is, to the fact of domination, to expose both its latent nature and its brutality. I then wanted to show not only how right is, in a general way, the instrument of this domination – which scarcely needs saying – but also to show the extent to which, and the forms in which, right (not simply the laws but the whole complex of apparatuses, institutions and regulations responsible for their application) transmits and puts in motion relations that are not relations of sovereignty, but of domination. Moreover, in speaking of domination I do not have in mind that solid and global kind of domination that one person exercises over others, or one group over another, but the manifold forms of domination that can be exercised within society. Not the domination of the King in his central position, therefore, but that of his subjects in their mutual relations: not the uniform edifice of sovereignty, but the multiple forms of subjugation that have a place and function within the social organism.

The system of right the domain of the law, are permanent agents of these relations of domination, these polymorphous techniques of subjugation. Right should be viewed, I believe, not in terms of a legitimacy to be established, but in terms of the methods of subjugation that it instigates...

Power must be analysed as something which circulates, or rather as something which only functions in the form of a chain. It is never localized here or there, never in anybody's hands, never appropriated as a commodity or piece of wealth. Power is employed and exercised through a net-like organization. And not only do individuals circulate between its threads; they are always in the position of simultaneously undergoing and exercising this power. They are not only its inert or consenting target; they are always also the elements of its articulation. In other words, individuals are the vehicles of power, not its points of application...

I believe that the manner in which the phenomena, the techniques and the procedures of power enter into play at the most basic levels must be analysed,

From Michel Foucault, "Disciplinary Power and Subjection," in *Power*, ed. Steven Lukes (New York: New York University Press, 1986), pp. 231–2, 234, 235–6, 239–40, 242.

that the way in which these procedures are displaced, extended and altered must certainly be demonstrated; but above all what must be shown is the manner in which they are invested and annexed by more global phenomena and the subtle fashion in which more general powers or economic interests are able to engage with these technologies that are at once both relatively autonomous of power and act as its infinitestimal elements. In order to make this clearer, one might cite the example of madness. The descending type of analysis, the one of which I believe one ought to be wary, will say that the bourgeoisie has, since the sixteenth or seventeenth century, been the dominant class; from this premise, it will then set out to deduce the internment of the insane. One can always make this deduction, it is always easily done and that is precisely what I would hold against it. It is in fact a simple matter to show that since lunatics are precisely those persons who are useless to industrial production, one is obliged to dispense with them. One could argue similarly in regard to infantile sexuality and several thinkers, including Wilhelm Reich have indeed sought to do so up to a certain point. Given the domination of the bourgeois class, how can one understand the repression of infantile sexuality? Well, very simply – given that the human body had become essentially a force of production from the time of the seventeenth and eighteenth century all the forms of its expenditure which did not lend themselves to the constitution of the productive forces – and were therefore exposed as redundant – were banned, excluded and repressed. These kinds of deduction are always possible. They are simultaneously correct and false. Above all they are too glib, because one can always do exactly the opposite and show, precisely by appeal to the principle of the dominance of the bourgeois class, that the forms of control of infantile sexuality could in no way have been predicted. On the contrary, it is equally plausible to suggest that what was needed was sexual training, the encouragement of a sexual precociousness, given that what was fundamentally at stake was the constitution of a labour force whose optimal state, as we well know, at least at the beginning of the nineteenth century, was to be infinite: the greater the labour force, the better able would the system of capitalist production have been to fulfil and improve its functions.

I believe that anything can be deduced from the general phenomenon of the domination of the bourgeois class. What needs to be done is something quite different. One needs to investigate historically, and beginning from the lowest level, how mechanisms of power have been able to function. In regard to the confinement of the insane, for example, or the repression and interdiction of sexuality, we need to see the manner in which, at the effective level of the family, of the immediate environment, of the cells and most basic units of society, these phenomena of repression or exclusion possessed their instruments and their logic, in response to a certain number of needs. We need to identify the agents responsible for them, their real agents (those which constituted the immediate social *entourage*, the family, parents, doctors etc.), and not be content to lump them under the formula of a generalized bourgeoisie. We need to see how these mechanisms of power, at a given moment, in a precise conjuncture and by means of a certain number of transformations, have begun to become economically advantageous and politically useful. I think that in this way one could easily manage to demonstrate that what the bourgeoisic needed, or that in which its system discovered its real interests, was not the exclusion of the mad or the surveillance and prohibition of infantile masturbation (for, to repeat, such a system can perfectly well tolerate quite opposite practices), but rather, the techniques and procedures themselves of such an exclusion. It is the mechanisms of that exclusion that are necessary, the apparatuses of surveillance, the medicalization of sexuality, of madness, of delinquency, all the micro-mechanisms of power, that came, from a certain moment in time, to represent the interests of the bourgeoisie...

This new type of power, which can no longer be formulated in terms of sovereignty, is, I believe, one of the great inventions of bourgeois society. It has been a fundamental instrument in the constitution of industrial capitalism and of the type of society that is its accompaniment. This non-sovereign power, which lies outside the form of sovereignty, is disciplinary power. Impossible to describe in the terminology of the theory of sovereignty from which it differs so radically, this disciplinary power ought by rights to have led to the disappearance of the grand juridical edifice created by that theory. But in reality, the theory of sovereignty has continued not only to exist as an ideology of right, but also to provide the organizing principle of the legal codes which Europe acquired in the nineteenth century, beginning with the Napoleonic Code.

Why has the theory of sovereignty persisted in this fashion as an ideology and an organizing principle of these major legal codes? For two reasons, I believe. On the one hand, it has been, in the eighteenth and again in the nineteenth century, a permanent instrument of criticism of the monarchy and of all the obstacles that can thwart the development of disciplinary society. But at the same time, the theory of sovereignty, and the organization of a legal code centred upon it, have allowed a system of right to be superimposed upon the mechanisms of discipline in such a way as to conceal its actual procedures, the element of domination inherent in its techniques, and to guarantee to everyone, by virtue of the sovereignty of the State, the exercise of his proper sovereign rights. The juridical systems – and this applies both to their codification and to their theorization – have enabled sovereignty to be democratized through the constitution of a public right articulated upon collective sovereignty, while at the same time this democratization of sovereignty was fundamentally determined by and grounded in mechanisms of disciplinary coercion.

Law and Society in Modern India

Marc Galanter

THE GAP BETWEEN 'HIGHER LAW' AND LOCAL PRACTICE

Every legal system faces the problem of bridging the gap between its most authoritative and technically elaborate literary products at the 'upper' end of

From Marc Galanter, *Law and Society in Modern India* (Delhi and Oxford: Oxford University Press, 1989), pp. 32–5.

the system and the varying patterns of local practice at the 'lower' end. It must decide on allowable leeways – how much localism to accommodate, how to deflect local to general standards. Hindu law solved these problems by willingly accommodating almost unlimited localism; it was willing to rely on acceptance and absorption through persuasion and example. These methods are too slow and irregular to appeal to a ruling group which aspires to transform the society radically and to build a powerful and unified nation. Even where specifically Hindu norms are made the basis of legislation – e.g. in prohibition and anti-cow slaughter laws – these norms are not implemented by the old techniques. Enforcing these matters by legislation, courts and the police, stands in striking contrast to allowing them simply to be adopted gradually by various groups in the society. Such change still takes place, but it operates outside the legal system. While the harsher British methods have displaced the methods of persuasion and example from the legal system itself, they persist alongside it in the form of propaganda, education and the widespread tendency to imitate urban and official ways.

But the demise of traditional law does not mean the demise of traditional society. Traditional notions of legality and methods of change still persist at a sub-legal level – e.g. in the area of activities protected by the doctrine of 'caste autonomy', in the form of accepted deviance, and in arrangements to evade or ignore the law. The modern legal system may provide new possibilities for operating within traditional society. Official law can be used not only to evade traditional restrictions, but to enforce them. Traditional society is not passively regulated by the modern system; it uses the system for its own ends. Traditional interests and groupings now find expression in litigation, in pressure-group activity and through voluntary organization.

TWO POLITICAL IDIOMS

Morris-Jones (1963) speaks of two contrasting political idioms or styles in contemporary India: the modern idiom of national politics with its plans and policies and the traditional idiom of social status, customary respect and communal ties, ambitions and obligations. He notes that 'Indian political life becomes explicit and self-conscious [modern] idiom . . . But this does not prevent actual behaviour from following a different path'. Similarly, all contact with the legal system involves the translation of traditional interests and concerns into modern terms in order to get legal effectiveness. For example, at the touch of the official law, a caste's prerogatives become the constitutionally protected rights of a religious denomination; a lower caste's ambitions become its constitutional right to equality; property can be made to devolve along traditional lines, and land-reforms can be frustrated by transactions in good legal form.

Traditional interests and expectations are thus translated into suitable legal garb, into nationally intelligible terms.[1] But the process of translation opens new possibilities for affiliation and alignment; new modes of action. If we regard tradition not as a stationary point, a way of remaining unchanged, but as a method of introducing and legitimizing change, we can say that the modern legal system has displaced traditional methods within the legal system itself while it has supplemented them outside it.

A DUALISTIC LEGAL SYSTEM

India has what we might call a dualistic or colonial-style legal system – one in which the official law embodies norms and procedures congenial to the governing classes and remote from the attitudes and concerns of its clientele. Such systems are typical of areas in which a colonizing power superimposes uniform law over a population governed by a diversity of local traditions. However, legal colonization may occur from within as well as from without, as in Turkey, Japan and in India since the departure of the British. The colonial legal situation prevails wherever there is unresolved tension between national and local, formal and popular law.[2] In a relatively homogeneous society, the law can be visualized as the expression of widely shared social norms. In a heterogeneous society (differentiated horizontally by culture, or vertically by caste or class), the law expresses not primarily the aspirations and concerns of the society, but those of the groups that formulate, promulgate and apply the law. A gap between the official law and popular or local law is probably typical of most large political entities with intensive social differentiation. To some extent this colonial legal situation obtains in most modern societies. But it is present with special force in the so-called new states. In the nineteenth and early twentieth centuries, the poorer parts of the earth were the scene of a reception of foreign law unprecedented in scope (even by the reception of Roman law in medieval Europe). In India, the incorporation of large blocs of common law and civil law in the nineteenth century was followed by the reception of new constitutional models in the twentieth century and by a post-independence wave of reform and rationalization. This process of borrowing, consolidating and modernizing national legal systems seems to involve certain common trends: application of laws over wider spatial, ethnic and class areas; replacement of personal by territorial law; the breakdown of corporate responsibility and the growth of individual rights; increasing generality and abstraction; greater specialization and professionalism, secularization, bureaucratization and replacement of moral intuition by technical expertise. In almost all of the newer countries, the legal system is comprised of these modern elements in uneven mixtures with traditional ones and the discrepancy between the different components of the legal system is strongly felt. This multi-layered legal situation involves common processes of the displacement of local by official law and seems to be accompanied by common discomforts.

FAILURE OF REVIVALISM

A certain irreversibility in this process of forming a modern legal system, even where it is based upon foreign sources (at least as long as a unified political power retains control of the law), seems indicated by other instances of the reception of complex law based upon foreign sources, as in the reception of Roman law in Western Europe or the massive borrowing of civil law in nineteenth-century Japan. This irreversibility is confirmed by the very limited success of revivalist movements. Attempts to purify and reconstruct Irish law fared no better than present attempts in Pakistan and Israel which have so far not succeeded in bringing about any fundamental changes in their respective legal systems. In Ireland, Israel and Pakistan, there is, if anything, more common law in the broad sense, i.e. law of the modern type, than before independence. In India, where the proponents of indigenous law are less attached to *dharmasastra* than nostalgic for the 'simplicity' of local-customary law – and where they tend to be persons who find detailed consideration of the law uncongenial – any change in this direction is even more unlikely.[3]

NOTES

1 'The use of the courts for settlement of local disputes seems in most villages almost a minor use of the courts. In Senapur, courts were and are used as an arena in the competition for social status, political and economic dominance in the village. Cases are brought to harass one's opponents, as a punishment, as a form of land specula-tion and profit making, to satisfy insulted pride and to maintain local political dominance over one's followers. The litigants do not expect a settlement which will end the dispute to eventuate from recourse to the State Courts'.
2 The colonial legal situation then stands midway between those systems where official law is reflective of, and well integrated with, popular law because it has been precipitated out of that law (or because it has completely absorbed and digested local law); and those where it is reflective of a well integrated folkways because no remote official law has ever differentiated itself institutionally from folk or popular law.
3 It should be recalled that the similar distaste for the law of former colonial rulers found in the early history of the United States is not to be observed in more recent American evaluations of our common law heritage. As India feels safely distant from her colonial past, a similar embrace of her legal heritage is at least a possibility.

Modernity and Self-Identity

Anthony Giddens

4

We may also trace a return of the repressed in a burgeoning preoccupation with the reconstruction of tradition to cope with the changing demands of modern and social conditions. Of course, in many sectors of modern life traditional elements remain, although they are often fragmented and their

From Anthony Giddens, *Modernity and Self-Identity* (Cambridge: Polity Press, 1991), pp. 206–8.

hold over behaviour partial. Moreover, some of the 'traditional' features of modern social life are in fact inventions dating only from the earlier period of modernity.' They are ways of encapsulating and representing modern trends rather than links with a deeply sedimented historical past.

Today, we see a definite tendency to seek to re-establish vanished traditions or even construct new ones. As was mentioned in a previous chapter, whether tradition can effectively be recreated in conditions of high modernity is seriously open to doubt. Tradition loses its rationale the more thoroughly reflexivity, coupled to expert systems, penetrates to the core of everyday life. The establishment of 'new traditions' is plainly a contradiction in terms. Yet, these things having been said, a return to sources of moral fixity in day-to-day life, in contrast to the 'always revisable' outlook of modern progressivism, is a phenomenon of some importance. Rather than constituting a regression towards a 'Romantic refusal' of modernity, it may mark an incipient move beyond a world dominated by internally referential systems.

5

As a phenomenon partly independent of the previous point we might mention the resurgence of religious belief and conviction. Religious symbols and practices are not only residues from the past; a revival of religious or, more broadly, spiritual concerns seems fairly widespread in modern societies. Why should this be? After all, each of the major founders of modern social theory, Marx, Durkheim, and Max Weber, believed that religion would progressively disappear with the expansion of modern institutions. Durkheim affirmed that there is 'something eternal' in religion, but this 'something' was not religion in the traditional sense: symbols of collective unity persist in more secular vein as the celebration of political ideals.

Not only has religion failed to disappear. We see all around us the creation of new forms of religious sensibility and spiritual endeavour. The reasons for this concern quite fundamental features of late modernity. What was due to become a social and physical universe subject to increasingly certain knowledge and control instead creates a system in which areas of relative security interlace with radical doubt and with disquieting scenarios of risk. Religion in some part generates the conviction which adherence to the tenets of modernity must necessarily suspend: in this regard it is easy to see why religious fundamentalism has a special appeal. But this is not all. New forms of religion and spirituality represent in a most basic sense a return of the repressed, since they directly address issues of the moral meaning of existence which modern institutions so thoroughly tend to dissolve.

6

New forms of social movement mark an attempt at a collective reappropriation of institutionally repressed areas of life. Recent religious movements have to be numbered among these, although of course there is great variability in the sects and cults which have developed. But several other new social movements are particularly important and mark sustained reactions to basic institutional dimensions of modern social life. Although – and in some part because – it addresses questions which antedate the impact of modernity, the feminist movement is one major example. In its early phase, the movement was pre-eminently concerned with securing equal political and social rights between women and men. In its current stage, however, it addresses elemental features of social existence and creates pressures towards social transformations of a radical nature. The ecological and peace movements are also part of this new sensibility to late modernity, as are some kinds of movements for human rights. Such movements, internally diverse as they are, effectively challenge some of the basic presuppositions and organising principles which fuel modernity's juggernaut.

NOTE

1 Eric Hobsbawm and Terence Ranger, *The Invention of Tradition* (Cambridge: Cambridge University Press, 1983).

7

Max Weber: The Evolution from Irrationality to Rationality in Law

Introduction

Weber (1864–1920) was trained as a lawyer, but economics, history, and philosophy were as much his territory as law and government. His illustrative examples are drawn from a wide variety of societies and periods of history, To handle these diverse materials and simplify them, he constructed a typologizing method, identifying what seemed to him the most important characteristics of a set of "ideal types." For example, he considered that politically legitimate domination could be usefully thought about in terms of three "ideal types," traditional/patriarchal, charismatic, and bureaucratic. Authority in the first was rationalized with reference to a valued, established order in which the ruler's place was explained. Authority in the second was attached to the particular gifts and qualities of a given political leader. The third, the bureaucratic type, found its justification in the logic of its rules and organization. Examples from actual societies often had mixtures of these types in varying degrees. A kind of evolutionary logic attended this scheme.

The bureaucratic structure is everywhere a late product of historical development. The further back we trace our steps, the more typical is the absence of bureaucracy and of officialdom in general. Since bureaucracy has a "rational" character, with rules, means-ends calculus, and matter-of-factness predominating, its rise and expansion has everywhere had "revolutionary" results, in a special sense still to be discussed, as had the advance of *rationalism* in general. The march of bureaucracy accordingly destroyed structures of domination which were not rational in this sense of the term. Hence we may ask: What were these structures?

In Weber's thought rationality had two meanings. It was applied to: (1) a logic-ally coherent system of ideas and/or rules; and also pertained to: (2) the most efficient means toward a given end (as in economic rationality). In the last sense, Weber was convinced that capitalism was the most rational economic system that had been devised, and that the rules of law associated with it were the only kind that could assure rational calculation. Thus Weber is often juxtaposed to Marx in their very different visions of economy and its meaning. But Weber was very much aware that capitalism has prospered under very different kinds of legal systems, blooming under codifying systems and common law logic. The rough approximations of the "ideal types" to actual realities was certainly something of which Weber was aware, and unperturbed by. Plainly "ideal types" were a methodological device, a way of identifying the issues and thinking about the material, and not a description of any particular reality.

> The differences between Continental and Common Law methods of legal thought have been produced mostly by factors which are respectively connected with the internal structure and the modes of existence of the legal profession as well as by factors related to differences in political development. The economic elements, however, have been determinative only in connection with these elements. What we are concerned with here is the fact that, once everything is said and done about these differences in historical developments, modern capitalism prospers equally and manifests essentially identical economic traits under legal systems containing rules and institutions which considerably differ from each other at least from the juridical point of view.

Yet, the high esteem and advanced status accorded to the idea of rational bureaucracy had its echoes in Weber's analysis of law and its evolution. From his point of view, the most advanced law was the most formally rational, i.e. the most guided by general rules. A legal system that was formally irrational would be guided by other criteria. It might use oracles, or revelations, ordeals or divination. Substantive rationality in law meant that general norms were applied to cases, general principles and policies were the guides. Substantive irrationality was marked by arbitrariness, personal evaluations of cases, rule by men, not by law. As Weber saw it, reliability and predictability were characteristics required by a capitalist economy. Irrational ity in law was inconsistent with such an economy and could not serve its purposes.

Weber was very much aware of the role of specialists and jurists in developing the kind of codified legal systems that developed in western Europe out of Roman law, and emphasized the economic transformations that paralleled some of those changes.

The enormous set of essays he wrote, entitled, *Economy and Society* (1922), has become one of the classics of sociological thought and contains much com-mentary on law. As will be evident from the ethnographic reports included later in this volume, Weber's rationality thesis does not do justice to the fact that such phenomena as witchcraft and divination and the use of talismans and the like, and indeed some personalized legal decision-making, themselves are part of particular systems of thought. They form part of an order of causal and social ideas that have their own logic. In the early days of colonially situated anthro-pology considerable anthropological effort was devoted to demonstrating that these "irrational" systems were not simply random and arbitrary, but were founded on explanatory models quite different from those of Europeans, but, in their way, were just as systematic. Lawrence Rosen, for example, has roundly criticized Weber for his assumption that what he called Islamic "khadi justice" was arbitrary. Rosen offers a different explanatory model which can be seen in an extract of his paper that follows the quotations from Weber himself.

S.F.M.

Chapter I The Economy and Social Norms

Max Weber

I Legal Order and Economic Order

A The sociological concept of law

When we speak of "law," "legal order," or "legal proposition" (*Rechtssatz*), close attention must be paid to the distinction between the legal and the sociological points of view. Taking the former, we ask: What is intrinsically valid as law? That is to say: What significance or, in other words, what *normative* meaning ought to be attributed in correct logic to a verbal pattern having the form of a legal proposition. But if we take the latter point of view, we ask: What *actually* happens in a group owing to the *probability* that persons engaged in social action (*Gemeinschaftshandeln*), especially those exerting a socially relevant amount of power, subjectively consider certain norms as valid and practically act according to them, in other words, orient their own conduct towards these norms? This distinction also determines, in principle, the relationship between *law* and *economy*.

The juridical point of view, or, more precisely, that of legal dogmatics aims at the correct meaning of propositions the content of which constitutes an order supposedly determinative for the conduct of a defined group of persons: in other words, it tries to define the facts to which this order applies and the way in which it bears upon them. Toward this end, the jurist, taking for granted the empirical validity of the legal propositions, examines each of them and tries to determine its logically correct meaning in such a way that all of them can be combined in a system which is logically coherent, i.e., free from internal contradictions. This system is the "legal order" in the juridical sense of the word.

Sociological economics (*Sozialökonomie*), on the other hand, considers actual human activities as they are conditioned by the necessity to take into acount the facts of economic life. We shall apply the term *economic order* to the distribution of the actual control over goods and services, the distribution arising in each case from the particular mode of balancing interests consensually; moreover, the term shall apply to the manner in which goods and services are indeed used by virtue of these powers of disposition, which are based on *de facto* recognition (*Einverständnis*).

From Max Weber, *Economy and Society* (Berkeley: University of California Press, 1978), pp. 311–14, 316–17, 889–90, 1002–3.

It is obvious that these two approaches deal with entirely different problems and that their subjects cannot come directly into contact with one another. The ideal "legal order" of legal theory has nothing directly to do with the world of real economic conduct, since both exist on different levels. One exists in the realm of the "ought," while the other deals with the world of the "is." If it is nevertheless said that the economic and the legal order are intimately related to one another, the latter is understood, not in the legal, but in the sociological sense, i.e., as being *empirically* valid. In this context "legal order" thus assumes a totally different meaning. It refers not to a set of norms of logically demonstrable correctness, but rather to a complex of actual determinants (*Bestimmungsgründe*) of human conduct. This point requires further elaboration.

The fact that some persons act in a certain way because they regard it as prescribed by legal propositions (*Rechtssätze*) is, of course, an essential element in the actual emergence and continued operation of a "legal order." But, as we have seen already in discussing the significance of the "existence" of rational norms, it is by no means necessary that all, or even a majority, of those who engage in such conduct, do so from this motivation. As a matter of fact, such a situation has never occurred. The broad mass of the participants act in a way corresponding to legal norms, not out of obedience regarded as a legal obligation, but either because the environment approves of the conduct and disapproves of its opposite, or merely as a result of unreflective habituation to a regularity of life that has engraved itself as a custom. If the latter attitude were universal, the law would no longer "subjectively" be regarded as such, but would be observed as custom. As long as there is a chance that a coercive apparatus will enforce, in a given situation, compliance with those norms, we nevertheless must consider them as "law." Neither is it necessary – according to what was said above – that all those who share a belief in certain norms of behavior, actually live in accordance with that belief at all times. Such a situation, likewise, has never obtained, nor need it obtain, since, according to our general definition, it is the "orientation" of an action toward a norm, rather than the "success" of that norm that is decisive for its validity. "Law," as understood by us, is simply an "order" endowed with certain specific guarantees of the probability of its empirical validity.

The term "guaranteed law" shall be understood to mean that there exists a "coercive apparatus" (in the sense defined earlier), that is, that there are one or more persons whose special task it is to hold themselves ready to apply specially provided means of coercion (legal coercion) for the purpose of norm enforcement. The means of coercion may be physical or psychological, they may be direct or indirect in their operation, and they may be directed, as the case may require, against the participants in the consensual group (*Einverständnisgemeinschaft*) or the association (*Vergesellschaftung*), the organization (*Verband*) or the institution (*Anstalt*), within which the order is (empirically) valid; or they may be aimed at those outside. These means are the "legal regulations" of the group in question.

By no means all norms which are consensually valid in a group – as we shall see later – are "legal norms." Nor are all official functions of the persons constituting the coercive apparatus of a community concerned with legal coercion; we shall rather consider as legal coercion only those actions whose intention is the enforcement of conformity to a norm as such, i.e., because of its being formally accepted as binding. The term will not be applied, however, where conformity of conduct to a norm is sought because of considerations of expediency or other material circumstances. It is obvious that the effectuation of the validity of a norm may in fact be pursued for the most diverse motives. However, we shall designate it as "guaranteed law" only in those cases where there exists the probability that coercion will be applied for the norm's sake. As we shall have opportunity to see, not all law is guaranteed law. We shall speak of law – albeit in the sense of "indirectly guaranteed" or "unguaranteed" law – also in all those cases where the validity of a norm consists in the fact that the mode of orientation of an action toward it has some "legal consequences"; i.e., that there are other norms which associate with the "observance" or "infringement" of the primary norm certain probabilities of consensual action guaranteed, in their turn, by legal coercion. We shall have occasion to illustrate this case which occurs in a large area of legal life. However, in order to avoid further complication, whenever we shall use the term "law" without qualification, we shall mean norms which are directly guaranteed by legal coercion.

Such "guaranteed law" is by no means in all cases guaranteed by "violence" (*Gewalt*) in the sense of the prospect of physical coercion. In our terminology, law, including "guaranteed law" is not characterized by violence or, even less, by that modern technique of effectuating claims of private law through bringing "suit" in a "court," followed by coercive execution of the judgment obtained. The sphere of "public" law, i.e., the norms governing the conduct of the organs of the state and other state-oriented activities, recognizes numerous rights and legal norms, upon the infringement of which a coercive apparatus can be set in motion only through "complaint" or through "remonstrance" by members of a limited group of persons, and often without any means of physical coercion. Sociologically, the question of whether or not guaranteed law exists in such a situation depends on the availability of an organized coercive apparatus for the nonviolent exercise of legal coercion. This apparatus must also possess such power that there is in fact a significant probability that the norm will be respected because of the possibility of recourse to such legal coercion.

Today legal coercion by violence is the monopoly of the state . . .

B. State law and extra-state law

A discussion of the various categories of such extra-state law would be out of place in the present context. All we need to recall is that there exist nonviolent means of coercion which may have the same or, under certain conditions, even greater effectiveness than the violent ones. Frequently, and in fairly large areas even regularly, the threat of such measures as the exclusion from an organization, or a boycott, or the prospect of magically conditioned advantages or disadvantages in this world, or of reward and punishment in the next, are under certain cultural conditions more effective in producing a certain behavior than a political apparatus whose coercive functioning is not always predictable with certainty. Legal forcible coercion exercised by the coercive apparatus of the political community has often come off badly as compared with the coercive power of other, e.g., religious, authorities. In general, the actual scope of its efficiency depends on the circumstances of each concrete case. Within the realm of sociological reality, legal coercion continues to exist, however, as long as some socially *relevant* effects are produced by its power machinery.

The assumption that a state "exists" only if the coercive means of the political community are superior to *all* other communities, is not sociological. "Ecclesiastical law" is still law even where it comes into conflict with "state" law, as it has happened many times and as it is bound to happen again in the case of the relations between the modern state and certain churches, for instance, the Roman-Catholic. In imperial Austria, the Slavic *Zadruga* not only lacked any kind of legal guaranty by the state, but some of its norms were outright contradictory to the official law. Since the consensual action constituting a *Zadruga* has at its disposal its own coercive apparatus for the enforcement of its norms, these norms are to be considered as "law." Only the state, if invoked, would refuse recognition and proceed, through its coercive power, to break it up.

Outside the sphere of the European-Continental legal system, it is no rare occurrence at all that modern state law explicitly treats as "valid" the norms of other organizations and reviews their concrete decisions. American law thus protects labor union labels or regulates the conditions under which a candidate is to be regarded as validly nominated by a party. English judges intervene, on appeal, in the judicial proceedings of a club. Even on the Continent German judges investigate, in defamation cases, the propriety of the rejection of a challenge to a duel, even though duelling is forbidden by law. We shall not enter into a casuistic inquiry of the extent to which such norms thus become "state law." For all the reasons given above and, in particular, for the sake of terminological consistency, we categorically deny that "law" exists only where legal coercion is guaranteed by the political authority. For us, there is no practical reason for such a terminology. A "legal order" shall rather be said to exist wherever coercive means, of a physical or psychological kind, are available; i.e., wherever they are at the disposal of one or more persons who hold themselves ready to use them for this purpose in the case of certain events; in other words, wherever we find a consociation specifically dedicated to the purpose of "legal coercion." The possession of such an apparatus for the exercise of physical coercion has not always been the monopoly of the political community. As far as psychological coercion is concerned, there is no such monopoly even today, as demonstrated by the importance of law guaranteed only by the church.

Classic Themes in New Forms

The Theory of Communicative Action

Jürgen Habermas

4   THE RATIONALIZATION OF LAW: WEBER'S DIAGNOSIS OF THE TIMES

In Weber's theory of rationalization the development of law occupies a place as prominent as it is ambiguous. The ambiguity consists in the fact that the rationalization of law makes possible – or seems to make possible – both the

From Jürgen Habermas, *The Theory of Communicative Action*, vol. 1 (Boston: Beacon Press, 1984), pp. 243–4, 254–5.

institutionalization of purposive-rational economic and administrative action and the detachment of subsystems of purposive-rational action from their moral-practical foundations. In contrast, the methodical conduct of life counts per se as an embodiment of moral-practical structures of consciousness; but the principled ethic of the calling remains influential, in Weber's view, only so long as it is embedded in a religious context. As we have seen, the dialectic of scientific and religious development is supposed to provide empirical grounds for the view that, in consequence of the shaking of religious faith, ethical action orientations can no longer be reliably reproduced. This explanation could not hold in an analogous way for modern law, since the latter appeared from the start in secularized form. Thus in his sociology of law Weber-pursues a different strategy than he does in his studies on the sociology of religion. Whereas in the case of the Protestant ethic he gives reasons why there can never be an enduring institutionalization of secularized moral-practical struc-tures of consciousness, he *reinterprets* modern law in such a way that it is detached from that evaluative sphere and can appear from the start as an institutional embodiment of cognitive-instrumental rationality. This strategy stands in the context of a diagnosis of the times based on the line of thought sketched in the *Zwischen-betrachtung*. Thus before I take up (B) the rational-ization of law, I would like to consider (A) the two most important elements of Weber's diagnosis.

A

In his diagnosis of the times Weber keeps closer than usual to the theoretical perspective in which modernization is represented as a continuation of the world-historical process of disenchantment. The differentiation of independent cultural value spheres that is important for the phase of capitalism's *emer-gence*, and the growing autonomy of subsystems of purposive-rational action that is characteristic of the *development* of capitalist society since the late eighteenth century, are the two trends that Weber combines into an existen-tial-individualistic critique of the present age. The first component is repre-sented in the thesis of a *loss of meaning*, the second in the thesis of a *loss of freedom*. These two theses together still determine the underlying ideology – with its scepticism concerning progress – of those neoconservative social scientists who do not want completely to sacrifice their need for a worldview to their declared scientism.

With the differentiation of autonomous cultural spheres of value, we also become aware of their inner logics. In Weber's view, this has two kinds of consequences. On the one hand, it first makes possible a rationalization of symbol systems under one (at a time) abstract standard of value (such as truth, normative rightness, beauty, authenticity); on the other hand, the meaning-giving unity of metaphysical-religious worldviews thereby falls apart. A com-petition arises among the autonomous value spheres which can no longer be settled from the superordinate standpoint of a divine or cosmological world-order. As soon as systems of action crystallize around those "ultimate ideas," these spheres of life "drift into the tensions with one another which remain hidden in the originally naive relation to the external world."[2]

B

These conflicting tendencies are reflected in his sociology of law. On the one hand (a), modern law, like the Protestant ethic, counts as an embodiment of posttraditional structures of moral consciousness. The legal system is an order of life that responds to the forms of moral-practical rationality. On the other hand (b), Weber attempts to view the rationality of law exclusively from the standpoint of purposive-rationality and to construe it as a parallel case to the embodiment of cognitive-instrumental rationality in the economy and the state administration. He succeeds in this only at the cost of an empiricist reinterpretation of the legitimation problematic and a conceptual separation of the political system from forms of moral-practical rationality – he trims back political will-formation to processes of acquiring and competing for power.

(a) First a word on the posttraditional character of bourgeois law. Social actions are institutionalized in the framework of legitimate orders; and the latter rest in part on consensus [*Einverständnis*]. This consensus is grounded in the intersubjective recognition of norms. To the degree that the normative consensus is based on tradition, Weber speaks of conventional social action [*Gemeinschaftshandeln*]. To the degree that conventionally bound action is replaced by action oriented to success, by purposive-rational action, there arises a problem of how the scopes of actions based on self-interest [*Interessenhandelns*], freed from convention, can in turn be legitimately ordered, that is, demarcated from one another in a normatively binding way. Normative agreement has to shift from a consensus pregiven by tradition to a consensus that is achieved communicatively, that is, agreed upon [*vereinbart*]. In the limit case, what is to count as a legitimate order is formally agreed upon and positively enacted; with this, rationally regulated action [*Gesellschaftshandeln*] takes the place of conventional social action.

> Naturally the transition from consensual action to rationally regulated action is fluid – after all, the latter represents only the special case of regulation by enactment...Conversely, almost every associative relationship [*Vergesellschaftung*] tends to give rise to consensual action among consociates which goes beyond the sphere of its rational purposes (this will be called "consensual action conditioned by associative relationship")...The more numerous the spheres to which the individual rationally orients his action, and the more varied these are as regards the kind of opportunities constitutive of them, the further "rational societal differentiation" has progressed; the more things take on the character of associative relationship, the further the "rational societal organization."

The ideal-typical case of the normative regulation of purposive-rational action is freely agreed-upon enactment with legal force; an institution based on an order achieved through enactment is an association [*Verein*] or, where a coercive apparatus permanently sanctions the original agreement, a compulsory association [*Anstalt*]. In these concepts Weber describes the tendency to societal rationalization: "On the whole...we find that the purposive-rational ordering of consensual action through enactment, and particularly the transformation of organizations [*Verbände*] into purposive-rationally ordered compulsory associations is ever on the increase." In this passage, Weber is not using the term "purposive-rational" in accord with his own definitions; he should have written "value-rational" instead.

Law and Social Science

Richard Lempert and Joseph Sanders

THE HERITAGE OF WEBER

During the last two decades work in law and social science has blossomed and a separate field of inquiry has been defined. The roots of law and social science[1] extend back into the nineteenth century, however, when the social sciences generally were in their cradle. Particularly important was the work of Max Weber, not only because he identified law as an important field of inquiry, but also because his ideas are still very much alive. Although you will find few citations to Weber in this book, our perspective is informed throughout by his work. In particular, we, like Weber, are concerned with the problems of *human action*, and we adopt Weber's favorite methodological device, *the ideal type*, as a mechanism for theoretical generalization (Weber, 1949).

By human action we mean human behavior that has some meaning for the person acting. It is the existence of *subjective* meaning for the actor that distinguishes action from mere behavior or reflexes. The social scientific understanding of human behavior cannot be reduced to some natural science understanding of the physical and biological processes we observe. For example, in viewing a film of someone shooting a gun and killing another person, we may be observing a murder, an act of self-defense, or a patriotic war deed. As behaviors these three possibilities may appear identical, but as actions they are profoundly different. The law is concerned with human action. The degree of concern is a variable that distinguishes both different types of law and different ways of applying it.

In making these and other distinctions, we have found it useful to proceed by the method of ideal types.[2] Weber described the ideal type:

> An ideal type is formed by the one-sided *accentuation* of one or more points of view and by the synthesis of a great many diffuse, discrete more or less present and occasionally absent *concrete individual* phenomena, which are arranged according to those one-sidedly emphasized viewpoints into a unified *analytical* construct. (Weber, 1949, p. 90)

The essence of the ideal type is twofold. First, it is a conceptual abstraction from reality which is sufficiently general that it cannot capture the whole of

From Richard Lempert and Joseph Sanders, *Law and Social Science* (Philadelphia: University of Pennsylvania Press, 1986), pp. 2–4.

any actual phenomenon. Second, it is a stylized construct that represents the perfect, and thus unreal, example – it is not the average case; it is the pure one. As a pure case the ideal type is an analytical yardstick against which we might measure actual actions, institutions, or societies. We use such pure types in each section of this book to create generalized statements and to help us understand the intricate workings of the legal order. In the final section our debt to Weber is compounded, for the types we develop are directly influenced by types Weber employed to identify essential differences between possible legal systems.

NOTES

1   There is now a professional association, the Law & Society Association, which specializes in this area, and several journals, including most importantly the *Law & Society Review*, which are devoted to work in law and social science.

2   Our reason for employing ideal types reflects another judgment we share with Weber. Weber not only defined human action as the core concern of sociology, he also rejected those social theories which held that social structure was ultimately determined by any one particular factor, such as economic relations, political power, or religious belief. This view of the world poses a problem. The combination of an action orientation and the absence of some fundamental determinant implies an indeterminancy of events and ultimately a science of human behavior that can only explore particular historical phenomena. But to understand law and the legal system, we must move from unique, historical accounts to more general social scientific accounts of causal relationships. The ideal type allows us to maintain this Weberian view of the social world and still generalize about the social order.

Equity and Discretion in a Modern Islamic Legal System

Lawrence Rosen

In *Terminiello v. Chicago* (1949), Mr. Justice Frankfurter, commenting on his own court, said: "This is a court of review, not a tribunal unbounded by rules. We do not sit like a kadi under a tree dispensing justice according to considerations of individual expediency." For Justice Frankfurter, as for many others, the image of the Islamic law judge, the *qadi*, is often that of a man sitting barefoot and turbaned under a tree or in the corner of a mosque dispensing justice off the top of his head. Even Max Weber (1967: 351), who appreciated that actual Islamic adjudication was neither capricious nor unrestrained, chose the term *Kadijustiz* to refer to a type of legal system in which judges have recourse to a general set of ethical precepts unevenly employed on a case-by-case basis rather than to a series of rules abstractly formulated and uniformly

From Lawrence Rosen, "Equity and Discretion in a Modern Islamic Legal System," *Law & Society Review*, 15 (2) (1980–81), pp. 217–18.

applied (see generally Turner, 1974: 107–121). Although the traditional role of the *qadi* has been greatly altered by the introduction of western codes and the development of bureaucratic structures, the quest in many Moslem countries for an authentically Islamic way of life has given renewed emphasis to classic precepts of Islamic jurisprudence. It is important, therefore, to appreciate that, far from being arbitrary or unsystematic, *qadi* justice partakes of regularities which reveal not only Islamic legal history but also the interplay between Islamic law and the society in which it is rooted.

Part II

The Early Classics of Legal Ethnography: The Real Thing – Fieldwork on Law, Rules, Cases, and Disputes

Introduction to the Early Classics of Legal Ethnography

Clearly the philosophers and social theorists from Plato to Weber cited here were concerned with what was morally "right," what was "best" and most "advanced," and how the law might have evolved. Not all of them were solely armchair theorists. Some referred to other societies to support their conclusions. Montesquieu and Morgan, for example, visited other peoples and compared their systems with their own. But it was not until much later that professional anthropologists began to practise their specialty. The gathering of new data about law in unfamiliar settings began to be a serious academic project in itself. Thus the books on observed law written by Malinowski, Schapera, Gluckman, Bohannan, and Pospisil (and the work of a few predecessors and contemporaries) were path-breaking endeavors which addressed anthropological problems of method and theory as well as gathering information on peoples whose way of life was not at all familiar to Europeans and Americans.

They all confronted basic questions. What were the local rules that made social order possible? Was that to be considered "the law"? How does an observer distinguish the rules that are law-like from those that are simply social conventions? Can such a distinction be made? And if the local people do not draw any such line, can the ethnographer do it without distorting the cultural facts? In one way or another, and in varying degrees, the anthropologists all operated by analogy to the law in the countries from which they had come.

In this period, all those interested in law were working in colonial situations. Colonial administrations invariably presumed that a local, indigenous, system of order existed parallel to the system they had imposed. This duality, as well as the foreign origin of the ethnographers, necessarily had a direct impact on the way the ethnographers saw their work, and their subject matter. Some considered themselves to be reconstructing a "traditional system," or observing what was *primarily* indigenous custom. In other instances, as was the case of Schapera, the ethnographer was very much aware that "the old tribal system had been greatly altered" (Schapera

1955:xviii). Schapera states that his purpose was "to place on record, for the information and guidance of government officials and the Tswana themselves, the traditional and modern laws and related customs of the Tswana tribes of the Bechuanaland Protectorate" 1955:xxv). He undertook his investigations at the invitation of the Administration, (p. xxv). By no means was this the purpose and circumstance of all the ethnographers quoted here, but at the very least, they all had to obtain permission from the local colonial administration to do fieldwork in their areas.

Besides the questions what part of local practices constituted law and how much of it was traditional, another major issue they all confronted was what Geertz has called the problem of "translation" (1983:36–54). There was more than the issue of finding words in English that would express indigenous concepts. It was a question of presentation and representation that would convey a totally different way of thinking about things, a different way of classifying and explaining people, ideas, and objects. Thus the concept of a kinsman in one society includes an entirely different set of relatives from the idea of a kinsman in another. And attached to the difference in categories is also a different idea of the obligations and expectations involved. Could one accurately present the way a New Guinean conceives his obligations to his family without explaining the whole context? That is, could particular Western legal concepts, such as inheritance or succession, be separated from the total cultural matrix in which they are used? That, in a nugget, is the problem of "translation."

Thus the two fundamental questions that either dogged these pioneering inquiries, (or should have dogged them) were: (1) the strains and definitional ambiguities surrounding "law" where the concept as we know it did not exist in the indigenous society, and, (2) the problem of "holism," of assuming that the whole social and cultural context is imbedded and implicated in every concept. Aspects of these issues will be evident in the passages quoted from these writers.

The Ethnographers

Malinowski's *Crime and Custom in Savage Society* (1926) marks the first fieldwork attempt by an anthropologist to look at law in a setting where there were no indigenous formal legal institutions, no courts, no police, no writing, no legislature. The question Malinowski took as his theme was to ask how such an order worked. How were the rules enforced? How was order maintained.

To address this question in the Trobriand Islands in the years 1915–18 he concocted his own working definition of law and the "legal forces." He said, "we shall try merely to discover and analyse all the rules conceived and acted upon as binding obligations, to find out the nature of the binding forces, and to classify the rules according to the manner in which they are made valid" (1926:15). He soon had to modify the scope of this definition when he examined the encompassing breadth of the idea of "custom." "If we designate the sum total of rules, conventions and patterns of behaviour as the body of custom, there is not doubt that the native feels a strong respect for all of them, has a tendency to do what others do, what everyone approves of, and, if not drawn or driven in another direction by his appetites or interests, will follow the biddings of custom rather than any other course. The force of habit, the awe of traditional command and a sentimental attachment to it, the desire to satisfy public opinion – all combine to make custom be obeyed for its own sake ... the rules of law form but one well-defined category within the body of custom" (1926:51–54). This part sounds very much like Durkheim, though Malinowski rejected the connection. Malinowski described the prevalent customary obligations in general terms. His book is both a statement of the general prescriptions for proper Trobriand behavior, and a theoretical commentary on them. But it provides only one or two illustrative instances.

What distinguished "law" as a sub-category of customary obligations? "Civil law, the positive law governing all phases of tribal life, consists then of a body of binding obligations, regarded as a right by one party and acknowledged as a duty by the other, kept in force by a specific mechanism of reciprocity and publicity inherent in the structure of their society" (1926: 58). Reciprocity was Malinowski's answer to the self-operation of the legal system. People who failed in their reciprocal obligations could be penalized by being frozen out of the essential system of exchange. Those who performed well would have their pride satisfied through social appreciation, and further favors. Malinowski's further attempt to describe criminal law in the Trobriands is rather disorganized and somewhat vague. Much punitive power had been taken over by the colonial administration which tried to limit the prerogatives of chiefs.

A major issue mentioned, but not discussed in Malinowski's legal analysis, was the significance of the colonial presence, and that of missionaries and traders. These dominant foreigners greatly modified the autonomy of the Trobriand people. It is clear that the system of order that Malinowski observed was, as he acknowledged, far from an untouched traditional one.

Yet what Malinowski concentrated on in the 1926 book was an attempt to reconstruct the whole fabric of reciprocal obligations as it might have been in pre-colonial times. Much emphasis was put on a major system of competitive ceremonial exchange, the inter-island *kula*. He gave scarcely any specific instances of disputes, or instances of punitive action, though in his text, there are undeveloped intimations of potential violence. Only one dispute account stands out, which is reproduced here.

A later ethnographer of the Trobriands explained that the full political meaning of the incident had been misunderstood by Malinowski (Powell 1960:167). Malinowski's interpretation was that it was a demonstration of the tension between matrilineality and the parental bond between fathers to sons, essentially a conflict between the norms of kinship and the imperatives of emotional attachment. Powell, instead, indicates that the son and the matrilineal nephew (the chief's heir) were in competition for a higher office, the headmanship of a cluster of villages. The son was trying to ruin the heir's reputation with the colonial administration in order to make himself more likely to eventually be named the village cluster headman. As can be seen from the passage quoted here, this attempt backfired. But Malinowski had not seen the affair in political terms at all. Throughout *Crime and Custom* the themes of reciprocity, social pressure, and tradition were the dominant explanations he offered.

An anthropologist who did not see overall explanations of an indigenous legal system as his objective was Isaac Schapera. He thought that reporting "the facts" was sufficient. His book, *A Handbook of Tswana Law and Custom*, was originally published in 1938. His initial period of fieldwork was done during the years 1929–35, among the Kgatla and the Ngwato of the Bechuanaland Protectorate, and he subsequently made information-collecting visits to six more Tswana "tribes." The population of the Protectorate according to the 1946 census was roughly 259,000 (1955:xxxi).

Schapera observed small local variations in the rules of each tribe, but concluded that they all had once had essentially the same laws and customs. However, of course, much had changed since contact with Europeans. By the turn of the century all the leading chiefs were converts to Christianity. "Missionaries first settled in the present Protectorate in 1846 and by about 1870 were established in all the larger tribes" (1955:xiii). The British Government established the Protectorate in 1885.

Schapera treated his task as a fact finding one, finding out about local practice as it was when he was there. He says, "I was invited in 1934 by the Administration of the Protectorate to undertake the compilation of such a record," (1955:xxv). He described Tswana social structure, the nature and sources of Tswana law, the tribal constitution, family law, the law of property, the law of contract, legal wrongs and procedure. This classification reveals his approach which was to treat each of these topics as a collection of rules. He did not provide narratives of cases in this law book, but only the kinds of rule statements that might have served as guidelines for a court. Nor did he make any attempt to identify a single dynamic social principle, in the manner of Malinowski, who argued that reciprocity was the key to conformity in the whole of Trobriand society. Schapera said that his objective was simply to "place on record, for the information and guidance of Government officials and the of the Tswana themselves, the traditional and modern laws and related customs of the Tswana tribes of the Bechuanaland Protectorate" (1955:xxv). This was to provide a reference for those chiefs who sat as judges in the courts or those colonial officials who had administrative responsibilities. It could not be assumed that they knew what they needed to know to decide cases of dispute. But there was another reason as well. Both the chiefs and the administration had made changes in the laws from time to time and Schapera suggests that, "It may well be that the time has already come for some attempt at standardization, otherwise, with eight tribes each producing its own local laws, confusion is unavoidable" (1955:xvii).

An entirely different approach, heavy with theoretical interpretation, can be found in two books of Max Gluckman's, *The Judicial Process among the Barotse* (1955) and *The Ideas in Barotse Jurisprudence* (1965). Like Schapera, he did his fieldwork in Africa. However, unlike Schapera, his first law monograph was a study of law *cases* tried in the colonially established Native Courts from 1940 to 1947 in what was then Northern Rhodesia (1955:32). Missionaries had been present in the area from 1885, and British authorities formally from 1900. The legislation establishing the courts was passed in 1936 by the British together with the Barotse King-in-Council, but the Barotse had had courts of their own for a long while – according to Gluckman, for two hundred years (Gluckman, 1955:2). Barotse authorities continued to be in charge locally, but were also supposed to be carrying out the policies of the Colonial Government as well as their own customs under the policy of "Indirect Rule." The population of the Barotse Province at that time was about

260–300,000. The Lozi people (the dominant tribe) comprised 70,000 or 80,000 of that number. The Barotse were organized as a centralized kingdom with many layers of administrative hierarchy.

In the appellate court which Gluckman studied most closely, the Lozi judges who presided together were also the Barotse political administrators. The government had formally limited their powers in various ways. They could not impose the death penalty nor unlimited flogging. They had the power to imprison. Prisons did not exist in pre-colonial times. They could not try capital cases, nor imprison for life. They did not have jurisdiction over cases in which a non-native was a party. There were other limitations. But they were still very powerful. They could not try witchcraft cases. But of course a popular belief in witchcraft continued, as well as a great fear of sorcery, and the belief that sorcery could be the source of success (1955:30, 98).

In reviewing the court cases, Gluckman was very much engaged in trying to explain the way judges reached their decisions, and to demonstrate that this was logical, and comparable to what happened in other societies. The theoretical framework used by Gluckman was derived from various sources. From the gaps in Maine's historical evidence, he got the idea that what the literature needed was a fieldwork example of an archaic system, and that in some ways, the Lozi material would fulfill that need (1965:xvi). While the societal circumstances surrounding the courts had changed considerably in the colonial period, Gluckman was convinced that the reasoning of the judges in applying Lozi principles to specific cases was a general continuation of indigenous practice, and that his study showed that it was "akin to our own judicial process [and involved] modes of reasoning which are found wherever men apply norms to varied disputes" (1955:33).

From Radcliffe-Brown Gluckman took the idea of a structural framework of social positions, each having a place in relation to all the others. This positional place he identified with Maine's notion of status. He concluded that what the judges were assessing was "whether particular people had behaved as reasonable incumbents of specific social positions" (1955:312, 1965:17). The "reasonable man" has a special place in Gluckman's argument as he contrasted this minimal normative standard with the higher standard of "upright behavior," to which leaders and officials ought to conform (1955:270).

Gluckman conceived the Lozi judge as strongly motivated to reconcile the parties, and thought that the production of amity and the acceptance of the decision as "right" was a judicial goal (1965:10). "Large parts of the judgments read like sermons, for they all lecture on the theme 'your station and its duties'" (1955:49). Many of the cases he encountered, either in the court records or in analysis of the hearings, were between persons who were linked together for life, sometimes as fellow villagers and kinsmen, sometimes in marriage relationships. About 80% of cases coming before Lozi kutas (courts) "are classed by the Administration as 'matrimonial cases'" (1955:64). He emphasized the flexibility of concepts like "reasonableness" and the fact that an unwritten legal system can adapt itself to changing conditions and reject customs unsuitable to modern life (1955:243). But he also makes it clear that "the first and the most prolific source of Lozi legal rulings is *custom*, defined in its everyday sense of 'usual practice', though it has too an ethical value, that it ought to be followed" (1955:236).

Throughout his comments on the cases he heard and read, Gluckman's preccupation was with describing the logic of the judges, the manner of their reasoning, and the way it compared with the practices in English courts and others. He was very keen to show that the Lozi were as logical, and as judicious in their decision-making as any European. Considering that his was the first book that recorded what transpired in an African court, examined cases of dispute, and tried to generalize about them, he was keen to make the political point that Africans were not intellectually primitive or crude.

The 1965 book, *The Ideas in Barotse Jurisprudence* was a much bolder analytic project. There Gluckman was not so much concerned with the formal logic of judicial reasoning as with the concepts used by the Barotse in their political life, in their dealings with property and debt, and in their transactions in general. He devised an original vocabulary for dealing with many matters. Thus he called the political sovereignty over a territory and its people an "estate of administration", and the right to use land as an "estate of production" (1965:90–91). This was a useful clarification of a situation in which words like "ownership" and "control" were not sufficiently specific.

Gluckman also proposed that relationships in tribal society were dominantly "multiplex" (1965:5). He meant that The same persons were involved in relationships with each other in multiple contexts: kinship, religion, economy, etc. Those relationships, he contended, were dominated by status. By contrast, he argued that in modern society, relationships were dominantly "single interest." He elaborated further that the law varied accordingly.

Numbers of other useful analytic suggestions appear in that book. It should have generated considerable professional debate. However, to debate these points requires some knowledge of comparative law which few anthropologists have. In fact, some anthropologists, such as Bohannan, thought the comparative effort almost impossible. His view was that each culture and its legal concepts were virtually unique. This position spared him the trouble of making comparisons, and provided a good staging area from which to attack Gluckman.

Paul Bohannan was openly critical of Gluckman's way of going about his analysis. Bohannan argued that the folk system of ethnographic fact should be sharply distinguished from the analytical system of comparative law, that it was a bad business to explain "a folk system of jural control" in terms of our own system of law (1957:5–6). Bohannan did a his study among the Tiv of northern Nigeria in 1952 and 1953. The Tiv population was about 800,000 at that time. The Tiv were a stateless people whose political organization was based on their system of localized lineages.

Bohannan worked in two kinds of courts, some that had been recognized by the colonial administration as official native courts, and some that he called "moots" which were more informal assemblies of the elders of the community, a group of neighbors and kinsmen who decided disputes. The Tiv lived in localized lineages, so the moots were composed of members of smaller or larger lineages depending on the nature of the case.

Throughout his ethnographic descriptions, Bohannan uses a Tiv vocabulary which readers are obliged to learn. Thus he speaks of the *jir* which means both the case and the court. The *tar* is the territory of the social group that lives in it. In one sense it means "district." A person who is quarrelsome spoils the *tar*. Courts repair the *tar*. But repairing the *tar* also has mystical meanings. The elders of a community, called *mbatsav*, are thought to form an organization. By day they repair matters through secular means. By night they act in mystical ways to protect the community, and look after its well-being, which includes making the land and women fertile and healthy, and thus to repair the *tar*. They do this by means of *tsav*, a witchcraft substance. A man of *tsav* is a man of power and talent.

By night, in some mysterious way which no Tiv can fully explain, the *mbatsav* sometimes kill. Because their power depends on the sacrifice of life from time to time, sometimes of a chicken or a goat, but sometimes also a human life, they are both revered and feared. "Moots are concerned with actions involving *tsav*, and hence often with charges against the elders of the community. The workings of *tsav* are known by the presence of illness, death, and evil omens" (1957:163). Oaths and curses are also matters to which much attention is paid. Oaths are made on *swem*, a cooking pot filled with ashes and other substances which is thought to kill anyone who swears on it falsely. *Swem* is used in the courts recognized by the colonial administration as well as in the moots. It is taken very seriously.

One can easily understand that hearings involving people and actions categorized in these ways would not lend themselves to the type of comparative description of the judicial process that Gluckman employed. One could re-present some of Bohannan's secular material in the government courts in such a way that it would fit into Gluckman-type description, but by no means would this apply to the moots. The emphasis on the mystical element, on witchcraft and its associated vocabulary, and on dispute as a community disturbance, simply is not present in the same degree in the Gluckman account. Is this because of a difference between Tiv and Barotse social structure, a difference between Tiv and Barotse cultural belief and practice, Tiv and Barotse modes of thought? Or is this a bias in Gluckman's analysis because of his politically inspired wish to present the Africans as being equal to European lawyers and judges in their ability to reason systematically?

In addition to his argument about cultural uniqueness, Bohannan made a more general contribution to the debates about law. He created a definition of law that put the burden on institutional processing. "A norm is a rule ... which expresses 'ought' aspects of relationships between human beings. Custom is a body of such norms ... that is actually followed in practice most of the time" (1967:45). "A legal institution is one by means of which the people of a society settle disputes that arise between one another and counteract any gross and flagrant abuses of the rules ... Every ongoing society has legal institutions in this sense, as well as a wide variety of nonlegal institutions" (1967:45).

Bohannan criticized Malinowski"s definition of law as "a body of binding obligations" (quoted above). What he said about it was this: "His error was in equating what he had defined with the law. It is not law which is kept in force by ... reciprocity and publicity." Law is, rather, "a body of binding obligations regarded as right by one party and acknowledged as the duty by the other" *which has been reinstitutionalized within the legal institution so that society can continue to function in an orderly manner on the basis of rules so maintained*. In short, reciprocity is the basis of custom: but the law rests on the basis of this double institutionalization" (1967:48). He also argued that stateless societies were bicentric power systems

(I would amend that to "multicentric") and that quarrels therefore had to end in compromise. "In short, the bicentric, unicultural system may not have a very great potential for organized, neat systems of 'law'" (1967:53). To the contrary, "It is characteristic of unicentric legal systems that they are empowered to reach and enforce decisions" (1967:55). The Barotse kingdom was by definition, unicentric. He does not pass up the opportunity to say, "We may, like Gluckman's first book, cut our insights short by defining the 'legal' too rigidly before we start to write" (1967:56).

The Trobriands and Africa were not the only sites of early legal analysis. Leopold Pospisil published his monograph on *Kapauku Papuans and their Law* in 1958. In it he included a definition-cum-theory of law. He asserted that this theory was based on his fieldwork together with the comparative study of the literature on many other cultures. As far as he was concerned, law had four attributes: (1) It had to have the *attribute of authority*. That is, the rule, or ruling, had to be propounded by persons who were in a position to exact compliance. They had to have the power to induce or force the members of their social group to conform to their decisions. They might be informal leaders or formally appointed officials. (2) It had to be a rule which had *the intention of universal application* (1971b:78). "Not only does a legal decision solve a specific case, but it also formulates an ideal – a solution intended to be utilized in all similar situations in the future" (1971b:80).

(3) It had to have the attribute of *obligatio*. "It refers to that part of a decision which states the rights of one party to a dispute and the duties of the other" (1971b:81). (4) The fourth attribute of a law was that it had to have an attached *sanction*. That is, a coercive element was necessary. But that might not be physical coercion. It could be shaming or some other non-physical punitive measure. These four definitional attributes of law did not find universal academic acceptance, but they stimulated a great deal of talk.

Pospisil's fieldwork was an astonishing achievement. He moved into "his village" in the interior of Netherlands New Guinea in 1954 and had to teach himself the language. The confederacy he studied was virtually without chieftainships, and was in an area barely touched by Western civilization. It was in this respect very different from the Trobriands, the Tswana, the Barotse, and the Tiv, whose contact with administrators in the colonial government and with missionaries and many other "outsiders" was considerable. The Kapauku welcomed Pospisil, helped him to learn their customs, built him a house, let him observe many goings-on including every-thing from the fighting of wars with bows and arrows to the buying and selling of pigs for cowries. They assisted him in gathering his legal data on disputes, which is quite detailed and of no small interest.

What should be added to Pospisil's rather formal definition of law is his theory of legal levels. Since the New Guinea people he studied settled disputes, and made decisions and rules at every subgroup level from the family to the household, from the village to the sub-lineage, from the lineage to the confederacy, all of the rules and rulings made by the leaders of these groups, Pospisil was ready to call "law." Presumably he saw all of those decisions as potentially exemplifying his four attri-butes. But he has a further modification to insert about rules, that in societies like the Kapauku the rules are not binding, but serve as "a help to the authorities in settling disputes. It is easier to adjudicate a case by a decision referring to a rule, thus depriving it of an air of arbitrariness, than simply to state one's own opinion" (1971a:253). If a Kapauku authority felt that a decision satisfactory to all parties would be one which did not comply with the appropriate rule, they would not hesitate to disregard it. "Thus a rule functions in the Kapauku process of settling disputes as a referential device rather than a ready-made answer applicable mechanically to corresponding cases" (1971a:254). "We can conclude that it is not the abstract rule that affects the Kapauku people, but the actual decision of the headman" (1971a:255).

S.F.M.

REFERENCES

Becker, Howard and Harry Elmer Barnes, 1961 *Social Thought from Lore to Science*. 3 vols. New York: Dover Publications.

Berman, Harold J., 1983 *Law and Revolution*. Cambridge, MA: Harvard University Press.

Bohannan, Paul, 1957 *Justice and Judgment Among the Tiv*. London. New York, and Toronto: Oxford University Press.

——, 1967 The Differing Realms of the Law. In *Law and Warfare* Paul Bohannan, ed. pp. 43–56 Garden City, N.Y., The Natural History Press. Reprinted from *American Anthropologist*, special publication, *The Ethnography of Law*. Laura Nader, ed. 67, (6), part 2: 33–42.

Bourdieu, Pierre, 1977 [1972] *Outline of a Theory of Practice*. Richard Nice trans. Cambridge: Cambridge University Press.

——, 1987 The Force of Law: Toward a Sociology of the Juridical Field. *The Hastings Law Journal* 38 (5): 805–854.

Cowan, Jane K., Marie-Benedicte Dembour, and Richard Wilson, eds., 2001 *Culture and Rights*. Cambridge: Cambridge University Press.

Durkheim, Emile, 1964 [1893] *The Division of Labor in Society*. London and Glencoe: Collier Macmillan Ltd. and The Free Press.

Engels, Friedrich 1969 [1884] *The Origin of the Family, Private Property, and the State*. New York: International Publishers.

Foucault, Michel, 1986 Disciplinary Power and Subjection. *In Power*. Steven Lukes, ed. New York: New York University Press.

Galanter, Marc, 1989 *Law and Society in Modern India*. Delhi: Oxford University Press.

Geertz, Clifford, 1983 *Local Knowledge*. New York: Basic Books.

Giddens, Anthony, 1991 *Modernity and Self-Identity* Stanford: Stanford University Press.

Gluckman, Max, 1955 *The Judicial Process among the Barotse of Northern Rhodesia*. Manchester: Manchester University Press.

——, 1965 *The Ideas in Barotse Jurisprudence*. New Haven and London: Yale University Press.

Habermas, Jürgen, 1984 *The Theory of Communicative Action*. Vol. 1. Thomas McCarthy, trans. Boston: Beacon Press.

Henkin, Louis, ed., 1981 *The International Bill of Rights*. New York: Columbia University Press.

Hobsbawm, E. J., ed., 1965 *Karl Marx: Pre-capitalist Economic Formations* Jack Cohen, trans. New York: International Publishers.

Lempert, Richard, and Joseph Sanders, 1986 *Law and Social Science*. New York and London: Longman.

Maine, Sir Henry, 1894 [1861] *Ancient Law*. London: John Murray.

Malinowski, Bronislaw 1951 [1926] *Crime and Custom in Savage Society* London: Routledge; New York: The Humanities Press.

Marx, Karl, 1956 *Selected Writings in Sociology and Social* Philosophy. T. B. Bottomore, trans. New York, Toronto, and London: Mcgraw-Hill Book Company.

Montesquieu, Charles Louis de Secondat, 1989 [1748] *The Spirit of the Laws*. Ann M. Cohler, Basia Carolyn Miller, and Harold Samuel Stone, trans. Cambridge: Cambridge University Press.

Morgan, Lewis Henry, 1963 [1877] *Ancient Society*. Eleanor Burke Leacock, ed. Cleveland and New York: Meridian Books, and The World Publishing Company.

Newman, Katherine, 1983 *Law and Economic Organization*. Cambridge: Cambridge University Press.

Pospisil, Leopold, 1971a [1958] *Kapauku Papuans and Their Law*. New Haven: Human Relations Area Files Press.

——, 1971b *Anthropology of Law*. New York: Harper and Row.

Powell, H. A., 1967 [1960] Competitive Leadership in Trobriand Political Organization. reprinted in Ronald Cohen and John Middleton, eds. Garden City: The Natural History Press.

Rosen, Lawrence, 1980–1981 Equity and Discretion in a Modern Islamic System. *Law and Society Review* 15 (2).

Rouland, Norbert, 1994 *Legal Anthropology*. Philippe Planel, trans. Stanford: Stanford University Press.

Schapera, Isaac, 1955 [1938] *A Handbook of Tswana Law and Custom*. London, New York, and Cape Town: Oxford University Press.

Weber, Max, 1968 *Economy and Society*. 2 vols. Berkeley and Los Angeles: University of California Press. (Being a translation of the 4th German edition of Wirtschaft und Gesellschaft, Grundndriss der verstehende Soziologie, Johannes Winkelmann, ed. Tubingen.)

8

Crime and Custom in Savage Society

Bronislaw Malinowski

III   Systems of Law in Conflict

Primitive law is not a homogeneous, perfectly unified body of rules, based upon one principle developed into a consistent system. So much we know already from our previous survey of legal facts in the Trobriand Islands. The law of these natives consists on the contrary of a number of more or less independent systems, only partially adjusted to one another. Each of these – matriarchy, father-right, the law of marriage, the prerogatives and duties of a chief and so on – has a certain field completely its own, but it can also trespass beyond its legitimate boundaries. This results in a state of tense equilibrium with an occasional outbreak. The study of the mechanism of such conflicts between legal principles, whether overt or masked, is extremely instructive and it reveals to us the very nature of the social fabric in a primitive tribe. I shall therefore proceed now to the description of one or two occurrences and then to their analysis.

I shall describe first a dramatic event which illustrates the conflict between the main principle of law, Mother-right, and one of the strongest sentiments, paternal love, round which there cluster many usages, tolerated by custom, though in reality working against the law.

The two principles Mother-right and Father-love are focussed most sharply in the relation of a man to his sister's son and to his own son respectively. His matrilineal nephew is his nearest kinsman and the legal heir to all his dignities and offices. His own son on the other hand is not regarded as a kinsman; legally he is not related to his father, and the only bond is the sociological status of marriage with the mother.[1]

Yet in the reality of actual life the father is much more attached to his own son than to his nephew. Between father and son there obtains invariably friendship and personal attachment; between uncle and nephew not infrequently the ideal of perfect

From Bronislaw Malinowski, *Crime and Custom in Savage Society* [SI] (Kegan Paul, 1926), pp. 100–5.

solidarity is marred by the rivalries and suspicions inherent in any relationship of succession.

Thus the powerful legal system of Mother-right is associated with a rather weak sentiment, while Father-love, much less important in law, is backed by a strong personal feeling. In the case of a chief whose power is considerable, the personal influence outweighs the ruling of the law and the position of the son is as strong as that of the nephew.

That was the case in the capital village of Omarakana, the residence of the principal chief, whose power extends over the whole district, whose influence reaches many archipelagoes, and whose fame is spread all over the eastern end of New Guinea. I soon found out that there was a standing feud between his sons and nephews, a feud which assumed a really acute form in the ever recurrent quarrels between his favourite son Namwana Guya'u and his second eldest nephew Mitakata.

The final outbreak came when the chief's son inflicted a serious injury on the nephew in a litigation before the resident government official of the district. Mitakata, the nephew, was in fact convicted and put to prison for a month or so.

When the news of this reached the village, the short exultation among the partisans of Namwana Guya'u was followed by a panic, for everyone felt that things had come to a crisis. The chief shut himself up in his personal hut, full of evil forebodings of the consequences for his favourite, who was felt to have acted rashly and in outrage of tribal law and feeling. The kinsmen of the imprisoned young heir to chieftainship were boiling with suppressed anger and indignation. As night fell, the subdued village settled down to a silent supper, each family over its solitary meal. There was nobody on the central place – Namwana Guya'u was not to be seen, the chief To'uluwa hid in his hut, most of his wives and their families also remained indoors. Suddenly a loud voice rang out across the silent village. Bagido'u, the heir apparent, and eldest brother of the imprisoned man, standing before his hut, spoke out, addressing the offender of his family:—

"Namwana Guya'u, you are a cause of trouble. We, the Tabalu of Omarakana, allowed you to stay here, to live among us. You had plenty of food in Omarakana, you ate of our food, you partook of the pigs brought to us as a tribute and of the fish. You sailed in our canoe. You built a hut on our soil. Now you have done us harm. You have told lies. Mitakata is in prison. We do not want you to stay here. This is our village! You are a stranger here. Go away! We chase you away! We chase you out of Omarakana."

These words were uttered in a loud piercing voice, trembling with strong emotion, each short sentence spoken after a pause, each like an individual missile, hurled across the empty space to the hut where Namwana Guya'u sat brooding. After that the younger sister of Mitakata also arose and spoke, and then a young man, one of the maternal nephews. Their words were almost the same as in the first speech, the burden being the formula of chasing away, the *yoba*. The speeches were received in deep silence. Nothing stirred in the village. But, before the night was over, Namwana Guya'u had left Omarakana for ever. He had gone over and settled in his own village, in Osapola the village whence his mother came, a few miles distant. For weeks his mother and sister wailed for him with the loud lamentations of mourning for the dead. The chief remained for three days in his hut, and when he came out looked older and broken up by grief. All his personal interest and affection were on the side of his favourite son, of course. Yet he could do nothing to help him. His kinsmen had acted in complete accordance with their rights and, according to tribal law, he could not possibly dissociate himself from them. No power could change the decree of exile. Once the 'Go away' – (*bukula*), 'we chase thee away' – (*kayabaim*), were pronounced, the man had to go. These words, very rarely uttered in dead earnest, have a binding force and almost ritual power when pronounced by the citizens of a place against a resident outsider. A man who would try to brave the dreadful insult involved in them and remain in spite of them, would be dishonoured for ever. In fact, anything but immediate compliance with a ritual request is unthinkable for a Trobriand Islander.

The chief's resentment against his kinsmen was deep and lasting. At first he would not even speak to them. For a year or so, not one of them dared to ask to be taken on overseas expeditions by him, although they were fully entitled to this privilege. Two years later in 1917, when I returned to the Trobriands, Namwana Guya'u was still resident in the other village and keeping aloof from his father's kinsmen, though he frequently paid visits to Omarakana in order to be in attendance on his father, especially when To'uluwa went abroad. The mother had died within a year after the expulsion. As the natives described it: "She wailed and wailed, refused to eat, and died." The relations between the two main enemies were completely broken and Mitakata, the young chieftain who had been imprisoned, had sent away his wife who belonged to the same subclan as Namwana Guya'u. There was a deep rift in the whole social life of Kiriwina.

The incident was one of the most dramatic events which I have ever witnessed in the Trobriands. I have described it at length, as it contains a clear illustration of Mother-right, of the power of tribal law and of the passions which work in spite of it.

The case though exceptionally dramatic and telling is by no means anomalous. In every village where there is a chief of high rank, an influential notable or a powerful sorcerer, he favours his sons and allows them privileges, which are, strictly speaking, not theirs. Often this produces no antagonisms within the community – when both son and nephew are moderate and tactful.

NOTE

1 Cf. *The Father in Primitive Psychology* (1926), originally published in *Psyche*, vol. iv. no. 2.

9

A Handbook of Tswana Law and Custom

Isaac Schapera

But the two terms are really not sharply discriminated in ordinary Tswana usage. The same rule of conduct may be spoken of on one occasion as *molao*, and on another as *mokgwa*. Nevertheless, if pressed to distinguish them, the Tswana will sometimes say that one can be punished by the tribal courts for breach of a *molao*, but not for breach of a *mokgwa*.

This particular distinction, although not invariably or even consistently maintained by the people, suggests a possible line of approach to the problem of what must be regarded as Tswana law and what must not. The Tswana employ various mechanisms to ensure that all members of a tribe conform to its recognized norms of conduct. Children are carefully taught by their parents the difference between right and wrong conduct. At the initiation ceremonies associated with the formation of age-regiments, more formal instruction of the same nature is given, certain definite rules of behaviour being firmly impressed upon the minds of the young people concerned. Later, as an adult, every man participates fully in the life of his tribe, and learns by actual experience what he may or should lawfully do and what is forbidden or resented. As husband, father, kinsman, subject, fellow tribesman, worker, and owner of property, he soon becomes aware, through his dealings with his family, neighbours, and political superiors, of the rights to which he is entitled and the duties he must fulfil.

Throughout a man's life, therefore, his behaviour is being either deliberately or unconsciously moulded into conformity with the social norms making for law and order. At every stage, moreover, pressure is brought to bear upon him in the form of sanctions, definite forms of social control restraining him from violating established rules of conduct. Diligent adherence to tribal usage earns for him the approval and respect of his fellows. Failure to comply with it is, on the other hand, penalized in

From Isaac Schapua, *A Handbook of Tswana Law and Custom* (London: Oxford University Press for the International African Institute, 1955), pp. 36–7, 138–9, 144, 145–6.

various ways, according to the nature of his offence. He may suffer loss of social esteem, or be treated with ridicule or contempt, as when a girl is notoriously promiscuous, or a man recklessly squanders his wealth or drinks too much. He may, as when he neglects his kinship obligations, be denied services akin to those he has failed to render. Or, if he breaks any of the numerous taboos pervading Tswana life, he will, it is maintained, be afflicted with sickness or some other misfortune by the offended ancestor spirits or some other supernatural agency.

The sanctions mentioned above do not involve any direct coercion on the part of the tribal authorities. They nevertheless serve the same function as material compulsion, in that they also help to secure compliance with established rules of conduct. Similar sanctions are found among all other peoples, both primitive and civilized. In many primitive societies, indeed, no other mechanism exists to bring people into line with the accepted standards of conduct. It has therefore been maintained by some writers that such societies do not have law, but only custom; while others would extend the use of the term 'law' to cover all rules of conduct, no matter what their sanction, which specify the rights of one person and the corresponding duties of another. This controversy need not detain us here; for the Tswana, like ourselves, have attained to a stage of legal development where certain rules of conduct can, in the last resort, be enforced by the material power of compulsion vested in the tribal courts. These courts can compel a man to carry out obligations he has neglected to fulfil, or to make restitution or pay compensation for damage he has done, or to suffer punishment for an offence he has committed. The rules of conduct distinguished from the rest by this ultimate sanction of judicial enforcement may for all practical purposes be regarded as the 'laws' of the Tswana.

One difficulty arises in this connexion. The courts come into operation only when some rule of conduct has been violated, or when there is a dispute regarding its nature or validity. But, as mentioned above, there is no codified body of law which the courts have to administer, or which is meant to guide them in their decisions. In all but a very few instances, they have to deal with customary rules of behaviour, with traditional usages habitually followed by the people and regarded as more or less binding and obligatory. In arriving at their decisions, they are guided as far as possible by precedent, by reference to the decisions of previous courts. But, save again in a very few instances of quite recent date, these judicial precedents are not recorded in writing. They are embodied in the personal and traditional recollections of people who vary considerably in range of experience and memory; and for this very reason are neither systematized nor comprehensive.

The lack of written codes and records of cases makes it impossible to isolate legal rules absolutely from other rules of conduct...

Bogadi

Significance

According to Tswana law, no marriage is regarded as complete unless *bogadi* has been given by the husband's people to the wife's people. This transfer has often been looked upon by missionaries and others as constituting a purchase of the woman, and as involving her in many humiliating consequences. As will appear from the information given below, this conception of *bogadi* is altogether wrong. There is no bargaining over the number of cattle to be given: the husband's parents give as many as they like and can, which fact alone should dispel the idea of a purchase. It is certainly true that a woman married with *bogadi* is under the control of her husband to a greater extent than a woman who has not; and that if she leaves him her parents will usually send her back, unless there is very good reason for her action. It is also true that in old Tswana law, when such a woman's husband dies, his younger brother or some other close male relative has the right to cohabit with her. On the other hand, a woman married with *bogadi* holds a far more honoured position in the tribe generally than a woman who has not been thus married. If she is ill-treated, or has any justifiable complaint against her husband, she can appeal to his parents and senior male relatives, who will protect her; whereas a woman for whom *bogadi* has not been given has no legal remedy against the actions of her 'husband'.

The Tswana themselves speak of *bogadi* as being a thanksgiving (*tebogô*) to the wife's parents for the care they have spent on her upbringing, and as a sign of gratitude for their kindness in now allowing her husband to marry her. Some say also that it is compensation to the wife's parents for the loss of her services, and others that it is a sort of register of the marriage, showing that the cohabitation of the man and woman meets with the full approval of their respective families. Others stress the fact that *bogadi* creates a special bond between the two family-groups, just as the transfer of cattle in other situations creates special relationships between Chief and subject, or owner and herdsman. The payment of *bogadi* is further said to give the children of the union certain privileges at the home of their mother's people to which they are not otherwise entitled. They have the right, e.g., to go or be sent to their mother's home to grow up there, and to be supported from the cattle given out as her *bogadi*.

But the main function of *bogadi* is to transfer the reproductive power of a woman from her own family into that of her husband. This fact is of considerable importance, for upon it rests the whole Tswana conception of legitimacy. Summarizing this briefly, it may be said that no form of cohabitation between a man and a woman is held to be a proper marriage unless it is accompanied by the transfer of, or understanding to transfer, *bogadi*. No man can claim, for any purpose, the children he has by any woman, until he and his family have agreed to transfer, and under certain circumstances until they have actually transferred, *bogadi*. On the other hand, all children borne by a married woman, no matter who their actual father may be, are held to be the legal offspring of the man on whose behalf *bogadi* for that woman was given out.[1] '*Bogadi*', in the words of one informant, 'is given out because the woman is coming *go agêla motse* (to raise up the village).' All the incidents flowing out of the *bogadi* transfer are directly derived from this conception.

Nature, amount, contributors

Bogadi almost invariably consists in cattle ...

Should a man die before having paid *bogadi* for his wife, the obligation to do so falls upon his eldest son, if old enough, or upon his own brother failing this. The boy brings cattle to his mother's people, with the words: *Ke nyadisa mmê*, 'I am causing my mother to be married.' Should he fail to do so, he must hand over the *bogadi* he receives when his first sister is married. If he has no sister, he must find the cattle elsewhere, as otherwise he himself with his brothers are held to belong to his mother's family. In such cases his father's relatives will generally come to his assistance.

Should a married woman die before *bogadi* has been paid for her, her children can be claimed by her parents or her linked brother, unless her husband prevents this by now handing over some cattle. The children, if they do go to their maternal relatives, can when grown up return to the home of their father if they wish, although strictly they have no legal rights there. Should the woman not have any children, and *bogadi* have not been paid, there is no obligation on the part of her husband to pay it after her death.

In all these instances, it is evident, a marriage is not regarded as complete until *bogadi* has been paid...

Recovery

Cases involving the return of *bogadi* cattle to the husband's people are apparently very infrequent. Theoretically, *bogadi* can be taken or claimed back only: (*a*) if the wife dies childless, and (*b*) in case of divorce, if she is barren...

Abandonment of the 'bogadi' practice

The usages described above in connexion with *bogadi* are still practised by most Tswana tribes. The only one which appears to have abandoned them completely is the Ngwato, where Kgama deliberately abolished them. His main reason for doing so, apart from the pressure put upon him by the London Missionary Society, appears to have been the fact that when a woman's husband died, she could not, under the old law, leave his home, and any children she subsequently bore were still regarded as those of her late husband. Even if she had been divorced and then gave birth to any children, these were also regarded as those of her former husband. Kgama now said: *Mongwe le mongwe a a itsalêlê*, 'Every man should be the father of his own children', i.e. if a woman is divorced or widowed, and then marries again, any children she bears should belong to her new husband. At the present time, the payment of *bogadi* among the Ngwato is said to be a punishable offence, and the practice is no longer openly carried out, although there are still said to be people who practise it secretly.

NOTE

1   Cf. G. P. Lestrade, 'Some Notes on the *Bogadi* System of the BaHurutshe', *S. Afr. J. Sci.*, vol. xxiii (1926), p. 938, from whom I have borrowed some passages in this paragraph.

10

The Judicial Process Among the Barotse of Northern Rhodesia

Max Gluckman

XII

There are a number of important implications in the Lozi use of the standard of reasonable behaviour, both as a measure for evidence and as the central issue in multiplex disputes.

First, it is largely through the concepts of *ngana* (reason, sense) and *kuluka* (uprightness) that the judges import their view of human nature – their psychology – into the law. There are, of course, many other Lozi legal terms which deal with intention and motivation: *kufosa* (to do wrong, to be guilty) and *kusafosi* (to be innocent), provocation (*lishamaeta*), negligence (*buswafa*), and so on. The judges always impute intention and motivation by the test of 'reasonable and customary' interpretation of actions. . . .

Indeed, though the judges rebuke parties for their wrongful feelings and intentions, they are not always concerned with these. The Violent Councillor had behaved wrongfully even if he had in fact been trying to stop the fight. A man who behaves familiarly with another's wife is usually found guilty of 'adultery' whether or not he is proved to have slept with her.

Case 40: The case of the incestuous action (from a text)

A young man was sitting with his sister in a hut with the door closed. Their kin accused them of committing *sindoye* (incest) and demanded a beast for sacrifice from him. He

From Max Gluckman, *The Judicial Process Among the Barotse of Northern Rhodesia* (Manchester: Manchester University Press for the Rhodes-Livingstone Institute, Northern Rhodesia, 1955), pp. 153, 154, 218–19, 376–7, 378.

insisted that he had done no wrong and appealed to SOLAMI, R3 at Lialui. SOLAMI said to him: 'I am sure you did nothing wrong with your sister, but you should not sit alone with her in a closed hut. You must give the beast for sacrifice'.

The Lozi apply this straightforward psychology in legal decision though they are well aware of the complexities, and in a sense of the unconscious pressures, in human motivation...

Secondly, this judicial psychology is an 'ethical psychology'. It is not concerned with an objective assessment of why people act as they do, but with how their actions and presumed motivations appear in comparison with legal and moral norms. The reasonable man (*mutu yangana*) is partially identified with the upright man (*mutu yalukile*). When actions have been considered against reasonable standards and accepted norms, they are judged as 'guilty' or 'innocent' – the Biassed Father and the Violent Councillor showed lack of judgment and partiality in ruling their dependants, and these emotions are disapproved of...

'Reasonable behaviour' thus covers different measures of conformity with ideal norms, as envisaged by the kuta. In part, it demands scrupulous observance of important modes of behaviour, and some conformity with unimportant modes. Even observances of etiquette and convention may enter into it. Since Lozi courts are largely concerned with the behaviour of parties occupying positions of status, each party should have conformed to the customary usages, etiquette and conventions which are appropriate to his social position in a specific relationship. Hence the reasonable man of Lozi law might be more accurately described as the reasonable and customary occupier of a specific position...

Lozi ideas of morality did not make them into Arcadian shepherds. They still do not consider their harrying raids on the persons and property of surrounding tribes to have been immoral, though missionaries' moral arguments helped to induce the Lozi to abandon those raids. These raids were carried out with slaughter and destruction. Captives brought to Loziland became serfs, though very few were sold to West Coast slavers. These serfs have largely now been absorbed into the nation but many returned home after Lewanika's edict of freedom in 1906. After civil wars kings killed their powerful adversaries: but Lewanika refused to punish the ordinary supporters of these adversaries. Lozi kings and councillors have been arbitrary tyrants: these always provoked rebellions in defence of justice and traditional custom. Sorcery trials, carried out by due process which for the Lozi established guilt, used to punish people whom we consider innocent, as did ordeals for strongly suspected thieves: here there was no judicial process (see above, p. 97 f.). Punishments were previously far harsher. British overlordship has restrained arbitrary actions and powers. As I emphasized in the *Introduction*, many suits arising out of social inequalities in relations with Whites go to British and not to Lozi courts. There is no doubt that these circumstances help to explain the kindly account I must give of the practice of Lozi trials: the present circumstances do not deny the validity of my analysis of the Lozi judicial process, in either the present or, *mutatis mutandis*, the past. Nor do these circumstances deny that the concept of laws of human-kind – natural law – is indigenous. These laws, and the equitable considerations which guide judges, appear to have been influenced by Christianity and other Western influences, and the judges occasionally quote from the Bible (see 'The case of the

Quarrelsome Teacher', pp. 74–5). But the last six Commandments, and the principles of the Sermon on the Mount, coincide with basic premises of Lozi ethics.

X

...The myth is that I forced the concepts and processes of Barotse law into a [Procrustean] mould of English terminology and, as some apparently hold, of Roman-Dutch law.

Take the following, from Nader's introductory 'The Anthropological Study of Law' to a recent symposium she edited on *The Ethnography of Law* (1965, p. 11): Bohannan

> implicitly charges Gluckman with having converted the Western legal folk system into an analytical system and having forced the Lozi folk concepts into a Western model...Nadel (1956) and Ayoub (1961) discuss the perplexing questions inherent in Gluckman's assumptions [see below], as does the whole body in ethnoscience... Gluckman's work has been characterized as analogous to that of a linguist who attempts comparison by jamming Barotse grammar into Roman Dutch [*sic*] categories [source not cited].

It is not clear how far Nader accepts this kind of statement: in her full text, she believes the answer to lie 'solely neither with Gluckman nor with Bohannan'. But whoever made the last statement, about Roman-Dutch categories, has accepted the myth implicit in Bohannan, and clearly knows nothing about Roman-Dutch law. There is not a single instance in this book where I have used a Roman-Dutch category and jammed into it Barotse grammar – or law. I have very occasionally, when discussing a trial and after showing a principle of Barotse law in that trial, stated that the principle can be compared with one in Roman (and hence Roman-Dutch, and here English) law. Thus the Barotse maxim that 'if you are invited to a meal and a fish-bone sticks in your throat, you cannot sue your host', clearly invites comparison with *volenti non fit injuria* (which is important in Roman, Roman-Dutch and English law) (pp. 206, 325). But the whole of my analysis is concerned to show that, even if the principles of law be similar in the different systems, they are 'permeated' by quite different economic and social conditions. This being so, it is nevertheless important to state that there are similar principles...

I was fully aware, like 'the whole body of ethnoscience', of the difficulties and dangers involved in any kind of translating of a word from one language into another language, of comparing an idea or custom in one culture with those in another, and of equating an official in one society with an official in another. I was aware too that each word in English carries with it certain general connotations, and words used in jurisprudence carry also technical connotations. I made my awareness clear in the very first sentence of my Preface: 'In analysing legal problems in an African society one has to use terms and concepts which have been employed by jurists through two millennia, and therefore one ought to be well aware of what these jurists have written...'

11

Justice and Judgment Among the Tiv

Paul Bohannan

Chapter III   A Day in Court

THE best way to get an idea of how a *jir* works, of the cases it handles, and its methods of handling them, is to follow through a single day in MbaDuku *jir*, to analyse the cases, and trace out the events. I have selected the *jir* held on 3 August 1952, because, although representative, it contains rather more colourful cases than usual.

That day the *jir* got started about 10.30. It had rained the night before and the day was hot and steamy. When the chief and the *mbatarev* were settled in their chairs and had called for silence, the man who had outshouted the rest, so that his case was to be heard first, yelled, 'I call Kwentse.' When making a complaint the standard phrase is: 'I call so and so.' The *mbatarev* often ask the man who omits this simple procedure, 'Whom do you call?'

Jir no. 1 Gbivaa calls Kwentse to get his wife back

Kwentse, who was called as defendant, to put it in our terms,[1] is one of the local tax-collectors. On being called, he took off his red felt fez and squatted in front of the *mbatarev*, a few feet from the man who had called him. He had to be reminded two or three times to sit on the ground instead of merely squatting. Gbivaa turned to Kwentse and said in a loud voice, 'Give me my wife.'

Kwentse was supercilious: 'I don't have her.'

Gbivaa repeated, 'Give me my wife.'

Neither was willing to explain any further, so the *mbatarev* had immediately to begin asking direct questions and to 'investigate' the case. After much probing they

From Paul Bohannan, *Justice and Judgement Among the Tiv* (London: Oxford University Press for the International African Institute, 1957), pp. 20–1, 196–203.

discovered that Gbivaa had married Kwentse's daughter several years ago. A few months before the case was called, she had run off with another man from Gav lineage, and the husband wanted either his wife or the bridewealth he had expended for her.

When the facts of the case were complete, Huwa, the youngest *ortaregh*, said that it was plain what was to be done: Kwentse must either go himself or send one of his youngsters to Gav to discover just what the woman, his daughter, intended to do; only then would it be possible to continue the case. Kwentse promised, with much reluctance, to send one of his sons to Gav within the next few days. This amounted to a postponement of the case. It would never be reopened unless Gbivaa again came shouting to the MbaDuku *jir*. Kwentse did not, I believe, send his son to Gav to find out his daughter's intentions.

Jir no. 2. Akpalu calls WanDzenge about a nanny goat

The next *jir* to catch the attention of the *mbatarev* was that of Akpalu, a youngster who had left a nanny goat with a man named WanDzenge. It is not customary in Tivland to keep one's own livestock at home, for then it is subject to the legitimate claims of one's kinsmen. Rather, livestock – and especially goats – are left with friends or distant kinsmen. Then one can say with truth that all the goats in one's own compound belong to someone else. This practice is called 'releasing' (*tuhwa*) your goat with the person who becomes its caretaker. As his reward he receives one kid in three. Obviously a very complicated debt structure is built up; certainly these practices are a very fertile source of litigation.

This particular dispute centred around the number of kids borne by the nanny goat. Akpalu, the owner, said that she had borne four kids, of which WanDzenge had taken two. WanDzenge said that she had borne only two, and that he had received nothing at all for keeping her. After some fifteen minutes of cross-questioning and haranguing, it was decided that WanDzenge owed the boy a small billy goat some three or four months old ...

The first Tiv funeral that I understood was Gesa's. I had been in Tivland about nine months and was yet without clerks; but I understood the language sufficiently well to follow ... some of the action and debate and to make exhaustive inquiries afterwards.

Moot no. V The death of Gesa

Gesa was not an MbaDuku man and his compound was several miles from mine, but I visited it occasionally. I went there one afternoon in March 1950, and found a moot ending: several of the principals were just finishing the rite of 'blowing out the curse'. I was told that they had been discussing the matter of MbaWuam, a young girl who had been brought back to the compound of her mother's brothers for treatment. Orya, the compound head, then asked me to come along to Gesa's reception hut and have a look at him.

Gesa was lying on a mat, breathing with difficulty. His senior wife told me, when I asked, that he hadn't eaten or drunk or been awake for over two days. He could still hear conversation, however, and when I, wondering if he had some sort of paralysis, asked his wife if he could still move his legs, he did so. I turned to him, and told him to move his fingers if he could hear me. He did so. Outside again, the compound head told me that about two or three months ago Gesa had been working together with his age-set in a communal task of road-building. Not feeling well, he had come home. He had got steadily worse and in the last three days his feet and his belly swelled up.

Orya described the symptoms in the words always used in describing the action of *swem* – 'your feet and your belly and your head swell, and you die'. I went back to look more closely at Gesa. He was a man in good physical condition, in spite of his illness, and there was no sign that any part of his body had swelled.

On my walk home, I was accompanied part of the way by the oldest man of Gesa's lineage, whose compound lay in my general direction. Once we were on the path, he turned to me and said simply, 'He will die.' I asked him what the trouble was. He said he didn't know. I asked if the divination apparatus had been consulted. He said that it had not, and added that it was unnecessary – this was a matter of the *mbatsav*.[2] I asked what I knew to be a rude question containing a serious charge: 'How do you know it is a matter of the *mbatsav?*' He forgave my 'ignorance' and replied evasively, but probably truthfully, that everyone in Orya's compound 'knew' it and that they had told him.

I thought that the old man was probably right – that Gesa would die. The next morning at dawn I started in that general direction soon after waking. On the way I encountered two youths bathing in a stream. One of them, whom I knew slightly, asked if I was going to the funeral. I asked who had died. He replied that it was Gesa; he had heard this from a woman who had come to the stream for water some time after having seen people from Gesa's compound. I walked on to the home of Orya and Gesa.

When I entered the compound, Gesa's corpse was outside the reception hut where he had been lying the day before. A small piece of hand-woven cloth was tied over the face. His half-brother, a few months his senior and a member of the same age-set, whom I knew fairly well, greeted me only with, 'It defeated him', using for 'it' the pronoun of the noun-class to which death belongs. Gesa's younger full brother, one of his MbaDuku affines, began to wash the body. When they had finished, they put Gesa's best cloth on it, wrapped the whole in a large white cloth of the sort that Tiv call *pupu*, wrapped a mat about that, and tied it. This process took almost an hour.

About 9 o'clock the members of Gesa's age-set began to arrive in numbers. The women, who had been in the kitchen gardens wailing, filed back into the compound, still wailing. They went into Gesa's reception hut, where the corpse had been placed. By about 10 o'clock, almost fifty members of Gesa's age-set had arrived. The largest collection of age-mates I have ever seen, they were drawn from a lineage containing some 8,000 people. They soon began to be restive, and shouted at Orya, the compound head, asking if he had not notified the elders. He insisted that he had done so, and that they would be coming. Half an hour later, when none of the elders had arrived, the age-mates began to complain that the elders were refusing to come to hear this *jir* and bury their dead. Orya, nervous and distrait, tried to reassure them. One of the age-mates said that, since the elders of his *ityô* wouldn't bury him, the age-set must bury Gesa's body in the bush. Orya answered patiently that he was himself the oldest man in his segment within the hut; therefore they could not say

1. Gesa's lineage – the elders – were sitting under and near a drying platform, set more or less in the centre of the compound
2. The age-set, who far outnumbered the lineage, sat in the shade of mango trees
3. Gesa's reception hut
4. The women of the compound, and women representing the wives of most of the compounds of the lineage
5. I sat with, but a little to the side of the age-set.

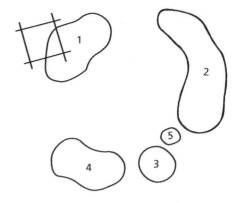

Figure 1 The seating arrangement

that the elders had not come. The eldest of the minimal *tar* – with whom I had walked the day before – would be along soon. He named several other elders whom he had notified. The seating arrangement was becoming apparent (see figure 1).

After another pause, when the most important elders of Gesa's lineage had still not arrived, Kwaghwam, the most respected member in the age-set, rose and said firmly, 'Gesa has no agnates (*ityô*). But he has an age-set. If all his agnates refuse to do anything for him, his age-set will do something.' They made a move to prepare the body for carrying.

The oldest member of Gesa's minimal *tar* present said tentatively that what they said wasn't a bad thing, but that they were very impatient and must want to keep something from the agnates, who were indeed coming.

Somebody in the age-set noted that this action, or lack of action, on the part of the elders spoiled the *tar*. Another added that the age-set had turned out early and in force, it was not the age-set who were spoiling the *tar*.

A few moments later, a few of the age-mates rose, and got a pole and some fibre rope. Others went into the hut where the body lay and bore it out; the wailing increased as the body emerged and was put down among the age-set. The few elders present tried to make them be patient; the age-set remonstrated. They were just beginning to fear that they might really have to make good their threat when the three most important elders of the lineage arrived together. They joined the other elders. The women came out of the reception hut and sat down silently. Now that all were present, they seemed reluctant to begin.

Finally Kwaghwam, easily the most commanding figure of the full age-set, rose and said to the elders, 'Did you ask Gesa before he died?'

The compound head also rose. 'We did not ask Gesa, but Gesa told us.'

Kwaghwam asked the elders, 'Does that satisfy you?'

One elder replied that it depended on what the age-set said. Another suddenly exploded and said that it did not depend on the age-set; they all knew that Gesa was their child and therefore he had done nothing wrong.

The age-set replied, 'We must know.' 'We want to see,' they chorused. Kwaghwam shouted above them all, 'If our age-mate was evil, we shall desist. If his agnates killed him, we shall never desist!'

The implications of this exchange became clear after detailed questioning later. A full sister of Gesa had died some three or four months earlier. The divination apparatus indicated that she had been killed by *tsav*, but nobody had asked the apparatus whose *tsav* had been responsible. At the funeral, her body was examined and it was found that she herself did not have *tsav* on her heart; therefore she did not die from her own evil, but was killed by someone else – either the elders *qua mbatsav* or by an evil man of *tsav*. Loud and bitter accusations had taken place among her close male kinsmen though only a small moot had been convened. At the end of this moot, *swem* had been dressed and broken, so that whosoever might have caused this death would be caught by *swem*.

Within a month, Gesa had fallen ill. By the time his death was imminent, most of the people nearby were describing his suffering in terms of the symptoms of *swem* [although I could not see them]. Therefore, the exchange among the agnates and the age-set amounted to: 'Did Gesa die by means of his own *tsav* and the force of *swem* that was, of course, stronger, or was he bewitched and killed as a sacrifice by his agnates or by one of them acting individually and *ipso facto* evilly?' There is only one sure way to determine this fact; the divination apparatus – except the sasswood ordeal – is fallible. That one sure way was to hold a post-mortem examination of Gesa's heart. If it were found to have *tsav* growing on it, then Gesa would be buried and it would be said that his own evil had killed him. If his heart was found to be sound and healthy, without *tsav* – if, as Tiv would put it, his chest was found to be empty[3] the age-set would know that he had been killed by his agnates: probably the same persons who had killed his sister and were trying to kill his second sister's daughter.

There were loud arguments, shouts, and accusations. The agnates constantly contradicted themselves, for it was necessary for them both to protest their own innocence and to uphold the innocence of their 'child'. The age-set, on the other hand, said repeatedly, 'We must know. Our duty is to protect and revenge our age-mate if he be innocent. But we must know if he is innocent before we dare to raise our hands for him. You are his agnates, but you are also our agnates.'

Had Gesa been found innocent, the age-set might – in the days before the effective government of the British Administration – have attacked, punished, and perhaps even killed those members of Gesa's lineage who were deemed to have caused his death. This institution, known as *hoyo*, is no longer practised. Today the age-set, if it were to do anything in such a situation, must either resort to magical means or hire someone else to do so.

By about half-past twelve the grave had been dug by the same men who had washed the corpse. The body was, after a series of moves requiring some twenty minutes, transported to its side. All sorts of delaying tactics were employed. The age-set was reluctant to perform the post-mortem operation; they would have been saved from doing so by a tacit admission from the elders that Gesa's death was 'natural' – that is, that they had needed his body for sacrificial purposes. But the elders, each knowing that such was not the case and that no decision had ever been reached about Gesa, would not make the admission.

The age-set and the elders faced one another grimly over the grave. Finally Kwaghwam said to the elders and Orya, 'Shall we look and leave?' The eldest replied, 'This is Orya's child. You must ask him. It is your matter and Orya's – but I should say, don't do it.' Orya said nothing. Kwaghwam decided to force the issue.

'We, his age-set, must know why he died. We will look.' One of the elders brought up the case of Gbannor, who, I discovered later, had been examined, and the examination didn't help him, his age-set, or his agnates; his chest had been empty, and Gesa's chest, this elder had implied, would also be empty.

Another elder, feeling himself supported, said, 'We know that our child is all right. We would bury him and break *swem*. But his age-set will not believe.'

Kwaghwam said, 'His age-set must know.' He thereupon dispatched some of his age-mates to find a suitable knife. 'Bring Gesa's own knife,' he told one of them.

Orya said sadly, 'Who will do it?'

Kwaghwam said, 'His agnates should do it, but they fear. His innocence must be proved by his age-mates, for his agnates have nothing but fear.'

A few of the elders and age-mates stood and watched; most of them withdrew. Kwaghwam appointed one of his age-mates to perform the operation. The operator unwrapped the corpse from its cloths and mats. It lay on its back in the sun on the pile of dirt beside its grave. Standing above the body, straddling it, the operator made a neat initial incision horizontally on the chest about two inches below the top of the sternum. Each corner, then, he turned down along the lower ribs so as to make the arc of an oval. The incision was deepened until he struck the bone of the ribs. He then drove the knife between two ribs, tapped its sides with an axe-handle, neatly cutting through each rib, one at a time, and finally through the top portion of the sternum. The knife was sharp and worked quickly. There was no sound except his tapping. When he had finished cutting, he took a hook (made from a forked branch which had been cut by another age-mate) and pried upwards the flap of flesh and bone. It rose with the slight sound of tearing perichondrium. It opened like a trap door and was laid down on the corpse's belly. Another layer of perichondrium was visible. The operator cut through it; the organs were exposed. He placed his knife and hook carefully below the trap-door of flesh and bone and reached in, slowly, with his right hand. Again, there were a few sounds of tearing ligament and pericardium. He lifted the heart out of the opening, turned it slowly and said, 'You see?'

They all looked. A few said 'Mmmmmm.'

Kwaghwam turned to me and said, 'Jim, do you see the *tsav*?'

I asked him to point it out precisely. He and the operator used their explanation to me as an excuse to describe it aloud so that all could hear, including those who would not come to look. *Tsav* is a growth on the heart. It looked to me as if blood had been forced into sacks in the pericardium. There were two such sacks on Gesa's heart. The larger, dull blue in colour, was about three inches long and half as wide. The smaller, about half that size, was bright red. I do not know what they were. If they were sacks of blood, one must have been arterial blood, the other venous.

'Do you see?' Kwaghwam repeated.

'Yes, I see,' I answered. 'And that is *tsav*?'

'You have seen *tsav*,' the operator said. 'You yourself have *tsav* to look on *tsav*.'

'But *tsav* need not be evil,' Kwaghwam added a moment later. 'But this *tsav* is evil. It is large and it is of two colours.'

The operator replaced the heart in Gesa's chest, closed the trap door and wrapped the chest about with a strip of cloth torn from that about Gesa's loins. The body was again wrapped in the mat, lowered into the grave, and moved with some difficulty on to the shelf that had been prepared for it. The white cloth was spread over it, and everybody present helped to cover the grave.

The operator took the knife he had used for the operation and, with the aid of a small stone, drove it point first up to its hilt into a tree. Such a knife must never be used again – if brought back into the compound, it might accidentally be used to cut food, in which case anyone who ate such food would have eaten the human flesh that had contaminated the knife. The wooden hook was buried with the corpse.

The tension was over. The moot could be finished quickly: Gesa had brought about his own death. Someone tried to joke about the elders and their knowledge that the situation would be as it was (i.e. one witch knows another); someone else tried to laugh. Then Orya began a dirge. He walked heavily back into the compound, singing as he came, those peculiarly Tiv dirges which start high and come down a minor scale for two octaves or more and end in formalized sobs. He sat down slowly and silently. The other agnates and the age-set also resumed their positions. The women, who had all gone down to the stream, did not return for another half-hour.

One of the elders said, 'It was the age-set. It was they who wanted him opened.'

Kwaghwam replied, 'I don't like it. But was it a lie (*yie*) which we did?'

One of the junior elders, a man very little older than the age-set, said that the whole thing was a matter of *swem*. '*Swem* killed him,' he noted through the other platitudes.

Slowly, over about fifteen minutes, they all admitted that this was indeed the case: *swem* had killed Gesa. Meanwhile, the women began to come back, a few at a time, into the compound.

There was nothing more to say. Someone in the age-set said, 'We have looked. We know. Let us go.' (*Se nenge mfe. Mough sha.*)

Then Kwaghwam rose and went before the elders. 'We must have his people,' he said.

This statement raised a turmoil again. Finally, however, Orya formally took each of Gesa's widows by the wrist and handed them to Kwaghwam, who grasped their wrists, thus signifying that he, for the age-set, was offering them protection. Gesa had a third wife, who had been absent for three months. The age-set asked several questions about her. Orya said he knew nothing about her, but would ask and be responsible for her well-being.

Kwaghwam said, 'What about Gesa's other people?' He referred to Gesa's younger full brother. The agnates shouted in anger, 'We did not kill Gesa. *Swem* killed Gesa. Why should Gesa's age-set seek to protect his brother, as if it had been we who killed Gesa?'

Kwaghwam was firm. Finally the agnates concurred, and the younger brother was handed to Kwaghwam, who grasped his wrist also, thus putting him under the protection of the age-set.

Kwaghwam then asked, 'What about the sick daughter of Gesa's sister?'

This time the agnates were more firm. 'She is here,' one elder said. 'She is safe with her mother's agnates. No one can harm her here, for we have refused to let them.' This point took almost ten minutes to settle. But the agnates were adamant – this child was not one of 'Gesa's people'. Had the elders let her go, it might some day be interpreted as an admission that they were bewitching her. If she remained 'in the palm' of her mother's agnates, then the assumption would be that it was Gesa who had bewitched her. The age-set eventually conceded the point.

The oldest man of the lineage then dressed a new *swem* in a large potsherd. He stood in the clear space, surrounded by all the participants, and held it high above his head. 'If we have not discussed this *jir* properly,' he said in a loud voice, 'and if we are wrong, then *swem* will catch anyone who has done evil deeds (*ishor i bo*) in this matter.' He dashed *swem* to the ground; the ashes in it raised a small cloud of dust which was carried away in the breeze.

The funeral – or moot, for it was both and could be called either *ku* or *jir* – was ended. It was a little after 4 o'clock in the afternoon. The whole procedure had taken about eight hours.

The first thing to note about this moot, as with the others, is that it was ended with a ritual: the dressing and smashing of *swem*. All the moots we have considered – and this applies, I believe, to all moots that are successfully concluded – ended with ceremonies of repairing fetishes, ceremonies of 'blowing out the curse', or ceremonies involving *swem*.

The second point of importance is that the moot settled a multitude of quarrels and fears among the people of the community: the volition for several past deaths was now 'known', and the atmosphere was cleared of suspicion. All the dependants of Gesa had been assured that they and their interests were being mystically protected by his age-set, for his wrongdoing did not relieve them of their responsibilities to his dependants: he was still their age-mate; his wives were still their *mtene*, and his sons were still their sons. The first steps toward re-establishing social relationships on a new footing, in the absence of the dead man, had been achieved. They grieved for Gesa and about Gesa, but now they 'knew'.

Again, the moot had 'repaired the *tar*' – the *tar* of the lineage which in Maine's terms can be called 'the entire little society'.[4]

NOTES

1   Tiv do not have words for plaintiff or defendant. During the process of the case, each is called the 'partner' (*ikyar*) of the other. The distinction between plaintiff and defendant is the distinction between the subject and the object of the verb 'call' (*yila*).

2   The implication here, that the divination apparatus cannot cope with matters of the *mbatsav*, is not true. There are, however, few diviners who have the courage to tackle this sort of problem. Most find it safer to profess ignorance.

3   The translation which East, following others, has given of this phrase – 'empty-chested' – is indeed correct, but the flavour is not conveyed. *Vanger gbilin* means two things: a man of no talent or consequence, if he is alive and healthy. Applied to a dead man, it means a person who died for some reason other than his own evil propensity. It resembles our word 'innocent' in that it has connotations of good, but in other usages the derogatory connotations of lack of experience are dominant.

4   Henry Sumner Maine, *Ancient Law*.

12

Kapauku Papuans and Their Law

Leopold Pospisil

Land ownership

In order to clarify the various aspects of organization of the sublineage we must digress for a moment and describe Kapauku land ownership in general. At the outset, we should recall the Kapauku individualism and the fact that all productive land is individually owned. Also, the land is classified into several categories according to its use and quality.

1. *Mude* is a type of land which is under cultivation or once has been cultivated. Thus, the concept includes gardens, which are called *bugi* and fallow land, either overgrown with secondary forest and brush, called *gapuuga*, or areas which have reverted to grass and reed land, called *geiga...*

Individual lots of *mude* land are owned by persons who may sell, lease, or work them as a garden. The owners are not limited in their ownership except in the case of an old man with adult sons who has to ask his sons' permission to sell the land. Violation of this requirement makes the deal invalid after the old man's death. The landlord is also restricted in the transference of his land to a member of a hostile confederacy. In such a case, the authority may invalidate the agreement and prevent the new owner from taking possession of the fields.

There are no prohibitions against trespassing on fallow land. To walk in a garden of a man from another sublineage, however constitutes a breach of law punishable by reprimand or beating. The shooting of game on anyone's *mude* land is permissible except for rats, for which permission from the owner has to be sought. Trapping and the felling of trees of a secondary forest on *mude* land is the exclusive right of the owner and a violation of this right may be punished even by shooting. Old trees can be felled by anyone from the same sublineage, a regulation reflecting the fact that in the past, or prior to the appearance of the iron ax, it was quite different and difficult

From Leopold Pospisil, *Kapauku Papuans and Their Law* (New Haven: Human Relations Area Files Press, 1971), pp. 97–9, 144, 145, 234–5, conclusion.

to cut an old tree with a stone ax or to fell it by burning. This seems to indicate a "legal lag" in which the law has not yet been adjusted to the recent introduction of the iron ax.

The acquisition of *mude* land is realized mostly through inheritance and, less frequently, through testament, sale or gift. For details on these methods, the reader is referred to the appropriate sections in the third part of this work. Boundaries between individual plots of land are marked by *ude*, Ti plants, all of which are carefully removed from the inside of the area in order to prevent confusion.

2. *Gamouda* is a type of land covered by forest in which most of the valuable trees, the wood of which is used for canoe and plank making, have already been cut and the rattan vines harvested. There are no laws against trespassing and cutting the old, economically unimportant types of trees. However, the individual owner retains the exclusive right to the few remaining "plank and canoe trees" and to all second growth which he cuts for fence construction or firewood. The game regulations are the same as for the *mude* land with one exception: rats can be shot by any member of the landowner's sublineage.

3. *Buguwa* refers to a type of land covered with virgin forest which is still full of rattan and wood usable for making planks and canoes. Even this territory is not commonly owned by a group but consists, legally speaking, of individually owned segments, whose boundaries are marked by cliffs, depressions, streams, large trees and crevasses. The owner has an exclusive right to trap game in his section and to cut the precious *moane* tree for making canoes. Plank trees and the more inferior canoe wood and rattan are accessible to all members of the sublineage. The cutting of firewood, hunting and collecting are theoretically free to all. In practice, however, a traditional enemy would not dare to use this right for fear of being accused of trapping or of stealing from the traps.

4. *Bega dimi*, the unproductive wastelands on top of the rocky mountains – which are covered with short grass, stones and a few bushes – are considered property of the sublineage as a whole. Here the right to trap belongs to the sublineage, the members of other groups being excluded. Any other use of the land, such as for hunting, is free to all.

5. Waterways. Navigable rivers are international and are free for anyone to fish or navigate. Streams which are too small for canoes are the property of the sublineage if they cut their beds through its territory. In such a case, the sublineage has the exclusive right to fish. If the stream marks the boundary between any two units, it is considered their property in common. The drinking of water is permitted to all. Lakes in the Kamu Valley, on the contrary, no matter where they are located, are always the property of some lineage but accessible for fishing to all members of the whole confederacy...

Part III: Rules and Disputes in the Kapauku Society

...If we turn for help from the confused situation in our literature to the Kapauku, we find that they themselves have not surpassed our writers on law in solving the problem of conceiving of a workable category of phenomena which could be called law. "*Kou dani te tija, kou dani daa,* one does not act like this, this is prohibited," is a common phrase one hears in various disputes coming from the lips of important *tonowi*. However, if we were to think of the word "*daa*, prohibited," as associated only with matters under dispute, we would be far from comprehending its meaning. It does not, by any means, confine itself to prohibitions made by the native authorities, or to those embodied in customary regulations of the relations between man and man. A nonpunishable breach of etiquette, a prohibition sanctioned by the supernatural as well as by the society, a purely religious taboo which defines a relation between an individual and the supernatural and the violation of which does not concern anybody else except the actor, and, finally, a moral but not enforced creed, all these various phenomena are assigned the same name... we shall present the ideal rule for behavior and the following cases will constitute the actual counterpart to the rule. In other words, the ideal "what should be done" in case of a violation of a prohibition will be juxtaposed to what actually is done.

The material on most of the 176 cases of disputes and all the 121 abstract rules has been obtained from informants. During the sessions with these informants there were always several, sometimes as many as twenty, individuals present who would check the narrator on his accuracy and who would fill in the gaps in his memory. An additional verification has usually been obtained from other people at a later date, in the absence of the original informants. There are also several cases which were witnessed by the author himself, which fact will always be indicated by an asterisk. Since the author does not see any reason for being secretive about the identity of the persons involved in the disputes, actual but abbreviated names of all the participants, together with the places and approximate dates will be made available to the reader. Because it would have involved unnecessary repetition, inclusion of impertinent data, and a way of expression not understandable to the reader who is not familiar with the Kapauku language and culture, both the rules and the cases are not presented in the original wording. If, for various reasons, it seems necessary to introduce the original version, the translation is marked by quotations.

All the disputes have been grouped into categories which have been assigned names by the author...

The rules and cases of disputes are presented in five main categories: offences against persons, against rights in things, against contractual agreement, against and by authority, and against society.

Delicts Against the Power of an Authority

All cases of non-subordination to the authority of any group will be listed below. Although the disobedience will be associated with various delicts, the fact of failure to follow a decision will be the primary reason for punishment in each case.

Rule 111

People should follow decisions and the advice of an influential and rich man (of their group). Failure to do so should be punished in accordance with the authority's opinion.

Case 144

Place: Aigi.
Date: ca. 1953.
Parties:
   a) *Defendant:* Ij Maa of Aigi.
   b) *Authorities:*
      Ij Eke of Aigi, confederacy's authority.
      Ij Kag of Aigi, village authority, father of the defendant.

Facts: Maa, son of the rich man Kag, was on trial for disobedience in a battle. During the questioning he became enraged and shouted at the village and confederacy's headman: "*ba*, feces."
Outcome: Both authorities beat the culprit with sticks so that he suffered two deep wounds on his head.
Comment: The punishment for the insult was severe because of the gravity of the delict for which the defendant was on trial.

Case 145

Place: Aigi.
Date: ca. 1953.
Parties:
   a) *Defendant:* Ij Nak of Aigi.
   b) *Authority:* Ij Eka of Aigi, confederacy's headman.
   c) *Authority's helper:* Ij Jok of Aigi.

Facts: The defendant fought intermittently for several days with Iib, his own brother. The authority wished to terminate the violence and asked the quarreling brothers to stop. Nak, in angry words, refused to comply with the request.
Outcome: The authority punished the man for disobedience by asking for the return of 120 Km which Nak owed him. Ij Jok of Aigi joined the authority in the act of punishment by asking for the return of his own loan of 10 Km. The defendant wept and pleaded to be excused. The authority insisted on his punishment, and the defendant had to kill two pigs to satisfy the creditors with the money received for the sold pork.

NOTE

1   The word is a compound of "*gaamai*, to split planks," and the suffix "*ida*, location." The word reflects the fact that the area was already exploited by cutting trees for making planks.

Conclusion

What can be made of the theoretical frameworks of these five ethnographers? One can only conclude that at this level they were competing to set the definitions and limit the analytical possibilities of their colleagues and students. Each wanted to produce a way of defining law that would fit *all* societies. Some of these ideas are interesting. None of them is really definitive. But all were clearly trying to show the intellectual capacities and achievements of the people they dealt with in the field. And all were reaching for some kind of a comparison between the legal arrangements of these predominantly non-literate peoples and the legal arrangements in their own societies. Legal evolution was not much on their minds. Legal difference was.

Which brings us to the main point of their work, their descriptions of what went on in the Trobriands, the Bechuanaland Protectorate, Barotseland, among the Tiv in Nigeria, and the Kapauku in New Guinea. This was detailed material of a kind that had not been available before. It tells us what kinds of rule-understandings there were, what kinds of disputes arose, and how these were handled. They all talk, in one way or another, about rule modification to accommodate the facts of particular cases. But they tell us very little about that other aspect of law that is so prominent in our world, the uses and modes of legislation. There are references, particularly in Schapera's book, indicating that there was indigenous legislation. But in the other ethnographies there is little on this point.

This matters, because the issue of tradition versus innovation looms so large in the way the history of these peoples is generally perceived. And making new law is not only a question of history, but also a question of the group's sense of autonomy, of change, and the sacredness (or not) of the things of the past. For some peoples, a sense of the potential of collective control of the future may well have existed until colonial interventions pre-empted the issue. Certainly, the tendency to see these peoples as largely stuck in their traditional ways and moving very little beyond them has been a persistent theme in the literature. There is an implicit evolutionism which lurks behind such ideas. To the extent that all these ethnographies give ample reason to believe that the peoples concerned had very practical arrangements, given their circumstances, and made what seemed to them, very practical decisions, the emphasis on tradition as the sole explanatory factor seems superficial.

The ethnographic contributions reviewed here did not talk about ideal systems, nor in any detail about moral or political values. They were not making the kinds of judgments that we see from Plato to Weber about what should be the law. The ethnographies they produced strove to be neutral on this point. What they achieved was flawed but remarkable. This work stands as a valued legacy, but not as the last word.

S.F.M.

Part III

Present Thematic Approaches

Introduction to Current Research and Interpretation in Legal Anthropology

In literate and industrial societies many legal rules, institutions, and practices, have a clear background. They are apt to have an identifiable time of inception, a known source. They are likely to have been promulgated with a declared intention, and are attached to some specific agency or milieu of enforceability. An inquiry into the context and consequences of this kind of act exposes the organizational structure of the society, and raises questions of power and legitimacy. The observer is drawn directly into political questions. Thus although the use of legal materials does not at first glance seem very different from other topic-specific inquiries in anthropology, it is quite distinctive in the breadth and direction of its implications. Apart from the political issues, studies of law lead to ancillary questions about conceptions of morality, the rightness and fairness of things, and the legitimacy of powerful asymmetrical relationships.

There are many examples of this kind of complex contextualization in anthropological studies. The necessary background material made them too long to include in this anthology, but a few words about the kind of problem addressed will illustrate the issues. A case in point is Borneman's comparison of the family law legislation in East and West Germany during the Cold War (1992). Each government strove to alter the family form that had prevailed in the Nazi era, and to accomplish this through law. East Germany, the GDR, tried to reshape the family to make it more compatible with the ideals of socialism. West Germany, the FRG, sought to reform the family to fit its ideas of the way the family should be constituted in a democracy. Another contextualizing comparative study by Greenhouse, Yngvesson, and Engel looks at law in three towns in the United States (1994). They characterize their work as exploring "the links between cultural ideas of community and individualism, focusing particularly on the place of law and the court in the cultural construction of community and hierarchy" (1994:174). These studies use law as a starting point for a search into the deep well of context. The context is characterized by contemporary conditions, and sometimes by the history of these conditions, but the link to the law depends on theoretical assumptions which postulate the causal connections. Assumptions of that kind, implicit models of process, are at the core of current work. Thus to analyze the articles that follow, the key questions in each instance have to do with the choice of the field materials assembled, and the author's way of addressing them.

The data available were very different in the classical days when anthropologists were observing the cultures of colonial subjects. Formerly, from what we know of non-literate societies, many of their enforceable norms could be identified, but the circumstances surrounding their origin and original rationale were cloudy. Their history was unknown. Observers and indigenes alike tended to think of these norms as "traditional" and of long standing. In the colonial period the laws of the colonizer were superimposed on such systems without completely eliminating them. Certain indigenous practices were acknowledged and ostensibly enforced by the colonial power as an acceptable part of "customary law." But, in fact, those which continued were often directly changed or subtly altered (Chanock 1985, 1998). Thus in agricultural settings, the introduction of cash crops and the monetization of parts of the economy altered the meaning of wealth and property, which had repercussions on the structure of the family, and on everything from landholding to marriage. Today all formerly non-literate societies, are sub-parts of an international system of literate states with formal laws and governments. The mixed legal arrangements in such settings have been tantalizing to anthropologists who look for the dynamics of social order. For an example see Gordon and Meggitt's *Law and Order in the New Guinea Highlands* (1985); Moore's *Social Facts and Fabrications: "Customary" Law on Kilimanjaro, 1880–1980* (1986); and Moors' *Women, Property and Islam: Palestinian Experiences, 1920–1990* (1995).

In studies of contemporary, modern societies, anthropology has ventured beyond these locally focussed studies to look at the legal links between locations. Some of these connections are embodied in formal treaties or regional organizations, in contractual relations between and among businesses, in financial institutions and their transactions, in the migration of populations, in transnational programs of economic development, in supra-local questions of public health and environment, in international courts, or in the conceptually overarching world domain of human rights. Studies of this kind are very different from the local ethnographies that formerly prevailed. Because crucial events in the world today are involved, anthropology is likely to move more and more in this direction. See for example Darian-Smith, *Bridging Divides: the Channel Tunnel and English Legal Identity in the New Europe* (1999). Also see her review article, "Structural Inequalities in the Global Legal System" (2000).

The abbreviated pieces that follow in this part are examples of the kind of work that is going on today. They have been chosen from a vast array of possibilities, and are illustrative instances, but are far from definitive of the scope of the field. The articles have been grouped around a few themes: the varieties of property, the pertinence of identity to legal standing and human rights, the creation of enforceable rules inside and outside of legal institutions, and legal elements in large scale settings: instances of globalism, pluralism, and international negotiation.

The section concludes with a synoptic overview of the shifting preoccupations in legal anthropology from 1950 to 1999.

S.F.M.

REFERENCES

Borneman, John, 1992 *Belonging in the Two Berlins: Kin, State, Nation*. Cambridge: Cambridge University Press.

Chanock, M., 1998 [1985] *Law, Custom and Social Order*. Cambridge: Cambridge University Press.

Darian-Smith, Eve, 1999 *Bridging Divides: The Channel Tunnel and English Legal Identity in the New Europe*. Berkeley, Los Angeles, and London: University of California Press.

—— 2000 Structural Inequalities in the Global Legal System. *Law and Society Review* 34(3): 809–828.

Gordon, Robert J. and Mervyn J. Meggitt, 1985 *Law and Order in the New Guinea Highlands*. Hanover and London: University Press of New England for the University of Vermont.

Greenhouse, Carol J., Barbara Yngvesson, and David M. Engel, 1994 *Law and Community in Three American Towns*. Ithaca: Cornell University Press.

Moore, Sally Falk, 1986 *Social Facts and Fabrications, Customary Law on Kilimanjaro, 1880–1980*. Cambridge: Cambridge University Press.

Moors, Annelies, 1995 *Women, Property and Islam: Palestinian Experiences 1920–1990*. Cambridge: Cambridge University Press.

A.   Struggles over Property

General Introduction

Property is a culturally constructed idea. As a socially held conception, it defines the relationship people have to each other with respect to things. What is classified as a "thing" or an "object" in which one may have property rights, varies from one society to another. Indeed there may be variation from one community to another. Moreover, the question of which people (individuals or groups) have property rights and which do not, and for how long they may enjoy them is equally variable. Property is often the subject of competition and conflict. Thus knowledge of a system of property holding, or of conflicts over property, can be an excellent entry-point into the structure, values, and practices of any society.

   Property usually has a political dimension. The regulation of property interests has occupied governments and administrators, chiefs and lineage leaders, judges and councils for eons. It is no wonder, then, that philosophers and jurists, designers of utopias and revolutionaries, have speculated on the origin of the idea of property, particularly private property. In the absence of evidence, in the seventeenth, eighteenth, and nineteenth centuries they created conjectural histories, reasoning from what they imagined to be the state of nature to the legal condition of property in their time.

   John Locke, the Natural Law theorist, in his *Second Treatise of Government* (1690) wrote, "God, who hath given the World to Men in common, hath also given them reason to make use of it to the best advantage of Life, and convenience. The Earth, and all that is therein . . . belong to mankind in common, as they are produced by the hand of Nature; and nobody has originally a private dominion" (1996:286) "Though the Earth and all inferior Creatures be common to all Men, yet every Man has a *Property* in his own *Person*. This no Body has any Right to but himself. The Labour of his Body, and the *Work* of his Hands, we may say, are properly his. Whatsoever then he removes out of the State that Nature hath provided... he hath mixed his *Labour* with and joyned to it something that is his own, and thereby makes it his *Property*" (1996: 288). "As much Land as a man Tills, Plants, Improves, Cultivates, and can use the Product of, so much is his Property. He by his Labour does, as it were, inclose it from the Common" (1996:290–291). As can be seen in the selection to follow from Coombe, these Lockean arguments are now reiterated in a doctrine of authorship in intellectual property law (Coombe 1998:94).

Blackstone, of the famous *Commentaries on the Laws of England* (1765–69 amended up to the sixteenth edition of 1825 as cited and quoted by Peter Fitzpatrick 1992:83–84) says, "There is nothing which so generally strikes the imagination, and engages the affections of mankind, as the right of property" (1825:I–II). He considered that the material bounty which God had provided was originally held in common, but that when men multiplied and became cultivators, private property became necessary.

"Had not therefore a separate property in lands, as well as moveables, been vested in some individuals, the world must have continued a forest, and men have been mere animals of prey... Necessity begat property: and in order to insure that property, recourse was had to civil society, which brought along with it a long train of inseparable concomitants; states, government, laws" (Blackstone 1825: 5, 7–11).

Jean Jacques Rousseau in his celebrated treatise on *The Social Contract* remarks about real property, that once the social contract has been formed, "the right which each individual has to his own estate is always subordinate to the right which the community has over all: without this, there would be neither stability in the social tie, nor real force in the exercise of sovereignty" (1762, tr., ch. IX).

It is evident that before the 20th century Western scholarship focussed on the development of private property as critical to the evolution of society. As we have seen in Karl Marx, in Lewis Henry Morgan, and in Sir Henry Maine, property was treated as the very motor that propelled social development from communal sharing to private ownership, and morally, from shared wealth to greedy accumulation. The societies of many non-Western peoples were long thought to represent early stages in this evolution, hence anthropological accounts were looked to as evidence. It is surely no accident that this way of thinking about the matter coincided with colonial expansion. All of this is the background of present anthropological work which is entirely different in its interests.

Property, then, has a long history in legal studies in anthropology. But in the current form of study, the questions of origins and of evolution have been totally dropped. For a while it looked as if comparative work would be the medium through which some general typologies would be attempted. For example, Max Gluckman, emphasized the classical Roman law division between immovable and moveable property. But he went further. He wrote about two kinds of interest in land, estates of production and estates of administration (1965:75–112). And he hypothesized that the dichotomy between immoveables and moveables had different functions in the system of social relations. He said that a social system was stabilized by the fact that immoveable property "provides fixed positions which endure through the passing of generations... moveables establish links between individuals occupying different immovable properties" (1965:116). He was of course thinking of the Barotse among whom he had done fieldwork, but thought the general outlines applied very widely. Jack Goody wrote on *Death, Property and the Ancestors* (1962) in the same decade, and a few years later Franz von Benda-Beckmann made property the very center of his ethnography of Minangkabau, West Sumatra (1979).

The present preoccupation is quite different. The *different* forms property takes in various contemporary societies and situations is emphasized rather than the general patterns. So one very widely read book, *The Social life of Things*, gives a cultural perspective on exchange (1986). In recent African studies there has been a strong interest in the common belief that those who acquire property and become rich quickly, obtain it through illicit, occult, means, thus giving a very modern twist to "witchcraft" beliefs as an expression of the powerful resentment produced by marked disparities in wealth (Geschiere, 1997; Comaroff, Jean and John, 1999). Issues of class and gender, the legacy of colonialism, and environmental issues also emerge, (see, for just a few examples, *de Moor and Rothermund (eds.), Our Laws, Their Lands*, 1994; Abramson and Theodossopoulos (eds.), *Land Law and Environment*, 2000; and Moors, *Women, Property and Islam* 1995)

On a large scale, the legal-anthropological interest today is in the connections among legally protected rights to property and the involvement of these property rights with economy, politics and power. This touches on private and corporate property, and national, as well as international and global arrangements. On a small scale the interest is often in the way property is intertwined with such matters as gender, race, kinship, ethnicity, inheritance, exchange, crime, and local power. Beyond the matters succinctly specified here are large additional categories, so large that it would be impossible to specify all the items that could fit within them. After all, we live in a time when patents may be obtained on genetic patterns, when it is possible to have property rights in the air space above a building, when one can be said to have a property interest in one's public reputation, when "property" describes a type of interest, and the "thing" involved could be almost anything.

The articles that follow in this section are a tiny sample of present and recent work. They demonstrate the breadth and variety of anthropological approaches, but by no means all of its extent. Coombe's chapter is about the control of cultural representations implicit in trademark law, Cohen's is about the inability of Indian law to change the market in human organs. Ruffino's concerns the informal legal system developed in Sardinia to deal with sheep theft, and Bowen's looks at court decisions about the division of family property in Indonesia. Almost any ethnography describes some property relations. But these papers go into detail. They show rule-making by authorities, but they go further and illustrate the meanings and behavior that surround the rules, behavior that conforms or resists the authorities, that may even invent alternative rule-patterns.

S.F.M.

REFERENCES

Abramson, Allen and Dimitrios Theodossoopoulos, eds., 2000 *Land, Law and Environment*. London and Sterling, VA: Pluto Press.
Appadurai, Arjun, 1986 *The Social Life of Things*. Cambridge: Cambridge University Press.

Benda-Beckmann, Franz von, 1979 *Property in Social Continuity.* The Hague: Martinus Nijhoff.

Comaroff, John and Jean Comaroff, 1999 Occult Economies and the Violence of Abstraction: Notes from the South African Post-Colony. *American Ethnologist* 26 (2): 1–25.

Fitzpatrick, Peter, 1992 *The Mythology of Modern Law.* London and New York: Routledge.

Geschiere, Peter, 1997 *The Modernity of Witchcraft: Politics and the Occult in Post-Colonial Africa.* Virginia: University of Virginia Press.

Gluckman, Max, 1965 *The Ideas in Barotse Jurisprudence.* New Haven and London: Yale University Press.

Locke, John, 1996 [1690] *Two Treatises of Government.* Peter Laslett, ed. Cambridge: Cambridge University Press.

Moor, Jap de, and Dietmar Rothermund, eds., 1994 *Our Laws, Their Lands.* Munster, Hamburg: LIT Verlag.

Moors, Annelies, 1995 *Women, Property and Islam: Palestinian Experiences, 1920–1990.* Cambridge: Cambridge University Press.

Rousseau, Jean Jacques 1971[1762] *The Great Legal Philosophers.* Clarence Morris, ed. Philadelphia: University of Pennsylvania Press.

13

Objects of Property and Subjects of Politics

Rosemary Coombe

Introduction: The Cultural Life of Intellectual Properties

This chapter by Rosemary Coombe is part of a book that addresses the relationships among law, culture, and the commodity form. She characterizes her approach as "postmodern," and this stylistic commitment is evident in her vocabulary and in her polemic constructions. What preoccupies Coombe is the bombarding of the postindustrial consumer with symbols of goods for which a demand is being created. What she sees as paramount is the production of cultural meaning through the marketing of goods. Her political sympathies are with subordinate social groups and their response. She makes the point that the words and images conveyed by the mass media create a collective inventory of marketed signs and meanings that form a large part of the cultural environment. She says, "such images so pervasively permeate all dimensions of our daily lives that they are now constitutive of the 'cultures' in which most people in Western societies now live" (1998: 57). The question who has the legal right to use this material, and to what purpose, moves her into a political discussion. She asks what dialogues are possible between subordinate social groups and the companies that own the words and images.

Our law makes many created "things" into property by granting exclusive rights to them to designated persons and organizations. This includes inventions, trademarks, copyrights, and other authored creations, even to the publicity rights of celebrities. Coombe emphasizes that once the non-material thing becomes a property-object, control of that property is in the hands of the owners. She calls attention to the unorthodox use of manufactured signs in popular culture, the

---

From Rosemary Coombe, "Objects of Property and Subjects of Politics," in R. Coombe (ed.) *The Cultural Life of Intellectual Properties* (Durham and London: Duke University Press, 1998), pp. 41–87, 316, 319, 323–5, 329–32, 334.

satirical presentation of slightly distorted trademarks which make fun of their intended meanings, and obliquely defy the owners. As an example (and she provides many others) she cites the children's song, "Comet, it makes you vomit. It makes your mouth turn green" and other forms of parody (1998:58).

Coombe argues that this popular "recoding" of the meanings of cultural signs should be encouraged and protected, because the signs are important cultural resources for the articulation of identity and community in Western societies. She pleads for permitting satirical or derogatory uses of trademarks because she interprets these uses as a means of dialogue between the powerless and the powerful. She argues that the appropriation and transformation of commercial symbols is a necessary form of commentary on political relations, and essential to democracy. But companies are apt to sue those who appropriate the media signs and successfully give them new parodied meanings. The courts back up the owners. Coombe asks, "Why should the most prominent symbols of corporate power be enabled to impart an exclusively favorable impression?" (1998:71). She stresses "the inequalities between those who have the resources to speak and those who must speak the languages of others" (1998:84). Where, she says, is the public interest?

Coombe's approach to law and anthropology is distinctive. With her talk about dialogic democracy, and her emphasis on the blockage of popular expression that results from intellectual property law, she uses trademark law as a metaphor for, or surrogate for, much broader political and economic relations. She calls attention to the market generated dimension of the culture that surrounds us, the role of law in protecting it, and the attempts by others to appropriate the symbols for their own uses. Her book is full of case illustrations, court decisions, and examinations of the various legal doctrines concerning intellectual property. It is also replete with illustrations of instances in which trademarks and other protected symbols were appropriated and integrated in popular culture in a recoded form. Certainly this approach is entirely different from that in the classical ethnographies in which the focus is on the practices and enforceable norms of a putatively culturally homogeneous community and their modes of dispute settlement. Here the topic is industrial society writ large, with its class divisions, the public interest issues associated with the control of cultural objects, the preconditions of democratic dialogue, the interpretations of the judiciary, and the contrasting opinions of Coombe and other social scientists.

S.F.M.

Coombe, *Objects of Property*

... A large group of legal scholars have developed and elaborated a critique of the dichotomous understanding of subjectivity and objectivity that characterizes liberal legal thought. Arguing that the objective world is the cultural construction of social subjects and that subjectivity itself is a product of language and cultural practice, this literature draws upon continental philosophy, North American pragmatism, cognitive theory, feminist theory, and cultural anthropology to support its claims. The idea of an objective world that can be known with certainty by a subject whose capacity for knowledge is independent of that world is repeatedly undermined. The world must be understood culturally in terms of the significance it is given by social groups who perceive, categorize, and act upon it according to socially conventional structures of meaning and language. Human beings may never speak in the name of the real, or grasp the world objectively, because the realities we recognize are shaped by the cultural contexts that enable our very cognizance of the world itself. Cultural categories provide the very possibilities for perception. What we experience as social reality is a constellation of cultural structures that we ourselves construct and transform in ongoing practice.

As Steven Winter once put it, legal objectivists treat the world as if it were "filled with determinate, mind-independent objects, with inherent characteristics unrelated to human interactions," understand categorization as inherent in the world or as a human subsumption of objects that have ascertainable properties that independently establish their commonality, and "treat reasoning as about propositions and principles that are capable of 'mirroring' those objects and accurately describing their properties and relations." Many legal scholars now argue that legal categories bear no accurate correspondence to a singular knowable reality, and that language, rather than mirroring or describing an objective state of things in the world, is constitutive of the world itself. Gary Minda, in an overview of "postmodern legal movements," suggests that second-generation critical legal studies scholarship is concerned to show how legal meaning about the world is created by interpreting subjects who are themselves constituted by particular social and cultural environments. These perspectives all emphasize the constitutive role of culture – socially maintained structures of meaning or relations among construable symbols or signs – in constructing the realities we recognize as well as our sense of self, community, and possibility. The imaginative making of meaning is the quintessential human act, and culture is both this practice and its products...

The idea of discursive production is crucial to any theory of the human subject; cultural construction is a practice in which the mediation of signifying practices forms both consciousness and the unconscious. Anthropologists, whose discipline was traditionally understood as "the study of man," have, ironically, always been in the vanguard of attempts to challenge the unity of this term and demonstrate the radically diverse ways in which personhood is culturally created and experienced. They contribute to a tradition of thought that recognizes that the individual subject always already finds itself in textualized realities, characterized by signifying systems as diverse as myths, kinship, religion, and commodities, although human language is often seen as the paradigm.

When the subject assumes language, forms belief systems, or develops an imaginary understanding of a "real" social position, enmeshings in realms of signification are realized. One of the central tasks of anthropology, conceived as a form of cultural critique, is to demonstrate the contingency of those things we find natural: to defamiliarize bourgeois culture in order to facilitate an enriched understanding of our human situation as social beings. Traditionally, anthropology accomplished this through the ethnographic rendering of others, but such an endeavor is just as necessary to understand contemporary Western social practices. A focus on cultural signification illuminates both how the subject is constructed in social formations and how human agency is accomplished. To understand contemporary subjects mandates an attention to cultural activities in which identities are forged and transformed, interpellated and resisted, maintained and challenged. It is with such practices that this volume will be concerned.

Historicizing the Subject

Legal theory tends to render its reconstitution of subjectivity and objectivity in utopian and optimistic gestures, as if legal tendencies to reify and dichotomize subjectivity and objectivity could be reversed with only a modicum of intellectual good faith and political good will. In the Dionysian social worlds they describe, dialogue is always already our state of being and consciousness. If judges and decision makers were simply to recognize this state of affairs as the human condition, better laws and better decisions would further realize this immanent potential. Such scholarship tends to project a purely theoretical subject, far removed from the social, political, and ethical realities in which human agents actually live and the material constraints they encounter. Legal theorists too frequently evade consideration of the social processes at work in everyday life to fix meaning and stifle dialogue. We need to examine the differential power that social agents have to make their meanings mean something, and the material factors that constrain signification and its circulation in contemporary societies. If, as human selves, in human communities, we are constituted by and constitute ourselves with shared cultural vehicles (as many of us are weary of having to assert), then it is important that legal theorists consider the nature of the cultural forms "we" "share" in consumer societies, and the recognition that the law affords them. If both objective social worlds and subjective desires, identities, and understandings are constructed with cultural resources, then legal attitudes toward these resources may have socially significant implications…

I will wander down some inviting tangents: considering language, texts, intertextuality, and subjectivity in a particular social and historical context – the so-called postindustrial consumer society that cultural theorists acknowledge to be the heartland of the postmodern. The intersection of law, postmodernity, and subjectivity I propose compels us to attend to the constitutive role of the law in creating spaces of power and resistance, constructing privileged authors and piratical thieves, distinctions between originals and copies, providing conditions that both promote and prohibit the creative bricolage, pastiche, and parody identified as a postmodern aesthetic. Intellectual property laws play significant roles both in generating and in regulating that prolific intertextuality celebrated as the signature of the postmodern. By creating objects of property, the law simultaneously creates subjects of politics.

Postmodern Culture

In postwar America, media images have dominated our visual language and landscape, infiltrating our conscious thoughts and unconscious desires. In a century that has seen the intrusion of saturation advertising, glossy magazines, movie spectaculars, and television, our collective sense of reality owes as much to the media as it does to the direct observation of events and natural phenomena. – Marvin Heiferman and Lisa Phillips, *Image World: Art and Media Culture.*

It is important to focus on the human capacity to engage in imaginative meaning-making, as many legal scholars have done, but it is necessary to go beyond abstract assertions about the nature of subjectivity and objectivity to examine concrete practices of self and world creation. To do so, it is imperative that we acknowledge the politics of making meaning and the conflictual nature of struggles to fix and transform meanings in a world where access to means and media of communication is limited. We need to consider, concretely, what the "optimal material and cultural conditions for participatory dialogue" might be in a world as media saturated as the one in which most North Americans live. As a modest contribution to an "ethics and politics based on the dialogical principle," I shall indicate how intellectual property laws often function to deprive us of possibilities for dialogic interaction with the cultural reality or life-world of postmodernity...

Social theorists identify the term postmodern both with a historical era of capitalist development and with particular forms of cultural practice characteristic to it. To simplify things, I will refer to the historical period as the condition of postmodernity, and to its cultural qualities as postmodernism, using the term postmodern or postmodernist to describe practices situated in these contexts. Postmodernity is distinguished by a dramatic restructuring of capitalism in the postwar period, a reconstruction of labor and capital markets, the displacement of production relations to nonmetropolitan regions, the consolidation of mass communications in corporate conglomerates, and the pervasive penetration of electronic media and information technologies. Such processes have coalesced in the Western world in societies oriented toward consumption, which is managed by the capacity of mass media to convey imagery and information across vast areas to ensure the production of demand. Goods are increasingly sold by harnessing symbols, and the proliferation of mass-media imagery means that we increasingly occupy a "cultural" world of signs and signifiers that have no traditional meanings within geographically contiguous communities or organic traditions...

Theorists of postmodernism suggest that we address the "textual *thickness* and the visual *density* of everyday life" in societies saturated with commodified forms of cultural representation. Such images so pervasively permeate all dimensions of our daily lives that they are constitutive of the "cultures" in which most people in Western societies now live...

Our children sleep in Barney® sheets, eat off Aladdin placemats, drink liquids they know only by brand name from plastic cups encircled by Disney characters (protected by copyright laws and character merchandising agreements). "All over the world, more and more of what children eat, drink, wear, ride, play with, and sleep on are influenced by such product promotions, the fruits of corporate licensing departments of Time Warner or Sony or Nintendo and the manufacturers of food, beverages, and toys." A child in the Philippines eats Batman cereal launched by Ralston Purina. Logos like Cabbage Patch Kids, Hot Wheels, and Ghostbusters mark American products as more desirable than local ones in a diversity of markets. When playing in clothing branded with names, images, and logos, children are marked as consumers (and, less obviously, as producers) of an incredible surplus of excess meaning, the value of which accrues to the corporate "authors" of these mass-media texts. The accomplishment of this expropriation of surplus signifying value is effected by intellectual property laws that restrict the right to reproduce these publicly identifiable texts to those who are deemed to "own" them and claim their social meanings under various legal fictions of authorship...

A central dimension of the study of postmodernism has, however, been a concern with the ways in which people "live and negotiate the everyday life of consumer capitalism" and the manner in which people use mass culture in their quotidian practices. If society is characterized by pervasive media imagery, and commodified cultural forms permeate all dimensions of our experience, then we must ask what people *do* with these representations. For "one of postmodernism's most provocative lessons is that terms are by no means guaranteed their meanings." Regimes of signification are used in numerous and unexpected ways; people don't use products only as advertised, and they don't necessarily use advertising as it was intended.

The consumption of commodified representational forms is productive activity in which people engage in meaning-making to adapt signs, texts, and images to their own agendas. These practices of appropriation or "recoding" cultural forms are the essence of popular culture, understood by theorists of postmodernism to be central to the political practice of those in subordinate social groups and marginal to the centers of cultural production. It is now evident that mass-media imagery and commodified cultural texts provide important cultural resources for the articulation of identity and community in Western societies where many traditional ethnic, class, and cultural indicia are fading and minority groups organize along alternative lines (commodity texts may also be deployed in reactivating identities).

Despite their pandemic presence in people's daily lives, insufficient anthropological attention has been directed to the use of commercial signs in capitalist cultures. Corporate trademarks are "friends from our childhood," "members of our extended modern family."[72] We grow up with the jolly Green Giant®, Mr. Clean®, the Lucky Charms®' leprechaun, and the Pillsbury Doughboy. Brand names have become so ubiquitous that they provide an idiom of expression and resources for metaphor. With phrases like the Coca-Cola-ization of the Third World, the Cadillac® (or the Edsel) of stereo systems, meeting with the Birkenstock® contingent (or the Geritol® generation), we convey messages easily and economically.

In practices of appropriation we may discern "indexes of the creativity that flourishes at the very point where practice ceases to have its own language." This is especially important in consumer societies where "marginality" is no longer a quality only of minority groups, but is pervasive, in the sense that most of us are nonproducers of the commodified culture within which we live. Cultural activity increasingly involves the recoding of commodified cultural forms. The tactics of subcultural recodings with respect to commodity/signs encompass a range of practices as diverse as children's songs ("Comet. It makes you vomit. It makes your mouth turn green..."), through adolescent satire magazines (*Mad* magazine's relentless spoofs on advertising), fanzine writing, graffiti artists' defacement of billboards, bootleg T-shirts parodying media figures for parochial purposes, to more intentionally political practices that appropriate commercialized forms in the visual arts, film, media activism, and community organizing...

Author(iz)ing the Corporate Persona

...The signs, symbols, and texts that academic practitioners of cultural studies take seriously as resources for cultural politics are legally defined as properties in which authors are bestowed privileges to preclude reproductions or imitations by others on the basis of their creation under rubrics of originality and distinction. Cultural forms thus become signs with an exchange value enabled and maintained by powers to prohibit uses by others. This was illustrated rather ironically to me while attending a conference on the semiotics of marketing in 1989. Advertising and marketing professionals were offered the theoretical equivalent of fast food – bite-size McNuggets® of Saussure, Pierce, Baudrillard, and Barthes were served up on flowcharts and overhead displays that promised a new science of meaning for the market. Hearing about my interest in trademarks, two marketing consultants eagerly sought me out. They were impatient to let me know that they had obtained federal trademark registration in the term *semiotics*. Although the exclusive protections they obtained pertained only to use of the term in association with marketing consulting services, it was clear that they were bemused by the potentials for exercising their proprietary rights: the possibility of transforming the name of a discipline of linguistic scholarship into an advertising logo. Legally they were enabled to claim royalties and even to enjoin others who might use the term semiotics in association with marketing services or associated wares and goods. The very conference at which we met, with its heavy usage of the term and the preponderence of marketing executives that formed its clientele, was potentially endangered by these preexisting rights. We joked about enjoining the next day's proceedings...

Although trademarks are not conventionally understood to have "authors" because they require no necessary genius, originality, or creativity, the legal recognition that trademark "owners" have a proprietary interest in marketing signs increasingly relies upon a reenactment of the author-function as described by Foucault. This is evident in judicial acceptance of the belief that through investment, labor, and strategic dissemination, the holder of a trademark creates a set of unique meanings in the minds of consumers and that this value is produced solely by the owner's efforts. Sociolinguistics and anthropological scholarship would suggest, instead, that meanings are always created in social contexts, among social agents, in social practices of communication, reproduction, transformation, and struggle: in short, that cultural distinction is socially produced.

Legally, however, the cultural value of a mark generated by such social practices may be expropriated by the owner of that mark and realized as exchange value (thus, companies with rights to trademarks with long histories and a tradition of affirmative advertising are targeted by potential corporate raiders for acquisition or merger). This is justified using rhetoric that mimics the author-function, seeing in the mark's social reproduction, transmission, and reactivation by others only the aura of the corporate persona and its exclusive authorial efforts. Unlike copyright or publicity rights protections, however, the right to control a trademark is potentially perpetual, so long as it continues to be used and retains its distinction in the social imaginary. Unlike human authors or celebrity personas, the corporation may live forever, and its embodied identity in the trademark form shares its potential immortality and, if assigned, will survive even the corporate demise...

By objectifying and reifying cultural forms – freezing the connotations of signs and symbols and fencing off fields of cultural meaning with "No Trespassing" signs – intellectual property laws may enable certain forms of political practice and constrain others.

This is most readily apparent in the exercise of trademark rights, but examples of the chilling power of intellectual property are also rampant in the publicity rights and copyright fields. In any case, in an era when characters, phrases, logos, and even names and faces from movies, novels, and television are the subject of merchandising rights and tie-in contracts, these distinctions become less relevant. Humphrey Bogart's estate, for example, could hold general publicity rights and trademark his name and face to sell cigarettes, and perhaps use Sam Spade to market raincoats, while MGM licenses Casablanca to hotel chains and collects royalties for commercial usages of copyrighted dialogue. These figures from our cultural history become private properties that we parody, proliferate, or politicize to our peril.

Let me give a few examples drawn from the trademark field. In 1977, an environmental rights group distributed materials critical of the practices of the electric utility industry. These materials contained a caricature of the Reddy Kilowatt trademark (a stylized cartoon stick figure). Confronted with a motion for an injunction, the Environmental Action Foundation argued that it was exercising its right of free expression.[110] The defense was rejected on analogy to cases affirming the right of private property owners to exclude picketers. In other words, you can't use someone else's property to express yourself. Trademark rights were never designed to bestow "ownership" over a sign or symbol in any and all contexts; judges, however, often authorize such proprietorship. The Manitoba Court of Appeal, for example, allowed the Safeway grocery chain to enjoin picketing workers from using the stylized S from the company's logo in its strike literature. Deciding that the insignia was known to the public, the court determined it was an asset connected with the company's goodwill, and thus that the company had proprietary rights in it: "there is no right under the guise of free speech to take or use what does not belong to [you]." It was, of course, precisely because the insignia was publicly linked to the company that the union wished to use it, to let the public know that the sign was associated with unfair labor practices as well as the more cheerful connotations projected by the store's management. They attempted to invest the symbol with another, alternative, set of meanings.

The ability to fix the signifier, because you "own" the sign, has expanded dramatically with increased judicial enforcement of state antidilution statutes. Traditional trademark theory protected rights in the sign only insofar as it was necessary to protect consumers from deception and confusion based upon their recognition of the mark as indicating the source of goods. If the public imagined in this legal arena was, as we have seen, largely one simulated to meet the economic demands of trademark holders, at least the protection of the mark was limited to such contexts, real or projected. Increasingly, however, holders of trademark rights are enabled to prevent "misappropriation" even where the use of the trademark is unlikely to cause public confusion and there is no competition between the goods marketed. Indeed, trademark holders may now enforce their rights to maintain their goodwill against public communicative uses of which they disapprove...

The dimensions of dilution now extend to include protection against "blurring" a positive image caused by "dissonant" usage, against "erosion" of the "magic" of the status of the mark, "tarnishing" the luster of a trade name, use of the mark in an "unwholesome or unsavoury" context, and the production of "unsavoury mental associations." The trademark owner is invested with authorship and paternity; seen to invest "sweat of the brow" to "create" value in a mark, he is then legitimately able to "reap what he has sown." The imaginations of consumers become the field in which the owner sows his seed – a receptive and nurturing space for parturition – but consumers are not acknowledged as active and generative agents in the procreation of meaning. When positive connotations grow in the promiscuity of social communication, the trademark owner reaps their benefit as goodwill. The generation of new, alternative, or negative connotations are ignored, denied, or prohibited because patrilineal rights of property are recognized as exclusive: no joint custody arrangements will be countenanced.

"Many of our culture's best known and most powerful symbols are trademarks." Moreover, the "owners" of trademarks are some of the most powerful and wealthy actors in North American society. Indeed, the more famous the mark, the more likely judges are to extend it protection against "dilutions" of its commercial aura. The more valuable the mark becomes, the more legal protection it receives, which of course means that it accrues even more value because it is granted further immunity from scrutiny, competition, or denigration. Protected because it is valuable, it is valuable primarily because it is protected. The production operations and management activities of the corporations that hold such powers may be increasingly invisible to us, but their signifiers permeate our senses and surround us with words and images, sights, sounds, and smells. Why should the most prominent symbols of corporate power be enabled to impart an exclusively favorable impression? Why should these symbolic forms be enabled to maintain a pristine innocence, abstracted from the history and the practices of the corporate bodies that produce them? Commodity fetishism is legally endorsed and sanctioned here in a fashion that is rarely so clearly enunciated.

The Coca-Cola Company, which polices its marks assiduously, is often (one could almost say routinely) successful in preventing unauthorized uses of its globally recognized bottles, logos, and trade dress. In 1972 it enjoined entrepreneurs from marketing "ENJOY COCAINE" posters using the famous script employed by the multinational in its "ENJOY COCA-COLA" advertisements. The court found that impermissible damage to Coca-Cola's reputation would be caused by this unwholesome association with an illegal drug. The injunction was granted, the judge commenting that people seeing the posters might "refuse to deal with a company which could seek commercial advantage by treating a dangerous drug in such jocular fashion." The court conveniently overlooked the company's historically established attraction of its early market through its more than symbolic associations with the drug at issue.

General Electric was granted an injunction against the use of "GENITAL ELEC-TRIC" on T-shirts and briefs in a decision that manipulated the confusion rationale to deal with the threat of tarnishment to the company's image. But what if one were to superimpose the company's advertising slogan, "GE, we bring good things to life," over a drawing of the missiles they produce, or on a photograph of carnage in Iraq (presuming it were established that GE played some role in manufacturing the bombs that inadvertently killed thousands of Iraqi civilians)? Would we be permitted to counter their media message with other mediations? Could we response to their dissimulations, even if we did have access to the same media channels and the same level of resources? Concepts as vague as loss of distinctiveness and tarnishment have the capacity to escalate into a general power to prohibit all reproductions of a mark and "grow into a powerful vehicle for the suppression of unwelcome speech."

The legal doctrine of dilution provides a potent means for corporate actors to manage their public personas. Perhaps the full implications of this have yet to be realized; it is difficult to know. No one is keeping a record of threatening phone calls and letters received by local parodists, political groups, and other "consumers" of corporate symbols, which are subjectively experienced realities rarely documented by those who quantify objectivities for the official record. The political effects of the exercise of these legal rights may well be (and may remain) invisible to us. In jurisdictions that enforce dilution laws, it would not be advisable to comment upon the sexual objectification of women in a bedding company's ads by way of a feminist film suggesting a rape on a mattress identified with its trademark. Nor could you be sure of your freedom to comment upon multinational capital if you depicted a Nestlé billboard in the midst of Third-World squalor and malnutrition. By controlling the sign, trademark holders are enabled to control its connotations and potentially curtail many forms of social commentary...

In 1996 the *New York Times* ran similar advertisements denouncing Joe Camel placed by antismoking activists:

> sponsorship purchases innocence by association for an industry that *should* be worried about its soul. Philip Morris, in particular, seems almost desperately concerned about its image of moral rectitude. Its "Good People do good things" ad campaign pictured Philip Morris employees who help the handicapped, protect animals, and so on... Philip Morris is a great champion of free speech except when it's used to criticize cigarettes. When Dr. Alan Blum of Doctors Ought to Care designed a series of public service announcements satirizing the company's ads, Philip Morris slapped him with a lawsuit. Philip Morris brought out its big legal guns to silence Peter Taylor, whose documentary film *Death in the West* showed real-life "Marlboro Men" – cowboys dying from lung cancer... Philip Morris successfully sued to gain possession of all copies of the film... [and] tried to impugn the film's credibility by questioning the men interviewed in the film about whether they were *really* cowboys.

It would seem that the "innocence" of the Marlboro Man must be maintained at all costs. Other cigarette advertisement parodies mimic the copy, format, and logos of "the real thing" but replace trademarked slogans with more pointed insinuations. Hence, Newport® becomes Newcorpse and its promise of being "alive with pleas-ure" becomes the warning "dead with cancer"; Joe Camel, the "Smooth Character," becomes a black-hooded "Smooth Reaper"; and Merit®'s "New crush-proof box" is represented by a coffin in artist/activist Bonnie Vierthaler's mock ads. Artist Robin Shweder asserts that advertising alterations should be considered a form of cultural interrogation; given their ubiquity as public forms of representation that present cultural content, they are also public forums for critique and arenas for cultural contestation. Shweder, however, simply assumes their availability for such appropriations.

Such artistic appropriations are diverse in terms of their intentions and may be politically distinguished by the public sphere domains in which they circulate and have consequence. Legally, however, they are more similarly situated. By subjecting copyright-protected works and trademarks to histories and meanings other than those their "authors" would claim (production processes, working conditions, employment policies, gender disparities, unemployment statistics, investment practices, pollution, and the social costs of military rearmament) and attaching them to an alterity they contain, disembody, and deny (an authorial persona and presence that is other to their publicity values), artists like Haacke, Vierthaler, and Shweder are put at risk. To reduce or avoid this risk they must, ironically, seek corporate consent: an authorial and authorizing signature must be acquired to secure the alterations of others . . .

More probable, however, is the likelihood that in most cases of politically creative cultural appropriations, freedom of expression arguments will never be asserted, and certainly not publicized. In many instances, the dispute will never be tried on its merits. Faced with the threat of litigation, most local parodists, political activists, and satirical bootleggers will cease their activities. Lawyers advising their clients as to whether to threaten an injunction when they find their copyright or trademarks used in an unwelcome fashion will not be considering the most liberal readings of Lockean natural rights theory, but the most conservative of judicial opinions. The more indigent their opponents, the less likely it is that they will have recourse to counsel sophisticated in intellectual property matters, and the more likely it is that intellectual property holders will be advised to project expansive claims about their own rights and threaten draconian measures of enforcement.

For instance, a local furniture store chain in southwestern Ontario wrote a threatening letter to a Toronto gay nightclub. The bar featured a weekly drag routine in which one performer impersonated and paro-died a comical middle-aged female character who was prominent in the furniture store's frequent television advertisements. The letter promised to seek a legal injunction to enjoin the performance on copyright grounds unless the establishment ceased to depict the female character in its entertainments. The copyright and trademark status of fictional characters in Canada is actually quite limited. With the exception of cartoon characters, whose graphic instances are recognized as works in their own rights, to attract legal protection characters must be so central to the work in which they figure, or be so well-known, that consumers associate them with the source of the goods and services for which they serve as marketing vehicles. It is not clear that in permitting the performance the club reproduced any "work" that might even potentially be protected by copyright. In this instance, there was clearly no registration of a trademark, the character had not been used as a trademark, and had not been so extensively employed as to develop secondary meaning. The likelihood of confusion was limited: the furniture store catered to a downscale, suburban clientele, not the urban gay community (although it is plausible that the company's perception of the homophobia of their market niche compelled them to end any suggestion of association with gay nightlife). However, in the absence of a parody defense, fair use provisions, or any judicial consideration of the intersection between intellectual property and freedom of expression in Canada, the furniture store was on fairly safe ground when it asserted its imagined rights.

Canadian courts granting injunctions in such matters rarely examine the niceties of the parameters of the textual properties in which owner-ship rights are claimed. Those who copy the expressive forms claimed by legally recognized authors may be visited with *ex parte* injunctions and even Anton Piller orders involving raids in which goods and records are seized and confiscated without notice. In circumstances such as these, those visited with accusations of "piracy" are unlikely to have the resources and wherewithal to engage in protracted constitutional litigation . . .

If what is quintessentially human is the capacity to make meaning, challenge meaning, and transform meaning, then we strip ourselves of our humanity through overzealous application and continuous expansion of intellectual property protections. Dialogue involves reciprocity in communication: the ability to respond to a sign with signs. What meaning does dialogue have when we are bombarded with messages to which we cannot respond, signs and images whose significations cannot be challenged, and connotations we cannot contest? . . .

Such centralizing forces of authority (those of the law, the state, the interests of capital) must always contend with alterity – unpredictable, centrifugal forces that find expression in practices like those of satire, parody, irony, quotation, collage, stylization, and polemic. For Bakhtin, the dialogic sphere is a fragile domain that remains in constant peril, threatened by forces of linguistic-ideological closure and centralization. Nonetheless, he continued to believe throughout his life that the carnivalesque tone was deeply embedded in human history and culture and managed to maintain a foothold, however tenuous, in contemporary life. Monologism is always infected by its opposite, the "parodic antibodies" of a transgressive dialogism that promises to rupture this "grey, monotonous seriousness" from within – or, to put it another way, semiotic contestation is immanent within linguistic and cultural practices themselves. These practices, like the appropriate recodings explored earlier, involve a generation of new meanings by unanticipated agencies engaged in metaphorical movements and recontextualizations of the sign.

Attempts to fix the meaning of signifiers or to disarticulate and rearticulate the meaning of texts are the essence of hegemonic struggle, a struggle in which certain social groups periodically *do* manage to fix the meaning of the sign and evoke closure. Because such closure is secured only through discursive practice, however, it is temporary and always open to future disarticulations. The struggles that take place on the terrain of the sign to define its symbolic boundaries are historically specific contentions in which those with divergent social interests strive to establish legitimate meanings for the sign and/or delegitimate the meanings established by others. The sign is dynamic; it maintains the capacity for development – a vitality and a social life – to the extent that it is open to reconfiguration. In postmodernism, I fear, we see fewer and fewer signs of life, but more and more monologic mouments – commercial tombstones marking the demise of the carnivalesque in the condition of post-modernity . . .

This ongoing negotiation and struggle over meaning is the essence of dialogic practice. Many interpretations of intellectual property laws quash dialogue by affirming the power of corporate actors to monologically control meaning by appealing to an abstract concept of property. Laws of intellectual property privilege monologic forms against dialogic practice and create significant power differentials between social actors engaged in hegemonic struggle. . . .

To convey a sense of the significance of those cultural forms protected by regimes of intellectual property, I have thus far posed legal enforcement of copyright, publicity, and trademark rights primarily as a source of danger for democratic dialogue. It would be reductionist, however, to see the power of intellectual property in purely prohibitory terms. The law is always simultaneously prohibitive and productive: it creates realities and constitutes possibilities. In this chapter I let the recoding of others show how law enables authorities to stifle the expressive activities of those who would create alternative, ironic, or oppositional meanings for the texts that circulate in the place of the corporate proper name. In the next two chapters, however, I will move beyond the claim that intellectual property laws potentially effect new forms of private censorship and show how intellectual property laws simultaneously constitute fields of signifying practice – shaping fields in which subjectivities are forged, communities and identities are framed, nations negotiated, and resistances to law's power performed and enacted in everyday life.

14

Where It Hurts: Indian Material for an Ethics of Organ Transplantation

Lawrence Cohen

Introduction

Since ideas can be owned, it comes as no great surprise that parts of bodies can be the property of the person in whose body they are situated. Indeed, parts that become separated from the person can also be owned, such as organs, or sperm, or ova, or blood. It follows, given the commercial turn of our world, that those body parts can be bought and sold, and that there is now an international traffic in organs for transplantation. Since, for the most part, in places like India, the poor are the persons selling their organs, there has been an effort to regulate this traffic.

Cohen's chapter tells us that legislation passed in India in 1994 made such sales illegal in general. However, there were some approved exceptions to the prohibition on live donors, namely that gifts of organs could be made by a close relation or friend. Authorization committees were set up in every state to examine each transaction and to approve appropriate donors who fell within the exceptions. The exceptions proved to be so broad and vague as to allow for general circumvention of the restrictions. Organ sales continued. Some involuntary donations resulted in kidney scandals. These erupted around stories of people anesthetized and tricked into giving organs. Trials have followed. But the question raised in this paper is whether these accusations are genuine, and founded on concern, or were trumped up because of corruption in the whole system.

Cohen inquires into the broad situation of the sellers and the buyers. What is the social milieu in which such sales take place. Could these organ donations be considered voluntary given the extreme poverty of many Indians. Was the eco-

---

From Lawrence Cohen, "Indian Material for an Ethics of Organ Transplantation," *Daedalus: The Journal of the American Academy of Arts and Sciences* 128(4) (1999), pp. 135–65.

nomic situation itself by implication, "coercive"? Cohen explains that there seems to be a gendered aspect of organ donation, women being more likely to give a kidney than men. And saddest of all, the motivation of kidney donation seems to be to get rid of indebtedness to moneylenders. In fact, Cohen speculates that it may be the aggressiveness of moneylenders that results in the decision to sell. And the families that sell are soon in debt again.

This paper shows that state regulation is difficult to enforce, that there are issues about civil liberties in the rights of a person to sell a body part, that the ethical issues are difficult to balance given that the persons who want a kidney transplant are in danger of dying without it and the poor want to sell. What this paper makes evident is that organ transplantation can be deeply enmeshed in everything from local politics to economic distress, and that regulatory law regarding such matters can only be understood in a wide landscape of human misery interlocked with ambition and greed.

This is an anthropological approach to law, ethics and their context in a contemporary milieu. It is in no way concerned with custom and tradition, but with the present day consequences of medical advances. It addresses extreme questions about the balance of interests in life-threatening situations, the ongoing practices and ideas about practices in families, clinics, state agencies, and beyond.

S.F.M.

Prologue: The Scar

WE ARE SITTING in a one-room municipal housing-project flat in a Chennai slum, in a room filled with photographs of the man of the house posing with Tamil political leaders. His wife, one of the persons I am interviewing this June 1998 morning, all of whom had sold a kidney several years earlier for 32,500 rupees (roughly $1,200 at the time of sale), is speaking about why poor people get into debt. Chennai used to be called Madras, and it has become the place where people come in search of a "selling-their-kidneys-to-survive" story. This woman has invited us – myself, the hospital orderly Felix Coutinho who hooked me up with her, and the four other sellers we have found – to use her place for interviews. All of the sellers are women, and all but one have gone through Dr K. C. Reddy's clinic to have the operation. "Operation" is one of the few words I recognize in the Tamil conversation that Mr. Coutinho is translating. I am used to working in north India and the United States, but neither English nor Hindi is of particular use at this moment. As they are cut out from the flesh, organs reconstitute the spaces of bodily analysis, and to delineate these spaces I have found myself continually moving about and ever more reliant, uncomfortably, on translation.[1]

Dr Reddy has been India's most outspoken advocate of a person's right to sell a kidney. His practice – until 1994, while it was arguably still legal to remove someone's kidney without a medical reason – was apparently exemplary: education for potential sellers on the implications of the operation, two years free follow-up health care, and procedures to avoid kidney brokers and their commission. My anthropological colleague Patricia Marshall, on her own and with the Omani transplant surgeon Abdullah Daar, studied the practice of Reddy and his colleagues.[2] She did not find evidence of the often-reported practices of cheating, stealing from, or misinforming sellers. Marshall introduced me to Reddy and to the general practitioner who had run his follow-up clinic for local sellers.

When I first visited the follow-up clinic, an estate with an abandoned air set back from the Poonamalai High Road, I met Coutinho sitting on the verandah with several other orderlies. He had previously been the go-between hooking up sellers with the clinic and knew where to find them. We talked for a while: there were not many patients. The follow-up clinic had closed when Reddy shut down his program in the wake of India's 1994 Transplantation of Human Organs Act, which made the selling of solid organs unambiguously illegal, authorized the harvesting of organs from the bodies of persons diagnosed as brain dead, and forbade the gift of an organ from a live donor other than a parent, child, sibling, or spouse. There were exceptions, approved by Authorization Committees set up in each state that implemented the Act to ensure that the donor was some kind of relation or close friend. *Frontline*, a Chennai-based newsweekly, had published an article the year before documenting how easily these committees were circumvented.[3] As long as the paperwork was in order, the investigative team argued, it was virtually impossible for committee members to differentiate an altruistic donation from a sale masquerading as such . . .

Few of the growing number of Villivakkam experts have commented on what is to the outsider a pronounced feature of the slum's topography: it is saturated with pawnshops where moneylenders buy and sell gold and other precious items. Outside many shops in the slum's central shopping area are boards noting the day's buying and selling prices. Women in particular examine jewelry they are considering buying to consolidate their earnings or bargain over the money and credit earned by pawning their gold. There are few banks.

I worried that Villivakkam might not be the place to begin, given the neighborhood's media glut and my sense of the emergence of information brokers offering investigators whichever version of the trade they seem to want to find. I asked Coutinho whether there were other neighborhoods, where one might learn something new. We ended up in the Ayanavaram municipal projects, in the room with the political pictures, listening to one woman after another recount her story. Similar stories, but different in quality from the various public accounts, *neither* tales of graphic exploitation nor heroic agency. There were obvious biases: Coutinho was identified with Reddy, and his presence might have dampened any accounts of malpractice or exploitation. Conversely, I was signifiably well-off – dressed like the middle class, foreign, and white – and the possibility of future patronage might have heightened accounts of poverty and disappointment. We came in the late morning, when many of the women were back from domestic service but the men were still out working or looking for day jobs; we may have overestimated the proportion of women to men sellers. But the one man we interviewed as well as all of the women said that few men in this neighborhood had undergone the operation. In each neighborhood, the stories we heard varied in the details of a body and its particular situation, but shared several common threads.[4]

What was common: I sold my kidney for 32,500 rupees. I had to; we had run out of credit and could not live. My friend had had the operation and told me what to do. I did not know what a kidney was; the doctors showed me a video. It passes water; it cleans the blood. You have two. You can live with one, but you may get sick or die from the operation or from something later. You have to have the family planning operation because without a kidney childbirth is very dangerous. I had already had *that* operation.

This, too: What choices did I have? Yes, I was weak afterwards, sometimes I still am. But generally I am as I was before. Yes, I would do it again if I had another to give. I would have to. That money is gone, and we are in debt. My husband needs his strength for work, and could not work if he had the operation. Yes, I also work . . .

For the question of contemporary kidney sales in Chennai, additionally relevant is the fact that the relation of medicine to what we might term the constitution of the citizen's body is gendered.

What might such a link between gender, citizenship, and the possibility of transplantation entail? Cecilia Van Hollen has studied the high usage of reproductive medicine and family planning by poor women in Chennai and other cities in the state of Tamil Nadu.[5] The situation differs significantly from much of north India, where women have been less likely to utilize state biomedical interventions like tubal ligations.[6] Many poor women in Chennai incorporate surgery and other obstetric and family-planning procedures into their lives, frequently electing extensive medical intervention. Van Hollen's findings suggest the ubiquity and intensive character of this medicalization as central to any account of agency in women's encounters with the state. *What they said* in Ayanavaram: I already had that operation. They told me I needed to have it before I could have the kidney operation, *but I already had it.*

Thus, most women have chosen to undergo tubal ligation before the decision to sell a kidney is imagined. The emergence of Chennai's various "Kidneyvakkams" must be located in the *prior operability* of these bodies. The operation here is a central modality of citizenship, by which I mean the performance of agency in relation to the state. It is not just an example of agency; it is agency's critical ground. In other words, having an operation for these women has become a dominant and pervasive means of attempting to secure a certain kind of future, to the extent that means and ends collapse: to be someone with choices is to be operated upon, to be operated upon is to be someone with choices. "Operation" is not just a procedure with certain risks, benefits, and cultural values; it confers the sort of agency I am calling citizenship.[7]

Intriguingly, in these interviews the operation was said to weaken men more than women. A prior moment of contest over operability was, of course, the nationwide "Emergency" more than two decades earlier with its legacy of coercive family-planning operations, and particularly vasectomies.[8] Current accounts of the operation's greater danger to men draw upon memories of that earlier time, as well as upon a more generalizable phenomenology of male anxiety in the face of imagined female regeneration.[9] In these women's accounts of their husbands' concerns, an operable citizenship came at far higher risk to men: it literally "unmanned" them. Regions like the "kidney belts" of rural Tamil Nadu feeding the Bangalore industry, where more sellers were men than in Chennai, often comprised settlements of mostly male migrant workers paying off large debts in the wake of the collapse of the booming power-loom industry. Women were back in the village, and were less likely than urban women to have been hospitalized in childbirth or to have had procedures like tubal ligations . . . [10]

Within the terms of such an imaginable gift, what language would pain take? One of the women in the room offers the beginning of an answer. Her operation, she says, caused her body to hurt. "It still hurts." She points to her flank, to the scar. "It hurts there." I ask her, through Coutinho, to describe the pain. There is no data in India on the effects of nephrectomy for these very poor sellers, most of whom lack long-term primary care. I begin to ask her more and more specific questions, sensing a symptom.

She looks at me, then at Coutinho. She had been talking, before my asking her about this pain, about her husband: a story of sporadic work, frustration, and drinking. Were we listening? She looks toward her scar again, and she says: "*That's* where he hits me. There. When I don't have any more money."

Arthur Kleinman has written of ethnography as the study of what is at stake, an elegant and deceptively transparent formulation. [11] The stakes in the postoperative scar differ for the women in the room, for the doctors in Bangalore, for the husband who hits, and for me. For the women, the scar has two moments: a recent past when it marked their successful efforts to get out of extreme debt and support their households, and an indebted present when it has come to mark the limits of that success. A sign of the embodiment of the loans one seeks to supplement wages and give life to one's family, the scar reveals both the inevitability of one's own body serving as collateral and the limits to this "collateralization." One has only one kidney to give, but the conditions of indebtedness remain. At some point the money runs out and one needs credit again, and then the scar covers over the wound not of a gift but of a debt.

For the doctors, the scar is the sign that nephrectomy can and does heal, given their knowledge of the operation, skills, and commitment to what they are doing. Life for life, another physician had said: the real wound is poverty and the operation provided the money to heal it. And yet there is the persistent fear, the counter-knowledge that things can and do go wrong, not only in the healing of the flesh but in the healing of the impoverishment the flesh stands for. Doctors know that sellers have little to no access to hospital care, that they often have to work at strenuous labor, that they are undernourished, and that they live in neighborhoods where infectious disease and alcohol are endemic. They know that much of the money passes quickly through the hands of sellers and goes to moneylenders and that many sellers lack bank accounts. In a different register, doctors also know the public is concerned about rumors of organ-thieving gangs, and rival hospitals might foment an accusation against one or another of them: both public anxiety and the strategies of rivals can bring the police in at any moment. No matter how good the surgery, the scar could still betray them, and sellers have to be kept out of sight. [12] Like de Sade's libertines, the doctors try to erase all evidence of the cut . . .

Life for Life

Contemporary debate on the ethics of the sale of organs surgically removed from the bodies of the poor is shifting. Increasingly, philosophers, physicians, and social scientists are willing to suspend concern and to consider the case for a market in human organs. In India – the most well known of what is now a large number of countries supporting an emerging market in kidneys – several prominent opponents of sales have reversed their position. One of the most vocal of these is R. R. Kishore, formerly a high-ranking medical bureaucrat and currently an active player in the multilateral conferences and task forces constituting the global expansion of the field of bioethics. An architect in the development of the 1994 Transplantation of Human Organs Act, Kishore, in a 1998 interview in Delhi with my colleague Malkeet Gupta and me, concluded that he had made a terrible mistake.

Kishore went through his reasoning carefully. Cadaveric donation will not work in our country, he said, repeating a frequently heard claim. The infrastructure is not adequate; the mentality will not support it. And even though in a few years "we will be able to grow fetuses like popcorn" – a tantalizing phrase – the use of clone technology may have its ethical limits. For the needs of our population, Kishore suggested, we have to reconsider our stance. He turned to a bit of role-playing: "Look, I'm a man dying of hunger. I ask this one for help, he does nothing. That one, nothing. Now I ask you. You say: I'm also dying. I need an organ. I'll help you if you help me." Allowing for an exchange of one man's surplus money for another man's surplus kidney is not really traffic, Kishore concluded, but "life for life." Everybody wins . . .

How do we steer between a flexible ethics that reduces reality to dyadic transactions and a purgatorial ethics that collapses real and imaginary exploitation in the service of complex interests? I am in the midst of a four-year study in Chennai, Bangalore, Delhi, and Mumbai (Bombay), and in lieu of a full answer I offer six points as part of a work in progress.

1   No data exists on the long-term effects of nephrectomy
to sellers or families

Many surgeons in these four cities reported an absence of long-term effects and then went on to insist that follow-up research was impossible since they have no way of knowing where the itinerant or illiterate sellers have gone. Yet the ability of activist physicians, fact-finding teams of ethicists, and journalists to locate sellers suggests that epidemiological research on such long-term effects is eminently possible and would seem to predicate any future calculations of risk-benefit ratios.

After Reddy, two of the most internationally prominent physicians who are advocates for organ sales are Drs S. Sundar and A. K. Huilgol of the Karnataka Nephrology and Transplantation Institute (KANTI), housed in Bangalore's Lakeside Hospital. All physicians in Bangalore and Chennai acknowledged the high standard of care KANTI offers: medically, it is an exemplary site. Like Reddy, Sundar and Huilgol make no secret of their commitment to organ sales as a win-win scenario in the context of local conditions. Like Reddy, they are carefully acquainted with Radcliffe-Richards's work and cite it to challenge opposing positions as both intellectually unsustainable and naïve. Unlike Reddy, however, Sundar, in several 1998 interviews, deflected my question each time I asked about meeting his former sellers. When pressed, he pleaded the impossibility of finding these people or learning much from them.

Many of the Bangalore sellers have come from the Salem-Erode kidney belt. According to social workers and small-town reporters working in that region, these sellers are primarily men who left unirrigated "dry" farming districts for the promise of steady work as the power-loom industry dispersed from cities like Chennai to cheaper production sites. Unlike the Ayanavaram and Villivakkam sellers, these men are more likely to be recent migrants who are indeed harder to follow. This difficulty has been used to forestall attempts to generate data.

Part of Sundar's cautiousness may arise from the possibility of KANTI's knowing or unknowing involvement in the trade. Sundar denies awareness of any illegalities: if his patients say the donor is a relative or family friend, and if the state authorization committee has concurred when necessary, it would be wrong, he argues, not to go ahead. Sundar is open about patients who seek out the committee. KANTI in fact makes a public display of its transparency. The waiting room is lined with large wall charts listing the numbers of every procedure carried out by KANTI and its sister clinics in the state. News clippings attesting to KANTI's popularity in Bangladesh are hung along with a computer-generated sign from Bangladeshi patients thanking the clinic.

Despite this transparent design, three members of the Karnataka State authorization committee who were interviewed acknowledged that few of the donors they were asked to consider were relations or friends, from KANTI or most other Bangalore clinics. Why do committee members approve these donors, then? The state secretary who runs the committee said in an interview with me that patients and physicians have political allies who pressure the committee to grant approvals. Reddy is but the most prominent of several transplant doctors who specifically accused Sundar and Huilgol of "going too far" in turning transplants into big business. Reddy claimed that KANTI has advertised in Sri Lanka and Bangladesh for patients and that Sundar and Huilgol had come to the Kidneyvak-kams of Chennai in search of sellers. Part of Reddy's concern might have been territorial: the urban Kidneyvakkams had for several years supplied Chennai clinics, while the rural kidney belts to the west had supplied Bangalore. "They have become greedy," he said – suggesting that, far from being unable to determine the provenance of kidneys, Sundar and Huilgol themselves served as procurers.

Sundar and Huilgol may well be the victims of false accusations by competitors. But their resistance to follow-up research is striking. The only things missing from the prodigious display of data shown by KANTI on its walls, in its publications, on its web site, and through its dealings with the press are the bodies and statistics of donors. The second time I tried to get Dr Sundar to talk about a possible follow-up study of donors he took out a copy of a Radcliffe-Richards article from his desk and asked me if I had read her. He read choice phrases of the article to me, dismissing my concerns over sellers as paternalist. But where were the donors? If the market structure of transplantation deflects attention from the actual bodies of sellers onto ideologically constituted proxies, how complicit are flexible ethics in maintaining postoperative inattention to sellers?

2   Decisions to sell a kidney appear to have less to do with raising cash toward some current or future goal than with paying off a high-interest debt to local moneylenders. Sellers are frequently back in debt within several years

The Ayanavaram slum dwellers who sold their kidneys described their reasons for selling and their desire to sell again if biologically possible in terms of a transaction not with the present or future – an operation to pay for, a house to buy, a shop to set up, a wedding to finance – but with the past. They were in debt, and could no longer manage their indebtedness and still feed and shelter a household. This finding is tentative, for as most of these borrowing and lending transactions are through private moneylenders and small shopkeepers as opposed to state or private banks or credit associations, data to confirm sellers' and nonsellers' patterns of indebtedness are difficult to generate. But the testaments of sellers do correlate with the work of investigative journalists in Chennai.[13] Furthermore, they make sense within the topography of credit in poor Chennai neighborhoods, in which moneylenders and pawnbrokers are ubiquitous.

None of the Chennai sellers interviewed claimed to have a bank account, and they offered the usual reasons: they were illiterate or poorly literate and of low status, and therefore could not negotiate the language and status practices of the bank bureaucracy with any certainty. Stories of money lost to bankers were common. Jewelry offered a seemingly more practical locus for saving, though stories of gold stolen or appropriated were not uncommon. Most of the kidney money went to pay off debt, and the expenses of husbands and children – education, marriage, medical costs, legal fees – took the rest. Several of the women interviewed mentioned men who drank up the savings.

Persons sell a kidney to get out of debt, but the conditions of indebtedness do not disappear. All of the thirty Chennai sellers with whom Coutinho and I spoke were back in debt again. Organs and blood, from the perspective of the debt broker, are but two of the multiple sites of the collateralization of the poor, ranging from patterns of debt peonage with lengthy pedigrees to expanding new markets in children for adoption, labor, and sex work. Technological transformation like that mediated by the emergence of cyclosporine offers new biosocial strategies for debt markets seeking under the logic of capital to expand.

The argument here is that the decision to sell may be set for debtors by their lenders, who advance money through an embodied calculus of collateral value. In other words, the aggressiveness with which moneylenders call in debts may correlate with whether a debtor lives in an area that has become a kidney zone. If so, the decision whether or not to sell is a response not simply to some naturalized state of poverty but to a debt crisis that might not have happened if the option to sell were not present. Based upon these interviews and discussions with historians, social workers, and journalists in Chennai, my hypothesis is that kidney zones – the vakkams and belts of Tamil Nadu – emerge through interactions between surgical entrepreneurs, persons facing extraordinary debt, and medical brokers. As a region becomes known to brokers as a kidney zone, their search for new sellers intensifies.

Persons in debt are approached. In urban areas, more women than men respond. Creditors, who must advance and call in loans with an eye to interest, collateral, and reproduction – that is, to how much of the debtors' resources to take while keeping them alive and healthy enough to be able to make future payments and take out more debt – also respond to these shifting circumstances... More analysis of local credit practices is needed...

"Manufactured" is deceptive here. If most transplant clinics have violated the letter and spirit of the Indian Penal Code and the later 1994 act in using sellers or passing them off as family or friends, and if sellers are provided minimal care and shunted back to the villages or slums, most clinics are therefore vulnerable to accusation – thus KANTI's strategy of performative transparency. But why police involvement? Most new clinics and hospitals have had to rely upon extensive political patronage to wade through regulations designed to promote a public health sector and limit private growth. Available urban land often has squatter colonies, and significant political capital is needed to move a potential "vote bank." Conversely, the new hospitals offer a variety of services to politicians and industrialists, ranging from a source of political patronage to a literal tax shelter where industrialists and others under trial for foreign exchange and tax violations can be admitted to defer a court date in perpetuity. Journalists and other cosmopolitans in each of the aforementioned cities where kidney scandals continue offered dozens of accounts of the nexus between the new medicine, politics, and industry – some substantiated, many not.

Transplantation, both because it is a critical site of publicity around which periodic panics emerge and because it often involves a nested series of illegalities and produces a class of potentially exploited persons, seems to have become a key node around which competition for control of medical, industrial, and political resources is negotiated. The paradox is therefore created of a politics that tries to quell kidney panics while abetting the periodic negotiation of scandals.

What is the relevance of these scandals to the sociology and ethics of the market in organs? First, they push us to take seriously the need for an ethnography of the state. Radcliffe-Richards and her colleagues make a classic transparency argument, parallel to those used to defeat prohibition or decriminalize prostitution and drugs: if there is exploitation, then legalizing and regulating the market cleans it up while allowing sellers their autonomy. But this argument presumes a state structure, one in which increased regulation has a specified effect and the organization of the state can address the organization of the market. But what if the organization of the trade *mirrors* the organization of the Indian state in its need for brokers? The presumption of the ethicists seems to be that once India is developed into a certain assemblage of rational bureaucratic forms, the current abuses will disappear. This presumption imposes a narrative of the development of the state with little empirical grounding. In consideration of the recent work of Akhil Gupta on the ethnography of the Indian state as well as the writing of Veena Das, Ravi Rajan, and others on the bureaucratic management of treatment for the Bhopal gas disaster victims, what seems more likely is that any new central bioauthority will generate a new class of agents demanding payments from sellers.[14] Such "bioethical brokers" may supplement, rather than eradicate, currently existing tissue brokers and debt brokers in the lives of the poor. At any rate, these are empirical questions that require ongoing ethnography before distanced consideration can be achieved...

The production of scandal, through sociologically complex linkages of state and market agencies and old and new media, maintains the image of a distinctive state apparatus that can intervene to regulate medical abuses against the poor. This image is central to ethical publicity, justifying its presumption of a universal and liberal state structure allowing the invisible hands of utility and reason to guide an individualist ethics of radical autonomy. The public productions of such an ethics are consumed and elaborated by transplant professionals and more generally by the corporate/political hybrid of contemporary health care.

To what world do such ethics speak? Midway through this research, we are left with scattered signs: a woman offering both of her kidneys to MGR; a man in a park begging to a Novartis representative; a postoperative complication of a painful scar that began to hurt when the money ran out.

NOTES

1 George Marcus has written several well-known essays on the risks and benefits of anthropology spreading itself thin, collected in *Ethnography through Thick and Thin* (Princeton: Princeton University Press, 1998).
2 Patricia A. Marshall, "Organ Transplantation: Defining the Boundaries of Personhood, Equity and Community," *Theoretical Medicine* 17 (1) (1996): R5-R8; Patricia A. Marshall and Abdullah S. Daar, "Cultural and Psychological Dimensions of Human Organ Transplantation," *Annals of Transplantation* 3 (2) (1998): 7–11.
3 "Kidneys Still for Sale," *Frontline* 14 (25) (23–26 December 1997); "Options before Kidney Patients," ibid.; "For a Cadaveric Transplant Programme," ibid.
    Raj Chengappa, "The Great Organs Bazaar," *India Today*, 31 July 1990, 60–7.
4 Interviews were recorded and are being transcribed. This summary comes from my written notes taken at the time of the interviews and checked against the tapes; it represents what was common to most interviews and is not verbatim.
5 Cecilia Coale Van Hollen, "Birthing on the Threshold: Childbirth and Modernity among Lower Class Women in Tamil Nadu, South India," Ph.D. dissertation, Department of Anthropology, University of California at Berkeley, 1998; and "Moving Targets: Routine IUD Insertion in Maternity Wards in Tamil Nadu, India," *Reproductive Health Matters* 6 (11) (1998): 98–106.
6 Patricia Jeffery, Roger Jeffery, and Andrew Lyon, *Labour Pains and Labour Power: Women and Childbearing in India* (London: Zed Books, 1989); Van Hollen, "Birthing on the Threshold."
7 The link of operative loss to citizenship has multiple referents in India. Perhaps the most illustrative is the case of castrated *hijras* ("eunuchs"), who claim to lift their saris and show the absence produced by an operation in order to travel on trains and buses and even to cross borders into Bangladesh: the absence is the *hijras*' "all-India pass" or "passport."
8 Van Hollen, "Birthing on the Threshold."
9 See Gilbert H. Herdt, *Guardians of the Flutes: Idioms of Masculinity* (New York: McGraw-Hill, 1981) and Klaus Theweleit, *Male Fantasies* (Minneapolis: University of Minnesota Press, 1987–1989).

10   Van Hollen, "Birthing on the Threshold."
11   Arthur Kleinman, *Writing at the Margin: Discourse between Anthropology and Medicine* (Berkeley: University of California Press, 1995), 98–9.
12   The aforementioned Dr. Reddy, here as elsewhere, is the exception. Unlike transplant physicians interviewed in Mumbai, Bangalore, and Delhi, Reddy made it very easy to locate his calls.
13   "Kidneys Still for Sale," *Frontline* 14 (25) (23–6 December 1997). This *Frontline* piece includes interviews with rural male sellers: "Subhash ran up a debt of Rs.35,000 after the tea shop he owned caught fire; Govindan, a powerloom worker, borrowed Rs.45,000 when his daughter was married. With their creditors pressing them to pay up and nowhere to go, each decided – not without reluctance and a feeling that it would all come to no good – to sell an asset he did still possess, a kidney. . . . Govindan received the promised amount of Rs.35,000 while Subhash received Rs.30,000, one-third less than he was promised. They paid back a part of their debt but began to borrow heavily once again. They were weak and unable to work as earlier. Neither has visited a doctor since the surgery. Subhash is already in debt to the tune of Rs.25,000, Govindan of Rs.10,000."
14   Akhil Gupta, "Blurred Boundaries: The Discourse of Corruption, the Culture of Politics, and the Imagined State," *American Ethnologist* 22 (2) (1995): 375–402; Veena Das, *Critical Events: An Anthropological Perspective on Contemporary India* (Delhi: Oxford University Press, 1995); S. Ravi Rajan, personal communication.

15

Disputing over Livestock in Sardinia

Julio L. Ruffini

Introduction

This is an account of the practices of Sard shepherds in the late 1960s and early 1970s, where they figure both as perpetrators of sheep-theft and as victims of sheep-theft. A flock of 150 to 200 ewes is considered small. The shepherds are alone with their animals up in the mountains for weeks at a time, far from town. They are obviously vulnerable to theft. As such stock-theft is not seen primarily as a crime, but rather as a dangerous, challenging, bravado act of valor by the young. What is dangerous about it is that it can escalate into feud, violence, and murder.

When a theft occurs the shepherd does not run to the Italian police. Though there is an Italian legal system available to them, with courts and codes and a system of sanctions for breaking the law, the shepherds consistently avoid those national institutions. This is partly because the *carabinieri* (the national military police) are the people who deal with stock theft. They are usually outsiders, not Sards, serving in the area for a temporary period of time, and the relationship between them and the shepherds is one of mutual hostility.

Instead of complaining to the *carabinieri* when sheep have been stolen, the shepherds set local institutions into motion. They prefer negotiation between the disputants, mediation, or arbitration. The Sard shepherd uses his social ties when he is in trouble. His kinship, ritual kinship, patron–client relations, neighborhood, and friendship bonds are those he relies on. This is his core action set. But beyond this he can mobilize a mutual aid society (*soci*), The whole of the village community of shepherds is ready to support him. They help search for the lost animals and for the culprit, using their own networks and operating through

From Julio L. Ruffini, "Disputing Over Livestock in Sardinia," in Laura Nader and Henry F. Todd (eds) *The Disputing Process: Law in Ten Societies* (New York: Columbia University Press, 1976), pp. 209–47.

intermediaries. Settlements are negotiated. In some cases the thief is only required to return the stolen animals. In others he must do so and must add some
of his own as compensation. This is what happens when the identity of the thief
is known and all are agreed that he is in the wrong. But if the animals cannot be
traced, and the thief succeeds in hiding his identity from the victim, sometimes
the victim must pay some form of ransom to get his beasts back.

If he belongs to an organization called the *barracellato*, he has an even better
support system available. The barracelli operate all year long and send out armed
patrols to protect against thievery. The community of shepherds of a village who
elect to have *barracelli*, also pay dues to support them. Such companies are
formed annually by local proprietors. Though voluntary and community based,
these organizations are regulated by the communal councils, the provincial
prefects, the Sard Region and the Italian government. They are thus, in a sense
a hybrid organization, recognized and regulated by government, but local in
their foundations. They are a kind of insurance company because if there is a
theft and they are unable to recover the animals, the *barracelli* are obliged to
pay the victim 75 percent of the value of the animals. If the barracelli have not
spent their treasury of dues on such disasters, at the end of the year they divide
what is left among the members. Thus they have a financial motive to be diligent
in their patrols and to locate thieves efficiently.

This is a case of a plural legal system, of many semi-autonomous social fields in
which the members sometimes operate independently of one another, sometimes in concert. And it is an instance in which there is some flexibility, some
choice of intermediaries, of remedies, and of alliances.

S.F.M.

SARDINIA is, except for Sicily, the largest island in the Mediterranean Sea. It is
approximately 170 miles long from north to south and ninety miles wide from east
to west.

The island is composed largely of mountains and upland plateaus intersected by
small rivers, most of which dry up in the summer (Guido 1963: 23–6). Most of the
high mountainous land, the Barbagia, is in the central and eastern part of the island,
the highest and most inaccessible region being the wild and bare peaks of the
Gennargentu range, which rise to 6,000 feet. This zone is mainly of granite, with
sharp, craggy summits and wide valleys. The vegetation is generally patchy scrub
dotted with oaks scattered over pasture land. The area is poorly watered (Guido
1963: 26).

Although Sardinia is now integrated into the social and cultural life of the Italian
nation, it maintains a strong sense of separateness, symbolized by its own language,
which is not comprehensible to continental Italians. In many respects the age-old
historical pattern of relations to its political and economic masters continues today.

Sardinia has been occupied and controlled by a long series of foreign powers that
did little for the local inhabitants, but exploited their resources – the Carthaginians,
Romans, Vandals, Byzantines, Genoese, Pisans, Spaniards, and Piedmontese. In
1861, Sardinia became part of unified Italy. In earlier times, the nature of the terrain
and the poorly developed systems of transportation and communication, in conjunction with the indifference of the rulers, meant that the mountainous interior zones

were relatively uncontrolled by the central governments. In this historical situation of neglect and exploitation, a number of indigenous responses to problems of social control were created, including a shepherds' legal system.[1]

The Setting

Mountainous Barbagia, called "an island within an island," is the heartland of pastoral Sardinia and the region where the legal system of the Sard shepherds described in this essay prevails. The region's economy remains almost entirely pastoral.[2] Shepherds are found all over the island, but most of them are from the Barbagia and other zones of the east-central mountains.

Here tens of thousands of shepherds, from several score of villages perched high atop bare rocks, follow their flocks of sheep and goats on the perennial search for scarce pastures. Most of these shepherds are transhumant; they migrate with their flocks each winter from their cold and snow-bound mountain homes to lower and warmer coastal and plains areas throughout the island. They may travel as many as ninety miles from home, and they may be gone for three to nine months of the year. It is not only the climate that necessitates their annual migration. The shepherds of the highest zones own vast flocks of animals, far too many for their sparse pastures, and so they are forced to seek pastures elsewhere. They obtain these pastures in a number of ways, by a variety of rental and share-cropping arrangements with peasants and landowners, and more recently by purchase.

Many of the winter pastures consist of stubble and other remains of harvested crops. In the mountains the vast majority of pastures consist of unimproved, wild grass growing on rocky soil, amid clumps of oak trees and low brush. Only in recent years have some shepherds had enough good land to sow with hay for winter feeding, and seldom do they plow and sow meadows. Consequently, the sheep are not kept in stalls and fed forage – hay and grains – but wander endlessly over vast stretches of wild, lonely mountain pastures.

This system of pasturage requires the constant attention of the shepherd. The animals, if not watched constantly, may die by falling off cliffs or may be eaten by predatory animals or stolen by thieves. The shepherd must remain close to his animals for an even more important reason. Unlike many other pastoral economies, where sheep are raised only for their wool and meat, and therefore huge flocks can be maintained by a few men, in Sardinia the sheep and goats are kept to be milked. The milk, which is made into cheese and shipped to Italy to be sold throughout Europe and America, has to be obtained twice daily from the ewes. Consequently, a shepherd must remain close to his animals, and the number he can maintain by himself is limited.

Nevertheless, even with a small flock – 150 to 200 ewes – a shepherd can earn a good living. The cheese made from the milk of these sheep, which feed only on wild grass and wild aromatic herbs, is in great demand, and the sheep are excellent producers. The shepherd augments his income from milk and cheese by the sale of male lambs and wool. However, the vast majority of shepherds are not prosperous. Most of them do not own their own pastures, or all the pastures they require, and they must pay extremely high rents for additional land.[3] They are also forced to sell their milk or cheese at prices fixed by the dairies and cheese merchants. This economic squeeze, along with the grave risks of stockbreeding in a zone with a harsh climate and poor soil, results in a highly risky life for the shepherd.

In the last few years the government has provided money to build some solid shelters for the shepherds in the countryside. These shelters serve as storage barns for feed and provisions (recently the government has subsidized purchase of grains during periods of drought), sleeping quarters for the men, and dry places for the production and storage of cheese. Most shepherds do not have these facilities, however, and continue to rely on the thatched stone huts of their ancestors.

Apart from their transhumance, the shepherds are gone from home weeks at a time, alone with their animals in the mountains. They must milk their animals twice a day and then either transport the milk to distant dairies or to roads where the dairy trucks pick up the milk, or make the cheese themselves. Winter is a particularly difficult time, as it is lambing season and scores of lambs may be born, often at night, while the shepherd is often still in the cold, wet mountains. The shepherd lives close to nature, and in Sardinia nature is harsh and unfriendly.

Since the shepherd lives in the open, far from town and its amenities, he is also at the mercy of his fellow man. If he does not maintain friendly relations with all and at the same time earn the wary respect of all, he is vulnerable to predatory attack. If he leaves his animals unguarded for long, or at regular, predictable periods, he may lose them to thieves or enemies. If he makes enemies, he is alone in the country and he and his animals are vulnerable to attack. This vulnerability of the shepherd – alone in the mountains with no police protection – is a very important reason for his behavior in disputes over livestock.

Social and Political Organization

Sardinia is an autonomous region of Italy, with its own parliament, authorized to pass legislation that does not conflict with Italian law. In contrast to the past, the Italian government devotes much money to the island, generally to buttress the burgeoning governmental structure and to encourage industrialization and tourism. Sardinia is also a recipient of Italian mass culture – movies, music, clothing styles. It is no longer a forgotten backwater.

Sardinia is divided into four provinces, each named after its capital city. Cagliari, the southern province, is largely agricultural and industrial and is the most populous.[4] Oristano, in the west, is largely agricultural. Sassari, in the north, is commercial, agricultural, and pastoral. Nuoro is central and mountainous, and mainly pastoral. The provinces are headed by prefects, who are appointed and are part of the central state bureaucracy.

The lowest administrative unit is the commune – city, town, or village. There were 354 communes in Sardinia in 1966. Of these, 212 were considered by the Sard regional government to be mainly pastoral (Brigaglia 1971: 332). About 98 percent of the Sard population lives either in cities or small rural nucleated settlements. Only

2 per cent lives dispersed in the countryside (L. Pinna 1971: 45). Most Sard communes are small and rural, with populations ranging from 1,000 to 5,000. The rural communes follow the typical Mediterranean pattern of a nucleated village surrounded by vineyards and orchards, vegetable gardens, and pastures.

Typically, the land used by a commune forms concentric circles about the settlement. In the nearest circles the land is used for vineyards, orchards, and vegetable gardens. Beyond these is the land used for grains. In the furthest circles, and comprising most of the land, are the pastures. Dotted throughout these pastures, in the mountains and valleys, are thousands of sheepfolds, the enclosures where the sheep, cows, and goats are milked, cheese is made, and other routine work of the shepherds is performed.

An important principle of organization below that of the village is that of the neighborhood. The *vicinato* (*ikinatu* in Sard) is a principle of organization of great importance in the Sard village. *Vicini* (neighbors) have definite and precise rules of behavior and mutual expectations. One's vicinato is carefully delimited geographically. A precise number of houses on each side of one's own and a certain number across the road constitute one's vicinato.

Basically, neighbors expect to help each other with such chores as breadmaking, to visit each other and exchange gifts, and to attend each other's life crisis ceremonies. They can also be depended upon for aid in other crises, such as sickness.

The concept of vicinato extends also to the countryside, where a shepherd has similar relations to the vicini of his sheepfold, who are expected to establish and maintain relations of trust. They help each other at shearing time, visit each other (an important function in the lonely countryside), and watch each other's animals during a shepherd's absence. Vicini of the sheepfold can also be called upon for information and assistance in searches when theft of animals has occurred. Above all, they are expected to refrain from stealing each other's animals.

The most important group in Sard rural political and social organization is the family. The family is generally nuclear, but very often, in pastoral areas, the flock management unit consists of the father and sons until the death or retirement of the father, after which the brothers continue to work together, at least until their own sons are mature. Efficient flock management requires several hands and, typically, flocks are managed by two to four or more adult brothers. Very often these brothers live together in a building, even though they may not share the same hearth.

Sons expect to receive equal amounts of the family estate when they marry. Shepherd brothers who marry continue to manage their animals together after division. Failure to divide the inheritance equally often results in bitter disputes (L. Pinna 1971: 53–60).

The structural tension between brothers and other close relatives, either actual or potential, means that the individual cannot always rely upon the support of a large kinship group. Even when kinship ties are strong, Sards consciously attempt to expand their ties within the village and in other villages. They do this through ties with vicini. Patron-client relations and ritual kinship (sponsorship of baptisms, weddings, and other religious events) are also extremely important in rural Sardinia as means of strengthening and creating social bonds. Friendship networks are also crucial in political and social organization.

All these types of social ties – kinship, ritual kinship, patron-client relations, neighborhood, friendship – are used by the Sard shepherd to strengthen his position as he competes for survival and advancement in a harsh environment. They are all of major importance in the Sard legal and political systems and play a central role in management of conflict over livestock. The importance of these social ties, as well as other institutions and processes which operate in disputes over livestock theft, is illustrated in the following case.

[. . .]

Livestock Theft

Livestock theft has probably been a salient feature of Sardinian history as long as pastoralism has been practiced. Any period of Sard history that is well documented discloses the incidence of theft of animals. Certainly in recent centuries it has been extremely widespread, and regarded locally and nationally as a major problem. It is difficult, if not impossible, to be very precise about the number of animals stolen. Official figures exist, but their value is limited, as very many, if not most, animal thefts are never reported to the authorities.

Sardinia has always been a poor region, especially in the rural zones. In periods of acute misery and poverty, livestock theft was widely viewed as a means of survival. It has also long been viewed as a means of enrichment and social advancement. It is seen locally as a legitimate and natural act of valor on the part of shepherds, especially young ones. Given these factors, it is not surprising that in an island with about 3,000,000 sheep alone, livestock theft should continue to be regarded as a serious problem.

Aside from the economic threat, livestock theft is serious because it may result in disputes that escalate to feud, violence, and even murder. Consequently, the Sards attempt to regulate livestock theft through their own legal and political systems, in an effort to minimize its disruptive effects.

The state authorities are also concerned about escalation of livestock theft and, in addition, its potential links with banditry. Suspected livestock thieves may have to become outlaws to avoid arrest. Outlaws, to support themselves, steal animals. As Pirastu (1973: 143) states it, "Theft of animals has nearly always been . . . the first link in the chain of banditry, original cause of vendetta, conflict between families and groups, or reprisals, and sometimes of homicides."

Legal Pluralism

. . . Sardinia provides an excellent example of a particular form of legal pluralism, in which two strong and thriving legal systems operate within the same society – that of the Italian state, and that of the Sard shepherds – but in which the legitimacy of the latter is not recognized by the state.

It might be expected that a Sard shepherd would be able to use either or both of these legal systems in his effort to settle disputes, resolve conflicts, defend his interests, or score against an opponent. In many areas of conflict Sards do indeed employ the mechanisms of the state legal system. In one crucial and important area, however – in disputes relating to animal theft[5] – Sard shepherds almost universally prefer to avoid the state legal system in favor of their own. There are a number of reasons why they prefer to choose one legal system over the other, and this paper attempts to examine the constraints upon Sard shepherds' freedom of choice in this area...

The Italian State Legal System

The national legal system is represented in Sardinia by the *carabinieri* (national military police) and the *pubblica sicurezza* (national police). Also present is the Italian court system, with its legal personnel (judges, lawyers, bailiffs), formalized codes of procedural and substantive law, norms and values, and system of sanctions (prison, probation, forced residence, fines). The national legal system is unitary, formal, and impersonal. Delicts are expressly defined, and so are the means by which they must be handled by all levels of legal personnel. The law is a body of specific prohibitions accompanied by specific procedures for dealing with infringements of the law.

Livestock theft is, according to the state legal system, a crime punishable by a series of penal sanctions, including prison. It is the duty of police officers to prevent livestock theft, apprehend thieves, arrest them, and compile evidence against them to be used in court proceedings. Disputes between parties over livestock are to be settled in court. Police are not dispute settlement agents.

The courts are not corrupt, but Sards generally agree that they are inefficient and understaffed. Delays are of legendary and awesome proportions. The nature of many Sard disputes, including disputes over livestock, is such that it is difficult, often impossible, for a judge to gain a clear picture of the situation. Crime may occur in the countryside with no witnesses. It is often the word of one man against that of another. It is easy to establish alibis and provide oneself with supporters who will claim to be witnesses.

Cases can be quite complex, with years of historical ramifications. The courts, with their harassed urban personnel, are ill equipped to cope with many of these cases. Thus judicial decisions may be seen by one or more of the parties to be arbitrary, unpredictable, and unrelated to reality. Furthermore, the decisions do not serve to reconcile the disputants. They do not establish peace between them but may actually cause further deterioration of relations between disputants and their supporters, who may have had to testify against each other.

Everyone to whom one speaks in Sardinia agrees that the judicial system has serious defects. The personnel of the system, the media, and organs of national public opinion, however, insist that this admittedly imperfect legal system is the only legitimate system for dealing with criminal activity, including livestock theft.

The major state legal effort against livestock theft is represented by the carabinieri. The carabinieri are outsiders in the rural communities where they work and are usually not Sards. They generally remain in one zone for only a few years before transferring to what they invariably consider more desirable stations.

The carabinieri, as part of their work, attempt to maintain a position of aloofness toward the local population, so that their dignity and impartiality cannot be compromised. They see themselves as outsiders who represent an impartial and impersonal legal system. When they act in the area of livestock theft and its related activities, they operate with a set of norms, rules, and procedures, all clearly defined by the national legal system.

They do not see themselves as locals enmeshed in the cultural and social life of the community. On the contrary, they see the shepherds' community as alien and hostile, a community they have to control and supervise, but one that is alien to the national Italian culture and its legal system. Carabinieri often conceive of shepherds as synonymous with criminals, guilty until proven innocent. Consequently, when carabinieri act in cases of livestock theft, they do not see themselves as mediators, arbitrators, or conciliators between disputants.

The attitude of the carabinieri toward the rural Sard population is reciprocated. In rural, and especially pastoral, communities the hostility toward the carabinieri is marked.

Consequently, the investigations of the carabinieri are hampered by a general unwillingness on the part of the rural population, and shepherds in particular, to cooperate with them in cases of livestock theft. Shepherds do not want to become involved in court proceedings against other shepherds, who might be imprisoned as a result of their testimony. They generally feel that disputes over livestock should be settled within the shepherd community rather than in the courts.

Because of these factors the carabinieri are not able to integrate themselves into the local friendship networks to obtain information. They sometimes employ police informers, who generally are not effective because they are unable to regularly integrate themselves into the networks. Consequently the police have to rely on patrols in the hope of apprehending thieves with stolen animals or butchers with stolen meat.

These patrols often find stolen animals, but usually the animals are wandering about freely and the thieves are not discovered. The patrols also further embitter shepherds whose sheepfolds they inspect. Moreover, these patrols are carried out during the day; the carabinieri seldom venture into the countryside at night, when livestock are usually stolen.

Sard Shepherds' Value and Legal Systems

A number of Sard legal scholars have written on the topic of the shepherds' value and legal systems.[6] What emerges from the writings of these and other scholars, as well as from my own fieldwork, is a well-defined, discrete system of values and norms of behavior in situations of conflict, with institutions and processes that can be called upon when needed. The ultimate sanction in the system is the threat of attack.

The shepherds themselves conceive of two distinct, competing legal systems, their own and that of the state, which they feel is alien, oppressive, and not responsive to the needs of their daily lives. The state law is imposed from without, while their own law emerges from their own social structure and is thus seen as "natural." The shepherds reason that the laws of the state are suitable for the towns and townspeople, where life is more "civil," but that in the harsh environment of the shepherds, laws must be flexible and more attuned to reality (G. Pinna 1967: 26–7).

Consequently, Sard shepherds continue to resort to their own indigenous legal system. The usual procedure for settling disputes is negotiation between disputants or mediation. Mutually acceptable agreements are effected, based upon normative rules and assessment of relative power. The community (village and shepherd) knows about the general provisions of the agreement, and the sanction of public opinion buttresses the agreement.

If the disputants are not able to effect an agreement, the dispute may escalate to feud or vendetta, or the disputants may continue, for years, to be in a state of enmity without resolution, in which they avoid each other. This lack of resolution of a dispute is disliked, as the disputants fear that they may at any time be the victims of attack, even years after the start of the dispute.

The preferred solution, therefore, when negotiation or mediation fails or even at the outset, is arbitration. The use of local arbitrators in many types of disputes is still widespread, because it is inexpensive and local arbitrators are familiar with the situation.

Arbitrators are called *sos homines*, "the men," with the connotation that they are mature men, dignified, able, and respected. In the most simple and frequent form of arbitration, *tres homines*, there are three arbitrators. Each disputant chooses one, and these two together choose the third, a man regarded as independent and objective. The disputants swear to accept the majority decision, and apparently they usually do, except in cases of suspected favoritism on the part of the arbitrators. Usually disputants are of the same or similar social class but often richer people use arbitration in disputes with poor people, who feel more confident with this system than with state could (G. Pinna 1967: 117–18) . . .

Pigliaru notes the Sard shepherds have values concerning the types of actions a man of ability should take, which are, lamentably, often regarded as criminal by state law (Brigaglia 1971: 167). Livestock theft is a case in point.

According to the experts, and my own data, livestock theft is viewed by shepherds of the Barbagia not as a crime, but as a "normal element" of pastoralism. It concerns only those directly interested – the victim and those who have close ties with him. Livestock theft is, for the shepherd, a traditional and normal practice. One steals to enrich himself. One also steals to prove one's valor – valentia – the fundamental virtue of the shepherd. The ability to steal animals has always been, in the Barbagia, a matter of pride (*L'Unione Sarda*, July 29, 1970, p. 8).

Livestock theft is not seen by the shepherds as a criminal offense, except under certain circumstances. If a thief steals from a ritual kinsman, friend, or neighbor, it is considered wrong (G. Pinna 1967: 49–50); it is also considered wrong if he steals the family goat or if he steals under circumstances meant to offend (Brigaglia 1971: 195–96). Otherwise, the theft is considered normal. In a case of "normal" theft, the victim attempts to obtain the return of the animals through his social networks within the shepherd community. He does not resort to the machinery of the state legal system, as that could be dangerous and expensive. It would also create enmity, while private accords eliminate these dangers (G. Pinna 1967: 49–50).

Pigliaru, Gonario Pinna, and other writers give much evidence to support the existence of these attitudes as well as the legal machinery concerned. It is not possible here to discuss this any further. I merely wish to emphasize that to the shepherd of the Barbagia, livestock theft is not regarded as a crime, but as the source of a dispute, which should be settled amicably without recourse to the state. The positive attitude of shepherds toward animal theft – one proves his worth by stealing animals; one can become rich by stealing animals; a poor man can eat only if he steals – is an extremely important factor in the way the indigenous legal system copes with livestock theft.[7]

The shepherds' political and legal systems as they relate to coping with the problem of livestock theft will be described briefly in terms of a number of structural characteristics: the levels or types of social organization which shepherds can mobilize to deal with the problem; the institutions – patterned forms of behavior and expectations – that they can mobilize to settle disputes over cattle; the values and goals that motivate actors within the shepherds' legal system; and the processes employed by shepherds to deal with livestock theft.

Levels of Organization

Within the shepherds' legal system are three subsystems of management of conflict over livestock which can be viewed as levels of organization, each incorporating a greater degree of community participation and responsibility. These three are ego-centered core action sets, mutual aid societies (*soci*; singular: *socio*), and organizations that combine the functions of insurance companies and armed patrols for self-protection (barracelli).

A shepherd who is the victim of livestock theft, acting on his own, with the support of his core action set, has the moral support of his village. All who hear of his plight may be expected to offer expressions of sympathy and solidarity. But only his closest supporters (kinsmen, ritual kinsmen, friends, and neighbors) will be actively mobilized to search for the animals and the thief and to support the victim in his often threat-laden negotiations with the thief. If the victim is ultimately unsuccessful in finding his stolen animals, he cannot always be sure that all the shepherds of the village, as distinct from his core action set, will contribute to restore his flock to its original size.

Furthermore, not all shepherds are equally able to mobilize action sets. Not all are equally popular. Not all have large, prosperous families with many members free to help the others. Not all have been in a position in the past to help others so that they may effectively call for a return for previous favors. Consequently, the use of core action sets, while almost universal in lifestock theft cases even when higher levels are simultaneously brought into play, is not always sufficient.

Soci, or voluntary mutual aid societies, are therefore often formed to provide more security for individual shepherds and to broaden the degree of community support. Soci may be composed of a number of shepherds from one village who agree to form them, or they may be commune-wide, all shepherds of the village being members.

In either case, the processes and institutions used by shepherds at the socio level of organization are the same as those used in the core action set level (and on the barracello level). The essential difference is that the entire village community of shepherds, or segments of it larger than the core action set, are formally committed, before the fact, to support a victimized shepherd. When a shepherd is victimized, the entire socio is mobilized to support him. All members (or representatives of all families) help search and provide support in the delicate negotiations. If the animals are not returned, all contribute to the restoration of the lost flock.

The barracelli differ from the other two subsystems in that they act not only after the fact but continually, all year long, with armed patrols designed to prevent theft. The community of shepherds of a village which elects to have barracelli is committed in the form of dues payments as well as preventive patrols. Furthermore, the barracelli, who are both state officials and shepherds, have more strength than shepherds alone, for behind them is the constantly menacing presence of the state. In the institution of the *barracellato*, the two legal and political systems meet, if not always in easy compatibility.

Companies of barracelli are a curious combination of local insurance companies for livestock and crops, and rural armed constabularies. The companies are organized yearly, on a communal basis, where the local proprietors decide to form them. Once a company is formed, all proprietors must insure their crops or animals, as the case may be, with the company. The barracelli, or members of the company, are generally the proprietors themselves, and they form an armed unit whose purpose is to patrol the countryside to prevent theft or vandalism.

While these associations are voluntary on a communal basis, once they are formed they are regulated by the communal councils, the provincial prefects, the Sard Region, and the Italian government. The barracelli, though an indigenous and unique Sard institution, are recognized by the Italian legal code[8] and regulated by the various levels of Italian governmental machinery.

Whenever the barracelli exist in a given commune, they represent the highest indigenous organizational level of formality and community involvement and solidarity. Yet it is important to realize that the people who become barracelli are shepherds and day laborers – the same people who participate in the core action sets and soci in the absence of companies of barracelli. They conceive of themselves as shepherds protecting their property. They do this in the same ways they did as actors in core action sets or soci, using the same processes and institutions, and with the same methods and motivations. The state, however, views the barracelli as public agents with the responsibility to enforce the state laws, in town as well as in the country, and as representatives of the Italian legal system. Under this mandate the barracelli are expected to keep the peace in town (breaking up fights, for example), help search for bandits, and arrest suspected livestock thieves. These duties the barracelli are loath to perform, as they violate the legal principles of their own communities.

The barracelli patrol the territory of the commune to prevent theft of animals insured with their company. If thefts do occur, all the barracelli participate in the search for the stolen animals and the thieves. If they are unable to return the stolen animals to the victim, they must pay him 75 per cent of the animals' value.

The barracelli are not paid salaries for their work. At the end of each year the treasury (consisting of the dues paid) is divided on the basis of the number of each member's tours of duty. If the barracelli have been successful in preventing thefts, each barracello has a considerable sum of money to supplement his income and defray the cost of his insurance. If the company has been inefficient and has had to pay for many thefts, the barracelli may have little or nothing. Legally they are responsible for paying victimized proprietors from their own pockets if the treasury is empty.

The barracelli, then, are motivated to prevent theft and return stolen animals, both because the animals are their own and because they will suffer financially if stolen animals are not returned. They are not motivated, however, to *arrest* thieves, which they are empowered and expected to do by state law.

Institutions of Settlement within the Sard Legal System

Friendship

Friendship, *amistade*, is a concept frequently used by Sards in a wide range of contexts, not only in reference to livestock theft. Sards of all strata, but particularly shepherds, consciously establish and maintain extensive friendship networks throughout the geographical zones of their activity. Together with consanguineal, affinal, and ritual kinship, and patron-client relations (which are often expressed in the idiom of friendship), friendship networks provide shepherds with a measure of security, information, and potential support.

Transhumant shepherds are highly mobile. The need to find pastures for their flocks requires them to seek friends and patrons throughout the island, in many communes. Ties which begin as relations of landlord and tenant are often trans-formed to ties of kinship, real and ritual, and they form the basis for further contacts as shepherds seek to establish nuclei of trusted supporters in each area. From these friends they can obtain information on pastures, rents, and prices, potentially useful social gossip, information on potential victims of theft if they are inclined to steal, support in their disputes with others, and companionship. Above all, friends are used by victims of livestock theft to attempt to find the stolen animals or establish contact with the thief, and by the thief to establish contact with the victim, if he desires to negotiate the return of the animals for a price. In a society in which it is necessary to establish an acceptable identity and be vouched for when in a strange town, and where it is impossible to obtain information or support from a stranger, a friend is an absolute necessity.

Friendship in Sardinia consists of an overlapping network, extending from the village to other communes and to other sheepfolds in the mountains. These net-works, often linked by casual acquaintances, extend through entire zones, and form, in the minds of the shepherds, social maps with which they can chart their journeys. These networks are consciously established, and the need to maintain and reinforce them by prestations, reciprocal hospitality, and expressions of goodwill and friend-liness, is consciously recognized.

Aside from the shepherds themselves, a number of others who play key roles in disputes over livestock have occasion to establish wide networks. Middlemen, buyers of cheese, milk, lambs, and wool, travel far and wide in their business and know many people. Butchers do also, and they are also potential receivers of stolen animals. Wealthy landowners often own land in a number of communes and employ servant shepherds from a number of communes. All these people, in addition to shepherds, may become links in the chain of friendship used in disputes over animals. Sometimes these links play an active role beyond seekers and providers of information, they become mediators.

Mediators play an important role in the process of negotiations between disputants over livestock. They are links in the friendship networks, employed by either the victim or thief, or both. People with wide networks, prestige, influence, and appropriate personalities are called upon or volunteer to be mediators. In every commune there are a number of people who everyone knows are the men to go to with a problem. They are respected men who cherish and value their role and reputation as men who can accomplish things. Typically they are rich landlords or merchants, but sometimes they are prosperous shepherds.

Their role is crucial because often agreements are reached without the victim and thief coming into contact, or the identity of the latter being known to the former. The mediator acts as a friend to both in the delicate negotiations.

The role of mediator or, for that matter, that of friend anywhere along the network between victim and thief, is not without its dangers. Often one doubts if he can trust his friend, and information given to a friend can result in reprisal. A friend to one man may be a spy to another. One shepherd expressed it this way: "Friendship is fine, but there are dangers also. There have been many killings because of this, because of spies. It is fine for a friend to say that somebody stole the animals, and the thief says, 'Yes, I have the animals, here they are,' but then the spy gets shot." The goal, obviously, is to effect an agreement suitable to all, so that a "friend" is not considered a spy or traitor by a disgruntled participant.

Accommodation

An accommodation (*acconzamentu*) is the Sard term for a verbal agreement between disputants to resolve their dispute amicably, with or without the aid of Sard mediators, conciliators, or arbitrators, and without recourse to the state authorities. It is also the term for the final agreement itself. Accommodation is closely related to friendship: it is the hoped-for result of the processes of friendship and depends upon it for its effectiveness. Simultaneously, a successful accommodation creates a new, or recreates an old, relation of friendship between the disputants. If an accommodation is to occur, the victim and the thief must be able to communicate, if not directly, then through intermediaries. The contact may be initiated by either the victim or the thief, but in either case it is established through the mechanisms, idiom, and ideology of amistade.

If no contact is made – because the thief either had to flee unsuccessfully without any animals, or fled too successfully and does not wish to negotiate with the victim, no dispute can be said to exist between them and no accommodation will occur.

Accommodation, then, occurs when the parties are in contact, through a situation of apprehension *in flagrante*; through successful searches and inquiries on the part of the victim, *soci*, or *barracelli*, utilizing friendship networks; or through the efforts of the thief himself to initiate contact, also through friendship networks.

These accommodations are patterned forms of behavior which occur within the framework of Sard pastoral culture and society. They emerge from the indigenous system of values and social relationships, and reflect the real economic and ecological facts of life. They are forms of settlement between people who share the same basic outlook and values and recognize that they live in the same society – *in* it not only physically, as the carabinieri do, but morally, emotionally, economically. The people making the accommodations live and work in the same society. So do their children, parents, brothers, cousins, friends. The well-being of the shepherds depends directly on the opinion others have of them. They are vulnerable to attack because they own animals, a form of wealth which is highly vulnerable. Consequently, they are willing to employ the institution of accommodation, even though, as we shall see, it often is not equally advantageous to both parties to a dispute.

The fact that disputing parties agree to an accommodation implies that all are reasonably satisfied with its outcome, even if each party is not equally happy with the degree of his gain or loss. The pessimistic outlook of the Sard shepherd predisposes him to expect less than the best solution. Even if one party feels that the details of the accommodation are not in his favor, he recognizes that, given the circumstances, the result is the best he can obtain.

The type of accommodation achieved may be related to factors of relative power (measured by the ability to inflict damage) and consequently to relative bargaining power, as well as to situational factors. Thus, while each accommodation is similar to others of its type in broad structural features, each is unique in content as a result of the differential situational factors associated with it. In this way the Sard legal institution of accommodation is directly related to economic, political, and cultural factors and is, therefore, closely attuned to the reality of the relations between the disputants, unlike proceedings carried out in the state courts.

Some accommodations are relatively advantageous either to the thief or the victim (asymmetrical accommodation), while others are more equally balanced in terms of cost and gains for both parties (symmetrical accommodation). The agreements finally hammered out also depend on such factors as the length of time that has elapsed between a theft and a confrontation; the relative costs to each party; and, most importantly, whether or not the thief has been able to conceal his identity and the whereabouts of the stolen animals.

Some accommodations are effected immediately between victim and thief when the thief is caught in the act. Usually in this situation the thief is allowed to flee as long as he leaves the animals to be restored to their owner. The victim keeps his animals and, as he has not been greatly inconvenienced, he is content to allow the thief to leave unharmed. Barracelli typically behave the same way. Their goal is to prevent theft, not to punish thieves.

Most accommodations occur some time after the theft. In one type, the thief is discovered, either through physical clues or through friendship networks. In such a case the thief must return the stolen animals, as he has been caught with the goods. He does not have the moral support of the community, as he obviously is not a successful thief. Because the victim has suffered through the loss of his animals and access to their products while he has had to continue to pay rent for pastures, the thief is expected to return the stolen animals plus a number of his own, often double the number of animals stolen, depending on the extent of the victim's loss. The accommodation may be effected through the barracelli or sos homines, or through negotiation or mediation. The outcome in all cases is affected by the willingness of the thief to comply with the conditions of the agreement which, in turn, is affected by his assessment of the dangers to himself if he does not comply.

Barracelli often enforce this type of accommodation, as their presence in a case means, first of all, that the supposed thief has been found out. The successful thief initiating contact with the victim for purposes of extortion would not bring in the barracelli. The presence of the barracelli tips the balance in the victim's favor. He is no longer relying only upon his core action set but upon the whole moral force of the village community on his behalf. Often the barracelli themselves arbitrate the details of the terms, or they may play a more passive role, allowing the thief and victim to negotiate in their presence. The exact nature of the participation of the barracelli in this type of accommodation varies with the circumstances, but in all cases their presence supports the position of the victim.

This kind of accommodation is not limited to situations in which the barracelli are present. However, the ability of a victim to enforce the terms of an accommodation is problematic if he is engaged in a dyadic (one-to-one) relation with the thief.

In the other type of asymmetrical accommodation, that favorable to the thief, the outcome is what may be called extortionate. In this situation, the thief has success-fully hidden the stolen animals and his own identity. He is in a strong bargaining position because the victim is in no position to retake his own animals or retaliate against the animals of the thief.

After a waiting period, the thief initiates contact with the victim through his network of friends and intermediaries, or he allows his friends and intermediaries to be approached by the investigating friends of the victim. The typical result of the ensuing negotiations is that the stolen animals are returned to the victim, who pays a sizable sum of money to the thief. Obviously this type of accommodation occurs only when the thief is willing to return the animals to the owner for a price. In reality, of course, thieves often steal to keep and use the animals themselves, consume them, or sell them to "fences." In such cases, no dispute exists between the thief and victim if the identity of the former is not known to the latter.

A number of variables may affect the relative positions of strength and thus the outcome of accommodations, but the factors that seem to be most salient and most consistent in my data are whether or not the thief has been successful in eluding pursuit or unmasking; the relative degree of cost expended by both parties; and the relative ability of each party to retaliate or escalate the conflict, that is, the relative vulnerability of each party to reprisal.

No matter what the variables, however, and no matter what the situation, an accommodation of some sort is the valued goal of participants and the shepherding community as a whole. Disputes of this sort should be settled "among friends," or "among ourselves." Recourse to the state authorities is considered to be wrong, except by the barracelli under certain circumstances (for example, if a thief has failed to carry out the terms of an accommodation felt to be reasonable). Recourse to state authorities is considered a dangerous escalation of the conflict by introduction of a new and forbidden weapon, not an attempt to resolve it, and therefore it calls for retaliation.

[. . .]

Summary and Conclusion

Pastoralism is an important aspect of the Sardinian rural economy. Many thousand shepherds care for the approximately 3,000,000 sheep and 400,000 goats, which form about one-third of the Italian total, in addition to large numbers of cattle and pigs. Many of these shepherds are transhumant; they move seasonally with their flocks and herds from their homes in the mountainous interior, often to distant lowland pastures throughout the island, forming, in the process, a perpetual movement of men and animals.

Because of the nature of the Sard topography and other ecological factors, the threat of livestock theft is ever present. At the same time that each shepherd must cope with the threat of theft of his own animals, a variety of factors operates to encourage him to steal the animals of his fellow shepherds.

While animal theft is generally regarded as justified under certain conditions, it is recognized by the pastoral community that such theft can be the source of interpersonal and intercommunal strife, with the danger of escalation from mutual theft to quarrels, feuds, and violence. Consequently, the Sard shepherd community has solved a number of institutions and processes, within its indigenous local-political system, to regulate livestock theft and to minimize the task of escalation.

The indigenous shepherds' legal system has a range of roles, mechanisms, procedures, norms, values, rules, and agencies for dealing with disputes over livestock theft. Groups that can be activated to scope with problems concerning animal theft range from ego-centered action sets to voluntary mutual aid societies organized on a group or village basis, to village-wide livestock insurance associations that have police powers, to respected elders who are mobilized to intervene between the disputants. The disputes themselves can be handled by direct negotiation between disputants or by mediation, conciliation, or arbitration.

Institutions that can be mobilized in the indigenous legal system include amistade (networks of friends) and acconzamentu (the ritualized amicable settlement of disputes). The actors participating in these institutions are guided by a clearly defined system of rules for appropriate behavior in disputes over livestock. At the same time, the rules are flexible as to the *content* (who gets what) of settlements in order to reflect actual or potential positions of power, while the *structure* (the form or procedure) of the dispute management process is fairly uniform. Regardless of the specific details of individual cases, the goal of participants within the indigenous legal system is to effect amicable settlements, which, while not necessarily regarded as "just" by all disputants, are accepted by them as reasonable and realistic attempts to restore harmony. The goal is to avoid escalation either from the feared state legal system or from feuds between the disputants.

The Sard shepherds' legal system, viewed by the pastoral community as legitimate and competent, is, however, an informal legal system in that it is not recognized or granted official status by the Italian state legal system, which insists upon exclusive jurisdiction over disputes involving animals and livestock theft. The state legal system has its own roles, mechanisms, procedures, norms, values, rules, and agencies for dealing with these disputes. State military police are given the responsibility of preventing livestock theft and arresting thieves. They engage in periodic patrols to search for offenders and stolen animals. State courts are empowered to adjudicate disputes over livestock, both civil and criminal. Police and other judicial actors within the state legal system define livestock theft as a crime rather than merely as a dispute between individuals, which is the shepherds' view.

Ideally, the Sard shepherd who is a disputant in a case involving animals is free to choose to use either or both legal systems. In fact, however, a number of constraints act upon his freedom of choice. The state legal system defines some of the procedures used in the shepherds' legal system as illegal. Nevertheless, the Sard shepherd almost always prefers to ignore the apparatus of the state legal system and to mobilize that of the indigenous system. A range of ecological, economic, cultural, and social factors act as constraints upon the shepherd's freedom of choice and cause him to resort to his own legal system in disputes over livestock.

NOTES

1   The fieldwork upon which this paper is based took place in Sardinia from August 1972 to June 1973. I also engaged in fieldwork in Sardinia during the summers of 1969 and 1970. Funds for this research were obtained mainly from the National Institute of General Medical Sciences, Training Grant Number GM-1224. Field work in 1970 was also funded by the Wenner-Gren Foundation for Anthropological Research, and the University of California, Berkeley. I gratefully acknowledge these sources of support. My fieldwork took place in the Barbagia and in the foothills to the west. Because the subject matter of this paper is a delicate one, I have decided to change the names of the villages in which I worked, as well as the names of the people who participated in the case discussed. This decision means that I cannot thank by name those men and women who so kindly and generously helped me in the field. They were many, and my debt to them is immense. I am also grateful to Laura Nader, Harry Todd, and Grace Buzaljko for reading and commenting on earlier drafts of this paper.

2   Over the last few decades the official figures for the number of sheep in Sardinia have fluctuated between about 2,500,000 and 3,000,000. As of the 1961 census, there were 2,860,000 sheep, 31.2 percent of the national total; 408,000 goats, 29.8 percent of the national total; and about 200,000 cattle, 2.1 percent of the national total (Brigaglia 1971: 173). Figures on the number of shepherds vary considerably. Luca Pinna (1971: 46) speaks of 60,000. Mori (1966: 413–14) mentions 50,000. Later figures cite 23,000 shepherding "firms," with 35,000 shepherds (*La Nuova Sardegna*, November 2, 1972, p. 3).

3   In Nuoro province, where the Barbagia is located, about 60 percent of land used for pastures is rented by shepherds, while only 40 percent belongs to the shepherds themselves (*La Nuova Sardegna*, November 2, 1972, p. 3).

4   The population of the island as a whole is 1,300,000 (L. Pinna 1971: 45).

5   This paper focuses on livestock theft rather than on the total range of disputes in pastoral Sardinia. Livestock theft is of major importance, and a study of processes concerning it leads inexorably to a study of much of the society as a whole. The institutions and processes described in this paper are often utilized in other kinds of disputes, such as abusive pasturage (trespassing). Because of the focus on disputes over theft of animals, the paper ignores the role of women, as the latter play no significant role in this area of disputing in the Barbagia.

6   Antonio Pigliaru, until his recent death, was a legal scholar at the University of Sassari, born in the Barbagia. He described a putative shepherds' legal system, with its own norms, values, personnel, procedures, and sanctioned by feud and vendetta. Pigliaru postulated a shepherds' legal code of twenty-three articles. The first ten consisted of general principles (e.g., an offense must be vindicated). The second part, consisting of seven articles, described offenses. Livestock theft is not regarded as an offense. The third part, six articles, dealt with vendetta (Brigaglia 1971: 194–97).

   Gonario Pinna, a practicing lawyer with many years' experience defending shepherds from his native Barbagia, has also written extensively on the topic of the Sard shepherds' legal system and their legal attitudes and values. His writings, more empirical and detailed, and well rooted in the daily social and economic life of the shepherds, support the thesis of Pigliaru.

7   I do not mean to imply that all Sard shepherds are livestock thieves. First of all, the fact that a shepherd does not view livestock theft as a crime does not necessarily mean he indulges in it himself. The attitudes and practices described here are well documented for many transhumant shepherds from the Barbagia. Even among them, however, there are many shepherds who consider themselves, and are regarded by others, as "serious" and "honest." While some shepherds freely admitted to me that they stole, or had stolen when they were younger, most spoke of others as thieves (usually those of other villages, while the shepherds of their own village had given up animal theft). Values are complex and situational. The same informant may, under different circumstances, express widely divergent opinions on the same topic. But, granted that not all Sard shepherds, or even most of them, are thieves the evidence is strong that most shepherds of the Barbagia would adhere to the values described in this section concerning *other* shepherds who *do* steal animals.

8   The present law concerning the barracelli, a revision of earlier ones, was written in 1898.

REFERENCES

Brigaglia, M. 1971. *Sardegna, perche banditi*. Milan: Edizioni Leader. A Lexico-Statistical Classification. *oceania* 37(4): 286–308.

Cagnetta, F. 1963. *Bandits d'Orgosolo*. Paris: Buchet/Chastel.

Graburn, N. H. H. 1969. "Eskimo Law in Light of Self- and Group-Interest." *Law and Society Review* 4(1): 45–60.

Guido, M. 1963. *Sardinia*. London: Thames and Hudson.

Kuper, H., and L. Kuper, eds. 1965. *African Law: Adaptation and Development*. Berkeley and Los Angeles: University of California Press.

Nader, L., and B. Yngvesson. 1974. "On Studying the Ethnography of Law and Its Consequences." In J. J. Honigmann, ed., *Handbook of Social and Cultural Anthropology*, pp. 883–921. Chicago: Rand McNally.

Pinna, G. 1967. *Il pastore sardo e la giustizia*. Cagliari: Fossataro.

Pinna, L. 1971. *La famiglia esclusiva: parentela e clientelismo in Sardegna*. Bari: Laterza.

Pirastu, I. 1973. *Il banditismo in Sardegna*. Rome: Editori Riuniti.

Pospisil, L. 1967. "Legal Levels and Multiplicity of Legal Systems in Human Societies." *Journal of Conflict Resolution* 11(1): 2–26.

Sutherland, E. 1949. *White Collar Crime*. New York: Holt, Rinehart & Winston.

16

Consensus and Suspicion: Judicial Reasoning and Social Change in an Indonesian Society 1960–1994

John R. Bowen

Introduction: Dividing Family Property in Islamic Courts in Indonesia

The discussion of judicial reasoning embodied in this paper is very different from what can be seen in Max Gluckman's work half a century earlier. Gluckman's ideas were set out in two books and various articles, and this is a single paper which complicates comparison. However, some features stand out. Gluckman was aiming for large theoretical generalizations about the logic of judges and the doctrinal concepts used in pre-industrial societies. As for the judicial logic, he contended that the abstract form of reasoning used by the African judges was not unlike that of European courts. With respect to the doctrinal concepts, however, his emphasis was on the difference between pre-industrial frameworks and those of modern society. Bowen does not generalize in the typological manner of Gluckman. Bowen's approach is much more particular and descriptive of a particular set of courts in a particular time and place. The explanation he gives of the judges' preference for rationalizing decisions in terms of the prior consensus of the parties is that such a tactic avoids a lot of prickly political issues, and has considerable legitimacy in a number of different social spheres, from village custom to Islamic law to Indonesian national ideology.

Bowen's article is about court cases involving the division of family property by the courts in the Gayo Highlands of Central Aceh, Indonesia. While he is presenting the reasoning of the judges in Islamic courts in the period 1960 to 1994 he is also giving readers some insight into the multiplicity of political meanings

From John R. Bowen, "Consensus and Suspicion: Judicial Reasoning and social charge in an Indonesian Society 1960–1994," *Law and Society Review* 34(1) (2000), pp. 97–127.

embodied in their doctrinal choices. For example, he explains that it was Dutch colonial policy to restrict the rights of religious courts, including their rights to decide inheritance cases in certain parts of Indonesia. Thus Islamic inheritance law became a symbol of the fight against colonial rule. Until 1989, the Islamic courts had no executory authority and had to rely on the general courts to enforce a decision. In 1989 the government expanded the jurisdiction and enforcement powers of the Islamic courts. There remain two distinct, formal, judicial systems: the Islamic which deals with marriage, divorce, and family property among Muslims, and the general judiciary which addresses all other civil matters and all criminal cases. Above both is the Supreme Court to which appellate decisions from either court system can be brought. So much for the bifurcate base of the formal system. But in addition there is the legacy of the colonial European civil code approach, which tried to convert *adat* into a rule system of positive law, and which recognized Islamic law only to the extent that it had been incorporated into *adat*. And there is, as well, a very great multiplicity of local customary practices and rules. The emphasis on dates in Bowen's title should give the reader instant insight into his historical approach. The law is seen as a product of its past and its present, not as a set of rules independent of its milieu and moment.

Sometimes the judges relied on local custom and sometimes on Islamic law in arriving at a decision. The judges' explanations are presented in a straightforward way, to illuminate the choices they had before them. There were a number of quite different legal doctrines on which they could rely. They could argue that local customary practice (*adat*) supported a particular division of property. But they could instead argue that the property should be divided according to Islamic law. Yet in the context of either form of reasoning, they could argue that there had been consensus, consent to some particular division of property in the kin-group or village, and the presumption about consensus was that it was voluntary and not coerced. The notion of the priority of consensus was a way out of openly choosing between *adat* rules and Islamic rules, an opposition the judges avoided.

Though presenting the judges' reasoning, Bowen goes behind the judicial rationales to explore three issues: one is the complex history of the law and the courts in this post-colonial part of Indonesia, the second is the very great economic changes that affected property holding in the period, and the third is the political context: political rebellion by an Islam-based movement, pressure from the state party, and a general shift toward greater control by the state. All three of these factors play into the perceptions and decisions of the judges, but how these cause particular case outcomes is very difficult to pinpoint. The logical reasoning offered by the judges themselves is much clearer, but the implication of Bowen's argument is that it probably masks other considerations. Thus the Bowen chapter is both methodologically and substantively of interest. It indicates that judicial reasoning in Indonesia, as in our own society, is a rationalized clue to case decisions, but not an explanation of them.

S.F.M.

Between 1960 and 1994, Islamic court judges in the Gayo Highlands of Central Aceh, Indonesia, radically changed the way they judged disputes over family property. Whereas once they had generally upheld local Gayo social norms (*adat*) about who received family property, by the early 1990s they consistently overruled settlements based on those same norms and redivided property according to Islamic law. From a conservative court that turned down requests to overturn past divisions of farm lands, the religious court became an activist court that routinely overturned such divisions. And yet over this time the relevant substantive law changed very little, and judges recognized that both *adat* and Islam provided legitimate bases for decisions...

Postcolonial societies offer particularly interesting places to study how judges have reasoned in the face of competing norms. Judges in these societies have been finding their interlegal feet amidst a multiplicity of statutes, court decisions, religious doctrines, and colonial-era treatises on "customary law."[1] Their public statements on laws and customs often become flash points for national cultural debates. In most societies with large Muslim populations, these debates turn on judgments about the relative legitimacy of secular and religious sources of law.[2] In Indonesia, a multi-confessional state with the world's largest Muslim population, not only have there been extensive public discussions about the validity of claims based on customary norms, Islamic law, statutes, and judicial decisions, but these discussions also have been part of a process of general, heightened reflection on the proper relation of Islam to national identity.

In the Gayo courts judges have paid particular attention to local processes of reaching consensus, and their evaluations of such processes are of significance to broader political discussions in Indonesia. Achieving consensus through deliberation," *musyawarah mufakat*, a central element in Indonesian ideology, bears some relationship, not yet well understood, to local ways of resolving disputes. In cases from the 1960s and from the 1990s, the Islamic court judges in the Gayo Highlands (and their colleagues on the neighboring general court) advanced theories as to how such local processes should be understood, and they based their decisions in great part on those theories. The theories themselves, however, changed radically. A close reading of the judges' justifications, and an attention to the political-economic context of those justifications can, I think, help us understand the historically-specific ways in which state legal institutions elaborate and extend the links between political ideology and local-level practices.

Indonesian Interlegality

The coexistence of several sets of legally-relevant norms has long been emphasized in studies of Indonesia. Indeed, Dutch colonial administrators conceptualized Indies social and cultural diversity through a legal lens. In their efforts to link colonial rule to local structures of authority, they demarcated naturally occurring culture areas in terms of what they took to be the prevailing "*adat* law" (*adatrecht*) (Ellen 1983; Benda-Beckmann 1984). Some Indonesianists have continued to view *adat* or *adat* law as the normative anchor of culture, the guarantor of locality and difference in the face of Islamic and European legal competition. For instance, in a series of lectures designed to highlight the cultural organization of legal reasoning, Clifford Geertz (1983) counterposed the local substance and symbols of *adat* to the other forms of law – "foreign machinery" (1983:214) – whose very presence was due to outside interventions. The assumption implicit in this counterposition is that certain ideas and practices can be construed as being more culturally embedded, more indigenous, than are their competitors.[3]

Viewing *adat* as the guarantor of local culture has its difficulties: are those men and women who choose Islamic norms thereby less culturally Indonesian? And yet, highlighting the conflict among norms does raise important analytical questions. How does a judge in a general court, following procedures and substantive law inherited from the European civil law tradition, apply Islamic norms? If a judge in an Islamic court gives Islamic legal rules priority, do local social norms no longer figure as legal norms? What arguments do judges employ in order to choose among, or to integrate, these competing normative systems?[4]

Indonesia has several distinct judicial systems; the two that concern us here are the Islamic judiciary (Peradilan Agama), which handles matters of marriage, divorce, and family property among Muslims, and the general judiciary (Peradilan Negeri), which handles all other civil matters and all criminal cases. (In most parts of Indonesia, Muslims may take inheritance disputes to either court.) Each system has its own set of first-instance and appellate courts. Appellate decisions in either system may be brought to the Supreme Court, which acts as a tribunal of cassation. Although the Supreme Court's decisions are not binding in the sense of *stare decisis*, some decisions are published in books called Yurisprudensi, and appellate courts often cite these decisions in overturning lower court findings. Despite a "separation of powers" doctrine inherited from European civil code ideology, Indonesian judges are multiply dependent on the government: all judges are civil servants, and thus financially dependent on the government; courts are administered by various ministries, not by the Supreme Court; the Supreme Court is highly subject to executive political pressure.[5]

Judges must take into account this complex legal and political context as a source of external constraints on their decision making as well as a source of substantive law. A judge on an Islamic court of first instance must consider past decisions of the appellate court and Supreme Court, publications issued by the Ministry of Religion (which are often critical of Supreme Court decisions), and instructions received from appellate court judges. He or she will be constrained by actions already taken at the neighboring general court, which may have decided the validity of a document or the prior ownership of a land parcel. The Supreme Court may have ruled on an appeal emanating from either the Islamic court or the general court, and this ruling, whether it appears intelligent or idiotic, represents a further constraint on the judge's decision.

A judge may decide that popular opinion makes certain decisions difficult to enforce. Prior to 1989, the Islamic courts had no executory authority and had to rely on the general courts to enforce a decision – and their willingness to oblige might have depended on their own interpretation of the law or the nature of influence on them or bribes paid to them. (Indonesian general court judges have been generally thought to be highly susceptible to bribery and to influence from political authorities; Islamic court judges less so.) Judges also must consider how to weigh local social norms vis-à-vis Islamic law or statutes. These norms may be directly relevant to the application of statutory law: for example, in suggesting what counts locally as a promise to repay a loan or as a consensus on a property division. They also may be a source of separate legal principles, but then judges may be forced to choose among alternative ideas of what *adat* really is. Is it a matter of long-standing local traditions, or a continually changing sense of propriety and justice? Whereas Dutch colonial practice was to codify *adat* as if it were a set of rules, unchanging but otherwise similar to positive law, the Indonesian Supreme Court has promoted the strikingly different idea of a "living *adat* law" among the people, a national *adat* that is gender-equal, revolutionary, and modern (Bowen 1988; Lev 1965). The view a judge holds on this question has implications for how he or she selects among competing norms. If the judge views *adat* as a set of unchanging rules, then testimony from local *adat* experts, a standard way for judges to discover the content of local *adat*, will trump other normative statements (and the older the expert, the better). If, however, he or she views adat as a "living law," then such testimony crumbles in the face of claims about modernity, particularly if supported by Supreme Court rhetoric (and the more recent the decision, the better).

Similarly, statutes may be seen as superseding *adat* norms, or, alternatively, as applying to those domains where *adat* and Islam are silent. For example, judges on the general court in the Gayo Highlands have ruled that local social norms give a right of first refusal to close relatives and neighbors of a landowner wishing to sell his or her land. A person in such a relationship may challenge a sale of land to a third party, and under certain conditions can win such a suit. But in recent cases, litigants have claimed that Indonesian statutes guarantee freedom to sell to anyone, and that such statutes override any local social norms. The issue of priority among alternative sets of legal norms is still unresolved.

It is in deciding cases about family property that such complexities most fully arise in Indonesia, where almost every conceivable type of indigenous inheritance system can be found. Among local systems that are tied to long-standing *adat* norms, some allocate a share to every child, others reserve shares of ancestral land either only to sons or only to daughters, and still others allocate ancestral lands to whichever children remain affiliated with the ancestral village after marriage. Most local systems consider the local corporate group, usually a village or lineage, to have some residual claim on ancestral lands. A considerable amount of property may be transferred *inter vivos*, via direct gifts of land, or bequests, or transfers of use-rights that then become ownership rights at the parent's death. Bequests, in particular, are a favored mechanism, because they allow the parents to finetune the transfer but retain the property, and through that property exercise some control over their children.

Islamic norms regarding inheritance stand in striking contrast to all *adat*-based systems.[6] Islamic jurisprudence knows nothing of village or lineage claims. Islamic law dictates that property be awarded in fixed ratios according to the gender of the claimants and their genealogical ties to the deceased. The Islamic jurisprudence currently dominant in Indonesia disallows any bequests to heirs and places limits on the giving of property (Bowen 1998).

Despite this sharp contrast between *adat* and Islamic inheritance norms, many Indonesian Muslims have been strong supporters of expanding the jurisdiction of Islamic courts to include the inheritance system, in part because the restricted jurisdiction of these courts was part of Dutch colonial policy. In 1937 the Dutch revoked the right of religious courts on Java and Madura to decide inheritance cases, thereby making Islamic inheritance law a symbol of the fight against colonial rule (Lev 1972).

These jurisdictional issues also have become arenas for postcolonial debate about national identity. In the 1970s, for example, Parliament considered allowing the general courts, not just the Islamic courts, to validate the marriages and divorces of Muslims. Heated debates ensued in the national press and in the streets on topics of national identity and religious freedom: some argued that the measure would contribute to creating an integrated national legal system; others, that it would abrogate the rights of Muslims. The proposals were abandoned, and a much different bill passed, one that preserved the monopoly held by the Islamic courts over Muslim marriage and divorce. When in 1989 the government successfully proposed expanding the overall jurisdiction and enforcement powers of the Islamic courts, a similar debate took place, with some parties warning that the bill heralded the creation of an Islamic state; others, that it finally undid the colonial wrongs perpetrated against Indonesian Muslims.

Many, though certainly not all, Indonesian Muslims today see the presence of strengthened Islamic courts as guarantors of their religious identity within a pluralistic, nonsectarian national context. From the many new political parties to have emerged in the wake of Suharto's fall in May 1998 have come a wide variety of platforms for Indonesia's future, but the parties that won significant shares of the vote in June 1999 agree on a view of a multiconfessional and legally pluralistic Indonesia.

Power and the Courts in the Gayo Highlands

The problem of implementing Islamic law in the context of local *adat* norms, and within a set of European-derived legal institutions, is nowhere more complex than in Aceh, the Indonesian province on the island of Sumatra containing the Gayo Highlands. Throughout Aceh's history, sultans, jurists, and judges have promoted Islamic institutions in the face of strongly held local norms and beliefs[7] The Darul Islam rebellion against the central government began shortly after independence, and newer versions of the movement have simmered ever since, kept alive in part by resentment at the export of highly valuable oil, gas, and forest resources, and at the heavy hand of the mainly Javanese troops stationed there since 1985. Vigorous, sometimes violent, calls for renegotiating the relationship between Aceh and Jakarta followed the fall of Suharto in 1998.

Since the 1970s, an Acehnese Islamic legal and political hierarchy – composed of members of the State Islamic Institute (IAIN, Institute Agama Islam Negeri), the appellate Islamic court, and the Council of Ulama (Majelis Ulama), all located in the provincial capital, Banda Aceh – has sought to tighten its control over local judges. Stricter supervision has led to frequent reversals of lower-court decisions and a higher degree of confrontation between the norms of *adat* and those of Islam. Local social changes, including more smallholder growing of commercial crops, and national legal changes, including the granting of broader legal competency and enforcement powers to the Islamic courts, have led to more litigation and to a higher profile for these courts.

In the central, mountainous part of Aceh lie the Gayo Highlands, whose largest town is Takèngèn. During the first fifteen years after independence, the highlands were in near-constant turmoil. The battles fought in northern Sumatra in the late

1940s against the returning Dutch and their allies involved many men and women from the highlands. The Darul Islam rebellion set villagers against one another and isolated the towns from the villages. The former were largely controlled by troops from Jakarta, and the latter were largely controlled by rebels. The massacres of the years 1965–66 followed on the heels of the rebellion and were exacerbated by still-raw resentments over betrayals and collaboration.[8]

The courts that were created in the highlands shortly after independence had very different histories and faced very different challenges, but they shared a commitment to create a more Islamic society and the problem of being weak institutions in a climate of turmoil and uncertainty. The general court (Pengadilan Negeri) succeeded a local colonial court and continued to hear all criminal cases and to accept litigation on a wide variety of civil matters. For its first three decades it was dominated by men from the Gayo Highlands or nearby northern Aceh, and its chief judges served for as long as ten years.

The Islamic, or religious, court (Pengadilan Agama), by contrast, was a new institution. During the colonial period no such courts had existed, and although in theory people could take inheritance cases to a religious official, they rarely did so. When the court was created in 1945, it was under provincial, not central, government authority. For its first few decades its legal basis remained unclear, it received little funding, and it had to rely on the general court to enforce its decisions. Although its authority to handle marriage and divorce matters was popularly accepted, such was not the case with its authority over inheritance disputes.[9] "Some people considered it a mock court," recalled one older judge. For staff and judges it depended on local talent, on those few Gayo men who had received training in Islamic law outside the region.

By the late 1970s, the backgrounds and interests of the judges on the two courts had diverged sharply. Today, all general court judges have law degrees and come from outside the region. Their career tracks involve Takèngën only incidentally. They spend three to five years in the town and dream of their next posting, which they hope will be in a larger city, or at least nearer to their birthplace. Islamic court judges, by contrast, remain tied to local concerns. Even as of the mid-1990s, the court only had two judges with law degrees; to make up the three-judge panel required to hear inheritance cases, a local man who had served as chief clerk in the 1950s and 1960s was appointed as judge, despite his lack of a law degree. These judges continue to perform the role of wise counselor, often speaking in Gayo to make a point more effectively, and rebuking witnesses who mistakenly describe Gayo *adat*.

Until 1970 disputes over inheritance – a general term I shall use to include estate divisions, gifts, and bequests – could be brought to either court, although this "forum shopping" possibility always aroused some discontent. Indeed, general court rulings on Islamic law were often overturned by the appellate court as overstepping the court's competence. In 1970, public protest against decisions taken by a general court judge in West Aceh led the two appellate courts to reserve to the Islamic court decisions on how an estate ought to be divided. However, because many inheritance disputes involve side issues that do fall under general court jurisdiction, such as the validity of a document or the ownership of a plot of land, some cases end up at both courts even today. (Several cases from Takèngën reached the Supreme Court twice during the 1990s, once from each of the two courts of first instance!)

Affirming Consensus in the 1960s

During the 1940s and 1950s, few Gayo people brought inheritance disputes to the Islamic court. This was so for a number of reasons: the institution was new, the region was in turmoil, and older *adat* procedures were strongly reinforced in the villages. By the 1960s, a handful of such cases began to show up in the court each year, but even then most suits were withdrawn after the two parties reached a settlement.[11]

When the parties failed to settle, the dispute usually involved a conflict between the Islamic norms cited by the plaintiff as the ground for requesting a redivision of wealth and the *adat* norms invoked by the defendant according to which the wealth had in fact been divided. It was precisely the stark opposition between the two sets of norms that made settlement in such cases difficult. However, the judges tried to avoid siding explicitly with either Islamic law or *adat*, but instead searched for a standard that could be reconciled with both normative systems. Sometimes they found that a prior agreement between all parties nullified the plaintiff's claim. Because the general idea of agreement, contract, or consensus is present in *adat*, in Islamic law, and in civil law, this finding allowed the judges to avoid giving priority to one or the other of the two normative systems.

Illustrative of the reasoning in this period is the 1961 case *Usman* v. *Serikulah* (PA 41/1961).[12] The case pitted the child of a sister against the child of a brother. Usman asked the court to redivide land once belonging to his mother's father, and to do so according to Islamic law. He admitted that two years earlier, in 1959, there had been an attempt to divide the rice fields by general agreement among the heirs, but he stated that now he was not satisfied with the results of this meeting. . . .

Taking a strong stand one way or the other might also have had immediate political consequences during a period of continued rebellion by an Islam-based movement. No judge wished to invite retaliation from the rebels by coming out against Islamic law, or risk accusations of rebel sympathies by coming out against *adat*. Furthermore, most judges on both courts saw their own tasks as incorporating norms of Islam and *adat*. Most considered their judicial roles to be part of a general effort to replace colonial-era institutions with new ones that better reflected the shared Islamic orientation of Gayo people. However, they also saw the norms of local *adat* as important safeguards of Islam – as the "fences guarding religion," in the words of one religious teacher.

In the end, the judges avoided framing the [1961] case as "Islam versus *adat*." Instead, they decided that in 1959 the two parties had already reached an agreement, a *penyelesaian secara perdamaian*, "bringing (the matter) to a close through reconciliation." The 1959 meeting had ended by awarding Sahim the rice fields. The judges noted that the plaintiff, Usman, was present at the meeting but that he had remained silent, even after the meeting's presider had called out three times to all present: "Don't anyone ever bring suit over these fields again." The judges concluded that Usman's silence had implied his consent to the agreement. They rejected his suit . . .

Inspecting Consensus: The Assumptions Behind the Decisions

These decisions by the Islamic and the general courts rested on two assumptions. The first was the empirical assumption that the village-level deliberations dividing the estates were consensual rather than coercive. The second assumption concerned the correct set of norms to apply: that the social norms understood and accepted by the parties to the original divisions at the time of those divisions are the correct legal norms on which to base a current decision. From these assumptions one could quickly infer the decisions themselves. Because the prior distributions of property did indeed comply with the norms of *adat*, and because they had been ratified at village assemblies attended by the plaintiffs, the plaintiffs lost their cases. Both assumptions are open to question and, indeed, both later were rejected by judges on both courts. Let us consider each in turn. The first is that meetings involved consensus and agreement. Such claims are ubiquitous in Indonesia; indeed, "consensus through deliberation" (*musy-awarah mufakat*) is a key plank in the state ideology. It is invoked daily in national political life, often as cultural cover for efforts to suppress popular dissent.[10]

Any legitimacy attached to these national claims is at least partly due to their resonance with long-standing local norms that decisions should be reached through consensus. In Gayo society, *mupakat* names the appropriate way of reaching all decisions through a consultation among village elders. Movement toward consensus is structurally part of the Gayo ritual-speaking that gave public conclusion and resolution to village-level disputes (Bowen 1991:139–68); this movement diagrammed the putative social process of people changing their opinions from divergent to convergent. So widespread in the archipelago are such norms that Clifford Geertz (1983) took Indonesian ideas of arriving at consensus through harmonious speaking as the defining feature of archipelagic *adat*.[11]

The frequency of claims that decisions were consensual does not make evaluating such claims any easier, however.[12] My own experience, most of it in the five-village complex of Isak, is that not only do different participants in village meetings evaluate the outcomes differently, but that even in the words of a single participant one can find more than one type of evaluation...In 1994, Tengku Daud Arifin, a former Isak religious official (*qadi*), whom I have known for two decades, explained, first, how these village deliberations produce a consensus and then, immediately afterward, how he and his siblings divided his parents' lands:

> When I was the Qadi we never had a case go to the Islamic court, nor has there been one since. I have often been called to resolve cases. I always first say what the divisions of the estate are according to Islamic law. But then some of those present will say, "But that is not fair (*adil*)," because the daughters get less then the sons. Or some of the children say, "I don't really need that," or the sons ask the daughters to renounce (*ikhlasën*, "give sincerely") their shares, because they are already provided for in their husbands' villages. So they work out a better arrangement peacefully. That's then fair and sincere.
>
> When my mother died [his father had died first] we all gathered together to divide the estate. One younger brother said if he did not find it fair he would not go along with what we did. Another suggested they divide it all up, and we worked out a division whereby I got the rice land way up in the weeds. But then I spoke, and as the eldest

I could say: "No; let's try again," and we redid it, and now I got the lion's share of the rice land close to the village [here he breaks into chuckles]. The other siblings have not used their shares: I work all the land, and now my children and grandchildren [work it], because they are all civil servants [rather than full-time farmers with their own lands].

Tengku Arifin's recounting of the process was complex. He initially described the village deliberations as moving from an application of the letter of the law toward an application of superior arrangements that responded to ideas of fairness. This movement was possible, he suggested, because some participants sincerely renounced their rights in order to respect the balance of needs. It is this sort of characterization of village deliberative processes that makes plausible legal judgments that agreements proceeding from such meetings ought to be taken as evidence of the sincere wishes of all participants, particularly in the absence of any public objections. I also heard villagers, usually men, counterpose the mechanical application of Islamic law to the morally superior recourse to feelings, needs, and sincerity.

But Tengku Arifin spoke in a different way later in the passage, when he chuckled over the way he, the eldest brother, could dictate which agreements would be acceptable and that he could also, even after the agreement, retain de facto control of most of the land, with the justification that his own children, with civil service occupations, did not have their own land. It is precisely this power of eldest brothers to defer divisions and retain control that has driven some children, or even grandchildren, to sue for redivisions in the court.

As the *qadi's* "double-voiced" recollections illustrate, one can infer from these meetings either consensus or coercion, or some combination thereof. Judges in the 1960s tended to practice a "consensus" reading of such meetings. To support their reading in any particular case, they would point to evidence indicating that, despite the plaintiff's subsequent dissatisfaction, at the time of the original agreement she or he was part of this consensus. This evidence could include testimony that the plaintiff had been silent when the deliberations were read aloud for final approval, or that the plaintiff freely accepted the result, as in the former judge's testimony that the plaintiff had been happy with the outcome.

Of course, the plaintiff's satisfaction at the time may have been because the then-prevailing social norms did not offer any alternative. As the former judge said, that was how things were settled at that time; no one who married outside of the village ever inherited wealth. That the satisfaction of the plaintiff some years earlier should be decisive brings into play the second major assumption underlying decisions of the 1960s, namely, that it was the role of the judges to render decisions according to what was appropriate under the local social norms prevailing at the time and not to challenge those norms on the basis of the plaintiff's rights under Islamic law or a new interpretation of *adat* law.

As applied by the Islamic court judges, this assumption, which may or may not have been publicly articulated, resembles the so-called reception doctrine advanced by colonial administrators, under which Islam was considered to be the law of the land only insofar as it had already been accepted into local *adat*. (This doctrine has become emblematic of colonial anti-Islamic policy, and for that reason a religious court judge would be horrified at my comparison.) The assumption justified the courts proceeding cautiously and conservatively at a time when that course may have seemed more prudent to the judges.

Hierarchy and Economy Since the 1970s

Changes in highlands (and national) political and economic life that began in the 1970s have presented the Islamic court with a new set of possibilities and constraints. The court's prestige and the volume of its tasks have risen since the mid-1970s, due in part to changes in the national legal environment.[13] The 1974 marriage law required all Muslims, men and women, to declare their divorces in the Islamic court; no longer could men simply pronounce the divorce utterance, the *talaq*, in order to be recognized as divorced. A 1989 bill created a uniform system of Islamic courts throughout Indonesia and gave the courts the power to enforce their own decisions. The Compilation of Islamic Law, given the force of a Presidential Decree in 1991, was intended to render the substance of religious court decisions uniform throughout Indonesia (see Bowen 1999; Cammack 1997).

At the same time that these measures gave greater powers to the Islamic judiciary, other measures were intended to increase the degree of hierarchy within that judiciary. The Ministry of Religion has required all courts to subscribe to its publication *Mimbar Hukum*, which presents critical reviews of decisions by lower, appellate, and the Supreme Court. In Aceh, the provincial appellate court began to subject local judges to more scrutiny outside of its appellate review process, through seminars and briefings held in the capital. Review itself became more likely, as litigants were more likely to persist in their attempts to redivide wealth, and to appeal to the appellate court in Banda Aceh, request cassation in Jakarta, and then start all over if they lost. Few cases in the 1960s were appealed; by the 1980s nearly all inheritance-related cases brought to either court were appealed. In Aceh, the appellate court has increasingly demanded that gifts, bequests, and other transactions be carried out to the letter of the Islamic law, as they see it, and they do not hesitate to rebuke the Takèngën judges when they err in this or in other regards. (I have witnessed rather sharp rebukes.)

But the broader political environment has also changed. The first decade of the New Order saw a gradually successful effort by the central government to suppress political dissent, to force local religious leaders into GOLKAR, the state party, and in general to penetrate civil society through state-run schools, mosques, foundations, and so forth. Interrogations of local religious leaders and the continual invoking of the "latent Communist threat" kept the level of fear high. Requiring general court judges to move from one posting to another at frequent intervals has been part of the strategy of greater central control; it prevents judges from developing sympathies with local movements and causes and emphasizes their financial dependence on the central government. Such dependence continued under the post-1998 Reform Era.

Finally, the decades since independence have witnessed a movement in economic activity and social norms away from a life focused on the village and on the ancestral land contained therein and toward a life focused on new cash crops and trading activities. In the 1950s and 1960s, even in villages near the town, farmland was usually ancestral rice land, tended by sons or daughters who had remained in the village after marriage. Households farming a group of contiguous plots shared the work of managing irrigation and performing rice rituals and saw the occasional outsider who acquired one of their plots as bringing disharmony to the land. Children who left the village after marriage had no continuing claim on village lands.

By the late 1970s, more and more villagers had chosen to pursue cash cropping, particularly of coffee, as coffee prices soared and as improved roads lowered transportation costs. Through the 1980s and 1990s, villagers left their home villages to open up new lands, some branching out into other crops such as patchouli or citronella. Sometimes they returned to their villages, but their movements had created a new sense of the relationship between village and land. Rather than something you inherited as part of your continuing membership in the village collectivity, land was more often than not something you obtained on your own. More people after marrying were living in neither the husband's nor the wife's village but somewhere else again, where the resources were: the town of Takèngën, the coffee-growing villages to its north, or in a new area of settlement.[14]

As movement among villages became more common, and land became more likely to have been purchased or cleared than inherited, norms about passing on land to children also changed. Awarding shares of an estate to children who had left the village came to be seen as less radical a move than it had been (see Bowen 1988). This shift in the culture of land and home was reinforced by state laws, which recognized villages only as residential and administrative units and recognized only ownership of land by individuals, with title or other written evidence of ownership outweighing any other kind of claim.

Moreover, as the commercial value of some land increased, so did the stakes of battles over inheritance. Litigation today over lands generally concerns coffee plots or areas located near the expanding commercial section of town. Whatever the social cost of suing for such lands might be, the potential economic benefits have risen dramatically.

Suspecting Consensus: The Islamic Court in the 1990s

These changes – toward greater religious court autonomy locally but more supervision from above, toward more effective central governmental control of local affairs, and toward a more individualistic idea of residence and property – have meant that judges in the 1990s faced a very different set of possibilities and constraints than did their predecessors in the 1960s. In the early period, judges, especially Islamic court judges, found themselves with a weak political base and a relatively strong set of local norms. Judges on both courts operated in an environment of legal unclarity, both about which laws were to be applied and about who had the power to decide whether the court was operating correctly or not. By the 1980s and 1990s, Islamic court judges were expected to apply religious law, spelled out for them in the new Islamic law code, in appellate decisions, and in ministerial publications. They could do so in a social environment in which older Gayo norms about the transmission and division of property were no longer clear to many actors, much less thought to be generally applicable. The overall legitimacy of the Islamic court in Takèngën had increased, and judges had less fear of retaliation for unpopular decisions.

In the 1990s judges considered themselves obliged to redivide an estate when the plaintiff was within her or his rights. In discussions with me in 1994, they explicitly denied that there was any temporal limitation on the right to bring suit. At the general court, I asked a judge from Java about a hypothetical case in which an estate had long ago been divided and the plaintiff had never raised the matter, but who then, ten or twenty or more years later, brought suit to the court for a redivision. I asked, "Does the delay weaken her case?" The judge's reply was "No, there is no statute of limitations in such civil cases. Furthermore, that she was silent would not signal that she had accepted the earlier division of wealth; she would have had to acknowledge that she agreed with that division." A judge at the Islamic court explained: "There is no statute of limitations in the religious court. In rights to land there is: for example if you and I work some land, and I let mine go, and after awhile you start working it, and 20 years later I demand it back, that's too late. But if the case is clear a division made a long time ago can be successfully challenged." I then asked, "What if the plaintiff was silent at a public meeting and sues much later?" The judge responded: "Well maybe she was silent because she was embarrassed (*kemèl*) about opposing her parents' wishes."

Following this logic, the Islamic court judges in recent years have generally divided estates when asked to do so, declaring that the plaintiffs have the right to demand an Islamic redistribution of the property even if prior agreements had been made. When defendants have protested that they had received portions of the estate as bequests (*wasiat*) or gifts (*hibah*), the judges usually have declared that the consent of all the heirs would have been required for those transfers to have been legitimate, and they have voiced suspicion about claims that consensus among the heirs was reached, even when a document to that effect was produced.[15]

Contributing to such suspicions is a greater litigiousness in Takèngën. Today "consensus" is difficult to make stick, even when an agreement is reached in court. Not that the courts do not continue to try. The head of the Islamic court, Judge Hasan, explained in 1994

> that when people come to us, they usually begin by asking what the law is, to see if they have a claim. Of course, the people who come are those who feel they have not received their due; they are equally likely to be men or women. We explain that heirs have a right to a share of the wealth, and they also have the duty to pay off debts. We urge them to work out something by searching for consensus in their village. Even if they make a formal request for a finding we send them off for two weeks or sometimes one week to try and work it out first, and only then let them come back. Sometimes they come and ask me to divide the estate before them in a familial manner (*secara kekeluargaan*), not in the form of a lawsuit, and then I do that in the Islamic way.

If the heirs reach an agreement outside the court (usually with the help of a legal scholar), they usually write down the result and have it witnessed by their village headman. The document (a *surat penetapan*) then has legal standing: it is, for example, recognized by the Office of Land Registration as the basis for a valid claim to own a plot of land...

I will consider the case of bequests here (see Bowen 1998 on gifts). Under standard Islamic law interpretations, which are followed in Indonesian Islamic courts, bequests to heirs are only valid if all the heirs agree to allow them. Under long-standing Gayo norms, however, parents may bequeath a parcel of land called *pematang* to whomever among their children cares for them as they are dying. The decision is up to the parents, and the siblings usually respect the bequest. Their consent to the bequest is not necessary for it to be considered valid under *adat* norms.

Sometimes, however, siblings do contest the claim that there was a bequest, and in the cases I read from the 1980s and 1990s, the judges then have disallowed the bequests on Islamic law grounds, even if considerable evidence exists that indicates agreement among the heirs . . .

As I mentioned earlier, the way the Islamic court currently interprets Gayo *adat* on bequests is inconsistent with village norms and practices, in the past and in most places today. A parent's bequest is ipso facto valid; its authority comes from the right of the owner to dispose of the wealth, not the consent of the other children. The rule enunciated by the court is, however, an accepted part of Islamic jurisprudence; what the judges did was to recategorize the Islamic rule as "local custom." They did not need to do so in order to rule as they did, because the Islamic law on the matter is clear. But their innovation made it possible for them to base their ruling not only on an Islamic rule but also on an agreed-upon local social norm. This claim made the decision not a matter of *adat* versus Islam but one of enforcing a rule found in both *adat* and Islam.

But on what grounds did the judges find that consensus had not been reached despite the existence of a document attesting to the contrary? Judges Hasan and Kasim explained to me in 1994 that the other heirs, principally the two daughters, could only have sincerely accepted the 1969 agreement if it had been in accord with their Islamic rights. But that agreement was clearly in contradiction with the contents of scripture, because it did not award them their rightful share, so it could not have been the product of consensus. Judge Kasim stated that he and the other judges had felt that the two daughters had been pressured into signing the 1969 document, even though such pressure could not be proven. Because no one would freely sign such an agreement if it were so clearly against her interests, he reasoned, there must have been pressure.

Consensus and Fairness

The Islamic court's invention of a Gayo *adat* norm concerning bequests calls to mind Judge Porang's earlier invention of a norm of adverse possession. These two inventions had opposite effects – letting past divisions stand in the earlier case, overturning them in the later one – but they both depended on a theory of consensus. In the older decision, consensus was said to be sufficient for the property division to stand, and it was presumed to have been achieved. In the second, consensus was deemed necessary for the division to stand, and it was presumed never to have existed.

In both cases, the court created a new norm, not only about consensus but also about how we can tell whether consensus has been achieved, in effect an evidentiary rule. In the first case, Judge Porang argued that waiting too long to bring suit was grounds for assuming that one had agreed to the preexisting state of affairs (the "adverse possession" rule). He argued that this was not only a rational supposition but also that it was part of Gayo *adat*. This was the invented part of his argument. It was reasonable to make the assumption, he said, because Gayo people adhered to the norm that people marrying out of the village lose claims to the estate. This norm was not invented by the judge; rather, a maxim that embodied it was slipped over and attached to the new, invented norm, giving "adverse possession in inheritance matters" the weight of a native custom. This slippage made it plausible to claim that when the plaintiff, and others in similar positions, had remained silent, they did so knowing that their silence showed their general agreement with the way the estate had been divided. Making the rule of adverse possession into a part of local *adat* made silence evidence for agreement.

In the later case, the Islamic court argued that the very fact that some heirs were suing in court added plausibility to the supposition that they never had agreed to the prior division of property. Such lack of consensus among heirs renders bequests invalid. Note that the court did not argue that the plaintiffs' agreement was not sought, as might have happened had such agreement been considered unnecessary, but that it was coerced. This claim is more plausible if at the time of the purported bequest of land the rule that bequests require the consent of heirs was a generally accepted Gayo social norm; that is if the defendants knew that consent was required.

As evidentiary rules, these inventions have their weaknesses. The Islamic judges today believe that community settings exert a great deal of pressure on individuals, and that Islamic social and legal sensibilities about the free assent of each heir are hardly well served in such settings. And yet written documents carry a lot of weight, especially when, as in the above case, they are ratified by judges on the general court (who tend to be less aware of village life than are their colleagues on the Islamic court). In the case in question, the existence of the document led the appellate court to overrule the Takèngën Islamic court.

With that problem in mind, in recent decisions the Takèngën Islamic court judges have emphasized the substantive issue of unfairness of the division of wealth recorded in a document. In a case that in mid-1994 was awaiting a hearing before the Supreme Court, Judge Kasim had ruled that an inheritance division backed by a signed document unfairly distributed land to heirs. "We are very interested in seeing whether the Supreme Court will support our judgment," he told me in 1994, "because it introduces a sense of justice into the court. No one is totally fair – just look at the fingers on one hand; they work together but all are different lengths [this image was made popular by a famous *didong* sung poetry composition of the 1950s]. And so it is with children; some will taste the sweet, some rich, some bitter foods. But there are limits."

The Islamic court's conflict with the appellate court is part of a more general pattern in which highlands institutions try to go over the head of the unhelpful Acehnese to a more responsive central government: voting for the state party, GOLKAR (when the rest of Aceh usually votes for the Muslim party); sending Gayo sons and daughters into civil service in Jakarta, rather than in Banda Aceh; and seeking trading partners in the large city of Medan to counteract ethnic Acehnese dominance of export trade networks in the province. But in this case, the conflict has a specific legal content, and it turns on the issue of whether general substantive considerations of equality can override the specific rules found in Islamic jurisprudence. This conflict is thus both part of a long-running debate about the appropriate relationship between *adat* and Islam and part of a continuing tension between the highlands and the powerful provincial institutions.

Conclusions

I have provided the material for more than one type of explanation for the changes in court decisions over this period. One could assume that over this entire time the Islamic court judges have held the same policy preferences – namely, encouraging behavior consistent with Islamic law – and that the changes in their decisions derive wholly from changes in the constraints they have faced. Certainly those changes have been significant ones. Between the 1960s and the 1990s, the state, largely through the military, increased its direct control over Indonesian social life; one effect of this greater state power has been to guard the Islamic court from reprisals against unpopular decisions. In this period, the Islamic courts gained independent executory powers and greater legitimacy (though this latter characterization would not be true of the general courts). At the same time, court decisions have been subjected to greater scrutiny for the faithfulness of their decisions to an increasingly codified form of Islamic law. The judges' increased tendency to apply Islamic law would then appear as the outcome of two changes: more power to overturn local social practices and more pressure from their superiors to apply Islamic law.

A quite different story may also be told, however, one that emphasizes alterations in how the judges perceive Gayo social life and how they perceive their own role in social life. The Islamic court judges today argue that changes in Gayo social norms not only justify but also require the application of Islamic law. They see Gayo people as wishing increasingly to be governed by Islamic rules and not by older ones; village meetings are seen as a means to coerce recalcitrant siblings rather than as emblems of democratic deliberation. The Islamic court judges also see Gayo men and women in a more individualistic, materialistic, light, and they are saddened by this perception. They derive it as much from their experience in divorce cases, which they see as reflecting a growing individualism, as from their noting the increase in bitterness and prolongation of inheritance disputes. They are also aware that economic and demographic behavior has changed in ways that support this shift in norms. They see their own roles in the 1990s as less about Islamizing the highlands than about urging people to act in a decent manner toward each other. They see Islamic law as a way to do that in accord with evolving social norms.

The first account emphasizes changes in the judges' constraints; the second, changes in their perceptions. The first explanation portrays Islamic court judges as newly empowered to apply Islamic law; the second, as letting their decisions reflect changing social norms. As is true in many such situations, the reason for the differing court decision is probably a result of some combination of the two sets of factors (see Bellow & Minow 1996).

I would emphasize, however, that these and other plausible explanations underscore the importance of the court as an institution concerned with the active interpretation of law and of society. The courts are not merely arenas for actors to implement "more basic" programs. The laws, the values and perceptions of the judges, and the powers of the court are all important in explaining the outcomes of the decisions.

Furthermore, the decisions themselves involve publicly accessible events of legal and social interpretation. We may never know what the judges "really thought"; what we can know, and, I believe, what most matters, is how they created new interpretations of law and of social life in their decisions. Let me emphasize three qualities of these interpretations.

First, judicial interpretations on both Takèngën courts have studiously avoided opposing *adat* to Islam, custom to law. Many of the more creative inventions advanced by the court involved precisely preventing such oppositions, either by claiming that the same rules are found in both *adat* and Islam (e.g., the rule that all heirs must agree to a bequest), or by claiming that rules of procedure precluded invoking one or the other (e.g., the rule that the right to bring suit had elapsed). Judges on both courts, over a considerable span of time, have endeavored to create a legal discourse that encompasses both sources of law. Efforts to separate *"adat"* from "Islam," then, whether carried out by anthropologists or by Islamic scholars, fail to capture the interpretive activities of, at least, these lower-court judges.

Second, across a long stretch of time the judges have continued to invoke the cultural category of "consensus." The judges interpreted "consensus" in distinct and changing ways, but the category remained constant, as a putative linkage between political ideology and ongoing social life. Clearly, the category of "consensus" (like "freedom" and "equality" in US political life) admits of a wide range of interpretations, but at the same time it signals a cultural and political rootedness. It is precisely this combination of consistent signaling and interpretive capaciousness that has allowed it to serve as a privileged cultural operator in the field of Indonesian law and politics.

Finally, the judges have provided consistent legal justifications for their decisions. The content of these decisions changed – from affirming long-standing social norms of property transmission in the older cases to overriding these norms in the later cases. But across these changes, the judges framed their decisions, and their various versions of what law was and what society was, in terms of law. Enfeebled by arbitrary state actions though it may be, the ideal of the rule of law in Indonesia has supported and continues to support the efforts of those who press for judicial reform and political accountability (Lev 1996). The importance of this ideal is hardly less at moments, such as those in the immediate post-Suharto period, when new foundations must be sought for political institutions and processes. In this respect, the interpretive history of judicial reasoning in this particular corner of Indonesia may prove useful, to the extent that it illustrates the capacity of judges to create a legal framework that can encompass multiple sources of law, amid rapidly shifting social norms.

NOTES

1   Although legal anthropology has developed quite an extensive literature on the ways ordinary people choose among several possible forums for resolving disputes, less

attention has been paid to judges' reasoning processes in the face of competing norms (Benda-Beckmann 1984 is one exception). Analytically closest to the perspective adopted here are ethnographic studies of how disputants manipulate legal norms and meanings (Comaroff and Roberts 1981; Just 1990), historical studies of how new legal norms are constructed, whether in the United States (Horwitz 1992; Karsten 1997) or in other settings (Moore 1986), and legal studies of how agreement is produced in appellate courts (Epstein and Knight 1998; Sunstein 1996). "Interlegal" is taken from Santos (1987); Merry (1992) reviews studies of law in postcolonial contexts.

2   Among recent studies of the interactions between Islamic and secular legal systems are Esposito (1982) on changes in family law and Brown (1997) on judicial systems in Egypt and the Persian Gulf states.

3   At the same time, Africanists were making quite distinct analytical points, high-lighting the invented character of customary law institutions (Chanock 1985; Moore 1986). The contrast may be due to the very different histories of creating political units in the two continents; I find, however, a nostalgia for authenticity more often among Indonesianists than Africanists. Why this is so is an interesting question not pursued here.

4   The issue is not a new one in Islamic history. Muslim jurists have incorporated "custom" into law through a variety of means (Libson 1997). However, the perception of a conflict between law and custom probably has increased with the codification of religious and secular laws.

5   The classic study of the Islamic courts is Lev (1972); for a recent analysis of the Supreme Court see Pompe (1996).

6   For the norms as found in classic jurisprudential literature, see Coulson (1971); Esposito (1982) documents modern reformulations of these norms.

7   Perhaps only in the province of West Sumatra, home of the Minangkabau people, has there been a similarly complex history of Islamic political and legal innovation (see Benda-Beckmann 1984).

8   For the political and economic history of the Gayo region to 1990, see Bowen (1991:60–135). For an analysis of recent uprisings in Aceh, see Kell (1995).

9   In 1953 the Aceh Chief Justice, Tengku M. Hanafiah, wrote to the head of the Office of Religious Affairs (*Kantor Urusan Agama*) in Banda Aceh, with copies to the religious courts throughout Aceh, that although the courts do have jurisdiction over inheritance disputes, settling them "makes things very difficult" (*sangat merumitkan*) because the court's status has not been clarified by the central government. "But we cannot just refuse to hear such cases," complains Judge Hanafiah, "so what should we do?" (letter in court archives).

10 So accustomed are political actors to deciding by "consensus," with varying degrees of de facto underlying coercion, that when in the post-Suharto era the national Parliament made a decision by "voting" (English in the original, in scare quotes), it was the headline story of the day (Kompas on-line, Sept. 1998).

11 A distinct theory about consensus comes from Islamic jurisprudence, in which the consensus (*ijma*) of jurists can be the basis for law. The validity of arguments from consensus is hotly debated within Islamic circles; on recent uses of the category in Indonesian legal reform, see Bowen (1999).

12 The problem is a general one for theories of deliberative democracy as well as for studies of specific political processes. On what grounds can one claim "consensus," given that any deliberative process will involve people changing their minds (perhaps by definition), and such changes involve influence, probably authority, and perhaps power?

13 Recall that after 1970 decisions on the proper division of an estate were reserved to the Islamic courts.

14 For example, the Isak village I have followed in most detail, Kramil village, had 55
    households in 1979 and had grown to 70 in 1994. But of those 70 households, only 47
    had their main house in the village or in the nearby Isak shop area; the rest lived in coffee-
    growing areas. In 1979 only 6 households grew coffee; in 1994, 37 did.
15 For a detailed analysis of the current and shifting jurisprudence on gifts, see Bowen
    (1998).

REFERENCES

Bellow, Gary, and Martha Minow (1996) "Introduction: Rita's Case and Other Law Stories,"
    in G. Bellow and M. Minow, eds., *Law Stories*. Ann Arbor: Univ. of Michigan Press.
Benda-Beckmann, Keebet von (1984) *The Broken Stairways to Consensus: Village Justice and
    State Courts in Minangkabau*. Dordrecht, the Netherlands: Foris Publications.
Bowen, John R. (1988) "The Transformation of an Indonesian Property System: *Adat*, Islam,
    and Social Change in the Gayo Highlands." 15 *American Ethnologist* 274–93.
——(1991) *Sumatran Politics and Poetics: Gayo History, 1900–1989*. New Haven, CT: Yale
    Univ. Press.
——(1998) "'You May Not Give It Away': How Social Norms Shape Islamic Law in
    Contemporary Indonesian Jurisprudence." 5 (Oct.) *Islamic Law and Society* 1–27.
——(1999) "Legal Reasoning and Public Discourse in Indonesian Islam," in D.F. Eickelman
    and J. W. Anderson, eds., *New Media in the Muslim World: The Emerging Public Sphere*.
    Bloomington: Indiana Univ. Press.
Brown, Nathan J. (1997) *The Rule of Law in the Arab World: Courts in Egypt and the Gulf*.
    Cambridge Univ. Press.
Cammack, Mark (1997) "Indonesia's 1989 Religious Judicature Act: Islamization of Indo-
    nesia or Indonesianization of Islam?" 63 *Indonesia* 143–68.
Chanock, Martin (1985) *Law, Custom and Social Order: The Colonial Experience in Malawi
    and Zambia*. Cambridge: Cambridge Univ. Press.
Comaroff, John, and Simon Roberts (1981) *Rules and Processes: The Cultural Logic of
    Dispute in an African Context*. Chicago: Univ. of Chicago Press.
Coulson, N. J. (1971) *Succession in the Muslim Family*. Cambridge: Cambridge Univ. Press.
Departemen Kehakiman (1973) *Masalah-masalah hukum perdata di Takengon* [Civil law
    issues in Takengon]. Jakarta: Direktorat Jenderal Pembinaan Badan-Badan Peradilan,
    Departemen Kehakiman.
——(1984) *Masalah-masalah hukum perdata adat di Daerah Bekas Kawedanan Takengon*
    [Adat civil law issues in the former subdistrict of Takengon]. Jakarta: Direktorat Jenderal
    Pembinaan Badan-Badan Peradilan, Departemen Kehakiman.
Ellen, Roy F. (1983) "Social Theory, Ethnography, and the Understanding of Practical Islam in
    South-East Asia," in M.B. Hooker, ed., *Islam in South-East Asia*, Leiden, Netherlands:
    E.J. Brill.
Epstein, Lee, and Jack Knight (1998) *The Choices Judges Make*. Washington, DC: CQ Press.
Esposito, John L. (1982) *Women in Muslim Family Law*. Syracuse, NY: Syracuse Univ. Press.
Geertz, Clifford (1983) "Local Knowledge: Fact and Law in Comparative Perspective," in
    C. Geertz, ed., *Local Knowledge: Further Essays in Interpretive Anthropology*. New York:
    Basic Books.
Horwitz, Morton J. (1992) *The Transformation of American Law, 1870–1960*. New York:
    Oxford Univ. Press.

Just, Peter (1990) "Dead Goats and Broken Betrothals: Liability and Equity in Dou Donggo Law." 17 *American Ethnologist* 75–90.

Karsten, Peter (1997) *Heart Versus Head: Judge-Made Law in Nineteenth-Century America*. Chapel Hill: Univ. of North Carolina Press.

Kell, Tim (1995) *The Roots of Acehnese Rebellion, 1989–1992*. Ithaca, NY: Cornell Modern Indonesia Project, Monograph No. 74.

Lev, Daniel S. (1965) "The Lady and the Banyan Tree: Civil-Law Change in Indonesia" 14 *American J. of Comparative Law* 282–307.

——(1972) *Islamic Courts in Indonesia: A Study in the Political Bases of Legal Institutions*. Berkeley and Los Angeles: Univ. of California Press.

——(1996) "Between State and Society: Professional Lawyers and Reform in Indonesia," In D. S., Lev, and R. McVey, eds., *Making Indonesia: Essays on Modern Indonesia in Honor of George McT. Kahin*. Ithaca, NY: Cornell Southeast Asia Program Publications, Studies on Southeast Asia No. 20.

Libson, Gideon (1997) "On the Development of Custom as a Source of Law in Islamic Law." 4 (June) *Islamic Law & Society* 131–55.

Merry, Sally Engle (1992) "Anthropology, Law, and Transnational Processes." 21 *Annual Rev. of Anthropology* 357–79.

Messick, Brinkley (1993) *The Calligraphic State: Textual Domination and History in a Muslim Society*. Berkeley and Los Angeles: Univ. of California Press.

Moore, Sally Falk (1986) *Social Facts and Fabrications: "Customary Law" on Kilimanjaro, 1880–1980*. Cambridge: Cambridge Univ. Press.

Pompe, S. (1996) "The Indonesian Supreme Court: Fifty Years of Judicial Development." Diss. at Leiden Univ., Faculty of Law, Netherlands.

Rosen, Lawrence (1989) *The Anthropology of Justice*. Cambridge: Cambridge Univ. Press.

Santos, Boaventura de Sousa (1987) "Law: A Map of Misreading, Toward a Postmodern Conception of Law." 14 *J. of Law and Society* 279–302.

Subekti, R., and J. Tamara, eds. (1965) *Kumpulan Putusan Mahkamah Aguing* [Collection of Supreme Court decisions]. 2d edn Jakarta: Gunung Agung.

Subekti, R., & R. Tjitrosudibio, eds. (1961) *Kitab Undang-Undang Hukum Perdata*. Jakarta: Pradaja Paramita.

Sunstein, Cass R. (1996) *Legal Reasoning and Political Conflict*. New York: Oxford Univ. Press.

Tamanaha, Brian Z. (1993) "The Folly of the 'Social Scientific' Concept of Legal Pluralism." 20 *J. of Law & Society* 192–215.

CASES CITED

Inën Deraman v. Inen Nur (PA 25/1962)
Inën Saidah v. Aman Jemilah (PN 47/1964)
Samadiah v. Hasan Ali (PA 381/1987)
Sulaiman v. M. Ali (PA 60/1973)
Usman v. Serikulah (PA 41/1961)

B. Identity and Its Legal Significance

General Introduction

In the United States in the early twenty-first century, there is continuous media talk of terrorists. Such talk alerts the public to dangers that may really exist. But many are also aware of the political uses that have been made of the reviled and feared "terrorist" identity. US laws have been changed. To free the hands of law enforcement and security personnel, exceptions have been ordered with regard to many basic civil protections. Suspected terrorists are now outside the normal workings of the legal system. Suspects can be held in prison without being charged with any offense. Who is a suspect? How is that condition defined? By whom? Under what authority?

In theory, the law of a polity applies to everyone, equally. Such ideas are enshrined in many constitutions. But now in the US there are to be official exceptions for persons who are suspected of being a threat to the state. Such political exceptions are well known in other parts of the world. In fact, there are other kinds of exceptions. In some countries there are special rights or disabilities that apply to ethnic groups, or religious categories, or to non-citizens. Women are denied equality in many countries in which the constitution guarantees equality for everyone. Also, in various states, there are special enclaves, or corridors, or abstract entities that make exceptions for business people. Such special laws are created to encourage investment, to stimulate commercial activity, and in general to advance economic development. Thus, even where there is a declared universality of state law, the anthropologist may well have to look closely at the question of identity to ascertain how and when the law uses special categories to construct privileges or disadvantages.

In addition to these politicized instances there are many mundane legal identities that are obvious in the ordinary course. The landlord, and the shopkeeper, the bus driver, are ordinary figures in our daily lives. They each have particular legal obligations as do the tenant and the customer and the passenger. No one should have any doubt that a person's identity is a critical definer of legal status and that the question of identity is ubiquitous, that it exists everywhere in the social environment, and that the identity issue is not only a matter of the roles of individuals, but of the categorization of groups, by the state, and by other groups.

In his well-known, path-breaking book *Ethnic Groups and Boundaries* (1969), Frederic Barth argued that self-identification was the best test of membership in an ethnic group. He was thinking of examples where that definition fits very well. However, once one starts thinking in legal terms, self-identification may be much less important than legal definition. Identities may be imposed from the outside.

Unni Wikan, writing about Pakistanis in Norway in *Generous Betrayal* (2002) confronts directly the issues that have emerged in the Norwegian welfare state in relation to their immigrants. When there is a conflict between Norwegian law and values and the values of the immigrants, what is the state to do? She particularly focuses on the question of gender equality, and describes instances of the forced marriages of some young girls from Pakistani families who had attended Norwegian schools and acquired Norwegian values, but found their fate sealed by their fathers who justified making the choice for them on the basis of a right to practice their culture. Wikan asks what Norwegian state policy toward the children of immigrants should be. She combines a fieldwork account with strong opinions about what measures should be taken.

To the extent that aspects of identity may be defined by the law, the state is implicated in the everyday lives of all persons. But that involvement is often not actively felt. It only comes to public notice when there are disputes, or when political activists focus on a particular set of persons or meanings.

What follows in this section of our reader are a great range of instances that involve identities and human rights in very different circumstances. The first is James Clifford's about a case in which a group of people tried to prove themselves to be Native Americans of the Mashpee tribe, and the way the court defined that identity, the second a chapter by Eve Daran-Smith on locating a reinvigorated Kentish identity. The next chapter by Anne Griffiths concerns gender and law in an African setting. And last, what follows are excerpts from a chapter by Richard Wilson on the way the Truth and Reconciliation Commission in South Africa sought to identify human rights offenders by giving victims a remedial mode of public expression. In the course of this process human rights talk expressed a national political rejection of the past. But while the Commission's work appeared to contribute to nation building and centralization, Wilsons' fieldwork in the townships shows that the human rights and reconciliation talk at the national level failed to permeate popular legal consciousness, nor did it alter violent local modes of meting out justice.

All of these articles involve the context of social practice on which the law of the state, or of an official court, has an impact. These anthropologists are thus breaking from earlier anthropological models. No longer is the law of a people seen as a seamless part of their tradition-in-practice, their social values and customary actions of long standing. The law is not just an internal part of some pre-existing "culture." The law is seen as something being made, as an entity in process, as something developing in historical time. The post-classical ethnographic model takes into account the fact that there are political institutions, the state, the official courts, the legislature, the institutions of enforcement, all implicated in defining the law and how and when it should be "applied." In the process of defining and "applying" the law, the institutions themselves are seen as sorting out their own political place and powers, and having an impact on the shape of the polity, and its "culture."

S.F.M.

REFERENCES

Barth, Fredrik, 1969 *Ethnic Groups and Boundaries*. Boston: Little Brown and Co.
Wikan, Unni, 2002 *Generous Betrayal: Politics of Culture in the New Europe*. Chicago: University of Chicago Press.

17

Identity in Mashpee

James Clifford

Introduction: The Mashpee Case – the Presentation of Identity

This is an account of the trial of lawsuit brought in 1976 in a federal court by a tribal council claiming 16,000 acres of land. Their claim to the land rested on their contention that the Mashpee were an Indian tribe. Methodologically, Clifford does three things in his treatment of this trial. He presents the testimony of various witnesses verbatim. These pages of testimony have been omitted in the excerpt that follows for reasons of space, but they are well worth reading for the sense that they give of the people who were involved. Secondly, Clifford classifies the lines of argument and types of witnesses who appeared. And he summarizes part of the evidence, particularly the historical evidence, giving his own opinion of what it shows.

Clifford describes the history of the ancestors of the people bringing the lawsuit in summary form. The gist of his argument is that there had been an earlier time when they were a much more organized and coherent collectivity. Later they could only be seen as geographically co-resident individuals with few things in common. He says that they had abandoned their tribal organization and many of their customs by the 1920s and become "individual citizen-farmers, workers and businessmen" (p. 300). They had no surviving native language. They intermarried with other populations in the area. A historian testified about their past, as did some anthropologists speaking to the question whether they were a "tribe" and whether they had been so continuously in the relevant period. The way anthropologists have filled this role and the problems they have faced is described in an article by Lawrence Rosen published in 1977, "The Anthropologist as Expert Witness," *American Anthropologist* 79:555–578.

From James Clifford, "Identity in Mashpee," in *The Predicament of Culture: Twentieth-Century Ethnography, Literature and Avt* (Cambridge, MA, and London: Harvard University Press, 1988), pp. 270, 278–80, 283–5, 288–91, 294–301, 302–10, 317, 321–3, 333–43.

Identity itself has at least two meanings, both of which were significant in this case. Identity can signify the way a person conceives him or herself, the kind of person he or she thinks himself to be. That is identity as the individual imagines himself. But, obviously, identity can have a social or collective meaning. Members of a group can see themselves as having the same social identity, can conceive themselves as being alike in some way. The testimony of the various Mashpee Indians in this case showed them to be very different individually, one from another, but it also shows them trying to make the argument that they nevertheless had institutions and practices in common, and therefore constituted "a tribe."

The difference between the legal definition of a "tribe" for the purpose of making land claims, and the Mashpee's conception of themselves is clearly brought out in this article. It is a useful demonstration of the attempt to create precise criteria for legal categorization. Yet it shows what a poor fit this may be for the actual accounts when lay people are testifying about their general sense of a situation.

S.F.M.

Clifford, *Identity*

In AUGUST 1976 the Mashpee Wampanoag Tribal Council, Inc., sued in federal court for possession of about 16,000 acres of land constituting three-quarters of Mashpee, "Cape Cod's Indian Town." (The township of Mashpee extends inland from the Cape's southern shore, facing Martha's Vineyard, between Falmouth and Barnstable.) An unprecedented trial ensued whose purpose was not to settle the question of land ownership but rather to determine whether the group calling itself the Mashpee Tribe was in fact an Indian tribe, and the same tribe that in the mid-nineteenth century had lost its lands through a series of contested legislative acts.

The Mashpee suit was one of a group of land-claim actions filed in the late 1960s and 1970s, a relatively favorable period for redress of Native American grievances in the courts. Other claims were being initiated by the Gay Head Wampanoag Tribe on Martha's Vineyard; the Narragansets of Charlestown, Rhode Island; Western Pequots, Schaghticokes, and Mohegans in Connecticut; and Oneidas, St. Regis Mohawks, and Cayugas in New York. The Mashpee action was similar... tribes laying claim to a large portion of the state of Maine. Their suit, after initial successes in Federal District Court, direct intervention from President Jimmy Carter, and five years of hard negotiation, resulted in a favorable out-of-court settlement. The tribes received $81.5 million and the authority to acquire 300,000 acres with Indian Country status.

The legal basis of the Penobscot-Passamaquoddy suit, as conceived by their attorney, Thomas Tureen, was the Non-Intercourse Act of 1790. This paternalist legislation, designed to protect tribal groups from spoliation by unscrupulous whites, declared that alienation of Indian lands could be legally accomplished only with permission of Congress. The act had never been rescinded, although throughout the nineteenth century it was often honored in the breach. When in the 1970s Indian groups appealed to the Non-Intercourse Act, they were attempting, in effect, to reverse more than a century of attacks on Indian lands. The alienations had been particularly severe for eastern groups, whose claim to collective land was often unclear. When court decisions confirmed that the Non-Intercourse Act applied to nonreservation Indians, the way was opened for suits, like those of the Maine tribes, claiming that nearly two centuries of Indian land transfers, even ordinary purchases, were invalid since they had been made without permission of Congress.

Although the Mashpee claim was similar to the Maine Indians', there were crucial differences. The Passamaquoddy and Penobscot were generally recognized Indian tribes with distinct communities and clear aboriginal roots in the area. The Mashpee plaintiffs represented most of the nonwhite inhabitants of what, for over three centuries, had been known as an "Indian town" on Cape Cod; but their institutions of tribal governance had long been elusive, especially during the century and a half preceeding the suit. Moreover, since about 1800 the Massachusett language had ceased to be commonly spoken in Mashpee. The town was at first largely Presbyterian then Baptist in its public religion. Over the centuries inhabitants had intermarried with other Indian groups, whites, blacks, Hessian deserters from the British Army during the Revolutionary War, Cape Verde islanders. The inhabitants of Mashpee were active in the economy and society of modern Massachusetts. They were businessmen, schoolteachers, fishermen, domestic workers, small contractors. Could these people of Indian ancestry file suit as the Mashpee Tribe that had, they claimed, been despoiled of collectively held lands during the mid-nineteenth century? This was the question a federal judge posed to a Boston jury. Only if they answered yes could the matter proceed to a land-claim trial.

The forty-one days of testimony that unfolded in Federal District Court during the late fall of 1977 bore the name *Mashpee Tribe* v. *New Seabury et al.*, shorthand for a complex, multipartied dispute. Mashpee Tribe referred to the plaintiffs, the Mashpee Wampanoag Tribal Council, Inc., described by its members as an arm of the Mashpee Tribe. A team of lawyers from the Native American Rights Fund, a nonprofit advocacy group, prepared their suit. Its chief architects were Thomas Tureen and Barry Margolin. In court the plaintiffs' case was argued by the trial lawyer Lawrence Shubow, with assistance from Tureen, Margolin, Ann Gilmore, and Moshe Genauer. New Seabury et al. referred to the New Seabury Corporation (a large development company), the Town of Mashpee (representing over a hundred individual landowners), and various other classes of defendant (insurance companies, businesses, property owners). The case for the defense was argued by James St. Clair (Richard Nixon's Watergate attorney) of the large Boston firm Hale and Dorr, and Allan Van Gestel of Goodwin, Proctor, and Hoar. They were assisted by a team of eight other lawyers.

The presence of the Town of Mashpee among the defendants requires explanation. It was not until 1869 that the community living in Mashpee was accorded formal township status. From 1869 until 1964 the town government was overwhelmingly in the hands of Indians. During this period every selectman but one was an Indian or married to an Indian. Genealogical evidence presented at the trial showed that the families of town officers were closely interrelated. No one contested the fact that before the 1960s Mashpee was governed by Indians. The disagreement was over whether they governed as an "Indian tribe."

This basic demographic and political situation, which had not altered drastically for over three centuries, was revolutionized during the early 1960s. Before then census figures showed a population in Mashpee fluctuating in the neighborhood of 350 Indians and "negroes," "coloreds," or "mulattoes" (the official categories shifted), and 100 or fewer whites. A reliable count of 1859, which served as a benchmark in the trial, listed only one white resident. After 1960 for the first time whites were recorded in the majority, and by 1970 whites outnumbered Indians and other people of color by 982 to 306. By 1968 two of the town's selectmen were whites, the third Indian. This proportion was in effect at the time of the lawsuit. Mashpee's white selectmen voted that the town should legally represent the non-Indian majority of property holders who were threatened by the land claim.

"Cape Cod's Indian Town" had finally been discovered. For centuries a backwater and a curiosity, in the 1950s and 1960s Mashpee became desirable as a site for retirement, vacation homes, condominiums, and luxury developments. Fast roads now made it accessible as a bedroom and weekend suburb of Boston. The new influx of money and jobs was first welcomed by many of Mashpee's Indian residents, including some of the leaders of the land-claim suit. They took advantage of the new situation. The town government, still run by Indians, enjoyed a surge in tax revenues. But when local government passed out of Indian control, perhaps for good, and as the scale of development increased, many Indians began to feel qualms. What they had taken for granted – that this was their town – no longer held true. Large tracts of undeveloped land formerly open for hunting and fishing were suddenly ringed with "No Trespassing" signs. The New Seabury development, on a choice stretch of coastline, with its two golf courses and expansionist plans, seemed particularly egregious. Tensions between traditional residents and new-comers increased, finally leading to the suit, filed with the support of most, but not all, of the Indians in Mashpee. The land claim, while focusing on a loss of property in the nineteenth century, was actually an attempt to regain control of a town that had slipped from Indian hands very recently.

[. . .]

Images

At the end of the trial Federal Judge Walter J. Skinner posed a number of specific questions to the jurors concerning tribal status at certain dates in Mashpee history; but throughout the proceedings broader questions of Indian identity and power permeated the courtroom. Although the land claim was formally not at issue, the lawyers for New Seabury et al. sometimes seemed to be playing on a new nightmare. At the door of your suburban house a stranger in a business suit appears. He says he is a Native American. Your land has been illegally acquired generations ago, and you must relinquish your home. The stranger refers you to his lawyer.

Such fears, the threat of a "giveaway" of private lands, were much exploited by politicians and the press in the Penobscot-Passamaquoddy negotiations. Actually small holdings by private citizens were never in danger; only large tracts of undeveloped land held by timber companies and the state were in question. In Mashpee the plaintiffs reduced their claim to eleven thousand acres, formally excluding all private homes and lots up to an acre in size. Large-scale development, not small ownership, was manifestly the target; but their opponents refused pretrial compromises and the kinds of negotiation that had led to settlement of the Maine dispute.

According to Thomas Tureen the sorts of land claims pursued in Maine, Mashpee, Gay Head, and Charlestown were always drastically circumscribed. At that historical moment the courts were relatively open to Native American claims, a situation unlikely to last. In a decision of 1985 permitting Oneida, Mohawk, and Cayuga Non-Intercourse Act suits the Supreme Court made it abundantly clear, in Tureen's words, "that Indians are dealing with the magnanimity of a rich and powerful nation, one that is not about to divest itself or its non-Indian citizens of large acreage in the name of its own laws. In short, the United States will permit Indians a measure of recompense through the law – indeed, it has done so to an extent far greater than any other nation in a comparable situation – but it ultimately makes the rules and arbitrates the game.

Seen in this light, the Mashpee trial was simply a clarification of the rules in an ongoing struggle between parties of greatly unequal power. But beneath the explicit fear of white citizens losing their homes because of an obscure past injustice, a troubling uncertainty was finding its way into the dominant image of Indians in America. The plaintiffs in the Non-Intercourse Act suits had power. In Maine politicians lost office over the issue, and the Mashpee case made national headlines for several months. Scandalously, it now paid to be Indian. Acting aggressively, tribal groups were doing sophisticated, "nontraditional" things. All over the country they were becoming involved in a variety of businesses, some claiming exemption from state regulation. To many whites it was comprehensible for Northwest Coast tribes to demand traditional salmon-fishing privileges; but for tribes to run high-stakes bingo games in violation of state laws was not.

Indians had long filled a pathetic imaginative space for the dominant culture; they were always survivors, noble or wretched. Their cultures had been steadily eroding, at best hanging on in museumlike reservations. Native American societies could not by definition be dynamic, inventive, or expansive. Indians were lovingly remembered in Edward Curtis' sepia photographs as proud, beautiful, and "vanishing." But Curtis, we now know, carried props, costumes, and wigs, frequently dressing up his models. The image he recorded was carefully staged. In Boston Federal Court a jury of white citizens would be confronted by a collection of highly ambiguous images. Could a group of four women and eight men (no minorities) be made to believe in the persistent "Indian" existence of the Mashpee plaintiffs without costumes and props? This question surrounded and infused the trial's technical focus on whether a particular form of political-cultural organization called a tribe had existed continuously in Mashpee since the sixteenth century.

The image of Mashpee Indians, like that of several other eastern groups such as the Lumbee and the Ramapough, was complicated by issues of race. Significant intermarriage with blacks had occurred since the mid-eighteenth century, and the Mashpee were, at times, widely identified as "colored." In court the defense occasionally suggested that they were really blacks rather than Native Americans. Like the Lumbee (and, less successfully, the Ramapough) the Mashpee plaintiffs had struggled to distinguish themselves from other minorities and ethnic groups, asserting tribal status based on a distinctive political-cultural history. In court they were not helped by the fact that few of them looked strongly "Indian." Some could pass for black, others for white.

[...]

Borderlines

Mashpee Indians suffered the fate of many small Native American groups who remained in the original thirteen states. They were not accorded the reservations and sovereign status (steadily eroded) of tribes west of the Mississippi. Certain of the eastern communities, such as the Seneca and the Seminoles, occupied generally recognized tribal lands. Others – the Lumbee, for example – possessed no collective lands but clustered in discrete regions, maintaining kinship ties, traditions, and sporadic tribal institutions. In all cases the boundaries of the community were permeable. There was intermarriage and routine migration in and out of the tribal center – sometimes seasonal, sometimes longer term. Aboriginal languages were much diminished, often entirely lost. Religious life was diverse – sometimes Christian (with a distinctive twist), sometimes a transformed tradition such as the Iroquois Longhouse Religion. Moral and spiritual values were often Native American amalgams compounded from both local traditions and pan-Indian sources. For example the ritual and regalia at New England powwows now reflect Sioux and other western tribal influences; in the 1920s the feathered "war bonnet" made its appearance among Wampanoag leaders. Eastern Indians generally lived in closer proximity to white (or black) society and in smaller groups than their western reservation counterparts. In the face of intense pressure some eastern communities have managed to acquire official federal recognition as tribes, others not. During the past two decades the rate of applications has risen dramatically.

Within this diversity of local histories and institutional arrangements the long-term residents of Mashpee occupied a gray area, at least in the eyes of the surrounding society and the law. The Indian identity of the Penobscot and Passamaquoddy was never seriously challenged, even though they had not been federally recognized and had lost or adapted many of their traditions. The Mashpee were more problematic. Partisans of their land claim, such as Paul Brodeur, tend to accept without question the right of the tribal council, incorporated in 1974, to sue on behalf of a group that had lost its lands in the mid-nineteenth century. They see the question of tribal status as a legal red herring, or worse, a calculated ploy to deny the tribe its birthright. However procrustian and colonial in origin the legal definition of tribe, there was nonetheless a real issue at stake in the trial. Although tribal status and Indian identity have long been vague and politically constituted, not just anyone with some native blood or claim to adoption or shared tradition can be an Indian; and not just any Native American group can decide to be a tribe and sue for lost collective lands.

Indians in Mashpee owned no tribal lands (other than fifty-five acres acquired just before the trial). They had no surviving language, no clearly distinct religion, no blatant political structure. Their kinship was much diluted. Yet they did have a place and a reputation. For centuries Mashpee had been recognized as an Indian town. Its boundaries had not changed since 1665, when the land was formally deeded to a group called the South Sea Indians by the neighboring leaders Tookonchasun and

Weepquish. The Mashpee plaintiffs of 1977 could offer as evidence surviving pieces of Native American tradition and political structures that seemed to have come and gone. They could also point to a sporadic history of Indian revivals continuing into the present.

The Mashpee were a borderline case. In the course of their peculiar litigation certain underlying structures governing the recognition of identity and difference became visible. Looked at one way, they were Indian; seen another way, they were not. Powerful *ways of looking* thus became inescapably problematic. The trial was less a search for the facts of Mashpee Indian culture and history than it was an experiment in translation, part of a long historical conflict and negotiation of "Indian" and "American" identities.

(This is how I came to see the Mashpee case, and the account I give of it reflects my way of seeing. As a historian and critic of anthropology I tend to focus on the ways in which historical stories are told, on the alternate cultural models that have been applied to human groups. Who speaks for cultural authenticity? How is collective identity and difference represented? How do people define themselves with, over, and in spite of others? What are the changing local and world historical conditions determining these processes?

At the Mashpee trial these were the kinds of questions that interested me and that now organize my account. I am not fictionalizing or inventing anything, nor am I presenting the whole picture. The reality presented here is the reality of a specific interest and field of vision.

I attended most of the trial, and I've used my courtroom notes as a guiding thread. I've read what has been published about the history of Mashpee and the litigation, notably Francis Hutchins' *Mashpee: The Story of Cape Cod's Indian Town* (1979), Paul Brodeur's *Restitution: The Land Claims of the Mashpee, Passamaquoddy, and Penobscot Indians of New England* (1985), and William Simmons' *Spirit of the New England Tribes* (1986). I've had access to Rona Sue Mazur's Ph.D. thesis in anthropology at Columbia University, "Town and Tribe in Conflict: A Study of Local-Level Politics in Mashpee, Massachusetts" (1980). And I have consulted the trial record. But I haven't systematically interviewed participants or done firsthand research in the archives or in Mashpee.

It should be clear from what follows that I am portraying primarily the trial, not the complex lives of Indians and other ethnic groups in Mashpee. Still, in the process I make strong gestures toward truths missed by the dominant categories and stories in the courtroom. Thus I invoke as an absence the reality of Mashpee and particularly of its Indian lives. I do this to maintain the historical and ethnographic seriousness of the account, a seriousness I wish both to assert and to limit.

I accept the fact that my version of the trial, its witnesses, and its stories may offend people on several sides of the issue. Many individual positions are more complex than I have been able to show. My account may be objectionable to Native Americans for whom culture and tradition are continuities, not inventions, who feel stronger, less compromised ties to aboriginal sources than my analysis allows. For them this version of "identity in Mashpee" may be about rootless people like me, not them.

It is, and is not only, that.

When I report on witnesses at the trial, the impressions are mine. Others I spoke with saw things differently. The trial record – which stenographically preserves, by a precise but not infallible technique, the meaningful, spoken sounds of the trial – provides a check on my impressions. It does not, of course, provide much information on the *effect* of witnesses or events in the courtroom. It omits gestures, hesitations, clothing, tone of voice, laughter, irony... the sometimes devastating silences.

I offer vignettes of persons and events in the courtroom that are obviously composed and condensed. Testimony evoked in a page or two may run to hundreds of pages in the transcript. Some witnesses were on the stand for several days. Moreover, real testimony almost never ends the way my vignettes do; it trails off in the quibbles and corrections of redirect and recross-examination. While I have included for comparison a verbatim excerpt from the transcript, I have generally followed my courtroom notes, checked against the record, and have not hesitated to rearrange, select, and highlight. Where quotation marks appear, the statement is a fairly exact quotation; the rest is paraphrase.

Overall, if the witnesses seem flat and somewhat elusive, the effect is intentional. Using the usual rhetorical techniques, I could have given a more intimate sense of peoples' personalities or of what they were really trying to express; but I have preferred to keep my distance. A courtroom is more like a theater than a confessional.

Mistrustful of transparent accounts, I want mine to manifest some of its frames and angles, its wavelengths.)

[...]

History I

The case against the plaintiffs was straightforward: there never had been an Indian tribe in Mashpee. The community was a creation of the colonial encounter, a collection of disparate Indians and other minorities who sought over the years to become full citizens of the Commonwealth of Massachusetts and of the Republic. Decimated by disease, converted to Christianity, desirous of freedom from paternalistic state tutelage, the people of mixed Indian descent in Mashpee were progressively assimilated into American society. Their Indian identity had been lost, over and over, since the mid-seventeenth century.[1]

The plague

When the English Pilgrims arrived at Plymouth in 1620, they found a region devastated by a disease brought by white seamen. The settlers walked into empty Indian villages and planted in already cleared fields. The region was seriously underpopulated. In the years that followed Puritan leaders like Myles Standish pressed steadily to limit Indian territories and to establish clear "properties" for the growing number of newcomers. Misunderstandings inevitably ensued: for example whites claimed to own unoccupied land that had been ceded to them for temporary use.

Richard Bourne of Sandwich, a farmer near what is now Mashpee Pond and a tenant on Indian lands, studied the language of his landlords and soon became an effective mediator between the societies. He was friendly to the area's inhabitants, remnants of earlier groups, who came to be called South Sea Indians by the settlers to the north. He believed that they needed protection; becoming their advocate, he negotiated formal title to a large tract adjoining his farm (which in the meantime he had managed to purchase). His ally in these transactions was Paupmunnuck, a leader of the nearby Cotachesset.

Bourne's "South Sea Indian Plantation" was to become a refuge for Christian converts, for as white power increased, it became increasingly dangerous for Indians to live around Cape Cod unless they came together as a community of "praying Indians." Under Bourne's tutelage the Mashpee plantation was a center for the first Indian church on the Cape, organized in 1666.

Thus Mashpee was originally an artificial community, never a tribe. It was created from Indian survivors in an area between the traditional sachemdoms of Manomet and Nauset – the former centered on the present town of Bourne at the Cape's western edge, the latter near its tip.

Conversion to Christianity

Badly disorganized after the plague and confronted by a growing number of deter-mined settlers, the Cape Cod Indians made accommodations. Live and let live was not the Puritan way, especially once their power had been consolidated. Tensions and conflicts grew, leading to war in 1675 with the forces of the Wampanoag Supreme Sachem Metacomet ("King Philip"). After Metacomet's defeat Indians who sympathized with him were expelled from their lands. Many, including some who had remained neutral, were sold into slavery.

The price for living on ancestral lands in eastern New England was cooperation with white society. The Mashpee, under Bourne's tutelage, became model Chris-tians. By 1674 ninety Mashpee inhabitants were counted as baptized, and twenty-seven were admitted to full communion. The "praying Indians" were entering a new life. They stopped consulting "powwows" (medicine men, in seventeenth-century usage); they respected the Sabbath and other holy days, severed ties with "pagans," altered child-rearing practices, dressed in new ways, washed differently. The changes were gradual but telling. They reflected not only a tactical accommodation but also a new belief, born of defeat, that the powerful white ways must be superior. When Bourne died in 1682, his successor as Protestant minister was an Indian, Simon Popmonet, son of Bourne's old ally Paupmunnuck. This was a further sign that the Indians were willingly giving up their old ways for the new faith.

"Plantation" status

Once the South Sea Indian Plantation had been established, its inhabitants' claim to their land rested on a written deed and on English law rather than on any aboriginal sovereignty. Like other "plantations" in New England, the community at Mashpee was a joint-ownership arrangement by a group of "proprietors." Under English law proprietors were licensed to develop a vacant portion of land, reserving part for commons, part for the church, and part for individual holdings. All transfers of land were to be approved collectively. This plantation-proprietory form, as applied to early Cape Cod settlements such as Sandwich and Barnstable, was intended to evolve quickly into a township where freemen held individual private property and were represented in the General Court of the colony. The white plantations around Mashpee did evolve directly into towns. From the late seventeenth century on their common lands were converted into private individual holdings in fee simple. Mashpee followed the same course, but more slowly. As late as 1830 its lands were the joint property of proprietors.

For complex historical reasons Mashpee's progress toward full citizenship lagged almost two centuries behind that of its neighbors. An enduring prejudice against Indians and their supposed lack of "civility" certainly played a part, for during the early and mid-eighteenth century the Indian plantation was governed in humiliating ways by white "guardians." Nonetheless, development toward autonomy, while delayed, did occur. In 1763, after a direct appeal to King George III, Mashpee won the right to incorporation as a district, a step on the road to township status and a liberation from oppressive meddling by white outsiders. Then, beginning in 1834 and culminating in 1870, a series of acts of the Massachusetts legislature changed the Mashpee plantation into an incorporated town. Its inhabitants had overcome the prejudice and paternalism that had so long hemmed them in. They were now full-fledged citizens of Massachusetts.

Taking the colonists' side

From early on the Indian inhabitants of Mashpee gave signs of active identification with the new white society. During King Philip's War a certain Captain Amos, probably a Nauset from near Sandwich, led a group of Indians against Metacomet. Amos became a prominent inhabitant of Mashpee after the conflict ended. A century later the district of Mashpee sent a contingent to fight in the Revolutionary War against the British, a commitment of troops even greater than that of the surrounding white towns. Reliable accounts estimate that about half the adult male population died in the war. A Mashpee Indian, Joshua Pocknet, served at Valley Forge with George Washington. At these critical moments, therefore, the descendants of the South Sea Indians showed something more than simple acquiescence under colonial rule. Their enthusiastic patriotism strongly suggests that they had identified with white society, relinquishing any sense of a separate tribal political identity.

Intermarriage

Mashpee's population showed two significant periods of expansion. During the 1660s and 1670s there had been an influx of Indians from elsewhere on the Cape. Then after a century of relative equilibrium the population rose again in the 1760s and 1770s. Census figures are inexact and subject to interpretation, but it seems clear that before 1760 the principal newcomers were a steady trickle of New England Indians: Wampanoags from Gay Head and Herring Pond, Narragansets and Mohicans from Connecticut, Long Island Montauks. Immigration was restrained by the tutelage of outside "guardians," some of whom had an interest in keeping Mashpee small so that "unused" Indian lands could be made available for whites. After 1763, however, the newly incorporated district opened its borders to a variety of new settlers. A few whites entered by marriage but maintained a separate legal status. Their progeny, if one parent was Indian, could become proprietors. At least one white man "went native," living in a wigwam – just as the Indian residents of Mashpee were abandoning the last of theirs. Four Hessian mercenaries stayed on after the Revolutionary War and married Mashpee women. It is recorded that they accepted Indian manners.

The 1776 census counted fourteen "negroes" in a total population of 341. Significant intermarriage with freed black slaves occurred in this period, but it is difficult to say how much since common parlance, reflected in the census, sometimes mixed diverse peoples of brownish skin color in categories such as "Indian," "mulatto," or "negro." Intermarriage between blacks and Indians was encouraged by a common social marginality and by a relative shortage of men among the Indians and of women among the blacks. The local racial mix also included Cape Verde islanders and exotic imports resulting from the employment of Mashpee men in the far-flung sailing trades and women in domestic service: a Mexican and an Indian from Bombay are mentioned in the written sources.

By 1789 Mashpee's white minister, the Reverend Gideon Hawley, had become so concerned about Mashpee being overrun by blacks and foreigners that he engineered a return to plantation status, with himself as guardian of the town's threatened authenticity. This return to a restrictive paternalism was a setback for Mashpee's ability to grow and develop into a distinctive, independent nonwhite community. It was not until the 1840s, after a long conflict with Hawley's successor, the Reverend Phineas Fish, that local leaders finally rid themselves of outside tutelage. The struggle for citizenship had been slowed but not stopped. By the time of the final transition from plantation to township status in the four decades after 1830 the American citizens of Mashpee had become a complex mix – "colored" in contemporary parlance – that included several American Indian, black, and foreign ingredients.

Mashpee becomes a town

In 1834, following a popular rebellion against the outside authority of the Presbyterian minister Fish, district status was again accorded by the Massachusetts General Court. The Mashpee were no longer wards of the state and, like other towns, were governed by three elected selectmen. But full citizenship did not follow, largely because the proprietors of Mashpee wished to preserve traditional restraints on the sale of lands to outsiders. Leaders such as Daniel Amos argued that many inhabitants of Mashpee were not yet ready for the responsibilities of citizenship and unrestricted property rights. They might sell their lands irresponsibly or be maneuvered into debt; the community would be invaded and broken up. In practice the entailment on property did not seal off Mashpee from growth. To qualify as a landowner one had to trace ancestry to at least one Indian proprietor; and by the midnineteenth century quite a few individuals around the Cape could make this claim. In 1841–2, at the urging of Indian entrepreneurs such as Solomon Attaquin, who had returned to Mashpee with the end of state tutelage, most of the district's common lands were divided among its individual proprietors – men, women, and children. Lands could now be freely bought and sold, but still only among proprietors.

This progress did not go uncontested. Mashpee was divided among those who, like Attaquin – self-made men reflecting the era's dominant laissez-faire capitalist ethos – wanted to move quickly to remove all barriers to individual initiative and others who wanted to move more slowly or who saw in the old plantation entailments a guarantee of community integrity. In 1868 matters finally came to a head. A petition to the General Court from two of Mashpee's three selectmen and twenty-nine residents requested an end to all land-sale restrictions and the granting of full state and federal voting rights. This petition was promptly countered by a "remonstrance" signed by the third selectman and fifty-seven Mashpee residents urging that the district's status not be altered. A public hearing was called to air the differing views.

The hearing, which took place in early 1869, marks a crucial turning point in Mashpee history. Records of its disagreements offer a rare access to a diversity of local voices and opinions. Those who spoke in favor of the proposed changes evoked centuries of degrading state tutelage and second-class status. It was time, they said, for Mashpee inhabitants to be full citizens, to stand on their own. If this meant that some would fail or be displaced from their lands, so be it. They spoke also of the commercial advantages to the region of making portions of its land available for outside capital investment. Representatives of Mashpee's "colored nonproprietors" (a status that gave certain mulattoes and blacks all rights of proprietorship except title to land) also favored the changes in legal status. As valued members of the community they felt the restriction on landholding to be an insult and a reminder of an inferior condition they had in every other respect left behind.

Others opposed the changes. They argued that the influx of outside capital would be a very mixed blessing, and without the present protections many who were not wealthy and wise to the ways of business would soon be displaced. They would find themselves, in the words of one speaker, "ducking and dodging from one city to another, and gain no residence." Some proprietors did not think the right to vote in state and federal elections worth the risk; the present system, providing real control over Mashpee's government, seemed sufficient to local needs. The Reverend Joseph Amos ("Blind Joe" Amos), the community's most influential spiritual voice and leader of a successful Indian Baptist movement three decades earlier, opposed the changes. He said that another generation of preparation was needed before the proposed step could safely be taken. Solomon Attaquin, who owned the Hotel Attaquin, a renowned hunting lodge in Mashpee, spoke for abandoning the district's special status. He evoked a lifelong dream of full citizenship and equality, a dream shared with others in the community. Those who had worked long and hard for this day should not have to die without gaining the status of free men in the commonwealth and the nation.

A vote was taken. Eighteen favored participation in federal and state elections, eighteen were opposed. The removal of land restrictions was sharply rejected, twenty-six to fourteen. Despite this vote by a minority of the total population the recorded discussions clearly showed a consensus in favor of ultimately ending Mashpee's special status, with dis-agreements only on the timing. The Massachusetts General Court, recognizing this fact and more impressed by Mashpee's "progressive" voices, in 1870 formally abolished the status of "Mashpee proprietor." All lands were henceforth held in fee simple with no restrictions on alienation. All residents, whatever their ancestry, now enjoyed equal status before the law. The transfer of town lands to outsiders began immediately.

This turning point marked the end of Mashpee's distinctive institutional status stemming from its Indian past. Though the community was divided on the change, the most dynamic, forward-looking leaders favored it; whatever their hesitations on timing, community members willingly embraced their future as Massachusetts and United States citizens.

Assimilation

During the years between 1870 and the 1920s Indians throughout the nation were forced to abandon tribal organizations and to become individual citizen-farmers, workers, and businessmen. This was the period of the Dawes Act with its extensive land-allotment projects west of the Mississippi. Not until the twenties was there much evidence anywhere of tribal dynamism. Mashpee residents continued to live as before, working as hunting and fishing guides, servants, and laborers in various trades. The town remained a backwater. To find steady work people often had to move to nearby towns or even farther afield. The historical record contains little evidence of any distinctly Indian life in Mashpee before the Wampanoag revival movements of the twenties. The town apparently did not undergo any major demographic or social changes and remained a rather cohesive community of long-term residents, most of whom were of varying degrees of Indian descent. Significantly, between 1905 and 1960 the category "Indian" disappeared from Mashpee's federal census records. The more than two hundred individuals who had previously been so classified were now listed as either "colored" (distinct from "negro") or "other." Only in 1970 would they again be called Indian. In the eyes of the state the majority of Mashpee's inhabitants were simply Americans of color.

Some of these Americans participated in the founding of the Wampanoag Nation in the late twenties. At that time various more-or-less theatrical revivals of Indian institutions were under way. People in Mashpee showed interest, but the daily life and government of the town were not materially affected. The Wampanoags did not, like many other Indian groups in the thirties, take advantage of the turnaround in policy at John Collier's Bureau of Indian Affairs (BIA) to reorganize themselves as a federally recognized "tribal" unit. The new sense of Indianness around Mashpee was a matter of county fairlike powwows, costumes, and folkloric dances.

The individuals of Indian ancestry from Mashpee who filed suit in 1976 were American citizens similar to Irish- or Italian-Americans with strong ethnic attachments. Individuals such as Earl Mills and John and Russell Peters had simply taken advantage of the latest wave of pan-Indian revivalism and the prospect of financial gain to constitute themselves as a Mashpee Tribe. Mashpee's distinctive history was in fact a story of Indian-Christian remnants who over the centuries had repeatedly given up their customs and sovereignty. Theirs had been a long, hard struggle for equality and respect in a multiethnic America.

[...]

History II

The case against the Mashpee plaintiffs was based on a reading of Cape Cod history. Documents were gathered, interpreted, and arranged in a coherent sequence. The story emerged of a small mixed community fighting for equality and citizenship while abandoning, by choice or coercion, most of its aboriginal heritage. But a different, also coherent, story was constructed by the plaintiffs, drawing on the same documentary record. In this account the residents of Mashpee had managed to keep alive a core of Indian identity over three centuries against enormous odds. They had done so in supple, sometimes surreptitious ways, always attempting to control, not reject, outside influences.

The plague

Aboriginally the concept of tribe has little meaning. The "political" institutions of Native American groups before contact with Europeans varied widely. Cape Cod Indian groupings seem to have been flexible, with significant movement across territories. Communities formed and reformed. In this context it is unclear whether the elders of local villages or sachems or supreme sachems should be identified as "tribal" leaders. These individuals had supreme power in some situations, limited authority in others. The plague was a disaster, but it did not decimate the Cape to the extent that it did the Plymouth area. In any event the response of the survivors at Mashpee, regrouping to form a cohesive unit, was a traditional political response, albeit to an unusual emergency. Written sources reflect only the views of whites, such as the evangelist Bourne, who saw his "praying Indians" paternalistically as passive remnants. The intentions of leaders such as Paupmunnuck and his kin are not recorded.

Thus it is anachronistic to say that the community gathered at what would later be called Mashpee was not a tribe. It is well known that the political institutions of many bona fide American Indian "tribes" actually emerged during the nineteenth and twentieth centuries in response to white expectations and power. Neat analytic categories such as "political organization," "kinship," "religion," and "economy" do not reflect Indian ways of seeing things. The simple fact remains that Bourne's South Sea Indian Plantation was a discrete community of Cape Cod Indians living on traditional Indian land – an arrangement that, through many modifications, survived until the mid-twentieth century.

Conversion to Christianity

Accounts of conversion as a process of "giving up old ways" or "choosing a new path" usually reflect a wishful evangelism rather than the more complex realities of cultural change, resistance, and translation. Recent ethnohistorical scholarship has tended to show that Native Americans' response to Christianity was syncretic over the long run, almost never a radical either-or choice. Moreover, in situations of drastically unequal power, as on Puritan Cape Cod, one should expect the familiar response of colonized persons: outward agreement and inner resistance.

The disruptions caused by disease, trade, and military conquest were extreme. All Indian societies had to adjust, and they developed varying strategies for doing so. Some passed through revitalization movements in the late eighteenth and early nineteenth centuries, led by messianic figures: the Delaware Prophet or Handsome Lake. These movements incorporated Christian features in a new "traditional" religion. Other groups renewed native culture by using Christianity for their own purposes. The white man's religion could be added on to traditional deities and rites.

Beliefs that appeared contradictory to Puritan evangelists coexisted in daily life. Native American religions are generally more tolerant, pragmatic, and inclusive than Christianity, a strongly evangelical, exclusive faith.

This is not to say that groups such as the South Sea Indians did not embrace Christianity in good faith or find there a source of spiritual strength. It is only to caution against the either-or logic of conversion as seen by the outsiders whose accounts dominate the written record. The gain of Christian beliefs did not necessarily mean the loss of Indian spirituality. It is easy to be impressed by surface transformations of clothing and public behavior and to forget that continuous kin ties and life on a familiar piece of land also carry potent "religious" values.

Adopting Christianity in Mashpee was not merely a survival strategy in an intolerant, hostile environment. The faith of the "praying Indians" kept a distinctly indigenous cast. Beginning with Richard Bourne's successor, Simon Popmonet, Indian ministers in Mashpee preached in Massachusett, a practice that continued throughout the eighteenth century. When white missionaries were imposed from outside, they were forced to use some Massachusett or to compromise, like Gideon Hawley, who conducted bilingual services in tandem with a respected Indian pastor, Solomon Briant. Moreover, the historical record before 1850 is filled with conflict between authoritarian missionaries and Indian church members. Hawley, who served from 1757 to 1807, progressively alienated his parishioners, especially after Solomon Briant's death in 1775. His successor, Phineas Fish, lost virtually all local support and in 1840, after a protracted struggle, was physically ejected from the Old Indian Meeting House by irate Indian Christians.

Baptist revivalism had already won over most of the congregation, a change tied to a political assertion of Indian power. As in many nativist revitalization movements, an Indian outsider took a leading role – in this case William Apes, a young Pequot Baptist preacher. Blind Joe Amos had already acquired a larger following for his all-Indian Baptist meetings than the Congregationalist minister, Fish.

The situation was volatile. Apes, a firebrand with a vision of united action by "colored" peoples against white oppressors, stimulated a Masphee "Declaration of Independence" in 1833 on behalf of a sovereign Mashpee Tribe. (This was one of the few times before the twentieth century that the word *tribe* appears in the historical record.) The effect of the declaration and of the political maneuvers that ensued was to wrest control of the town's religion from the outsider Fish, reclaiming the Meeting House and funds from Harvard University supporting Indian Christianity for the majority faith, which was now Baptist. Mashpee returned to district status, free of outside governors.

Over the centuries Indians in Mashpee fought to keep control first of their Presbyterian and then their Baptist institutions. Religion was a political as well as a spiritual issue. Well into the 1950s the New England Baptist Convention habitually referred to Mashpee as "our Indian church." The exact nature of Mashpee Christian belief and practice over the centuries is obscure. The historical record does not inform us, for example, of exactly what took place in Blind Joe Amos' insurgent Baptist services during the 1830s; but even the partial written record makes it clear that Christianity in Mashpee, symbolized by the Old Indian Meeting House, was a site of local power and of resistance to outsiders. At recurring intervals it was a focus of openly Indian, or "tribal," power.

"Plantation" status

Leaders of the South Sea Indians probably recognized, with Bourne, that title to land under white law was needed if it was not to be despoiled by an aggressive colonization; but seventeenth-century English proprietory forms did not unduly restrict their ability to function as an Indian community. Collective ownership of land, with individual use rights, could be maintained. The legal status that to some appeared an impediment to progress in fact protected the traditional life ways of Indian proprietors.

Although eastern Indians were not accorded reservation lands, Mashpee's plantation status created a de factor reservation. Unlike all its neighbors Mashpee did not quickly become a town but had the status forced on it in 1869. The plantation was widely considered to be Indian land held collectively in a distinctive manner. The reasons for keeping Mashpee "backward," a pupil of the state, were often racist and paternalist; but from the viewpoint of a small group struggling to maintain its collective identity, the proprietorship arrangement was an effective way of having legal status while also maintaining a difference. While there was internal disagreement at times, the majority of Mashpee proprietors consistently favored keeping the plantation land system. This was changed only by legislative fiat in 1969, against their expressed wishes. Until then an "archaic" status had been effectively used to preserve Indian lands in a collective form through rapidly changing times. The land-claim suit aimed to restore a situation illegally altered by the Massachusetts legislature.

Taking the colonists' side

The fact that some South Sea Indians fought against Metacomet in King Philip's War does not prove that they were abandoning their Indian sovereignty or independence. More did not fight, and the motivations of those who did are a matter of speculation. There was nothing new about Indians making war on other Indians. Moreover they may have had little choice. Puritan authorities were on the warpath, and even "loyal" Indians were punished during and after the war by loss of lands and slavery.

As for the war against England, again we should be wary of imputing motives. The Mashpee Indians who served in the Revolutionary Army may not have done so primarily as "American" patriots. They were, among other things, rebelling against the authority of their missionary Hawley, an ardent Tory. Moreover, as Indian status has evolved in the United States, it has been legally recognized that the privileges of citizenship (including the decision to unite in war against a common enemy) do not contradict other arrangements establishing special group identity and status. One can be fully a citizen and fully an Indian.

To expect Cape Cod Indians to hold themselves apart from the historical currents and conflicts of the dominant society would be to ask them to commit suicide. Survival in changing circumstances meant participation, wherever possible on their own terms. Staying separate or uninvolved would be to yield to the dangerous fantasies of protectors, like Hawley, who worked to keep the Mashpee pure – and under his tutelage. The inhabitants of Mashpee again and again resisted this restrictive "authenticity." The record confirms that they wanted integrity but never isolation.

Intermarriage

There was a good deal of racial mixing in Mashpee, but the exact extent is hard to determine, given the shifting categories of different censuses and doubts about how race was actually measured. Mashpee was a refuge for misfits, refugees, and marginal groups. At certain times a natural alliance against dominant white society formed between the town's Indian "survivors" and newly freed blacks. The crucial issue is whether the core Indian community absorbed the outsiders or were themselves absorbed in the American melting pot.

Historical evidence supports the former conclusion. Since whites and people of color who settled in Mashpee during the eighteenth and most of the nineteenth centuries could not become proprietors, this limited the influx; non-Indians remained a significant but small minority. Children with one Indian parent could become full community members. Intermarriage frequently occurred, and thus the purity of Indian blood was much diluted; but the legal and social structure consistently favored Indian identification. With land entailment and the maintenance of close kin ties among property holders a core was maintained. In any event blood is a debatable measure of identity, and to arrive at quotas for determining "tribal" status is always a problematic exercise. There are federally recognized tribes as mixed as the Mashpee, and organized Indian groups vary widely in the amount of traceable ancestry they actually require for membership.

Ethnohistorical studies show that in New England the mixing of different communities was common well before the Pilgrims' arrival. Adoption was frequent, and it was customary to capture and incorporate opponents in war. Indians were in this respect color blind. In colonial times a large number of white captives stayed with their captors, adopting Indian ways, some even becoming chiefs. Mashpee's later openness to outsiders – as long as the newcomers intermarried and conformed to Indian ways – was a continuation of an aboriginal tradition, not a loss of distinct identity.

In 1859, after more than a century of intermarriage and sporadic population growth (the dilution of Indian stock lamented by the missionary Hawley), a detailed report by the commissioner for Indian affairs, John Earle, offered a census of the "Marshpee Tribe" that included 371 "natives" and 32 "foreigners." The latter were people living on the land without proprietary rights and not lineal descendants of Indians. They were described as "Africans" and "colored." Only one "white" was listed. The names of "natives" listed on the 1859 census served in the trial as a benchmark of continuous "tribal" kinship ties.

Mashpee becomes a town

There is strong documentary evidence that most of the proprietors between 1834 and 1869 wanted to hold on to Mashpee's special land restrictions. Commissioner Earle asserts this in his report. "Progressives" such as Attaquin were more vocal, and their testimony thus receives more weight in the record than the less articulate majority who in 1869 voted decisively against township status. Spokesmen (note how few female voices are "heard" by history, although the role of women at the center of community life was undoubtedly crucial) such as Blind Joe Amos and his brother Daniel urged postponing the transition. They argued that most people in Mashpee were too "immature," not "ready" to dispose of their land individually. Give us just one more generation, Daniel Amos asked in the 1830s. His brother asked the same thing in the late 1860s. What do these arguments signify?

For those who see Mashpee's "development" and assimilation as inevitable, such statements require no interpretation: they simply show that even the traditionalists in Mashpee were ready eventually to give up their special status. But this is to assume the historical outcome. The Indian proprietors of Mashpee valued community integrity and possessed effective public and informal leadership. They had shown much strength and initiative in dealing with their various "protectors." The early historical record reveals a steady stream of petitions – 1748, 1753, 1760 – on behalf of the "poor Indians of Marshpee called the South Sea Indians" protesting abuses by the agents appointed to watch over them. More recently they had successfully asserted their autonomy against the missionaries Hawley and Fish. They were hardly "immature." Yet throughout the mid-nineteenth century Mashpee proprietors temporized, hesitated in the face of an "inevitable" progress. Their ability to protect their community from the coercions and enticements of white society was evidently precious to them.

The modified plantation status they had secured in 1834 gave them a way of keeping collective control over land and immigration while not isolating the community from interaction with the surrounding society. Even the "allotment" of lands sanctioned at that time reproduced an aboriginal land arrangement. Parcels were traditionally given to families for exclusive use while ultimate collective ownership was maintained. (In 1834, moreover, three thousand acres were formally kept as common land.) Continuing entailments on land sales outside the community guaranteed a flexible nineteenth-century tribalism. In this context public arguments about Mashpee's "immaturity" should be seen as ways of addressing an outside audience, the Massachusetts General Court, which still thought of the plantation as a ward of the state and which had already decided and again would arbitrarily decide its fate. It would be impolitic in addressing this body to say that Mashpee rejected full township status in the name of a distinctive vision of Indian community and citizenship. An argument for delay couched in paternalist rhetoric was more likely to succeed.

This interpretation of the debates in 1869 is at least as plausible as a literal reading of the recorded public utterances. Mashpee, like Indian communities throughout their recent history, was split between modernists and traditionalists. The traditionalists prevailed in the vote, but the modernists swayed the authorities. In changing Mashpee's land entailment the legislature violated both simple democracy and the Federal Non-Intercourse Act of 1790. But even the forced change – although it ultimately brought much land into non-Indian hands – was not fatal. The Mashpee Indians used their new imposed status as they had their former one. For almost a century local government was kept firmly in the hands of a closely interrelated group of town officers. Mashpee remained "Cape Cod's Indian Town."

Assimilation

The Mashpee Indians did not "assimilate." The term's linear, either-or connotations cannot account for revivalism and for changes in the cultural and political climate between 1869 and 1960. There have been better and worse times in the United States to be publicly Indian. The late nineteenth and early twentieth centuries were among the worst. Government policy strongly favored tribal termination and the dispersal of collective lands. It was not until the late 1920s that the failure of allotment schemes was recognized and a "New Indian Policy" instituted at the BIA that favored tribal reorganization. If there is little evidence in the historical record of "tribal" life in Mashpee between 1869 and 1920, it is no surprise. Many groups all over the nation that would emerge later as tribes kept a low profile during these years. Mashpee seemed to be simply a sleepy town run by Indians, known for its good hunting and fishing. There was no political need or any wider context for them to display their Indianness in spectacular ways. Everyone knew who they were. A few attended the Carlisle Indian School in Pennsylvania during this period. Traditional myths and stories were told around kitchen tables; the piles of sticks at Mashpee's "Indian taverns" or "sacrifice heaps" grew into enormous mounds; life close to the land went on.

The history of Indian tribes in the United States has been punctuated by revival movements. The 1920s saw the organization of the Wampanoag Nation, with various explicit tribal institutions including a supreme sachem and a renewed interest in more public Indian displays: dances, regalia, powwows, and the like. As in all revitalization movements "outside" influences from other Indian groups played a major role. Eben Queppish, who had once ridden with Buffalo Bill's Wild West Show, taught traditional basket making and on demand donned his Sioux war bonnet. Individuals from Mashpee participated in nationally known groups such as the Thunderbird Indian Dancers. The effects of these revivals were largely cultural. There was little need for political reorganization in Mashpee, for the town was still governed by an unchallenged Indian majority. Political reorganization of a more explicit "tribal" structure would occur during a later revivalist period, the ferment spurred by the loss of town control after 1968.

Like other tribal groups the Mashpee have been opportunists, taking advantage of propitious historical contexts and undergoing external influences. They have survived as Indians because they have not conformed to white stereotypes. They have lived since aboriginal times in a traditional locale. They have maintained their own hybrid faith. Over the centuries they have controlled the rate of intermarriage and have fought for the political autonomy of their community. Explicitly tribal political structures have sometimes been visible to the outside world, as in 1833, the 1920s, and the 1970s, but for the most part these structures have been informal. Often the "tribe" in Mashpee was simply people deciding things by consensus, in kitchens or at larger ad hoc gatherings where no records were kept. The chief in Mashpee, when there was one, shared authority with a variety of respected leaders, women and men. Politics was not hierarchical and did not need much in the way of institutional forms. The "tribe" in Mashpee was simply shared Indian kinship, place, history, and a long struggle for integrity without isolation. Sometimes the Baptist parish served as

an arm of the tribe; so did the town government. When the Mashpee Wampanoag
Tribal Council, Inc. filed suit in 1976, it did so as a new legal arm of the tribe.
[...]

The Experts

Expert testimony by professional anthropologists and historians played a major role
in the Mashpee trial. The defense rested much of its case on the historical testimony
of a single scholar, while the plaintiffs depended more on anthropologists. Indeed the
trial can be seen as a struggle between history and anthropology.
[...]

An adversary system of justice, the need to make a clear case to counterbalance an
opposing one, discourages opinions of a "yes, but," "it depends on how you look at
it" kind. Experts on the stand were required to answer the question: Is there a tribe
in Mashpee? Yes or no? On cross-examination, confronted with evidence that their
disciplines had no rigorous, commonly accepted definitions of key categories such as
tribe, culture, and acculturation, the experts could only smile or wince and stick to
their guns.[3]

Anthropologists speaking as scientific experts could not explain to the court that
theirs was a historically limited and politically enmeshed discipline. They could not
admit that many fieldworkers were now testifying in court on behalf of resurgent
indigenous cultures as part of a postcolonial context governing how researchers
from one society could represent or "speak for" another group. (There was a time
when an anthropologist could casually refer to "my people"; now indigenous groups
can speak of "our anthropologist"!) On the stand it was difficult to explain that the
word *tribe* could mean different things to a scholar discussing a range of aboriginal
systems, reservation Indians of the nineteenth century, and legally reorganized
groups of the 1930s, or that the term was unlikely to mean the same thing for an
author of evolutionist theories writing in the 1950s and an expert evaluating the
aspirations of eastern Indian communities in the 1970s ...

The anthropologists on the stand were clearly more comfortable with a polymorphous notion of culture than with the political category of tribe. And given the
court's unwillingness to establish a rigid initial definition, much, if not most, of the
testimony at the trial concerned the status of Indian "culture," broadly conceived, in
Mashpee. This cornerstone of the anthropological discipline proved to be vulnerable
under cross-examination. Culture appeared to have no essential features. Neither
language, religion, land, economics, nor any other key institution or custom was its
sine qua non. It seemed to be a contingent mix of elements. At times the concept was
purely differential: cultural integrity involved recognized boundaries; it required
merely an acceptance by the group and its neighbors of a meaningful difference, a
we-they distinction. But what if the difference were accepted at certain times and
denied at others? And what if every element in the cultural melange were combined
with or borrowed from external sources?
[...]

The Verdict

When Hutchins finished, the defense rested its case. The two principal attorneys, St. Clair and Shubow, then delivered their summations. Each was a review of the trial's evidence in the form of a compelling story. Life in Mashpee over the centuries was given two heroic shapes and outcomes. Shubow recounted "an epic of survival and continuity." St. Clair celebrated a "slow but steady progress" toward "full participation" in American society.

Judge Skinner then gave his instructions. He reviewed the course of the trial, mentioning briefly each witness. He reminded the jurors that the burden of proof was with the plaintiffs; they must prove by preponderance of the evidence (but not, as in a criminal case, beyond a reasonable doubt) the existence of a tribe in Mashpee. In its decision the jury was free to rely on inference and circumstantial evidence. They should not be unduly swayed by the authority of experts but must trust their own common sense judgment of the witnesses' credibility, weighing how well their conclusions matched the evidence presented, observing their way of speaking, even their "body English."

The jurors would be asked to decide whether the proprietors of Mashpee were an Indian tribe on six dates pertinent to the land-claim suit: (1) July 22, 1790, the date of the first Federal Non-Intercourse Act; (2) March 31, 1834, when Mashpee achieved district status; (3) March 3, 1842, when land was partitioned to individuals; (4) June 23, 1869, the end of all alienation restraints; (5) May 28, 1870, incorporation of the Town of Mashpee; and (6) August 26, 1976, commencement of the present suit.

Skinner told the jurors that they would also be required to decide on a seventh question: Did a tribe in Mashpee exist *continuously* during the relevant historical period? If not, the plaintiffs would fail. Moreover the judge instructed the jurors that if at any time they found tribal status in Mashpee to have been voluntarily abandoned, then it could not be revived. Once lost, it was lost for good.

The judge specified the legal definition of *tribe* that would apply, a matter about which there had been considerable suspense. Skinner opted for a relatively loose formula preferred by the plaintiffs and drawn from the case of *Montoya v. United States*, 1901: "*A body of Indians of the same or similar race united in a community under one leadership or government and inhabiting a particular, though sometimes ill defined, territory.*" For the plaintiffs to win, all the key factors of race, territory, community, and leadership had to be continuously present.

Skinner reviewed the testimony related to key factors of the definition.

Race. Exogamy and an influx of outsiders into a tribe is normal and necessary. The crucial question was whether the outsiders had been incorporated. If the jurors found that the group had Indian ancestry and had opted to focus on that ancestry rather than others, this could satisfy the racial requirement.

Territory. By holding land legally under an English proprietorship, Indians did not thereby become English. Without a reservation system there was no other way to secure land in New England. The jury had to decide whether the Mashpee proprietors used the English arrangement to preserve their tribal form or whether they preferred the English way, and thus abandoned the old form. Skinner warned against the "Catch-22" of requiring a formal land base in this case, since that was precisely what the suit was about.

Community. An "Indian community," Skinner cautioned, is not just "a community of Indians." Boundaries are crucial and can be maintained in various ways. The jury had to decide on the basis of incomplete historical evidence whether Mashpee constituted a discrete community with a definite boundary. A community for the purposes of *Montoya* is something more than a neighborhood.

Leadership. At this small scale leadership can be informal. Sovereignty, a requirement raised by the defense, is inappropriate; but tribal leadership should have roots in a once-sovereign Indian political community. The jury was to rely on its common sense about participation and leadership, the balance of core enthusiasts and people peripheral to the group. There must be more than a coterie claiming to speak for an Indian community. There is no inherent contradiction between serving as a tribal leader and functioning in the wider society, for example as a businessman. Skinner pointed to the gaps in the historical record. Evidence of tribal leadership in Mashpee between 1870 and 1920 is particularly scarce.

The issue of tribal existence is complex, the judge concluded, but it is not more so than issues of sanity or criminal intent, which are routinely decided by juries. Skinner expressed confidence in this jury's ability to weigh the evidence, argue freely, persuade, and finally reach unanimity on the seven yes-or-no questions.

The jurors were sequestered, accompanied by a large pile of documents. After twenty-one hours of deliberation they emerged with a verdict:

Did the proprietors of Mashpee, together with their spouses and children, constitute an Indian tribe on any of the following dates:

July 22, 1790? No.   June 23, 1869? No.
March 31, 1834? Yes.   May 28, 1870? No.
March 3, 1842? Yes.

Did the plaintiff groups, as identified by the plaintiff's witnesses, constitute an Indian tribe as of August 26, 1976? No.

If the people living in Mashpee constituted an Indian tribe or nation on any of the dates prior to August 26, 1976, did they continuously exist as a tribe or nation from such date or dates up to and including August 26, 1976? No.

The verdict was a clear setback for the Indians' suit. But as a statement about their tribal history it was far from clear. Judge Skinner, after hearing arguments, finally decided that despite its ambiguity – the apparent emergence of a tribe in 1834 – the jury's reply was a denial of the required tribal continuity. His dismissal of the suit has since been upheld on appeal.

The verdict remains, however, a curious and problematic outcome. We can only speculate on what happened in the jury room – the obscure chemistry of unanimity. What was done with the pile of historical documents during the twenty-one hours of discussion? Did the jurors search for a false precision? Asked to consider specific dates, did they conscientiously search the record for evidence of tribal institutions, for mention of the word *tribe*? If so, their literalism was nonetheless different from that encouraged by the particularist history of the defense, for the jury found that Mashpee Indians were inconsistently a tribe. Violating the judge's instructions, they found that a tribe first did not, then did, then did not again exist in Mashpee. Historical particularism does not by itself yield coherent developments or stories. Entities appear and disappear in the record.

The jurors' response contained an element of subversion. In effect it suggested that the trial's questions had been wrongly posed. Asked to apply consistent criteria of tribal existence over three centuries of intense change and disruption, the jury did so and came up with an inconsistent verdict.

Afterthoughts

The court behaved like a philosopher who wanted to know positively whether a cat was on the mat in Mashpee. I found myself seeing a Cheshire cat – now a head, now a tail, eyes, ears, nothing at all, in various combinations. The Mashpee "tribe" had a way of going and coming; but something was persistently, if not continuously, there.

The testimony I heard convinced me that organized Indian life had been going on in Mashpee for the past 350 years. Moreover a significant revival and reinvention of tribal identity was clearly in process. I concluded that since the ability to act collectively as Indians is currently bound up with tribal status, the Indians living in Mashpee and those who return regularly should be recognized as a "tribe."

Whether land improperly alienated after 1869 should be transferred to them, how much, and by what means was a separate issue. I was, and am, less clear on this matter. A wholesale transfer of property would in any case be politically unthinkable. Some negotiation and repurchase arrangement – such as that in Maine involving local, state, and federal governments – could eventually establish a tribal land base in some portion of Mashpee. But that, for the moment, is speculation. In the short run the outcome of the trial was a setback for Wampanoag tribal dynamism.

In Boston Federal Court, Cape Cod Indians could not be seen for what they were and are. Modern Indian lives – lived within and against the dominant culture and state – are not captured by categories like tribe or identity. The plaintiffs could not prevail in court because their discourse and that of their attorneys and experts was inevitably compromised. It was constrained not simply by the law, with its peculiar rules, but by powerful assumptions and categories underlying the common sense that supported the law.

Among the underlying assumptions and categories compromising the Indians' case three stand out: (1) the idea of cultural wholeness and structure, (2) the hierarchical distinction between oral and literate forms of knowledge, and (3) the narrative continuity of history and identity.

The idea of cultural wholeness and structure

Although the trial was formally about "tribal" status, its scope was significantly wider. The *Montoya* definition of tribe, featuring race, territory, community, and government, did not specifically mention "cultural" identity. The culture concept in its broad anthropological definition was still new in 1901; but the relatively loose

Montoya definition reflected this emerging notion of a multifaceted, whole way of life, determined neither by biology nor politics. By 1978 the modern notion of culture was part of the trial's common sense.

In the courtroom an enormous amount of testimony from both sides debated the authenticity of Indian culture in Mashpee. Often this seemed to have become the crucial point of contention. Had the Mashpee lost their distinct way of life? Had they assimilated? In his summation for the plaintiffs Lawrence Shubow took time to define the term *culture* anthropologically, distinguishing it from the "ballet and top hat" conception. Closely paraphrasing E. B. Tylor's classic formula of 1871, he presented culture as a group's total body of behavior. He said that it included how people eat as well as how they think. Using the anthropological definition, he argued that ecology, the special feeling for hunting and fishing in Mashpee, the herring eaten every year, spitting on a stick at an "Indian tavern," these and many other unremarkable daily elements were integral parts of a whole, ongoing way of life.

It is easy to see why the plaintiffs focused on Indian culture in Mashpee. Culture, since it includes so much, was less easily disproven than tribal status. But even so broadly defined, the culture concept posed problems for the plaintiffs. It was too closely tied to assumptions of organic form and development. In the eighteenth century culture meant simply "a tending to natural growth." By the end of the nineteenth century the word could be applied not only to gardens and well-developed individuals but to whole societies. Whether it was the elitist singular version of a Matthew Arnold or the plural, lower-case concept of an emerging ethnography, the term retained its bias toward wholeness, continuity, and growth. Indian culture in Mashpee might be made up of unexpected everyday elements, but it had in the last analysis to cohere, its elements fitting together like parts of a body. The culture concept accommodates internal diversity and an "organic" division of roles but not sharp contradictions, mutations, or emergences. It has difficulty with a medicine man who at one time feels a deep respect for Mother Earth and at another plans a radical real estate subdivision. It sees tribal "traditionalists" and "moderns" as representing aspects of a linear development, one looking back, the other forward. It cannot see them as contending or alternating futures.

Groups negotiating their identity in contexts of domination and exchange persist, patch themselves together in ways different from a living organism. A community, unlike a body, can lose a central "organ" and not die. All the critical elements of identity are in specific conditions replaceable: language, land, blood, leadership, religion. Recognized, viable tribes exist in which any one or even most of these elements are missing, replaced, or largely transformed.

The idea of culture carries with it an expectation of roots, of a stable, territorialized existence . . . the *Montoya* definition of tribe was designed to distinguish settled, peaceful Indian groups from mobile, marauding "bands." This political and military distinction of 1901 between tribe and band was debated again, in technical, anthropological terms, during the Mashpee trial. How rooted or settled should one expect "tribal" Native Americans to be – aboriginally, in specific contact periods, and now in highly mobile twentieth-century America? Common notions of culture persistently bias the answer toward rooting rather than travel.

Moreover the culture idea, tied as it is to assumptions about natural growth and life, does not tolerate radical breaks in historical continuity. Cultures, we often hear, "die." But how many cultures pronounced dead or dying by anthropologists and other authorities have, like Curtis' "vanishing race" or Africa's diverse Christians, found new ways to be different? Metaphors of continuity and "survival" do not account for complex historical processes of appropriation, compromise, subversion, masking, invention, and revival. These processes inform the activity of a people not living alone but "reckoning itself among the nations." The Indians at Mashpee made and remade themselves through specific alliances, negotiations, and struggles. It is just as problematic to say that their way of life "survived" as to say that it "died" and was "reborn."

The related institutions of culture and tribe are historical inventions, tendentious and changing. They do not designate stable realities that exist aboriginally "prior to" the colonial clash of societies and powerful representations. The history of Mashpee is not one of unbroken tribal institutions or cultural traditions. It is a long, relational struggle to maintain and recreate identities that began when an English-speaking Indian traveler, Squanto, greeted the Pilgrims at Plymouth. The struggle was still going on three-and-a-half centuries later in Boston Federal Court, and it continues as the "Mashpee Tribe" prepares a new petition, this time for recognition from the Department of the Interior.[2]

The hierarchical distinction between oral and literate

The Mashpee trial was a contest between oral and literate forms of knowledge. In the end the written archive had more value than the evidence of oral tradition, the memories of witnesses, and the intersubjective practice of fieldwork. In the courtroom how could one give value to an undocumented "tribal" life largely invisible (or unheard) in the surviving record?

As the trial progressed the disjuncture of oral and literate modes sharpened. The proceedings had been theatrical, full of contending voices and personalities, but they ended with a historian's methodical recitation of particulars. In the early portions of the trial the jurors had been asked to piece together and imagine a tribal life that showed recurring vitality but no unimpeachable essence or institutional core. Indianness in Mashpee often seemed improvised, ad hoc. The jury heard many wishful, incomplete memories of childhood events and debatable versions of recent happenings. In what may be called the "oral-ethnographic" parts of the trial many – too many – voices contended, in its "documentary" ending too few. A historian's seamless monologue was followed by attorneys' highly composed summations, two fully documented stories. There was no way to give voice to the silences in these histories, to choose the unrecorded.

The court imposed a literalist epistemology. Both sides searched the historical records for the presence or absence of the word and institution *tribe*. In this epistemology Indian identity could not be a real yet essentially contested phenomenon. It had to exist or not exist as an objective documentary fact persisting through time. Yet oral societies – or more accurately oral domains within a dominant literacy – leave only sporadic and misleading traces. Most of what is central to their existence is never written. Thus until recently nearly everything most characteristically Indian in Mashpee would have gone unrecorded. The surviving facts are largely the records of missionaries, government agents, outsiders. In the rare instances when Indians wrote – petitions, deeds, letters of complaint – it was to address white authorities and legal structures. Their voices were adapted to an imposed context. The same is true even in the rare cases in which a range of local *voices* was recorded, for example the public debates of 1869 on township status.

History feeds on what finds its way into a limited textual record. A historian needs constant skepticism and a willingness to read imaginatively, "against" the sources, to divine what is not represented in the accumulated selection of the archive. Ultimately, however, even the most imaginative history is tied to standards of textual proof. Anthropology, although it is also deeply formed and empowered by writing, remains closer to orality. Fieldwork – interested people talking with and being interpreted by an interested observer – cannot claim to be "documentary" in the way history can. For even though the origin of evidence in an archive may be just as circumstantial and subjective as that in a field journal, it enjoys a different value: archival data has been found, not produced, by a scholar using it "after the fact."

The distinction between historical and ethnographic practices depends on that between literate and oral modes of knowledge. History is thought to rest on past – documentary, archival – selections of texts. Ethnography is based on present – oral, experiential, observational – evidence. Although many historians and ethnographers are currently working to attenuate, even erase this opposition, it runs deeper than a mere disciplinary division of labor, for it resonates with the established (some would say metaphysical) dichotomy of oral and literate worlds as well as with the pervasive habit in the West of sharply distinguishing synchronic from diachronic, structure from change. As Marshall Sahlins (1985) has argued, these assumptions keep us from seeing how collective structures, tribal or cultural, reproduce themselves historically by risking themselves in novel conditions. Their wholeness is as much a matter of reinvention and encounter as it is of continuity and survival.

The narrative continuity of history and identity

Judge Skinner instructed the jury to decide whether the Indians of Mashpee had *continuously* constituted a tribe prior to filing suit in 1976. For the land claim to go forward the same tribal group had to have existed, without radical interruption, from at least the eighteenth century. The court's common sense was that the plaintiffs' identity must be demonstrated as an unbroken narrative, whether of survival or change. Both attorneys in their summations duly complied.

St. Clair's story of a long struggle for participation in plural American society and Shubow's "epic of survival and continuity" had in common a linear teleology. Both ruled out the possibility of a group existing discontinuously, keeping open multiple paths, being *both* Indian *and* American.

An either-or logic applied. St. Clair argued that there had never been a tribe in Mashpee, only individual Indian Americans who had repeatedly opted for white society. His story of progress toward citizenship assumed a steady movement away from native tradition. Identity as an American meant giving up a strong claim to tribal political integrity in favor of ethnic status within a national whole. Life as an American meant death as an Indian. Conversely Shubow's Mashpee had "survived" as a living tribe and culture from aboriginal times; but the historical record often contradicted his claim, and he sometimes strained to assert continuity. The plaintiffs could not admit that Indians in Mashpee had lost, even voluntarily abandoned, crucial aspects of their tradition while at the same time pointing to evidence over the centuries of reinvented "Indianness." They could not show tribal institutions as relational and political, coming and going in response to changing federal and state policies and the surrounding ideological climate. An identity could not die and come back to life. To recreate a culture that had been lost was, by definition of the court, inauthentic.

But is any part of a tradition "lost" if it can be remembered, even generations later, caught up in a present dynamism and made to symbolize a possible future?

The Mashpee were trapped by the stories that could be told about them. In this trial "the facts" did not speak for themselves. Tribal life had to be emplotted, told as a coherent narrative. In fact only a few basic stories are told, over and over, about Native Americans and other "tribal" peoples. These societies are always either dying or surviving, assimilating or resisting. Caught between a local past and a global future, they either hold on to their separateness or "enter the modern world." The latter entry – tragic or triumphant – is always a step toward a global future defined by technological progress, national and international cultural relations. Are there other possible stories?

Until recently the "history" accorded to tribal peoples has always been a Western history. They may refuse it, embrace it, be devastated by it, changed by it. But the familiar paths of tribal death, survival, assimilation, or resistance do not catch the specific ambivalences of life in places like Mashpee over four centuries of defeat, renewal, political negotiation, and cultural innovation. Moreover most societies that suddenly "enter the modern world" have already been in touch with it for centuries.

The Mashpee trial seemed to reveal people who were sometimes separate and "Indian," sometimes assimilated and "American." Their history was a series of cultural and political transactions, not all-or-nothing conversions or resistances.[3] Indians in Mashpee lived and acted *between* cultures in a series of ad hoc engagements. No one in Boston Federal Court, expert or layperson, stood at the end point of this historical series, even though the stories of continuity and change they told implied that they did. These stories and the trial itself were episodes, turns in the ongoing engagement. Seen from a standpoint not of finality (survival or assimilation) but of emergence, Indian life in Mashpee would not flow in a single current.

Interpreting the direction or meaning of the historical "record" always depends on present possibilities. When the future is open, so is the meaning of the past. Did Indian religion or tribal institutions disappear in the late nineteenth century? Or did they go underground? In a present context of serious revival they went underground; otherwise they disappeared. No continuous narrative or clear outcome accounts for Mashpee's deeply contested identity and direction. Nor can a single development weave together the branching paths of its past, the dead ends and hesitations that, with a newly conceived future, suddenly become prefigurations.

NOTES

1   The two "histories" that follow represent the best brief interpretive accounts I could construct of the contending versions of Mashpee's past. They draw selectively on the expert testimony presented at the trial – testimony much too long, complex, and contested to summarize adequately. The overall shape of the two accounts reflects the summation provided at the end of the testimony by each side's principal attorney. "History I" owes a good deal to Francis Hutchins' book *Mashpee: The Story of Cape Cod's Indian Town* (1979). This book takes a somewhat more moderate position than the courtroom testimony on which it is based. "History II" owes something to the general approach of James Axtell's book *The European and the Indian* (1981). Axtell was witness for the plaintiffs.

2   In the preceding discussion I am not suggesting that the ethnographic categories of culture and tribe, however compromised, should be subsumed in the recent and more mobile discourse of ethnicity. Ethnicity, as usually conceived, is a weak conception of culture suitable for organizing diversity within the pluralist state. The institution of *tribe*, still trailing clouds of aboriginal sovereignty and reminiscent of its eighteenth-century synonym *nation*, is less easily integrated into the modern multiethnic, multiracial state. The resurgent cultural-political identity asserted by Indian tribes is more subversive than that of Irish-Americans or Italian-Americans: Native Americans claim to be both full citizens of the United States *and* radically outside it.

3   William Simmons' collection and analysis of New England Indian folklore, *Spirit of the New England Tribes* (1986), not available at the time of the trial, provides much evidence for the productive interpenetration of Christian and Native American sources. It shows how Indian "tradition" was maintained through appropriation and interaction, transmitted both orally and in writing. Simmons provides background on the Mashpee Wampanoag culture hero, the giant Maushop, who, in Ramona Peters' testimony, unexpectedly turned into Moby Dick. The plaintiffs' lawyers and experts made little appeal to continuing Indian folklore, perhaps because of its evident implication in the religious traditions and fairytales of surrounding ethnic groups.

18

Locating a Reinvigorated Kentish Identity

Eve Darian-Smith

Introduction: Identity in Kent

The claims of the Mashpee Indians to a particular territory rested on their original loss, their subsequent long local residence, and their allegedly continuous tribal identity. In contrast, many of the residents of Kent, on the English Channel, have acquired their Kentish identity by recently moving to Kent from the London region. There are also, of course, some families with old local ties, but durable presence is not the identity issue here. The area has, of course, a long history, parts of which the residents celebrate and cherish. Darian-Smith takes note of some of these and examines their revival in the presence of the much newer elements that enter present-day ideas of Kent.

Darian-Smith's book is about the shifting place of the Kent she observed around the time of the establishment of the Channel Tunnel, agreed to by Treaty in 1986, and built a few years thereafter. She writes about the changing legal status of the area, as well as about reactions to those alterations of political place, some of which were expressed in a reconstructed modern form of "traditional" localism. A number of factors led to a re-emergence of Kent as an active and self-conscious unit. One factor was the restructuring of local government by Margaret Thatcher under whose leadership local bodies lost most of their autonomy. There was increasing centralization of control in the 1980s and 1990s, and much tension in central–local government relationships. Another factor was the development of more and more contacts with the European Union. In 1987 Kent Country Council established an office in Brussels. The same year the KCC signed a cooperation agreement with the Counseil Regional du Nord–Pas de Calais which

From Eve Darian-Smith, "Locating a Reinvigorated Kentish Identity," in Eve Darian-Smith, *Bridging Divides: The English Channel and the English Legal Identity in the New Europe* (Berkeley and London: University of California Press, 1999), pp. 160–6, 168–75, 177, 179–81, 184–8.

was formalized as the Transmanche Region. In 1989, a grant of six million pounds was given to the Transmanche by the European Union for cross-border projects. By the mid-1990s over thirty-five million pounds had been granted for the same purposes. Thus Kent was not only within the jurisdiction of London, but also within that of the European Union.

In Kent itself, many residents were not particularly aware of these considerable political shifts. Yet at the same time they were observed to be enthusiastically engaged in various celebrations of localism and commitments to community, from movements to preserve the landscape to activist attempts to maintain communal rights to public property. By describing these movements, Darian-Smith engages the question of Kentish identity as it connects with changes in the law, the economy, and popular organizations and movements. Identity is not presented as a static or as wholly a traditional construct, but is rather seen as an assemblage of loosely connected practices at a particular period in recent history. That these are continuing to shift is presaged in a number of Darian-Smith's speculations about the future. This work presents a compressed, multi-perspectival account of contemporary history through the encompassing optic of identity.

S.F.M.

Darian-Smith, *A New Kentish Identity?*

Today, Kentish identity represents many different things to different people. Some academics at the University of Kent in Canterbury – particularly in the anthropology department – assured me that a Kentish identity did not exist. Steve Dawe, the Green party candidate for East Kent who ran for the European parliamentary elections in May 1994, strongly declared, however, that the academics at the university live "in a village up there on the hill, and have no sense of what really goes on in any way." According to Dawe, there is a sense of Kentish solidarity, which "is a remarkably strong identity and should not be underestimated when something controversial comes up" (interview, 7 Mar. 1994). In his view, actions around the conservation of land highlighted this Kentish sensibility. He spoke of a petition of 10,000 local residents protesting the Shepway Council's plan to destroy the largest remaining single tract of English forest in 1993 . . .

Of course it is almost impossible to articulate what the Kentish identity is and how to recognize it. As pointed out to me by Steve Dawe's wife, Hazel, "you have a coast identity and a town identity and a rural identity all criss-crossing here" (interview, 7 Mar. 1994). And compounding the complexities between local communities within Kent are the external contexts through which these local negotiations are played out – namely, an encroaching and omnipresent London to the north, and the increasingly interventionist European Union to the east. And these two sources of pressure are not mutually exclusive nor unrelated to the operation of each other.

What can be said with some confidence is that there is currently a heightened consciousness of Kent as a regional entity, distinct from London, that is not determined by political party lines . . .

Perhaps as a counter to this, the Kent County Council published a list of reasons why Kent is unique among counties, which include, amongst other things:

> It is England's front line. In the second World War the Battle of Britain was fought above the fields of Kent.
>
> Kent is a peninsula. The sea forms much of its border. This has helped make the county feel separate from the rest of the South.
>
> Nowhere else in Britain has such strong links with the Continent. People in Kent travel to France regularly, people living elsewhere do not.
>
> There was a Kingdom of Kent in the Dark Ages when the county was a bastion of the Jutes. The rest of England was run by the Angles and the Saxons.
>
> Christianity arrived in England via Kent. St. Augustine was received by the Kentish King Ethelbert in the year 597.
>
> William the Conqueror did not conquer Kent. He had to reach an agreement with its people: hence the motto Invicta [unconquered]. (*Kent Messenger*, 11 Feb. 1994, p. 54)

Against this list's reiteration of a mythologized historical past, another impulse currently informing Kentish identity speaks to a much more open and flexible future. Particularly among younger generations who have no clear memories of World War II, there is a more open receptivity to and enthusiasm for change ...

In education, there are escalating opportunities for cultural exchange, and among school programs, links between Kent and Calais are rapidly expanding. Children go across the Channel to learn French, receive French friends into their homes, learn French history, and generally are encouraged to take an active interest in EU developments. Kent County Council has been prominent in promoting change. Given the recognized centrality of geographical education in the creation of a national identity (Foucault 1980: 73–4), it is revealing that the Kent County Council has its own geography curriculum consultant. According to this consultant, Marcia Foley:

> Schools with a strong European dimension and proximity to north east France will want to include it as part of their "home region." If you live in Dover and your mum or dad has been working on a cross-Channel ferry or may be soon employed driving a Channel Tunnel shuttle from Cheriton to the Coquelles terminal, then north east France is much more part of your home's region than Essex (*Kent Messenger*, 12 Nov. 1993, p. 12)

These links between Kent and Nord–Pas de Calais are also occurring through cultural organizations and music exchanges, such as the Education Art Link, the Cross Channel Photographic Mission, and a constant crossing of theater and dance groups from mainland Europe into Kent. And it is also happening at the level of business with networks such as the East Kent Initiative, cross-Channel farmers' cooperatives, English companies opening up offices in Calais, and the vast number of twinning schemes between Kent villages and European villages sponsored by groups such as the Kent Rural Community Council through their European Partners Competition. Indicative of wider changes is the seriousness with which these twinning schemes are approached.[1] Often representatives of local municipalities come together to sign an official treaty, usually somewhere aboard a ferry symbolically moored in mid-Channel, and double receptions are often presided over by a member of the European Parliament. Canterbury's chief executive, Christopher Gay, affirmed the development of these schemes:

> Each town has a twin; we are twinned with Rheims, Whitstable and Herne Bay have separate relationships, and so on, and all these things tend to be done on a voluntary basis not run by council. One particularly good link has been set up between Herne Bay and a town just outside Bologne. These are two seaside towns, both with the desire to do works to beautify their seafronts and provide related facilities, and it has been a very good relationship, developed effortlessly and people have got on very well. (Interview, 21 Dec. 1993)

...In this chapter, I explore some of the new connections and divisions emerging in Kent that have in part been brought about by the building of the Channel Tunnel. As a result of increasing communications across the Channel and the attenuation of national jurisdictional borders, broad changes are occurring both in the institutional frame of the European Union and informally through personal networks. In contrast to the feeling of despair expressed by many Kent residents at the signing of the Channel Tunnel Treaty in 1986 (see chapter 5), today, in the late 1990s, there is a new sense of optimism about the opportunities being opened up by the EU. Transnational exchanges between people living in Kent and on the European mainland now characterize local businesses and educational and cultural programs in towns such as Canterbury. For many people in Kent, the presence of the EU is becoming more accepted and acceptable over time.

However, simultaneously with the increasing connections between people and places on either side of the Channel, new boundaries are emerging and old divisions are being redefined. Kent is experiencing a need to reclaim its own identity and to assert its own independence as a region within England and a borderland with France...My focus is on some of the very new methods by which Kent people are claiming independence for themselves, which have only become available under the increasing impact of the EU on Kent. What I suggest is that historical narratives are being revamped and merged with new political and economic strategies into a dynamic, complex mix of local, regional, national, and transnational exchanges.

Having begun this chapter by describing how some Kent residents are expressly trying to define themselves as Kentish, and looking at what it might mean to have a "Kentish identity," I switch gears to examine EU politics and law, which are changing the Kent County Council's local forms of government. Specifically, the EU has been critical in helping Kent create a trans-border administration over the past decade. From this level of transnational policy and law, I move again to local changes and focus upon the revitalization in Kent of the ritual called "beating the bounds." Finally, I discuss the introduction into Kent by the EU of a new crop, rapeseed, which has dramatically altered the aesthetics of Kent's country landscape. Like the Tunnel itself, the growing of rape (*Brassica napus*), a crop of the mustard family, underscores the presence of the European Union on English soil. Throughout these explorations, my aim is to highlight the myriad ways in which Kentish people and their respective localized identities are increasingly being pulled into the EU's orbit, and how this ultimately affects social practices and what we construe as law.

My oscillation between so-called "global" and "local" spheres of action is deliberate, if somewhat confusing. There now exists a great deal of theoretical literature on local and global politics within which an analysis of Kent, England, Britain, and Europe can be situated. Yet much of this work takes for granted that we all recognize and know what "local" and "global" mean and represent. On the one hand, formal institutional change is presumed to operate at the global level, while on the other hand, personal perceptions relating to cultural identity and subjective interpretation of place occur at local levels. The problem with this model is that global (structure) and local (agency) are too often neatly distinguished as separate processes. In fact, these arenas of exchange and transition are interdependent. For despite the appearance of local and global as extreme opposites, they depend upon and mutually define each other.

The following analysis of activities in Kent over the past decade suggests that it is impossible to differentiate spatially where the global ends and the local begins, and what gets bracketed within these categories (see Buchanan 1995, 1996; Santos 1995; Darian-Smith 1996, 1998; Cvetkovich and Kellner 1997; Brenner 1997). Instead, I argue that new connections and new divisions are constantly being forged in push-and-pull relational processes that redefine the meanings people attribute to Kent's place in the New Europe. These meanings, of course, shift across the global/local continuum according to the various perspectives, at any particular moment, of any one individual. But what they underscore are the explicit challenges to the modernist notion that there is one law relevant to any one agent, that this is the nation-state's law, and that it correlates to a unified legal system within a particular state territory that itself has a unified identity.

Local Government in the New Europe

The Channel Tunnel provided the political and economic impetus for Kent County Council to take advantage of the new opportunities for local government bodies introduced by the EU.

[...]

European Influence on Britain's Local Government

The rupture in relations between Britain's central and local governments was accompanied by the perception of encroachment by the Europe Union, as reflected in Councilor Gay's remarks. Surprisingly, the impact of the EU is still often unappreciated in commentaries on British local government (e.g., Kingdom 1991). But as much as central government practices cannot be understood without attention being given to their implementation at the local level, so too the intervention of the EU throughout English and British government has to be taken into account. This is despite the refusal of the British government to sign the European Charter of Local Self-Government (1986),[2] and despite the assertion of Michael Portillo, British minister of local government in 1990, that "[l]ocal government is not a suitable subject for regulation by an international convention" (quoted in Crawford 1992: 69).

By the end of the 1970s, a number of English local authorities, including some in Kent, had close informal relations with bureaucrats in Brussels. This steadily increased, with some local bodies establishing offices there. Kent County Council was one of the first to take advantage of these informal processes and established a department in Brussels in 1987. It became increasingly apparent that British local authorities could both lobby Brussels to apply pressure on Whitehall and seek EU support for projects of explicitly local significance:

> There is no doubt that the link between EC powers and the local government authorities is becoming greater in terms of substantive issues. On the one hand ... powers will be transferred to the European level, "reinforcing trends towards supranational decision-making and curtailing local and regional autonomy in specific fields." On the other hand, Europe has sometimes found it useful to bypass recalcitrant central governments of member states and deal directly with local governments, such as in the area of regional assistance. (Crawford 1992: 83; also see Duchacek 1986)

The EU explicitly calls into question its member states' conventional central and local governmental frameworks. In short, it is no longer possible to accept as given a hierarchy in which local governments are exclusively subject to a central national state system. Of course, this raises further questions about what constitutes sovereignty (Appadurai 1996; Rosas 1993; MacCormick 1993; Wæver et al. 1993: 68–71; Camilleri and Falk 1992: 4, 98; Santos 1992: 134). New forms of politics, new centers of power, new conceptions of social space, and how these spaces relate to multiple layers of legal meaning, simultaneously show that the concept of sovereignty is changing. Today, "it seems obvious that no state in Western Europe any longer is a sovereign state," despite John Major's declaration in the House of Commons as recently as 1993 that "[t]he sovereignty of this House is not up for grabs" (MacCormick 1993: 1, 8).

The shift in legal and political relations between central and local governments is most evident since the Maastricht Treaty of 1992, which introduced both the Committee of Regions and the principle of subsidiarity, both aimed at creating a new balance of power more favorable to local authorities. At this stage it is difficult to determine how effective these measures will be in altering conventional center/periphery state relations. Nonetheless, the Committee of Regions and the subsidiarity principle are significant in that they procedurally and theoretically formalize a shifting relationship between national capitals and local authorities in the New Europe. Certainly, these innovations have attracted a great deal of attention in Scotland and Wales, where many people are anxious to reassert their independence of English political institutions. Also encouraging a growing sense of regional independence has been the shift in government policy toward decentralization and devolution of state power initiated by Tony Blair and his Labour party. In 1997, Scottish voters voted over-whelmingly for the return of their own parliament and its right to raise taxes. The referendum subsequently in Wales was not nearly so dramatic a success, with the "yes" vote for devolution just coming out ahead.

Nonetheless, despite concerns about the full implications of a transfer of power to regional entities, people in Wales and Scotland are envisioning new opportunities in their future relationships with London and Europe.

The Committee of Regions and the Principle of Subsidiarity

...Since subsidiarity implies a vertical division of political power, it has been referred to as the basic characteristic of federalism. However, its conceptual ambiguity, such that it could be used by the EU to increase its sovereign powers as much as to redistribute them to subnational entities, makes it questionable whether it can ever become justiciable and so constitute a ground for reviewing the legality of actions taken by the council or the commission. Still, some analysts do see subsidiarity as a principle of noncentralization, and so a way of institutionalizing direct contacts between the EU and substate governments, including interest groups and citizens, without too much concern for the opinions of member states (Emilliou 1994: 67). How subsidiarity will play out in the future is a question of much debate. Certainly at the level of local and regional governments, it has raised many hopes, and perhaps nowhere more so than in England, where local governments experienced a steady decline of their relative autonomy under the Conservative party, which governed Britain for eighteen years between 1979 and 1997.

Kent County Council in Brussels: Creating the Euroregion

The principle of subsidiarity in a sense formalizes an evolving and deepening relationship between some English local authorities and the EU's administrative offices in Brussels. In the mid 1980s, as fears mounted in England about the effects of the Tunnel, and as Britain's central authority refused all economic responsibility for needed infrastructural improvements, the Kent County Council decided it had to act for itself...

KCC agents in Brussels thereupon negotiated with the Conseil Régional du Nord – Pas de Calais and signed a cooperation agreement with it in April 1987 that resolved "to promote as far as possible across the border the development and strengthening of the friendship and ties which already unite the populations of their two regions ... [and to] contribute thus to the economic and social progress of the two border regions and to the solidarity which unites the people of Europe." This agreement was formalized to create the Transmanche Region, joining Kent and Nord–Pas de Calais (map 3), which received a grant of £6 million from the EU's Interreg Agency in 1989 for cross-border projects.

In 1991, the Transmanche Region was reconstituted to form a new Euroregion with the addition of the three Belgian regions of Flanders, Wallonia, and Brussels Capital. The Euroregion is more extensive in its networks and powers than the Transmanche Region, and its larger institutional and administrative framework qualifies it as an Economic Interest Group. This in turn provides it with a legal status sanctioned by the EU, easing "the problems which would otherwise stem from collaboration within a multitude of different legal systems and regulations" (Sinclair

and Page 1993: 482; see also Martin and Pearce 1993). With 15.5 million inhabitants, the Euroregion is one of the most densely populated areas in Europe, and it is
often called the "heartland" of Europe. Although it also handles tourism, employment, transport, and spatial planning, the Euroregion authority is particularly
concerned with the environment. On the basis of Interreg funding and the securing
of other European regional development funds, Kent County Council and its co-
operative partners on the European mainland had secured well over £35 million
pounds from the EU for trans-border programs by the mid 1990s. The Euroregion
initiative has also brought to the attention of other local British authorities
the financial benefits that may be gleaned from the EU (see Church and Reid
1994). In the words of Christopher Gay: "We are playing the system for what
it's worth. We have been getting grants from Europe with some success recently,
and we are regrouping ourselves to make what we can of that, forming links with
cities in Nord–Pas de Calais areas and putting up joint projects" (interview, 21
Dec. 1993).

Fingerprinting a New Identity?

...There certainly exists a new awareness of Kent as a regional entity neither
categorized as English nor contained entirely by the present British state. Kent and
Nord–Pas de Calais market themselves to foreign investors as a single region, and
international travel agents are beginning to promote the region "as a single overseas
holiday destination." As part of a frontier region with France and Belgium, and as a
corecipient of EU funds with the other territories of the Euroregion, Kent is in many
small ways somewhat independent of the rest of Britain. In effectively extending
Britain's border across the Channel with the sanction of EU law, Kent County
Council has reconfigured both the country's spatial territory and its political, economic, and social positions. At the same time, it has challenged the concept of the
bounded territory of the state, which Max Weber, among others, has argued to be a
critical characteristic of modern statehood (Weber 1946: 78)...

Beating the Bounds

While many of the economic and political links being forged by Kent County
Council with the wider Euroregion may pass unnoticed by the majority of Kent
residents, indirectly these connections do have significant local repercussions. With
the EU's penetration, which has greatly enhanced the power of British local governments, there is a concurrent move by some people in Kent to retreat to reassuring
rituals of localism and community. One of these is the current revival of a peculiar
ceremony called "beating the bounds." What is significant about this ritual to do
with land is that it is one way of "laying down" the law locally that does not
necessarily bear a clear relationship with either the British nation-state's legal system
or that of the New Europe...

Beating the bounds was a public spectacle designed to demarcate who had rights
(or not) to charity, access to common lands, and historically to a lord's knights for

military protection. "Those within the boundary were a part of a particular moral world and those without were outsiders" (Bushaway 1992: 126)

Beating the bounds helped solidify social relations within the local community.[8] This consolidation was important, given that England's medieval system of feudal tenure was based on a hierarchy of reciprocity and exchange. Thus beating the bounds was one of numerous rituals that helped establish people's place in society and their mutual responsibilities.[9]

Beating the Bounds in 1994

...In Kent, the revival of beating the bounds is one of many expressions of a popular anxiety to preserve the landscape, and specifically the communal right to public property. Beneath this anxiety, however, runs the related but deeper English identification with the land. This is linked historically to the loss of empire and more currently to the diminishing of Britain as a political and economic world leader. In recent years, this fear has become even more intense, as illustrated by the commodification and commercialization of heritage, which has become a huge English industry (Walsh 1992; Ashworth 1994).

Against the background of popular obsession with all things to do with English heritage, the resurgence of interest in beating the bounds becomes both more complicated and more interesting. This is particularly so when its main advocates tend to be, not natives of Kent, but recent arrivals from London and other urban areas, escaping the city in search of a sense of morality, community, and locality in which to play out their rural fantasies...

Yet I argue that the current impetus, especially by "city" people,[13] to revive a practice so central to the production of locality in premodern life is more telling of deep social and political undercurrents than is immediately apparent. Maintaining ritual is about more than merely the asserting of continuities. Customary ritual is also a way of remaking the world, of changing the present, of redirecting a sense of history.

Other Local Community Activities

Beating the bounds is only one of many local events in Kent that seek to lay down and reinstate a sense of local community imagined through a rural landscape and aesthetic sense of order. The Open Spaces Society, Common Ground, and other charities fear that the privatization schemes promoted by recent Conservative governments threaten the remaining common lands accessible to the general public. And as anyone who has traveled in southern and other parts of England can attest, common land in the form of the village green is the focus around which village life circulates. It is the site of festivals, fairs, and markets, and on summer weekends it may function as a cricket pitch, providing a centralized space for the local community's sport and leisure activities. Other forms of common land are parks and gardens, nature reserves, and beaches. All of these sites are theoretically collectively owned by the crown in the name of the people. And they help substantiate a sense of community justice, in a similar vein to the commons of medieval England, which provided a plot of land for individual tenant farmers and affirmed a community right to graze one's cow on common pasture.

Groups such as the Open Spaces Society and Common Ground inevitably came into conflict throughout the 1980s and 1990s with the capitalist ideology and the so-called "enterprise culture" fostered under Thatcherism (Heelas and Morris 1992). Under Thatcher, substantial tracts of common land were sold off to private owners. Against such action, in 1993, the Open Spaces Society launched an "Open Spaces – Special Places" campaign and established a charter proposing legislation to guarantee the protection of open land for collective recreational purposes. The Open Spaces Society advocates that local authorities be vested with the control of common land, which contests the efforts over the past decade of the Tory government to divest local bodies of power, as discussed above. With the Labour party voted into office in 1997, the extent to which these centralizing trends will continue remains an open question. For my purposes here, what is important is that the Open Spaces Society and other organizations like it, in seeking to legally reinstate the value of localism by generating interest in common lands and village greens, promote an alternative sense of justice that in theory rejects exclusive property rights and selfish individualism...

This brings the discussion back to the wider symbolism embodied in customary rituals such as beating the bounds. Just as beating the bounds rearticulates the village space, these other activities, be it a hedgerow restoration project or the setting up of a recycling scheme, are also consciously committed to building up a locality and carving out a sense of place. Revealingly, for the first time, many people from various political perspectives are becoming involved in local politics and have helped push green issues to the forefront. It seems that many individuals are clearly feeling a need to participate in the "laying down" of law and order in localities and for reasserting a "law of the countryside" in the old footpaths and rights-of-way that criss-cross the local landscape. For instance, the Kentish Stour Countryside Project has put out a pamphlet calling on landowners, farmers, community groups, Parish councils, and schools to become involved in the conservation and preservation of hedgerows. The pamphlet states that "[w]ith the disappearance of hedges, Rights of Way can be threatened as many follow original hedge boundaries. Footpaths may be ploughed up, making public access more difficult. Traditional field systems are lost, and the sense of place altered" (Kentish Stour Countryside Project, Wye, Kent).

Yellow Horizons

Fields of rape, a prolific crop, grown for the production of rapeseed oil (called canola oil in America), are one feature that Kent shares with many other counties in Britain and much of mainland Europe...

Since 1960, the Common Agricultural Policy has encouraged uniform European agricultural practices and policies directed toward maximum food productivity. In the past decade, this has meant that for English farmers to compete economically against their mainland neighbors, they had to pull out an estimated 42,000 kilometers of hedgerows in order to plant wheat, rape, and other crops producing oil and grain. As a result, smaller specialized crops like blackcurrants, hops, grapes, and English apples such as Cox's Orange Pippin have suffered dramatic setbacks. In Kent, rape has a substantial presence, standing out against the soft white and pink blossoms of the steadily diminishing apple orchards and vertical poles of Kent's hop gardens. According to one Kent native: "Perhaps if they would grow the old types of cattle food instead of the foreign rape, the glaring colour of which blots out a lot of the lovely green slopes of the Downs in Spring and spreads into the roadside hedges, it would be better for cattle, and for us. Will someone please soon declare that margarine made from rape seed is poisonous" (Laker 1992: 72).

Such monoculture runs directly counter to the aims of environmentalists and groups such as the Countryside Commission and the Council for the Protection of Rural England, which in recent years have sought new environmental legislation to introduce, among other things, regulations to protect hedgerows. British legal authority is being evoked against the widespread changes in the agricultural land-scape that illustrate the EU's attempts to create sustainable local economies. In Kent, the building of the Channel Tunnel, while dramatically polarizing public opinion, has had less visible impact on the countryside than the widespread, pervasive changes in farming. In certain areas, "[European] Community legislation may profoundly affect the use of the British landscape," observes J. D. C. Harte (1985: 52; and see also *Guardian*, 11 May 1998, pp. 8–9)...

Changes in the landscape provide a constant reminder that European law can have a material and startling impact. Whereas in the past, landscape may have been taken for granted, legal intervention has forced a new consciousness of its presence and significance, altering people's "forms of subjectivity and sociability and their aes-thetic appreciation of nature, landscapes, townscapes, and other societies," observes John Urry, who calls this a "growth of an aesthetic reflexivity" (Urry 1992: 127–8). Alongside continuing open resistance by the British government and many English citizens to the idea of a united Europe, there is thus increasing public awareness of an alternative and more authoritative local legal power.

Trains, roads, crops, pollution, beaches, noise, car exhaust, seat belts, bicycle helmets – in England all of these are increasingly regulated by the EU, affecting how one moves through, gazes upon, and perceives the environment and one's place and identity within it. Horizons of relations of power are shifting, expanding, and contracting, as well as accommodating new political centers and new modes of spatial operation. "The modern absence of actual physical horizons or boundaries poses its own set of problems, including possible loss of identity," remarks Dale Segrest (1994: 224). The national myth of a cohesive community looking out over a landscape delimited by Britain's coasts has thus received an "interruption," to use the terminology of Jean-Luc Nancy (1991: 43–70).[4] In other words, the need to forget the artificiality of Britain's fictitious national identity, sustained by an ideology of sovereign law and natural island borders, is now competing with the need to maintain equally fictitious resurrected local identities and new forms of trans-national European identity.

Concluding Comments

In seeking to establish a united territory – a European legal, political, and social community – the European Union is employing all sorts of tactics and strategies. Whether or not the EU technically qualifies as a state is immaterial to the realities of it emerging as the most regulatory and the most powerful of all modern institutions in contemporary Europe. In Michel Foucault's terms, it embodies new techniques in the art of governmentality, both over states and in the managing of individuals. And control over the landscape is, I have argued throughout this book, a critical dimension in the construction of what the New Europe will look like. Hence the legal presence of the EU, in the form of fast trains, yellow rape fields, clean beaches, and exhaust-free cars, may be subtly affecting a range of people and their perceptions of the landscape as an aesthetic symbol of their identity and a possible icon of national allegiance. One consequence is that the nature of English law, its intimate connection to the land, and its relationship to the conceptualization of Britain as an autonomous island nation are being seriously challenged.

Foucault's concern with the "workings of power" and the "techniques for 'governing' individuals" cannot be separated from the constructions of territory through which people are managed as a population (Foucault 1984: 337–8). Territory, according to Foucault, is merely a variable in the practices of modern government, because governmentality extends beyond the limits of the state – a conceptualization of territory that presumes its conflation with nation-state borders (Foucault 1980: 122; 1991: 93–4). I have tried to show that focusing on landscape as the cultural practice of territory shows the link between territory and state to be problematic. Landscape is not bound to territory any more than governmentality is to the state. Landscape should be conceived of as an instrumental strategy of power among various actors and agencies – as a contested domain through which individuals seek to manage their own destinies, "not as an object to be seen or a text to be read, but as a process by which social and subjective identities are formed" (Mitchell 1994: 1).

In the context of England in the New Europe, issues of law, territory, and identity are coming to the fore in unprecedented ways. Certainly, with the building of the Channel Tunnel and the impact of EU agricultural and environmental law in Kent, it is now more difficult to imagine the nation's mythologized green landscapes and link them to an identity that is exclusively and quintessentially English. At the same time, at least for some people, this symbolic destablizing makes even more pertinent the sustaining of an English nationalist, or more specifically Kentish, landscape imagery. Evident too throughout Kent are the variety of ways in which different people, with different interests and needs, are trying to manage a membership of Kent in Europe. Across these push-and-pull processes, landscapes, always political, contested, and dynamic, spill out across borders and seas, linking and confronting peoples and nations, shaping and being shaped by new forms of governmentality and spatial aesthetics.

NOTES

1 More than 1.5 million Europeans, in 4,000 towns, have so far been involved in town
   twinning, which has an EU budget of 10 million ecus for 1998.
2 Ireland is the only other EU member not to have signed.
3 Other anthropologists have pointed to the irony of incomers to small villages and towns
   taking over local committees and groups in an effort to "keep alive" local customs that
   natives are not particularly concerned about (see Forsythe 1982: 94–5; Rapport 1993).
4 But as Jean-Luc Nancy points out, this does not necessarily mean that the myth of nation-
   state is "demythologized" or abandoned. In the very act of acknowledging its absence,
   "myth says what is and says that we agree to say that this is" (Nancy 1991: 50). The
   recognition that Britain is no longer a unified nation-state affirms the possibility of such a
   state existing, albeit in another form.

REFERENCES

Albrechts, L., F. Moulaert, P. Roberts, and E. Swyngedouw, eds. 1989. *Regional Policy at the Crossroads: European Perspectives*. London: Jessica Kingsley.

Amin, Ash, and Nigel Thrift. 1994. "Living in the Global." In id., eds., *Globalization, Institutions, and Regional Development in Europe*, pp. 1–22. Oxford: Oxford University Press.

Appadurai, Arjun. 1996. "Sovereignty without Territoriality: Notes for a Postnational Geography." In P. Yager, ed., *The Geography of Identity*, pp. 40–58. Ann Arbor: University of Michigan Press.

Armstrong, H. W. 1993. "Subsidiarity and the Operation of European Community Regional Policy in Britain." *Regional Studies* 27, 6: 575–606.

Ashworth, G. J. 1994. "From History to Heritage: From Heritage to Identity: In Search of Concepts and Models." In G. J. Ashworth and P. J. Larkham, eds., *Building a New Heritage: Tourism, Culture and Identity in the New Europe*, pp. 13–30. London: Routledge.

Barber, Stephen, and T. Millns. 1993. *Building the New Europe: The Role of Local Authorities in the UK*. London: Association of County Councils.

Brand, John. 1795. "Rogation Week and Ascension Day." In id., *Observations on the Popular Antiquities of Great Britain*, rev. H. Ellis, pp. 197–212. London: Henry G. Bohn, 1853.

Brenner, N. 1997. "Global, Fragmented, Hierarchical: Henri Lefebvre's Geographies of Globalization." *Public Culture* 10, 1: 135–68.

Buchanan, Ruth. 1995. "Border Crossings: NAFTA, Regulatory Restructuring and the Politics of Place." *Indiana Journal of Global Legal Studies* 2, 2: 371–94.

Bushaway, R. W. 1992. "Rite, Legitimation and Community in Southern England, 1700–1850: The Ideology of Custom." In B. Stapleton, ed., *Conflict and Community in Southern England*, pp. 110–34. New York: St. Martin's Press.

Camilleri, Joseph A., and Jim Falk. 1992. *The End of Sovereignty?: The Politics of a Shrinking and Fragmenting World*. Aldershot, Hants.: Edward Elgar.

Crawford, C. 1992. "European Influence on Local Self-Government." *Local Government Studies* 18, 1: 69–85.

Cvetkovich, A., and D. Kellner. 1997. "Introduction: Thinking Global and Local." In id., eds., *Articulating the Local and the Global*, pp. 1–32. Boulder, Colo.: Westview Press.

Darian-Smith, Eve. 1996. "Postcolonialism: A Brief Introduction." In id. and Peter Fitzpatrick, eds., *Social and Legal Studies*, special issue, *Law and Postcolonialism* 5, 3: 291–9.

——ed. 1998. With Peter Fitzpatrick. *Laws of the Postcolonial*. Ann Arbor: University of Michigan Press. In press.

Duchacek, I. D. 1986. "International Competence of Subnational Governments: Borderlands and Regions." In O. J. Martinez, ed., *Across Boundaries: Transborder Interaction in Comparative Perspective*, pp. 11–30. El Paso: Texas Western Press / Center for Inter-American and Border Studies, University of Texas at El Paso.

Emilliou, Nicholas. 1994. "Subsidiarity: Panacea or Fig Leaf?" In T. O'Keeffe, ed., *Legal Issues of the Maastricht Treaty*, pp. 65–83. London: Chancery.

Forsythe, Diana. 1982. *Urban-Rural Migration, Change and Conflict in an Orkney Island Community*. London: Social Science Research Council.

Foucault, Michel. 1980. *Power/Knowledge: Selected Interviews and Other Writings 1972–1977*. Edited by C. Gordon. New York: Pantheon Books.

——. 1984. *The Foucault Reader*. Edited by P. Rainbow. New York: Pantheon Books.

Gray, John. 1993. *Beyond the New Right: Markets, Government and the Common Environment*. London: Routledge.

Harte, J. D. C. 1985. *Landscape, Land Use and the Law*. London and New York: E. & F. N. Spon.

Harvey, David. 1989. *The Condition of Postmodernity*. Cambridge, Mass.: Blackwell.

——. 1990. "Between Space and Time: Reflections on the Geographical Imagination." *Annals of the Association of American Geographers* 80: 418–34.

Harvie, Christopher. 1991. "English Regionalism: The Dog that Never Barked." In B. Crick, ed., *National Identities: The Constitution of the United Kingdom*, pp. 105–18. Oxford: Blackwell.

——. 1994. *The Rise of Regional Europe*. London: Routledge.

Heelas, Paul, and Paul Morris, eds. 1992. *The Values of the Enterprise Culture: The Moral Debate*. London: Routledge.

Laker, Mary. 1992. *Kent and England*. London: Brookside Press.

Ley, D. 1989. "Modernism, Post-Modernism and the Struggle for Place." In J. Agnew and J. Duncan, eds., *The Power of Place: Bringing Together Geographical and Sociological Imaginations*, pp. 44–65. Boston: Unwin Hyman.

Lyotard, Jean-François. 1984. *The Postmodern Condition: A Report on Knowledge*. Translated by Geoff Bennington and Brian Massumi. Foreword by Fredric Jameson. Minneapolis: University of Minnesota Press. Originally published as *La Condition postmoderne: Rapport sur le savoir* (Paris: Éditions de Minuit, 1979).

MacCormick, Neil. 1993. "Beyond the Sovereign State." *Modern Law Review* 56: 1–18.

Marquand, David. 1991. "Nations, Regions and Europe." In B. Crick, ed., *National Identities: The Constitution of the United Kingdom*, pp. 25–37. Oxford: Blackwell.

Marsh, D., and R. A. W. Rhodes. 1992. "Implementing Thatcherism: Policy Change in the 1980s." *Parliamentary Affairs* 45, 1: 33–50.

Martin, S., and G. Pearce. 1993. "European Regional Development Strategies: Strengthening Meso-Government in the UK?" *Regional Studies* 27, 7: 681–96.

Mellors, Collin, and Nigel Copperthwaite. 1990. *Regional Policy*. London: Routledge.

Mitchell, W. J. T. 1994. "Introduction." In id., ed, *Landscape and Power*, pp. 1–4. Chicago: University of Chicago Press.

Murphy, Alexander. 1993. "Emerging Regional Linkages within the European Community: Challenging the Dominance of the State." *Tijdschrift voor Econ. en Soc. Geografie / Journal of Economic and Social Geography* 84, 2: 103–18.

Nancy, Jean-Luc. 1991. *The Inoperative Community*. Translated by Peter Connor, Lisa Garbus, Michael Holland, and Simona Sawhney. Edited by Peter Connor. Minneapolis: University of Minnesota Press. Originally published as *La Communauté désoeuvrée*.

Norton, A. 1992. *The Principle of Subsidiarity and its Implications for Local Government*. Birmingham: Institute of Local Government Studies and the School of Public Policy, University of Birmingham.

Rapport, Nigel J. 1993. *Diverse World-Views in an English Village*. Edinburgh: Edinburgh University Press.

Reed, Michael. 1984. "Anglo-Saxon Charter Bounders." In id., ed., *Discovering Past Landscapes*, pp. 261–306. London: Croom Helm.

Robinson, A. H. 1990. "Regional Identity in Tomorrow's EC and the Case of North England." *EIU European Trends* 2: 68–76.

Rosas, A. 1993. "The Decline of Sovereignty: Legal Perspectives." In J. Iivonen, ed., *The Future of the Nation-State in Europe*, pp. 130–58. Aldershot, Hants.: Edward Elgar.

Salem, T. F. 1991. "Regionalism: The Awakening Paradigm in World Politics." *Journal of History and Politics*, special issue, *Regionalism and Theory*, 9: 143–60.

Santos, Boaventura de Sousa. 1992. "State, Law and Community in the World System: An Introduction." *Social and Legal Studies* 1: 131–42.

——. 1995. *Toward a New Common Sense: Law, Science and Politics in the Paradigmatic Transition*. New York: Routledge.

Schaefer, G. F. 1991. "Institutional Choices: The Rise and Fall of Subsidiarity." *Futures* (September): 681–94.

Segrest, Dale. 1994. *Conscience and Command: A Motive Theory of Law*. Atlanta: Scholars Press.

Sinclair, M. T., and Page, S. J. 1993. "The Euroregion: A New Framework for Tourism and Regional Development." *Regional Studies* 27, 5: 475–83.

Thrift, Nigel. 1995. "Taking Aim at the Heart of the Region." In D. Gregory, R. Martin, and G. Smith, eds., *Human Geography: Society, Space, and Social Science*, pp. 200–31. Minneapolis: University of Minnesota Press.

Urry, John. 1984. "Englishmen, Celts, and Iberians: The Ethnographic Survey of the United Kingdom, 1892–1899." In G. W. Stocking, ed., *History of Anthropology*, vol. 2: *Functionalism Historicized: Essays on British Anthropology*, pp. 83–105. Madison: University of Wisconsin Press.

——. 1990. *The Tourist Gaze: Leisure and Travel in Contemporary Societies*. London: Sage.

Wæver, O., B. Buzan, M. Kelstrup, and P. Lemaitre, 1993. *Identity, Migration and the New Security Agenda in Europe*. New York: St. Martin's Press.

Walsh, Kevin. 1992. *The Representation of the Past: Museums and Heritage in a Post-Modern World*. London: Routledge.

Weber, Max. 1946. "Politics as a Vocation." In H. H. Gerth and C. W. Mills, eds., *From Max Weber: Essays in Sociology*. New York: Oxford University Press.

19

Academic Narratives: Models and Methods in the Search for Meanings

Anne M. O. Griffiths

Introduction: Gender and Justice in an African Community

The excerpt which follows was taken from a book by Anne Griffiths. She indicates that in writing about women among the Kwena of Botswana she has two objectives. One is to describe the varied situations in which women find themselves. The other is to show in some detail how law and society are intertwined and mutually constitutive. Instead of describing a normative system and leaving it at that, Griffiths describes the large differences in circumstance that determine which norms women may invoke, and in which forums they may do so. Thus, some privileged Kwena women who make claims in relation to marriage, inheritance or other resources are able to do so in the formal system of courts. They may use legislative rules to advantage, yet while doing so may also rely on the ubiquitous customary social practices. However, most women have neither the money nor the education to resort to the formal law, and rely entirely on their social networks and the customary system of authorities and mediators as they try to manage their lives. The large categories by which Griffiths characterizes these two types of circumstance she calls, "the salariat" and "the peasantariat." In emphasizing their economic and educational differences she shows that "the law" available is also different.

Griffiths' fieldwork was done in the years 1982–89, but she sketches an earlier historical background and its legacy. She points out the enduring importance of the major divide made in colonial times between colonial law and customary

From Anne M. O. Griffiths, "Academic Narratives: Models and Methods in the Search for Meanings," in Anne M. O. Griffiths, *The Shadow of Marriage* (Chicago and London: University of Chicago Press, 1997), pp. 11–15, 17–29, 35–8.

law. In its colonial origins, common law was supposed to apply to Europeans, while customary law was for Africans. But when the Protectorate became independent in 1966, a single national legal system was established. The chief's *kgotla*, was incorporated into the national legal system as the lowest ranking juridical institution in the newly unified system. The *kgotla* had very limited jurisdiction, specified by statute. A new set of legal meanings came to be attached to common law and customary law. Common law was a residual category encompassing "any law written or unwritten, in force in Botswana, other than customary law" (p. 33).

All Botswana became theoretically eligible to use the magistrates court and the High Court, as well as to resort to the chief's *kgotla* and other indigenous dispute hearing agencies. But in practice the meaning for women was less than the apparent granting of universal access. The decision to resort to litigation, and the choice of forum depended on the pre-existing social networks of women, and on their education and wealth, not simply on the content of the normative rules set down in the formal system. The resulting gendered outcomes of dispute showed most women at a considerable disadvantage compared with males. These results were produced by a combination of the features of the female social situation and the structure and content of the legal system. It is in this connection that Griffiths says, "By focussing on actors' perspectives and use of legal forums [links can be made] between social and legal domains which underline their mutually constitutive nature," (p. 35).

Thus Griffiths underlines a theoretical point that has been made by many others, that the conception of the law as an autonomous system of rules that dominate society and successfully prescribes the framework for the social order is a mistaken one. Griffiths stresses that such a model of law, variously called a centralist or a positivist one ignores the interdigitated nature of legal and social norms. She shows again and again that it is impossible to understand the position of Kwena women simply in terms of formal legal rules or formal institutions. The pivotal issue here is the differentiated access to law, which depends on the social situation of women, not on their formal equality before the law. Kwena women live in a gendered social world. Their social differentiation from, and dependence on men is "reflected and reinforced" in legal settings, despite the fact that the notion of formal legal equality is imbedded in various parts of the legal system (p. 38).

S.F.M

Griffiths, *Family Law in Botswana*

This book addresses the question of women's procreative relationships with men and their access to family law in Botswana. It examines the role that marriage plays in the social construction of such relationships and the ways in which marital status affects the kinds of claims that women pursue with respect to their male partners. Such claims – which include compensation for pregnancy, maintenance, and rights to property – operate at both social and legal levels. They revolve around the links that exist between gender, procreation, and marriage and their relationship with one another. These issues are common to both social and legal studies which are concerned with the construction and regulation of family life. My study underlines the social contexts within which these claims arise. This has particular implications for women, given the gendered nature of the social world with which they are faced in Botswana. In addition, the study analyzes the impact that these social contexts have on an individual's (especially a woman's) ability to access and manipulate a legal system which incorporates Tswana customary and European law. This raises issues about legal identity which revolve around the colonial/postcolonial dimension of law and how it is played out in terms of national, regional, and local domains.

My analysis is based on an ethnographic study carried out in one area over a number of years (1982–9), which is grounded in everyday life and ordinary people's perceptions and experiences of their social and legal universe. The narrative and interpretive form of this book, drawn from detailed life histories and extended case studies, highlights the gendered world in which women and men live and how this affects women's access to law. Access to resources (including family histories) plays a key role in constructing different forms of power which affect individuals' abilities to negotiate with one another and the types of discourse they employ. Such power informs the kinds of claims that women and men can make on one another in both social and legal terms. Given the gendered nature of the world from which such power derives, this creates challenges for women which extend to their use of both Tswana customary and European law. In marking what these challenges entail, my form of analysis not only undermines any remnants of the old model of legal pluralism based on distinctions drawn between customary and European law but forms part of wider feminist critiques of law.

In this book, links are made between legal and social identities. These derive from an analysis of power which is not limited to the study of formal legal institutions, officeholders, or disputes but is grounded in everyday life. How individuals are situated in networks of kinship, family, and community and the features which affect their position within material and symbolic hierarchies is crucial. Such elements form some of the multiple ways in which individuals are inscribed. As such, they have an impact on the forms of expression or types of discourse that individuals employ and that affect their ability to negotiate status and to articulate claims with respect to one another.

This kind of analysis not only highlights the circumstances under which people do or do not have access to legal forums, but also accounts more generally for the conditions under which individuals find themselves silenced or unable to negotiate with others in terms of day-to-day social life. Such an analysis also provides for diverse accounts of power relations, not only between but within the sexes. However, an understanding of what gives rise to power in Botswana and how it operates is particularly significant for women, due to the gendered environment on which social and legal practices rest.

The issues of identity, gender, and power are raised in the context of my research in Molepolole. Moreover, these issues form part of a broader set of theoretical concerns that involve ongoing debates within legal and feminist theory. The book presents and analyzes the results of the ethnographic study within the framework of a number of more general theoretical questions. These questions concern the relationship between gender and power and how this relates to law and legal pluralism.

Families and Marriage

These broader debates are situated within discussions on familial relations. Both law and the social studies have stressed the importance of marriage in this context. This raises questions about the significance of marriage, not only in empirical terms, but also from an ideological perspective. With respect to Tswana polities there is a long and distinguished tradition of scholarship on this subject, dating back to Botswana's colonial past as a British Protectorate (1885–1966), involving lawyers and anthropologists such as Schapera, Kuper, the Comaroffs, and Roberts. Their work has, however, focused exclusively on one aspect of marriage, that is, marriage in terms of mekgwa le melao ya Setswana, often referred to as Tswana law and custom or customary law. According to John Comaroff (personal communication, 14 July 1994), much of Comaroff and Roberts's marriage data referred to in their book *Rules and Processes* (1981) derived from his research material, which was gathered mainly in South Africa between 1965 and 1975. At that time most people did not go to official churches or to the Bantu Commissioners to get married, for a whole range of reasons including political and economic concerns. As these types of formal marriages were in practice virtually nonexistent among Africans in practice, Comaroff and Roberts ignored them in their discussion of marriage and dispute processing.

But under the formal legal system of Botswana, individuals have a choice as to how they marry, which includes but is not restricted to customary law. Another option under the Marriage Act [Cap.29:01] is registration of civil as well as religious marriages. My research shows that a significant number of persons opt for marriage under this act, which has legal repercussions, especially where divorce is concerned. Yet my research, like that of a number of contemporary studies in Botswana (Kocken and Uhlenbeck 1980:53; Molenaar 1980:12; Molokomme 1991:1; see A. Griffiths 1989:587), also notes a growing gap between the incidence of pregnancy and the marriage rate along with a corresponding increase in the numbers of unmarried women with children. This was something that Schapera (1933) commented on as early as the 1930s while at the same time continuing to place marriage at the center of his discussion on family life (Schapera [1940] 1955:225). This raises the issue of how far marriage continues to have preeminence in family life today.

My study is the first ethnography of its kind to handle procreative relationships and marriage within a framework which incorporates customary and statutory law. As such it adds a new dimension to earlier work in that it addresses issues which are pertinent to the postcolonial state, not only of the nature of the formal legal system but also of the role that gender plays in providing access to law. On an empirical level, my data document a whole range of relationships involving procreation. Marriages are in the minority among all such relationships. But this is not to say that marriage is not a powerful force, for at an ideological level it provides the frame of reference in terms of which individuals' relationships are characterized – by the partners themselves as well as others – at any moment, particularly where law is concerned...

The ideological component of marriage strategies is derived from a concept of the household founded on male and female linkages, represented by the principles of agnation and matrilaterality, which were used to define the Tswana social world. In this world marriage played a central role in the construction of male and female linkages which came to be invested with symbolic attributes. These attributes were gendered in the sense that networks constructed through men, in terms of agnation, were characterized as hostile, assertive, and competitive relations embodied in the public sphere. In contrast, networks constructed through women, in terms of matri-laterality, were characterized as nurturing, supportive, and nonaggressive sets of relations which operated in the private domain.

This account of social relations is one that depicts a male-centered universe where women's only purpose is to create links in a set of relations that are primarily formulated around men and male access to power. My data endorse this view at one level and contest it at another through the narratives that women present of their encounters in daily life and in disputes. Their narratives highlight the ideological power that this construct of social life continues to wield (with material repercussions) especially with regard to law, while at the same time challenging the foundations upon which it is based...

Economic and Social Transformations

Before turning to this issue, however, it is necessary to say something about the economic and social transformations which have their foundation in the colonial past and influence family life in Botswana today. They represent the prolonged contact that Tswana polities have had with Europeans in the nineteenth and twentieth centuries. This contact precipitated changes in the structure of such polities through the imposition of colonial overrule and Christianity, as well as the introduction of a cash economy and sustained participation in migrant labor over many years. (For a more detailed historical account of these transformations see Nangati 1982; Ncgoncgo 1982a, 1982b; Parsons 1977; Schapera 1938, 1943, 1947; Shillington 1985; and Tlou 1972, 1985.)

Many of these elements were already in existence prior to the British establishing colonial overrule through the founding of the Bechuanaland Protectorate in 1885...

By the 1940s, access to European goods and migrant labor had become consolidated to such an extent that Schapera (1947:8) commented: "The people have been drawn into an elaborate system of exchange economy, through which they are linked up with and even dependent upon the markets of the world. New commodities of many kinds have been introduced, many of which can be obtained only from traders and other external sources of supply. The acceptance of these goods has greatly extended the range of desirable acquisitions, and created new standards of wealth and social status. Money has also become established as the principal medium of exchange."...

Not all migrants went to South Africa or to work in the mines, notwithstanding that the majority, according to Schapera, went to the mines and were concentrated on the Witwatersrand (1947:49). Some men went to Zimbabwe (at the time, Southern Rhodesia) to work in the mines there or went to work on farms as agricultural laborers. Others found employment in an urban context in South Africa as laborers or municipal employees. Women, who were ineligible for mine recruitment, tended to work as domestic servants or as agricultural laborers, particularly in the western Transvaal. They tended to congregate in the urban and rural areas there or in Mafeking (Schapera 1947:69). Many of these women who went to urban areas made a living through illicit beer brewing or prostitution. However, while women did engage in migrant labor, it was not at the same scale as that of men (Schapera 1947:64)...

One effect of this labor migration was a severe reduction of male labor power in the rural areas. This led dikgosi (chiefs), who had previously been active in the recruitment process, to seek to constrain it.

This concern for control extended to young boys and to women as dikgosi attempted to regulate their migration through a series of measures. These included pushing for adoption of a quota system (Schapera 1947:96) and having a representative at the railway station to check that any woman had her kgosi's permission to leave the area (Schapera 1947:90). These attempts to exert control, particularly over women, were a common phenomenon during this period in other African countries subject to colonial penetration (Channock 1985:145–60). This need to exert control was exacerbated as dikgosi found their powers being eroded by colonial authorities...

While a wage earner remained dependent on a family network to oversee his interests, his direct control over cash put him in a more powerful position with regard to the older male members of his family than formerly, when all he controlled was his own labor. Acquisition of an asset from an external source contributed something new to the process of exchange in the family context, allowing relationships to be mediated in new ways. This brought its own tensions, with fathers complaining about their lack of authority over sons and brothers acting out the inherent tensions in families through conflicts over what was owed by the migrant to brothers who stayed behind to maintain a family base...

Impact on Families, Households, and Marriage

Within this broader picture, marriage was inevitably affected. As a result of sustained labor migration, with young adults, especially men, away from home for long periods of time, marriage became postponed until a later stage in an individual's life cycle (Schapera 1947: 173; Kocken and Uhlenbeck 1980:55; Molenaar 1980:17; Timaeus and Graham 1989:392), at an age much later than that recorded for many other parts of Africa (Bledsoe 1990:117). This was accompanied by a decline in polygyny (Schapera 1950:45; Schapera and Roberts 1975:266; Kuper 1970:473; Comaroff and Roberts 1977), which was brought about by different factors. These included the influence of Christian missionaries,[1] but even more significant was the absence of eligible marital partners of the appropriate age and the shrinking resources which were available to service marital obligations within an extended family network. In this context the benefits of marriage had to be assessed in terms of its prospective returns...

These features set the contexts in which contemporary procreative relationships and the claims arising from them are negotiated today. Thus, power not only resides in ideological constructions concerning marriage but also is grounded in the material realm of resources. Indeed, the two are linked, as is demonstrated in Botswana by the way in which gendered control over access to resources, which gives men power over women in material terms, also operates to place women at a psychological disadvantage in their dealings with men. This disparity between the sexes is reflected by such well-established sayings as "Women should work and leave the *mahuku* (words) to men alone" (Kinsman 1983:49) and comments by scholars such as Alverson (1978:12), who observes that "generally men dominate women psychologically. The relations between the sexes are seen as based on proper inequality."

Family Histories and Networks: Women's Access to Resources

This material world informs relations of power documented in this book through an ethnography of one social unit, Mosotho kgotla, in Molepolole...

Although most women have access to land, their ability to utilize it as an agricultural resource depends on their ability to raise cash to buy the seeds and other items necessary for its maintenance (Kerven 1982), as well as their ability to mobilize the labor necessary for its cultivation (whether through kin or by hire: Izzard 1982:712; Cooper 1980:14). In both respects women tend to be dependent on men (Solway 1980; Kerven 1984), especially where they form part of the peasantariat, because of the nature of the social system and their poorer prospects of employment compared with those of men.

Households form the basis for the political structure of the kgotla[2] and customary law; authority is based on age and status. Children defer to adults, who acquire greater status with marriage and age. But women do not have authority comparable with that of men, and this is underlined by the fact that although they may act as heads of households,[3] they can never qualify for the position of head of a group of households which form a kgotla, the basic unit in the political structure of the morafe.[4] At each stage of her life a women falls within the shadow of male authority. When unmarried, it is the authority of her father and her brothers; when married, it is that of her husband; and when widowed or in old age (if never married), it is that of her sons. Material and social circumstances combine to create a situation where it is hardly surprising that households of married men and women prove the most effective in agricultural production.

The agricultural domain is closely allied to that of livestock, and here again women find themselves at a disadvantage when it comes to acquiring stock. This is due, in part, to the laws of succession according to which the largest category of cattle, referred to as estate cattle, is handed down from father to sons. Although a daughter can and not infrequently does acquire some livestock (where such cattle exist) her share is never on a par with that of her brothers, especially her eldest brother, who takes over responsibility for the family group on his father's death. Women may inherit livestock from their mothers, but a mother's opportunities for acquiring her own stock tend to be limited, as these can only derive from certain sources of labor. Cattle owned by women are mainly produced from their own (not their husbands') inherited land, which may be exchanged for livestock; or the produce of that land may be used to make beer, which in turn may be sold to provide the cash for cattle purchases...

Access to wage employment is one of the most important factors affecting the social and economic position of women in Botswana today (Brown 1983; Kerven 1984:267; UNICEF 1993:19–20). This is because cash, so essential for survival, is less generally available to women for a number of reasons. In the formal sector, certain basic types of employment on which the majority of the male population rely, for example, in the mining and construction industry, are not open to women. Others, particularly those of a more professional nature, require a certain degree of education, which limits their availability to both sexes. Only a minority of women have the necessary qualifications, yet they are beginning to outnumber the jobs available. Moreover, women in Botswana generally fall short of these qualifications compared with men (UNFPA 1989:13), a finding that has been documented elsewhere (Adepoju 1994:163–4; H. Moore 1988:104).

Women's lack of higher educational achievement compared with that of men (Alexander 1991:33; Botswana 1988a) is due to a number of factors. The high level of pregnancy among adolescents is paramount (Botswana 1988b), especially as education policy demands that these adolescents leave school as soon as they become pregnant regardless of the stage that they have reached in their studies. This has important consequences given that "more than one quarter of the females in the population become pregnant while teenagers" (Botswana 1988b:1) and that once young women drop out of school they find it hard to reenter the education system. Lack of money to meet the costs of secondary and tertiary education is also critical for the increasing numbers of impoverished female-headed households. Those who can afford the costs, on the other hand, may be unwilling to invest in education for women beyond a basic level. Whatever the reason, the kind of employment open to the majority of women is at the level of domestic service (Alexander 1991:49) or working as barmaids or shop assistants. There is competition for such work, which in any case is insecure and poorly paid. In this situation women find it hard to negotiate or enforce their terms of service, even where these are laid down by law. Men also have these difficulties, but have more options with regard to potential employment...

Under these conditions, life histories demonstrate that women's access to resources is heavily dependent upon the type of network to which they belong. So women within the peasantariat, who operate within the matrix of domestic, agricultural, and unskilled labor, find themselves heavily reliant upon the male networks and structures of authority which provide the mainstay for their existence. While their contributions in terms of labor and reproduction play an important role in sustaining such a network, those contributions are not invested with the same degree of power and authority as are those of men. Women associated with the salariat, however, who have stable employment and who focus less on the agricultural domain, place less reliance on the type of network that women within the peasantariat most depend on and so experience a greater degree of independence from men.

How women are situated within such networks has implications for the types of choices that they may make with respect to procreative relationships, the negotiation of status, and the terms upon which a relationship may take place. Such options have an impact upon the kind of claims that women make on their male partners, whether these involve compensation for pregnancy (chap. 4), rights to support (chap. 5), or other property rights (chaps. 6 and 7). Where claims are made, the majority occur as part of ordinary social life. But there are other options that go beyond this sphere into particular institutional forums, such as the magistrate's court, the High Court, and the chief's kgotla, that form part of the formal legal system of Botswana. This raises questions about the relationship between the social contexts in which such claims arise and their relationship with the formal legal system upheld by the state.

Confronting Law: Working with the Formal Legal System

Such questions involve an analysis of law, which in turn raises issues about the ways law is defined and perceived. Such differences in their perception of law gave rise to the dispute over the nature of rules and processes that exists between Schapera and Comaroff and Roberts, discussed earlier. So Comaroff and Roberts (1981:18) contest any presentation of mekgwa le melao ya Setswana as a formally differentiated and structured set of rules, where the "suggested causal connection between rule and outcome is thus closely similar to that envisaged in the more conservative accounts of Western legal systems." Indeed, their research leads them to conclude that such "assumptions are impossible to sustain, for it became clear, in the parallel contexts in which we studied them, that the rules consisted of a loosely constructed repertoire rather than an internally consistent code" (Comaroff and Roberts 1981:18)...

The Power of Law: A Legal Centralist Model

All legal studies stand in the shadow of what is often referred to by Galanter (1981:1) and J. Griffiths (1979, 1986) as a "legal centralist" or "formalist" model of law. Baldly stated, the characteristics of this model, which derive from a modern Western legal paradigm, are that it promotes a uniform view of law and its relationship with the state (J. Griffiths 1986:3), one which places law at the center of the social universe and which endorses normative prescriptions for interpreting society. In this model legal norms are set apart from, and privileged over, social norms (Roberts 1979:25; Galanter 1981:20) and used to determine outcomes where conflict arises (Roberts 1979:20; Comaroff and Roberts 1981:5). All these attributes combine to create an autonomous legal field, one which presides over the hierarchy of social relations...

Displacing the Centralist Paradigm: The Social Context of Law

...By focusing on actors' perspectives and use of legal forums, my study makes links between social and legal domains which underline their mutually constitutive nature. Understanding the nature of these multiple links or connections is central to my account of law, which makes visible features that are otherwise overlooked in a legal centralist account of law. For while legal centralists find no incompatibility between identifying law in formal terms and acknowledging the social sources of its content, their focus remains firmly on the former. This means that the social basis upon which law operates is largely ignored, because such a focus creates exclusionary boundaries. What counts as law, in terms of particular sources and institutions, along with the context in which law is situated remains circumscribed. So it is that approaches to law in what Franz von Benda-Beckmann (1989: 142) calls legal science produce accounts very different from those of social science.

It is at this level that discussions on power and how it is constituted are important. Here a discussion of life histories is key, as such histories illustrate the ways in which power operates to produce certain forms of discourse with regard to familial relationships and property. These inform the terms upon which parties speak and how they formulate claims in respect of one another in everyday life. Such discourses amount to law (at the very least in centralist terms) when they are located within particular institutional settings. But the power to shape such discourses is not confined to, or derived solely, from these legal settings, as it is generated within a broader arena which carries authority beyond such settings in the operation of everyday life. In other words, law is in fact reflecting and reinforcing social processes and the boundaries to which they give rise. In this context, women as individuals find themselves at a disadvantage in pursuing claims against men because of the gendered social world that gives rise to differential power relations between men and women. Such relations derive from the sexual division of labor within the household and the family, as well as differential access to employment and other resources within and beyond the family.

Analysis of how power and the discourses it gives rise to are constructed allows for a discussion of the conditions under which power and its discourses may alter or be transformed – a discussion lacking in a centralist account of law. Not only that, but by engaging with what is otherwise left out of account by legal centralism, namely, the world of economic and social differentiation, another image of law takes shape. This is one which challenges the claims to autonomy, neutrality, and equality which are attributed to the centralist model of law, without rejecting some of the formal aspects of law on which it is based. Such an approach radically transforms the way in which law is perceived, for although the familiar sources, institutions, and personnel associated with a centralist model of law continue to be factored into legal narratives, the ways in which they do so can no longer sustain only one representation of law.

REFERENCES

Adepoju, A. 1994. Women, Work and Fertility in Swaziland. In *Gender, Work and Population in Sub-Saharan Africa*, edited by A. Adepoju and C. Oppong, 157–72. Published on behalf of the International Labour Office, Geneva. London: James Currey; Portsmouth, N.H.: Heinemann.

Alexander, E. 1991. *Women and Men in Botswana: Facts and Figures*. Ministry of Finance and Development Planning, Central Statistics Office Gaborone: Government Printer.

Alverson, H. 1978. *Mind in the Heart of Darkness: Value and Self-Identity among the Tswana of Southern Africa*. New Haven, Conn.: Yale University Press.

Benda-Beckmann, F. von. 1989. Scapegoat and Magic Charm: Law in Development Theory and Practice. *Journal of Legal Pluralism and Unofficial Law* 28:129–47.

Bledsoe, C. 1990. Transformations in Sub-Saharan African Marriage and Fertility. *Annals of the American Academy of Political and Social Sciences,* July, 115–125.

Botswana, Republic of. 1988a. *Education Statistics*. Ministry of Finance and Development Planning, Central Statistics Office. Gaborone: Government Printer.

———. 1988b. *Teenage Pregnancies in Botswana: How Big Is the Problem and What Are the Implications?* Gaborone: National Institute of Development Research and Documentation and the University of Botswana.

Boyd, S. 1989. From Gender Specificity to Gender Neutrality? Ideologies in Canadian Child Custody Law. In *Child Custody and the Politics of Gender,* edited by C. Smart and S. Svenhuijsen, 126–57. London: Routledge.

Channock, M. 1985. *Law, Custom and Social Order: The Colonial Experience in Malawi and Zambia.* Cambridge: Cambridge University Press.

Comaroff, J. L. 1980. Bridewealth and the Control of Ambiguity in a Tswana Chiefdom. In *The Meaning of Marriage Payments,* edited by J. L. Comaroff, 161–195. New York: Academic Press.

Comaroff, J. L., and J. Comaroff. 1981. The Management of Marriage in a Tswana Chiefdom. In *Essays on African Marriage in Southern Africa,* edited by E. J. Krige and J. L. Comaroff, 29–49. Cape Town: Juta.

Comaroff, J. L., and S. A. Roberts. 1977. Marriage and Extra-marital Sexuality: The Dialectics of Legal Change among the Kgatla. *Journal of African Law* 21:97–123.

——1981. *Rules and Processes: The Cultural Logic of Dispute in an African Context.* Chicago: University of Chicago Press.

Cooper, D. M. 1979a. *Migration to Botswana Towns: Patterns of Migration of Selebi-Pikwe Mine Workers prior to and including Coming to Pikwe.* National Migration Study Working Paper no. 3. Gaborone: Government Printer.

——1979b. *Economy and Society in Botswana: Some Basic National Sociotics.*

——1980. *How Urban Workers in Botswana Manage Their Cattle and Lands: Selebi-Pikwe Case Studies.* National Migration Study Working Paper no. 4. Gaborone: Government Printer.

——. 1982. *An Overview of the Botswana Class Structure and Its Articulation with the Rural Mode of Production: Insights from Selebi-Phikwe.* (Dated 1980.) Cape Town: Centre for African Studies, University of Cape Town.

Datta, K. n.d. *Research on Women in Economy and Its Impact on Policy Making in Botswana.* Gender Research Programme. Gaborone: University of Botswana and National Institute of Development Research and Documentation.

Delphy, C., and D. Leonard. 1992. *Familiar Exploitation: A New Analysis of Marriage in Contemporary Western Societies.* Cambridge: Polity Press.

Field, R. F. 1982. Batswana Labour in South Africa: Migration to the Mines. In *Migration in Botswana: Patterns, Causes and Consequences.* Final report of the National Migration Study, 3:719–80. Gaborone: Government Printer.

Fineman, M. A. 1983. Implementing Equality: Ideology, Contradiction and Social Change – A Study of Rhetoric and Results in the Regulation of the Consequences of Divorce. *Wisconsin Law Review* 4:789–886.

——1991. Introduction. In *At the Boundaries of Law: Feminism and Legal Theory,* edited by M. A. Fineman and N. S. Thomadsen, xi–xvi. London: Routledge.

Galanter, M. 1981. Justice in Many Rooms: Courts, Private Ordering and Indigenous Law. *Journal of Legal Pluralism and Unofficial Law* 19:1–47.

Goldschmidt-Clermont, L. 1994. Assessing Women's Economic Contributions in Domestic and Related Activities. In *Gender, Work and Population in Sub-Saharan Africa,* edited by A. Adepoju and C. Oppong, 76–87. Published on behalf of International Labour Office, Geneva. London: James Currey; Portsmouth, N.H.: Heinemann.

Griffiths, A. 1988a. Support among the Bakwena. In *Between Kinship and the State,* edited by F. von Benda-Beckmann, K. von Benda-Beckman, E. Casino, F. Hirtz, G. R. Woodman, and H. F. Zacher, 289–316. Dordrecht: Foris Publications.

——. 1989. Women, Status and Power: Negotiation in Family Disputes in Botswana. *Cornell International Law Journal* 22(3):575–622.

Griffiths, J. 1979. The Legal Integration of Minority Groups Set in the Context of Legal Pluralism. Unpublished paper. (Revised as What Is Legal Pluralism, 1986.)

—— 1986. What Is Legal pluralism? *Journal of Legal Pluralism and Unofficial Law* 24:1–55.

Gulbrandsen, O. 1980. *Agro-Pastoral Production and Communal Land Use*. Gabor-one: Government Printer.

Harris, O. 1981. Households as Natural Units. In *Of Marriage and the Market: Women's Subordination in International Perspective*, edited by K. Young, C. Wolkowitz, and R. McCullagh, 49–67. London: CSE Books.

Izzard, W. 1979. *Rural-Urban Migration of Women in Botswana*. Final fieldwork report for National Migration Study Botswana. Gaborone: Government Printer.

——. 1982. The Impact of Migration on the Roles of Women. In *Migration in Botswana: Patterns, Causes and Consequences*. Final report of the National Migration Study, 3:654–707. Gaborone: Government Printer.

Kerven, C. 1982. The Effects of Migration on Agricultural Production.

——. 1984. Academics, Practitioners and all Kinds of Women in Development: A Reply to Peters. *Journal of Southern African Studies* 10(2):259–68.

Kinsman, M. 1983. "Beasts of Burden": The Subordination of Southern Tswana Women, ca. 1800–1840. *Journal of Southern African Studies* 10(1):39–54.

Kocken, E. M., and G. C. Uhlenbeck. 1980. *Tlokweng, A Village Near Town*. ICA Publication no. 39 Leiden: Leiden University, Institute of Cultural and Social Studies.

Kooijman, K. F. 1978. Social and Economic Change in a Tswana Village. M.A. thesis, Leiden University.

Kuper, A. 1970. The Kgalagari and the Jural Consequences of Marriage. *Man*, n. s., 5:466–482.

——. 1975a. The Social Structure of the Sotho-Speaking Peoples of Southern Africa. *Africa* 45, pt. 1:67–81; pt. 2:139–49.

——. 1987. The Transformation of Marriage in Southern Africa. In *South Africa and the Anthropologist*, edited by A. Kuper, 134–47. London: Routledge and Kegan Paul.

MacKinnon, C. 1983. Feminism, Marxism, Method and the State: An Agenda for Theory. *Signs* 8(2):635–58.

Maine, Sir Henry S. 1861. *Ancient Law: Its Connections with the Early History of Society and Its Relation to Modern Ideas*. 1st ed. London: J. Murray. (Reprinted as no. 734 in Everyman's Library. London: J. M. Dent and Sons, 1965.)

Minow, M. 1986. Consider the Consequences. *Michigan Law Review* 84:900–918.

—— 1990. *Making All the Difference: Inclusion, Exclusion, and American Law*. Ithaca, N.Y.: Cornell University Press.

Molenaar, M. 1980. Social Change within a Traditional Pattern: A Case Study of a Tswana Ward. M. A. thesis, University of Leiden.

Molokomme, A. 1991. *"Children of the Fence": The Maintenance of Extra-marital Children under Law and Practice in Botswana*. Research report no. 46. Leiden: African Studies Centre.

Molokomme, A., and B. Otlhogile. 1987. *Cases on Family Law and Succession*. Gaborone: University of Botswana, Department of Law.

Moore, H. L. 1988. *Feminism and Anthropology*. Minneapolis: University of Minnesota Press.

Nangati, F. 1982. Early Capitalist Penetration: The Impact of Precolonial Trade in Kweneng (1840–1876). In *Settlement in Botswana*, edited by R. Hitchcock and M. Smith. Marshall-town:Heinemann.

Ncgoncgo, L. 1982a. Impact of the difaqane on Tswana States. In *Settlement in Botswana*, edited by R. Hitchcock and M. Smith, 167–71. Marshalltown: Heinemann

——. 1982b. Precolonial Migration in South Eastern Botswana. In *Settlement in Botswana*, edited by R. Hitchcock and M. Smith, 23–30. Exeter, N.H.: Heinemann Educational Books.

O'Donovan, K. 1985. *Sexual Divisions in Law*. London: Weidenfeld and Nicolson.

Okin, S. M. 1989. *Justice, Gender, and the Family.* New York: Basic Books.

Olsen, F. 1983. The Family and the Market: A Study of Ideology and Legal Reform. *Harvard Law Review* 96(7):1497–1578.

Oppong, C. 1994. Introduction. In *Gender, Work and Population in Sub-Saharan Africa,* edited by A. Adepoju and C. Oppong, 1–16. Published on behalf of International Labour Office, Geneva. London: James Currey; Portsmouth, N.H.: Heinemann.

Parson, J. 1981. Cattle, Class, and State in Rural Botswana. *Journal of Southern African Studies* 7:236–55.

Parsons, Q. N. 1977. The Economic History of Khama's Country in Botswana, 1844–1930. In *The Roots of Rural Poverty in Central and Southern Africa,* edited by N. Parsons and R. Palmer, 113–43. Berkeley and Los Angeles: University of California Press.

Pateman, C., and M. L. Shanley, eds. 1991. *Feminist Interpretations and Political Theory.* Cambridge: Polity Press; Oxford: Basil Blackwell.

Petersen, H. 1992. On Women and Legal Concepts: Informal Law and the Norm of Consideration. *Social and Legal Studies: An International Journal* 4(1):493–514.

Ramsay, J. 1991. The Rise and Fall of the Bakwena Dynasty of South Central Botswana, 1820–1940. Ph.D. diss., Boston University.

Roberts, S. A. 1977. The Kgatla Marriage: Concepts of Validity. In *Law and the Family in Africa,* edited by S. A. Roberts, 241–60. The Hague: Mouton.

——. 1979. *Order and Dispute.* New York: St. Martin's Press.

Robertson, A. F. 1991. *Beyond the Family: The Social Organization of Human Reproduction.* Oxford: Polity Press.

Schapera, I. 1938. *A Handbook of Tswana Law and Custom.* London: Oxford University Press for the International African Institute.

——. [1940] 1955. *Married Life in an African Tribe.* London: Faber.

——. 1943. *Native Land Tenure in the Bechuanaland Protectorate.* Alice: Lovedale Press.

——. 1947. *Migrant Labour and Tribal Life: A Study of the Condition of the Bechuanaland Protectorate.* London: OUP.

——. 1950. Kinship and Marriage among the Tswana. In *African Systems of Kinship and Marriage,* edited by A. R. Radcliffe-Brown and D. Forde, 140–65. London: Oxford University Press for the International African Institute.

——. 1963a. Agnatic Marriage in Tswana Royal Families. In *Studies in Kinship and Marriage,* edited by I. Schapera. Occasional Paper no. 16. London: Royal Anthropological Institute.

——. 1963b. Kinship and Politics in Tswana History. *Journal of the Royal Anthropological Institute* 93(2):159–73.

Schapera, I., and S. A. Roberts. 1975. Rampedi Revisited: Another Look at a Kgatla Ward. *Africa* 45(1):258–79.

Shillington, K. 1985. *The Colonisation of the Southern Tswana 1870–1900.* Braam-fontein: Ravan Press.

Smart, C. 1984. *The Ties That Bind: Law, Marriage and Reproduction of Patriarchal Relations.* London and Boston: Routledge and Kegan Paul.

——. 1989. *Feminism and the Power of Law.* London: Routledge.

Solway, J. 1980. *People, Cattle and Drought in the Western Kweneng District.* Rural Sociology Report Series, no. 16. Gaborone:?

Timaeus, I., and W. Graham. 1989. Labour Circulation, Marriage and Fertility in Southern Africa. In *Reproduction and Social Organization in Sub-Saharan Africa,* edited by R. Lesthaeghe, 365–400. Berkeley and Los Angeles: University of California Press.

Tlou, T. 1972. A Political History of Northwestern Botswana to 1906. Ph.D. diss., Department of History, University of Wisconsin.

——. 1985. *A History of Ngamiland 1750 to 1956: The Formation of an African State.* Madison: University of Wisconsin Press.

United Nations Population Fund (UNFPA). 1989. *Gender, Population and Development.* Report on the High-Level Seminar for Chiefs and District Commissioners. Edited by L. Divasse and G. Mookodi. Gaborone: Ministry of Labour and Home Affairs, Women's Affairs Unit.

UNICEF. 1993. *Children, Women and Development in Botswana.*

Vaughan, M. 1985. Household Units and Historical Process in Southern Malawi. *Review of African Political Economy* 34:35–45.

Wylie, D. 1991. *A Little God: The Twilight of Patriarchy in a Southern African Chiefdom.* Hanover, N.H.: Wesleyan University Press.

20

Human Rights and Nation-Building

Richard A. Wilson

Introduction: Officializing Truth and Reconciliation in South Africa

One of the dilemmas of a new government after a major regime change is how much to keep of the previous regime's law. The new state must decide what to keep and what to reject. As we have seen in Griffiths' chapter, once colonial rule had come to an end in anglophone Africa, one of the projects of the independent successor states was to do away with the dual system of law and courts, one set for whites, one for Africans. National governments combined them, made one structure of courts and norms of what had previously been two. In practical effect this juridical unification met with variable success, but in every case what unification did succeed in doing was to communicate that, in principle, racially based justice was rejected by the new government. In practical fact, the jurisdiction of the local courts (the formerly African customary courts) was extremely limited. How much had changed? And what about constitutional change? And the law of property, the laws of inheritance, the nature of family law? What about taxation? What about the legal structure of administration? And no small matter, what about the criminal law? What about tort law? In Tanzania these were addressed slowly, considerably after the moment of independence.

It is neither an easy nor a quick task to totally review and revise a legal system in a modern polity. It takes many trained persons and much time to draft revisions, let alone to get them approved through the appropriate political process. But new regimes are characteristically in a hurry to legitimize themselves, and thus have a need to make dramatic political points through the legal system almost at once. Truth Commissions are one such strategy, undertaken in many countries in recent times. Where a part of the population had suffered

From Richard A. Wilson, "Human Rights and Nation Building," in Richard A. Wilson, *The Politics of Truth and Reconciliation in South Africa* (Cambridge, MA: Cambridge University Press, 2001), pp. xvi–3.

serious injustices under the old regime there was an urgency about instituting some publicized means of rectification. Post-authoritarian governments have had to respond, and many have done so.

What happened in South Africa is a particularly interesting instance. The Truth and Reconciliation Commission was a temporary forum whose main work was done between 1995 and 1998 (though the amnesty commission continued to 2001). There were hearings on Human Rights Violations, but the commission had no power to sentence anyone, and had no funds of its own with which to compensate victims. It made recommendations to the Reparation and Rehabilitation Committee (another section of the commission) but even after such recommendations were made, there was a big lag in reparations payments by the government. And no wonder, since the Commission had recommended payments to 22,000 victims. The third sub-unit of the TRC was the Amnesty Commission which could under certain circumstances grant amnesty to perpetrators of crimes who came forward and confessed. The granting of amnesty made it impossible for the perpetrators to be sued by their victims, or prosecuted by the criminal justice system, and it lay in the discretion of the government whether to give any compensation to victims. Thus from the point of view of the victims, the TRC sounded much more effective than it was. What it achieved was at least this: the TRC gave an opportunity for many persons to put their grievances on the record, and it gave the new government material for a moralizing national discourse about truth and reconciliation, both of which probably were politically useful.

What was the South African public reaction? Wilson says that public opinion surveys showed that "the overwhelming majority of those interviewed preferred not forgiveness or amnesty, but punishment and the right to sue through the courts" (p. 25). This is what Wilson's fieldwork in the African townships of the Vaal region to the South of Johannesburg confirmed. He was looking to see what impact the TRC had on local courts and local opinion. There were a great variety of responses, but he says, "One of the main results of my ethnographic inquiries was the centrality of emotions of vengeance in popular legal consciousness and practices of revenge in local justice institutions" (p. xx). Thus there was a substantial disjunction between the national ideology of reconciliation and the local practice.

The material in this book is fascinating and important. Furthermore, it points to major methodological issues for present day anthropological work, particularly work on legal/political matters. For those who want to address large scale questions, the demands made by the anthropological requirement that there be long-term close contact with persons in the researched area is not the same as the requirement that broad information be gleaned from a large number of interviewed individuals, and from the analysis of documentary materials. Combining them is something else again.

S.F.M.

Wilson, *Human Rights and Nation-Building*

In democratizing countries of Latin America from the mid-1980s and Eastern Europe from 1989, the language of human rights emerged as a universal panacea to authoritarianism. Human rights were demanded by ordinary citizens massed in the squares of

Leipzig or on the streets of Bisho, and they became symptomatic of the kind of 'procedural' liberalism established in post-authoritarian states. Human rights based legislation became a central component in the transformation of repressive institutions and in the establishing of the rule of law after the distortions of authoritarian legality. Each society had to face the question of how to deal with the gross human rights violations of the past, and new institutions and commissions were set up to reaffirm human dignity and to ensure that violations would not occur again. Increasingly, human rights talk was detached from its strictly legal foundations and became a generalized moral and political discourse to speak about power relations between individuals, social groups and states. This broad extension of human rights talk was exacerbated as democratizing regimes with crumbling economies and fractured social orders grasped for unifying metaphors, and human rights talk seemed to provide an ideological adhesive through terms such as 'truth' and 'reconciliation'.

By the 1990s, it was time to take stock and to evaluate critically the role of human rights ideas and institutions in democratic transitions. It became possible to move on from simply extolling human rights to examining what happened when human rights institutions were established in complicated contexts of political compromise, where neither opposing side in a civil war had won an outright military victory, where key perpetrators of the era of repression (from Vice-President FW de Klerk in South Africa to Senator Augusto Pinochet in Chile) still occupied positions of political power and where the former bureaucracies of death (especially the criminal justice system and security forces) were still staffed by personnel from the authoritarian era.

In the literature on democratization, liberal visions of 'democratic consolidation' often adopted a model-building and technicist tone. 'Transitology' attempts to isolate the variables that reinforce or undermine democratic consolidation and build universal mechanistic models that treat democratization as if it were a matter of correctly arranging pieces of a puzzle. Transition theory in mainstream political science often accepted a minimalist liberal understanding of democracy as indicated by constitutions enshrining individual civil rights, political party competition and periodic elections.

The establishing of a bare functioning minimum is not to be lightly dismissed, as it was an important objective of the struggles of opposition and dissident movements. Yet this book emphasizes a more sociological standpoint which places justice in transition in the context of nation-building and a hegemonic project of state formation. A focus upon how the rule of law is established and maintained must be complemented by an analysis of the concrete ideological and administrative difficulties which new regimes found themselves in. This requires a greater awareness of how new regimes used human rights to re-imagine the nation by constructing new official histories, and how they sought to manufacture legitimacy for key state institutions such as the criminal justice system.

Human rights discourses and institutions in South Africa such as the Truth and Reconciliation Commission, Human Rights Commission and the Commission for Gender Equality are central to creating a new moral and cultural leadership, that is to say, a new hegemony. This new hegemony is initially asserted in relation to accountability of past state crimes and whether to punish and/or pardon previous human rights violations. The study of transitional truth and justice has been too dominated by philosophical discussions abstracted from specific contexts, and we should instead examine how the politics of punishment and the writing of a new official memory are central to state strategies to create a new hegemony in the area of justice and construct the present moment as post-authoritarian when it includes many elements of the past.

In South Africa, human rights talk became ever more compromised as it was dragooned by an emergent bureaucratic elite into the service of nation-building. Ostensibly, the language of rights represented a departure from old ethno-nationalist models of nationalism with their romantic images of blood and land. Post-authoritarian nation-building, in contrast, appealed to civic nationalism as the new basis for moral integration and a redefined conception of nation. Yet this process of nation-building also had its normative injunctions and included elements of moral coercion. The constitution and subsequent legislation deprived victims of their right to justice and retributive justice was defined as 'un-African' by some, such as former Archbishop Desmond Tutu. Human rights became the language of restorative justice and forgiveness of human rights offenders in South Africa, whereas at the same time in international contexts, human rights were developing in just the opposite (punitive) direction with the creation of an International Criminal Court and the prosecutions brought by the UN war crimes tribunal for the former Yugoslavia and Rwanda.

There were some unintended consequences of the reliance upon human rights talk for nation-building and state centralization. Due to amnesty laws and a lack of prosecutions of human rights offenders, the high expectations expressed in human rights talk by both politicians and citizens were left unfulfilled, as transitional institutions seemed to protect perpetrators more than they fulfilled victims' hopes for justice and reparation. Human rights came not to represent ideal and inviolable principles (such as justice for victims and punishment for offenders), but instead expressed the problematical nature of the elite-pacted political settlement. The new promises of the constitutional order outstretched the capacity of the legal system, as human rights were enshrined in the Constitution that were unrealizable by the majority of impoverished black citizens. Given the yawning gap between human rights ideals and the grim realities of criminal justice delivery, the conditions were ripe for a crisis of legitimacy. Rather than resolving the crisis of legal institutions, human rights talk came to symbolically epitomize the legitimation crisis of post-authoritarian justice. Finally, the place of human rights talk in a project of legal unification and centralization brought them into conflict with local justice institutions and popular legal consciousness in a legally plural setting.

These reflections on human rights institutions in democratization processes urge us to look beyond the formal, legalistic and normative dimensions of human rights, where they will always be a 'good thing'. A sociology or ethnography of rights will look instead at how rights are transformed, deformed, appropriated and resisted by state and societal actors when inserted into a particular historical and political context. This shifts our attention away from the transcendent moral philosophy of rights to a rigorous examination of the history and social life of rights.

This book results from a twelve-month ethnographic study (over a four-year period) inside and outside of one of the main human rights institutions in transitional

South Africa – the Truth and Reconciliation Commission (TRC). During this time I was a lecturer and visiting associate in the anthropology department at the University of the Witwatersrand in Johannesburg. My research started in 1995, before the TRC began functioning, and continued into 1996–7, while it was in full swing; it ended in late 1998 after the main regional offices had been closed. I attended three weeks of Human Rights Violations hearings in Klerksdorp, Tembisa and Kagiso and three weeks of amnesty hearings for Northern Province security policemen in Johannesburg. I interviewed nearly half of all the TRC Commissioners, the TRC executive secretary, and many staff workers, such as lawyers, researchers and investigators. I would also include as 'research' the conference evaluating the TRC which I co-organized with Merle Lipton at the University of Sussex in September 1998, which included a TRC Commissioner, members of the Research Unit and Investigative Unit and a former judge of the Constitutional Court of South Africa.

Much of my research, however, took place outside the TRC process and concentrated on the impact of the TRC on the African townships of the Vaal region to the south of Johannesburg. In the Vaal, I carried out in-depth interviews with over 50 victims of political violence, many of them members of the Khulumani Support Group, as well as local religious personnel, local court officials, political leaders, legal activists and policemen. In the beginning, my contacts were mainly aligned to the African National Congress, but as time went on I actively sought out leaders and ordinary members of minority parties such as the Pan Africanist Congress and the Inkatha Freedom Party. I also tried to glean views from those who were not aligned with any political tradition at all. As for 'perpetrators', it is worth pointing out that some of my 'victim' informants were also implicated in acts of public violence during the apartheid era. Only a few were willing to speak openly about their involvement in such acts, but I did interview three Inkatha Freedom Party members who had been convicted in the courts for their participation in the 1992 Boipatong massacre, as well as a policeman representing amnesty applications from within the Vaal police force, and an Amnesty Committee investigator of the TRC for the Vaal region. Finally, my interviews in the Vaal were complemented by several weeks' archival work in the William Cullen Library, which holds many useful historical records of human rights monitors such as Peace Action and the Independent Board of Inquiry which worked in the Vaal in the late 1980s and early 1990s.

Truth commissions are now standard post-conflict structures set up in over seventeen countries in the last 20 years to investigate unresolved cases arising from past human rights violations. As one strand of the globalization of human rights, they have taken on a transnational validity as one of the main mechanisms for announcing a new democratic order. Truth commissions have fascinated international audiences and led to a voluminous literature acclaiming their promises of truth and restoration, mostly from law, political science and moral philosophy. The South African truth commission, as the largest and most ambitious in scope, is perhaps the zenith of this trajectory, and has attracted the most attention and discussion so far. The literature evaluating the achievements of truth commissions has mostly been positive and laudatory, claiming these commissions heal the nation by providing therapy for a traumatized national psyche. They break a regime of official denial of atrocities by ending the public silence on violence and violations. They expose the excesses of the previous political order and so discredit it, aiding in democratic consolidation. In Latin America, where disappearances were more widespread, they revealed the fate of the disappeared and led to exhumations of clandestine mass graves.

This book concentrates on the two main functions of the South African Truth and Reconciliation Commission: truth-telling about the apartheid past and the reconciliation of 'the nation'. The TRC Report published in 1998 on the gross human rights violations of a 34-year period provided a valuable starting point for discussions about moral responsibility during that era. However, the TRC's account of the past was constrained by its excessive legalism[4] and positivist methodology, which obstructed the writing of a coherent socio-political history of apartheid.

The TRC worked with many different understandings of reconciliation, but one came to dominate in the dozens of televised Human Rights Violations hearings held around the country. The religious-redemptive vision of reconciliation stressed public confession by victims, and it created meaning for suffering through a narrative of sacrifice for liberation. Finally, it encouraged the forsaking of revenge. Chapters 5 to 8 examine the consequences of the TRC's version of reconciliation for individual victims who appeared at hearings and others outside the TRC process in the African townships of Johannesburg. In many of these urban townships, political strife was ongoing during the period of fieldwork (1995–8), and it was possible to see the effect of the TRC on these conflicts.

At this point the book begins to shift its focus away from the TRC towards the surrounding social context, in order to evaluate the impact of human rights using ethnographic methods. This approach follows in the tradition of legal anthropology, documenting the moralities, discourses and everyday practices of ordinary citizens when they engage in rights processes and institutions. The TRC's language of 'reconciliation' elicited a variety of local responses and most could be placed in three categories: adductive affinities, where local values and human rights overlap and reinforce one another; pragmatic proceduralism, where survivors participate in human rights procedures to pursue their own agendas and without necessarily taking on human rights values; and relational discontinuities, where local actors are resistant to a restorative vision of human rights and assert a more retributive model of justice.

The variety of responses among the main ANC-supporting township constituency of the TRC demonstrates how human rights institutions are caught in a web of centralizing and pluralizing strategies simultaneously. Human rights talk is a contested discourse which draws popular legal consciousness closer to that of the state, while at the same time encountering resistance from localized organizations and moralities which assert the autonomous right to define and enforce justice. One of the main results of my ethnographic inquiries was the centrality of emotions of vengeance in popular legal consciousness and practices of revenge in local justice institutions. Despite the existence of many rarified national institutions dedicated to protecting human rights (not only the TRC, but also the Gender Commission, the Constitutional Court and the Human Rights Commission), enclaves of revenge controlled by militarized youth and punitive elders continued to shape the character of justice in the townships of South Africa. Because it was guided by a religious-redemptive notion of reconciliation, the TRC was never able to engage with, much less transform, these emotions and structures.

Understanding why the TRC struggled to accomplish its stated mission of 'reconciling the nation' requires a historical explanation which locates the TRC in a history of legal pluralism in South Africa in the twentieth century. The work of the TRC was shaped by the history of state attempts to consolidate the administration of justice and attempts by Africans to preserve control over local institutions of justice and social order. The racialized and dual legal system consolidated in the twentieth century led to a fracturing of justice and moralities which endured after the first multi-racial elections in 1994. The persistence of legal pluralism is closely linked to the historical failure to create a South African nation, reminding us of the concrete links between nation-building and state-building.

Instead of succumbing to state attempts at centralization, urban African residents continued to use local justice institutions to create social order in conditions of urbanization, industrialization and mass migration from rural areas. In the new South Africa, human rights talk was inserted into a context of a massive crime wave, profound social and economic inequality and disillusionment with ineffective criminal justice institutions. Human rights thus emerge as part of a pragmatic policy of state-building and centralization of justice in a milieu where state legality is still often perceived by township residents to be external and alien to the 'community'.

An ethnography of human rights evaluates new institutions of the nation-state 'from below' and compels us to understand them from a position of institutional fragmentation and legal pluralism. In concrete terms, it draws our attention to how human rights institutions and discourses in the 'new South Africa' have often failed to connect with local moralities and justice institutions and thereby transform them. As we come to realize that the new 'culture of human rights' is very thin indeed, we may need to temper celebrations of another seeming triumph for the model of liberal human rights. In a comparative perspective, the new human rights institutions of post-apartheid South Africa are impressive for their ability to shape the public debate on truth and reconciliation. It remains to be seen whether they have altered, over the long term, concrete social practices and discourses of violent conflict, justice and punishment.

The Civic State versus Ethno-Nationalism

The quest to build a 'culture of human rights' in South Africa after the multi-racial elections of 1994 needs to be understood in the context of a sea-change in global politics, and the rise of human rights as the archetypal language of democratic transition. A revived language of liberal democracy became increasingly prevalent in the mid-1980s, and was accentuated by the demise of the former Soviet Bloc and the rise of ethno-nationalist conflict in the Balkans. Since 1990, nearly all transitions from authoritarian rule have adopted the language of human rights and the political model of constitutionalism, especially in Latin America and the new states of Eastern Europe.

The end of the Cold War and the threat of irredentist nationalism led many intellectuals in Europe from a variety of political traditions to promote human rights and a return to the Enlightenment project. Among them, those as recondite as Jürgen Habermas (1992), as erudite as Julia Kristeva (1993) and as media-friendly as Michael Ignatieff (1993) advocated the establishment of constitutionalist states based upon the rule of law. All converge on the view that nations must not be constituted on the basis of race, ethnicity, language or religion, but should be founded instead on a 'community of equal, rights-bearing citizens, united in patriotic attachment to a shared set of political practices and values' (Ignatieff 1993:3–4). In this formulation, human rights are portrayed as the antithesis of nationalist modes of nation-building.

Habermas made one of the most influential constitutionalist statements of the 1990s in his paper 'Citizenship and National Identity' (1992). Here, he sees political change in Eastern Europe as having restored an older Enlightenment political tradition and recaptured the language of rights. Rights must do a great deal in Habermas' formulations: they underwrite an Aristotelian conception of participatory citizenship; they create a barrier to the totalitarian pretensions of states; and they resolve the awkward relationship between citizenship and nationalism:

> The meaning of the term 'nation' thus changed from designating a pre-political entity to something that was supposed to play a constitutive role in defining the political identity of the citizen within a democratic polity. The nation of citizens does not derive its identity from some common ethnic and cultural properties, but rather from the praxis of citizens who actively exercise their civil rights. At this juncture, the republican strand of 'citizenship' *completely parts company* with the idea of belonging to a pre-political community integrated on the basis of descent, a shared tradition and a common language [my emphasis]. (1992:3)

Habermas' aim is to recover a republican tradition of rights from the grasp of the nationalist traditions which once seemed to own it. In his formulation, the rule of law and the 'praxis of citizenship' transcend nationalism in its cultural and tradition-bound form. The allure of rights in the post-Cold War era is that they prescribe basic human rights as an antidote to ethnic nationalism. As Ignatieff states: 'According to the civic nationalist creed, what holds society together is not common roots but law' (1993:4). The concrete practice of claiming citizenship rights creates a political culture which displaces ethnic nationalism and deflects the romantic politics of ethnicity, culture, community or tradition.

Constitutionalist discourse among political commentators within South Africa bears a close resemblance to its European counterpart. South African constitutionalists also see democracy as the antithesis of any sort of nationalist project, which is associated solely with the previous apartheid state. Supporters of constitutionalism argue that an overarching moral unity cannot be achieved through cultural symbols since there is no 'ethnic core' in South Africa around which an overarching ethno-nationalism could be built, even if this were desirable. Instead of creating unity and identity out of cultural nationalism, the state should create a culture of rights based upon an inclusive and democratic notion of citizenship.

Some South African writers have gone a step further than their European colleagues by arguing that human rights should not be a form of nation-building at all. They argue that nation-building is not a guarantee of democracy, and they point to the failure of nation-building in other parts of Africa and the checkered history of nationalism in Europe. Instead of nation-building, they encourage the state to build legitimate and representative state institutions which respect fundamental human rights. Rather than attempting to build a nation, the new regime should build a working constitutional democracy so as to replace destructive nationalist sentiments with constitutional patriotism to a civic state. Fundamental rights and their protection by state institutions are an alternative to nationalism, but they perform similar functions–by creating national reconciliation and a sense of belonging and unity.

National identity unfolds not through ancient symbols but through the practice of claiming basic rights. As Johan Degenaar wrote: 'In one sense we can still speak of the nation as the congruence of culture and power, but now culture has shifted from a communal culture to a democratic culture' (1990:12). South African constitutionalists were generally quite confident that the constitutionalist state would enjoy legitimacy and this would lead to a civic national identity. Over time, as the Bill of Rights, backed up by the legal system and Constitutional Court, protects citizens in a neutral manner, then a national consciousness and sense of belonging will emerge 'naturally' over time.

Finally, human rights have the capacity to resist the limitation of rights to any one group of people; that is, they are seen as pan-ethnic, and irreducible to forms of ethnic particularism. The individualism of human rights chimes with the Charterist non-racialism professed by the ruling African National Congress[7] which won the 1994 and 1999 elections. Both political philosophies assume South Africa to be a society of individual citizens, not a society of racial communities with group representation and minority rights.

REFERENCES

Davis, Dennis 1998 "Democracy and Integority: making sense of the Constitution." *South African Journal on Human Rights* 14: 127–145.

Degenaar, Johan J. 1990 "Nations and Nationalism: The Myth of the South African Nation." *Occasional Paper* no. 40, IDASA, Mowbray.

Dworkin, Ronald 1977 *Taking Rights Seriously*. London: Duckworth.

Fagan, Anton 1995 "In Defense of the Obvious: Ordinary Language and the Identification of Constitutional Rules." *South African Journal on Human Rights* 11: 545–570.

Habermas, Jürgen 1992 "Citizenship and National Identity: Some Reflections on the Future of Europe," *Praxis International* 12(2): 1–19.

Ignatieff, Michael 1993 *Blood and Belonging: Journeys into the New Nationalism*. London: Chaffo and Windus/BBC Books.

Kristeva, Julia 1993 *Nation without Nationalism*. Leon S. Roudicz, trans. New York: Columbia University Press.

Truth and Reconciliation Commission of South Africa 1998 Report, vols. 1–5. Cape Town: Juta and Co. Also on internet site http://www.stuths.org.za/

C.   Enforceable Rules Inside and Outside the Formal Law

General Introduction

In an encyclopedia article on the sociology of law Philip Selznick alludes to the foundations of a legal order: "The special interest of sociology in these matters rests on the basic assumption that law and legal institutions both affect and are affected by the social conditions that surround them" (1968, vols 9–10:50). He conceives of law as "contributing to the fulfillment of social needs and aspirations" of a society (p. 50). With Philippe Nonet, Selznick wrote a book about "responsive law" (2001). In this conception, law can be consciously fashioned to respond to social demands, change society, and solve social problems. Such a "social engineering," view of the law, especially of legislation, appeared in the work of many writers on jurisprudence in the twentieth century. Law in this light is treated as distinguishable from the "social conditions" that surround it.

However, anthropologists tend not to approach law in this way. In an anthropological approach law does not appear distinct from social context, but as a part of it, whether the anthropologist approves of the observed legal system or not, and whether the population submits willingly or not. Anthropologists are trained observers loaded with some comparative knowledge. They also carry a library of useful conceptual frameworks in their heads. The primary objective of their fieldwork is to "tell it the way it is," and to understand the local logic for what they see. This set of intellectual premises makes it possible to inquire broadly into the part that law and legal institutions play in a society at a particular time. Whether the anthropologist also approves or disapproves of what he/she sees, and whether that evaluation is expressed, varies with the individual and the situation. The old ideal used to be that the social scientist should be an "objective" observer, not a judgmental one. That ideal no longer has the force and following it once had, and social critique has become a central preoccupation of some anthropologists.

In liberal societies, emphasizing the dichotomy between law and society appeals to optimistic professional reformers of law. Since the legal seems to define a distinct domain of control, it presents itself as a favored location for launching constructive social change. Freedom of expression empowers activism along these lines. Some anthropologists engaged with projects of social reform speak out, at the very least to the extent that they take a stance in what they write. Human rights concepts and institutions have given them encouragement. However, other anthropologists feel obliged to be wary of political commentary when they are precariously situated guests in a foreign country. Others do not find the complex and globally interdependent situations they observe appropriate for simple advocacy.

Should law be inspected as a repository of generally held ideas and social values? Not necessarily. The law and its institutions may represent the interests of only one sector of the population. The field of anthropology contains much background knowledge of such instances: law in colonial societies and in other authoritarian regimes, to say nothing of knowledge of the mandatory in the domain of corporate groups, of organized religion, or of ethnic practice. It seems evident that in many settings the rules made by an authority are imposed on sectors of a population which does not necessarily share all of the same objectives. The law cannot be assumed to be the essential expression of a homogeneous culture.

Nor is the law the repository of all forms of mandatory rules. The rules and institutions attached to governments are only one category of a vastly more extensive set of sites producing rules and obligations. In a particular locale, anthropologists ask such things as: how and by whom are particular obligations generated, what are the sources of their authority, how they are explained and enforced, and when and how and by whom they are obeyed or violated. Behavior and practices loom large, and so do the ideas that people have about what they are doing. What are the options and choices and restrictions that shape what people can do? How does their range of choice intersect with the obligatory requirements of the institutions of their society?

In our society, rules made by legislatures and enforced by the state are only one piece of the existing system of obligatory norms. There are many other ways in which enforceable rules are created, some of which intersect with the formal system. Contract, for example, is one. In the American legal system, you may hire a builder to construct a garage for you, and you and he decide on the terms, the design, the deadline for construction, and the price and timing of payment. If he does not do the work it is understood that he will not be paid. And if he does the work and you do not pay as agreed, he may sue you. The courts can be mobilized to enforce the terms of the contract, or to oblige a party to compensate for non-performance. In this matter one set of rules is devised by the contracting parties, but the state, in the form of its courts, entering the case at the behest of one of the parties, though attentive to the terms of their agreement, has its own rules as well, and "applies" them.

Beyond the realm of contract, many obligatory rules are made in non-government organizations. This is as true of industrial companies as of universities. In general, such non-official rules are socially enforced. Members of the social milieu must conform or get out. If people want to work for or belong to the organizations in question, or want to do business with particular people, the privilege of doing so may depend on adhering to the norms that have been set. An organization can expel a member, and a business person may not want to do business with someone who does not play the game. Thus the capacity for enforceable rule making is not found in the courts alone, nor in the legislature, nor in administrative agencies, nor in the police, but also in myriad unofficial sites of policy-making. Norm setting and enforcing is found in many legitimate social settings outside of government, and is also found in illegal organizations. Drug distributors have their rules and modes of enforcement as do the sellers of forged documents such as passports and social security numbers. The social and legal implications of this multiplicity of arenas of organized action have long been recognized as a major factor in the social milieu in which formal law operates.

In anthropology, when a multiplicity of enforceable rule systems operate concurrently this circumstance has been called "legal pluralism." An example would be a state which has a secular national legal system to address most legal issues, yet simultaneously, has Islamic law courts to deal with all family law matters. These days the same term, "legal pluralism," is often used more broadly to describe the multiplicity of formal and informal obligatory rules that can co-exist in a variety of social fields. This use of the term emphasizes the multiple *sources* of binding rules, and neglects a more sociologically significant dimension: the compelling characteristics of the various social milieu in which where they are operative.

A definitional debate has arisen in connection with the idea of legal pluralism. Some social scientists and lawyers treat all enforceable norms as "law" (see Griffiths, 1986). Others continue to emphasize the distinction between an official legal system with the force of government behind it (laws) and unofficial locations of rule making and enforcement ("informal" but enforceable rules). Thus legal pluralism is a term which can be analytically blurring. It can allude to such things as the international context where there are different national legal systems operating in the same arena, it can refer to state law and federal law in a federal system, to colonial law and customary law in a colonial situation, to religious law where there are a multiplicity of officially recognized religions, to ethnic laws where ethnic groups are officially recognized to have some legal autonomy, and so on.

Pluralism was first applied to cultural differences in colonial situations (Furnivall, 1948). It then was reconceived as emphasizing the difference in the legal systems that applied to colonial and indigenous populations (Hooker, 1975). Sally Merry, in an influential article, speaks of this as "the old pluralism" (1988). According to her the "new" pluralism is the one that packs official and unofficial rule making in the same basket. That broad application of the term is now in wide use. For a detailed and illuminating discussion of the controverisal issues that surround this terminology, including the political haze that envelops it, see Benda-Beckmann (1997).

A prominent area for research in recent decades has been the intentional interdigitation between official government law, and non-official organizations. In the papers in this part, we see Sally Merry's observations on the way courts in Hawaii referred some of the cases before them to non-government entities for resolution, interlocking the two systems. Jane Kaufman Winn tells us that small businesses in Taiwan would rather not use the official law to collect the payments of debtors. Instead, they use theatrically enacted threats of force. Susan Bibler Coutin describes the Sanctuary movement in the early 1980s. It gave aid and sanctuary to escaping Salvadorans and Guatemalans whom they classified as legitimate refugees, while the

US government considered them illegal aliens. Janet Gilboy describes the work of immigration inspectors at various points of entry into the US. Her concern is with the way the inspectors generate the criteria according to which they classify foreign travellers as suspect or non-suspect persons. Thus, this group of articles gives a small taste of the intermeshing between government-backed law and the mandatory element in "informal" social fields. This approach acknowledges the composite nature of society and gives full attention to its multiple sites of control.

REFERENCES

Benda-Beckmann, Franz von, 1997 Citizens, Strangers and Indigenous Peoples: Conceptual Politics and Legal Pluralism. *Law and Anthropology International Yearbook for Legal Anthropology*, vol. 9. The Hague, Boston, and London: Martinus Nijhoff.

Furnivall, J., 1948 *Colonial Policy and Practice*. London: Cambridge University Press.

Griffiths, J., 1986 What Is Legal Pluralism? *Journal of Legal Pluralism and Unofficial Law* 24.

Hooker, M., 1975 *Legal Pluralism*. Oxford: Oxford University Press.

Moore, Sally F., 2000 [1978] Law and Social Change: The Semi-Autonomous Social Field as an Appropriate Subject of Study. *Law as Process*. 2nd edition. Oxford: James Currey, for the International African Institute.

Merry, Sally, 1988 Legal Pluralism. *Law and Society Review* 22: 869–896.

Nonet, Philippe, and Philip Selznick, 2001 *Law and Society in Transition, Toward Responsive Law*. New Brunswick: Transaction Publishers.

Selznick, Philip, 1968 The Sociology of Law. *International Encyclopedia of the Social Sciences*, pp. 50–58. New York and London: The Macmillan Company and the Free Press, Collier Macmillan.

21

Rights, Religion, and Community: Approaches to Violence Against Women in the Context of Globalization

Sally Engle Merry

Introduction: Three Approaches to Violence Against Women

In this article Sally Merry examines the response to violence against women developed by three non-governmental but institutional entities in the town of Hilo in Hawaii. The research on which it is founded covered the period 1991–2000. One of the institutional entities was a "feminist batterer intervention program" (Alternatives to Violence) to which the court referred certain cases. The court had a secular, rights-based approach grounded in the criminalization of violence in which the feminists concurred. A second institution was a Pentecostal Church, New Hope, which considered the solution to wife beating to be found in spiritual experiences and the power of God. The third institution was a Native Hawaiian group which relied on a putatively traditional ritual-like procedure called *ho'oponopono* to bring the values of family and community to bear on the discordant scenes they addressed. The court referred cases to all three entities as an alternative to its own remedies.

Merry summarizes the history of these three institutions and the transformations they underwent over time in their ways of addressing violence against women. This brings forward the major large-scale themes of Merry's paper: globalization, modernization, the technology of self-formation, and the growing orientation to psychotherapeutic explanations and remedies. The argument she makes is that these apparently local changes are linked to transformations occurring in many other places. The further she goes from her ethnographic

From Sally Engle Merry, "Rights, Religion and Community: Approaches to Violence Against Women in the Context of Globalization," *Law and Society Review* 35(1). (2001), pp. 39–49, 53–60, 62–3, 65–6, 68, 70, 72–5, 77–9, 81–8.

observations the more she moves into the interpretation of local events as exemplifications of world processes.

She argues that each institution was anti-modern in its beginnings, the feminist movement being anti-patriarchal, the Pentecostal Church emphasizing its separation from, and antipathy to the secular world, and the Native Hawaiians considering themselves more genuinely family and community oriented than "modern society." She speaks of each these as embodying "a radical critique of modernity" (p. 42). One might raise the question what is meant by "modernity" in this context. Certainly, all three institutions were critical of key aspects of the world around them and tried to distinguish themselves from the larger society.

The argument offered is that these "local struggles among gender violence initiatives in the small town of Hilo, Hawaii, are an instance of a more general transnational competition among rights, religion, and community" (p. 46). Yet, Merry sees in the willingness of each of these groups to adopt "similar technologies of personal transformation based on the ideal of a self that can choose not to be violent and can understand his/her own feelings" an indication of the "homogenizing face of globalization" (p. 46). She speaks of this tendency as caused by institutionalization, funding and the market" which produces homogeneity "subtly colonizing apparently culturally diverse projects and organizations" (p. 46). But however grand the scale of her interpretation, she confesses that "I have not examined to what extent similar processes are occurring globally" (p. 46). So we have two statements, a provocative one by the author of a set of strongly asserted interpretations about globalism, followed by a confession by the same author that comparisons have not actually been investigated.

One might note that this work on the way institutions deal with cases of violence against women is in some respects a continuation of Merry's study of Alternative Dispute Resolution in the USA where courts referred some of their case load to other agencies for resolution through mediation (Merry 1990). In that work Merry also noted the bias toward psychological explanations and solutions and spoke of mediation as "a process of cultural domination exercised by the law over people who bring their personal problems to the lower courts" (1990:9).

Merry's interesting suggestions in this paper and in her earlier study are made in a challenging manner. She links local, highly specific material to putative large-scale trends. There are some bits of evidence about the large scale, but the general substantiation of the connections would be another project. What could be argued is that the vocabulary and psychologically founded ideas relating to a conscious remaking of the self do not in any way undermine the other tenets of the ideology of the three groups. Thus they can conform to the new remedies without giving up ther fundamental creeds. Thus when the courts resort to these "informal" resolutions of cases of wife beating, they are assured of working in a contemporarily acceptable mode. Whether the homogeneity of approach is more nominal than actual is not as certain as that the forms adopted have a great deal in common.

S.F.M.

REFERENCE

Merry, Sally, 1990 *Getting Justice and Getting Even*. Chicago: Chicago University Press.

Merry, *Violence Against Women*

In order to understand the differences among these competing models, I studied three approaches to gender violence – one based on rights, one on religion, and, one on community – coexisting in Hilo, a small town in Hawai'i. I focused on a feminist batterer intervention program (Alternatives to Violence), a Pentecostal Christian church, and an indigenous Hawaiian form of family problem-solving called ho'-oponopono. The first is a statefunded social service agency, the second a large church, and the third a network of practitioners offering services for drug treatment and other social problems, as well as providing informal help to Native Hawaiian families. The courts refer cases of gender violence to all three, although mostly to the first.

I was intrigued by how differently each group defines the problem of gender violence and its elimination and how differently each envisages ideal gender relationships. The first, based on feminism and a concept of rights, foregrounds women's safety and advocates an egalitarian gender order. Women who are in danger are encouraged to separate from their partners. Husbands and wives are taught to negotiate decisions with the promise of increased trust, love, and sexual pleasure for men who refrain from violence. This approach criminalizes the batterer and encourages the victim to think of herself as having rights not to be beaten regardless of what she does.

The second, growing out of conservative Christian notions of salvation, healing, and the authority of Biblical texts, uses a process called scriptural counseling based on Biblical quotations. This church stresses gender complementarity and firmly resists divorce. The ideal family is under the authority of the husband, who is in turn under the authority of God. The Christian model teaches women to submit to their husbands, to turn away wrath with gentle words, and to pray to dislodge demons that hide in strongholds created by resentment, grudges, and hostility.

The third, ho'oponopono, which descends from an ancient Native Hawaiian family problem-solving process, recently revalorized as part of a broader renaissance in Native Hawaiian values and cultural practices, is based on concepts of repentance, forgiveness, and reconciliation. It emphasizes the family and the community's responsibility for conflict. Though the process seeks reunification of a family experiencing conflict, an unrepentant person can be exiled from the family altogether. In this model, ideally, husband and wife should treat each other with mutual respect. The Native Hawaiian process emphasizes the value of every person as a child of God and the importance of treating others in one's family with respect and forgiveness for wrongdoing. The second and the third models are much more similar to each other than either is to the secular feminist rights-based program...

I soon discovered that each was part of a transnational movement. As I traced the formation of each group and the development of its conceptions of gender violence, I realized that each drew on an imported set of ideas about violence and gender, translated into the local context. Global feminism, the worldwide spread of Christian fundamentalism, and the global movement for self-determination and cultural rejuvenation of indigenous people inspired these local groups. The process of appropriation and translation differed, of course. Ho'oponopono, for example, is originally a traditional Hawaiian process, recently infused with ideas from psychiatry and alternative dispute resolution. In contrast, the founders of the church and the feminist program came from the mainland United States and worked with local people to develop a locally rooted institution.

As I examined this local struggle, impressed by the differences among these groups in their ideas about marriage, family, and violence as well as law and religion, I noticed a surprising similarity in their technologies of personal transformation. All emphasized making choices and holding people accountable, knowing and control-ling feelings, and building self-esteem for those who batter as well as for their victims. In all three settings, men and women were told they could make their own choices about how they feel, how they view situations, and how they respond to them. They were encouraged to be responsible for their choices. Clients were given names for feelings and encouraged to recognize these feelings as a way of managing them. They were encouraged to develop self-esteem. Clients were taught to think of themselves as worthwhile because of some identity – as a Christian, a native person, or a man or a woman – rather than in terms of more conventional understandings of achievement, class, status, or power. There are differences: Self-esteem because God created all humans and finds them worthy is different from self-esteem because one is Native Hawaiian or because one is a woman with rights. But, despite their wide ideological divergence, all approaches focused on the entrepreneurial creation of the self. At the heart of the competition among rights, religion, and community was a shared practice of self-creation: a technology associated with the creation of the modern subject (see Rose 1989; Collier et al. 1995; Foucault 1980 a and b) . . .

The convergence on techniques of forming the modern self is particularly ironic, since the initial impetus for each of these efforts was a radical critique of modernity. The feminists argued against a modernist patriarchy; the church against a secular, materialist world from which it felt profoundly alienated by the expectation of an imminent Second Coming; the Native Hawaiians against an assimilationist modern-ity that suppresses indigenous cultural and spiritual life. Why then did such disparate approaches converge on similar technologies of the self?

I think that, in establishing a program and gathering clients, each was driven in a different way to adopt self-management as a solution to the problem of gender violence. The need for financial support—for clients or members—led these organiza-tions to professionalize their leadership, tone down their rhetoric, and develop reform programs that seemed reasonable to their leaders and funders. As they sought to protect women from male violence, leaders and funders alike turned to psychothera-peutic techniques of self-management as familiar strategies for accomplishing this goal. They imported apparently successful ideas and practices from other parts of their transnational networks. The market was a major force . . .

By adopting these technologies, all three approaches contributed to the absorption of marginal populations into the project of modernity even as they simultaneously, and importantly, contributed to the protection of women.

Based on the stories they tell about their lives, it appears that many of those in all three settings are afflicted with unmanageable rage; have recurring difficulties with alcohol and drugs; and face educational deficits. They are also people who have trouble controlling their violence.

Thus, those who end up in such self-management programs have failed to consti-tute themselves according to the demands of modernity. They are in some ways living outside the disciplinary confines of modern society. The technologies they are taught seek to protect women from male violence but also to produce better workers and citizens. These technologies are resisted, of course. This is a major redefinition of masculinity for many perpetrators and is energetically challenged. Men brag about their sexual prowess, their desirability to women, and their overall attractiveness and joke about controlling women and continuing to batter them. Women sometimes turn down the offer of a rights-based self, protected by the law, because they hope that their partners will change on their own or because they are afraid to go forward with the prosecution and do not expect that the courts will protect them. This is not a smooth and uncontested domain of personal transformation for its practitioners or for its subjects...

The criminalization of gender violence similarly uses rights to define who belongs by punishing those who batter and by conferring rights on their victims. This new allocation of rights to women not to be hit is routinely resisted by men who say they were simply acting as they always had. Many fail to appear in court or for the batterer intervention program, or drop out quickly. And many try to persuade their partners to drop the charges, thus resisting the legal regime that defines them as criminals. Legal practitioners may also resist this use of rights to criminalize batterers by failing to impose sentences, failing to punish those who do not participate in mandated programs, and allowing perpetrators to select treatment programs that will not track their participation and report back to the court...

In sum, the local struggles among gender violence initiatives in the small town of Hilo, Hawai'i, are an instance of a more general transnational competition among rights, religion, and community. Despite these radically different ideologies, groups in Hilo adopt similar technologies of personal transformation based on the ideal of a self that can choose not to be violent and can understand his/her own feelings. These changes tailor the individual to fit into the modern nation and economy.

Despite the ideological contestation among rights, religion, and community in global society, there may be a growing similarity in technologies for producing the self. It is in the technologies of self-creation rather than in the ideologies of marriage, gender, and family that it is possible to see the homogenizing face of globalization...

Gender Violence in Windward Hawai'i

Hilo is a small port city of about 45,000, serving a sprawling agricultural region and providing a hub for governmental, educational, medical, and retail services, as well as some tourism. Although the town has a university campus, a hospital, and the county government and courts, it is also home to a large population of poor people, both homeless and unemployed town dwellers and people surviving in remote agricultural areas by hunting, fishing, and farming illegal as well as legal crops. The dominant ethnic groups in the town are descendants of Japanese, European, Filipino, Portuguese, Korean, Chinese, Puerto Rican, South Pacific Islander, Mexican, and Native Hawaiian ancestors. Extensive intermarriage means that most people have mixed ancestries and that identities are the product of social processes and self-identification as well as imposition. The large majority of native-born residents view themselves as "local," a culturally mixed identity that is associated with speaking the English creole called pidgin. The region experienced colonial processes in the 19th century that have marginalized and impoverished many of

the Native Hawaiian residents of the area (see Merry 2000). The intensive missionary work of the 19th century left a strong legacy of Protestant Christianity, particularly among the Native Hawaiian population.

In the late 19th and early 20th centuries, the entire windward coast of the island of
Hawai'i, where Hilo is located, was converted to sugar plantations manned by sugar
workers from Europe and Asia. The children and grandchildren of these plantation
workers are now prominent in education, government, and the judiciary. The plantations are now disappearing, replaced by massive unemployment and a new economy
of tourism. This is a postindustrial, postplantation society. There is now a significant
population engaged in the production of marijuana on fertile and well-watered soils.
There was always a population on the fringes of the plantation economy: families
living on the beaches, people who survive by hunting, fishing, and occasional construction jobs, along with welfare, and people who supplement their incomes by
growing marijuana. Many rural and some urban residents share a culture of guns,
drugs, fishing, and hunting; for some portion wife beating is a natural way of life.

The number of cases of violence against women in the courts in Hilo has expanded
dramatically over the past 25 years, particularly during the early 1990s. Although
the population of the county surrounding this town has doubled over the past 25
years, the number of calls to the police for help has grown eight times, the number of
requests for protective orders has jumped from one or two a year to 710 in 1998,
and the number of arrests for abuse of a family or household member has gone from
zero to more than 1,200 reports to the police and 855 cases in the courts in 1998. In
East (windward) Hawai'i, there were 499 temporary restraining orders in 1994, but
by mid-2000 an estimated annual total of 556. Criminal spouse abuse cases were
also at record-high levels in mid-2000, with an estimated 548 for East Hawai'i,
based on the numbers from the first half of the year. The dramatic increase in the
number of court cases of wife beating probably reflects an increase in battering, but
it also shows a major increase in help-seeking from the law. In most cases, the victim
has taken the initiative to call the police for help or to ask the Family Court for a
restraining order. If there is an arrest, the victim must usually provide evidence for
the prosecution. Thus, this burgeoning caseload indicates a new understanding of
the meaning of gender violence as a crime and a willingness by victims to complain
to the police and to seek restraining orders.

This research covers changes in the feminist violence control program between 1991
and 2000 and the simultaneous shifts in the church approach and the Native Hawaiian
program. It is based on ethnographic observations of the feminist programs for men
and for women as well as ho' oponopono and church services. I also conducted
extensive interviews with practitioners in each process as well as with referral sources,
such as the probation department and courts. Additionally, I observed both civil and
criminal court proceedings, the violence control program, the probation office and
prosecutor's office, and interviewed perpetrators and victims. . . .

Rights: The Alternatives to Violence Program

. . . But in 1986, the Family Crisis Shelter imported the newly developed Duluth model
as the basis for a program called Alternatives to Violence (ATV), which included a

batterer intervention program and a women's support group. The Director discovered that funds were more readily available for retraining men than for providing shelter services for women and children. The judiciary funded the ATV programs for batterers and paid staff to assist victims filing restraining order (TRO) petitions. ATV funding between 1992 and 1994 was relatively high, with approximately $700,000 for about 20 employees, almost all with Judiciary Department contracts, with a small amount of support from United Way (Chandler and Yu 1994: 102–6)...

In the late 1980s and early 1990s, the judiciary enthusiastically supported the program and referred all the battering cases to it. It was the only non-prison option for batterers in town. In the years 1992–3, the program reported serving 647 clients referred by the judiciary (Chandler and Yu 1994: 124). The high point of funding was 1994. By 2000, the program was still supported by the judiciary and United Way, but was experiencing financial shortfalls. As early as 1993, the judiciary was asking questions about its effectiveness. In 1993, it funded a research study to investigate the effectiveness of the men's programs statewide (Chandler and Yu 1994). This study found that program statistics were generally sparse, reflecting the press of work and lack of staffing. The difficulty of gathering recidivism data from police reports was insurmountable (Chandler and Yu 1994: 17). In the only program where some tracking of cases was possible, it appeared that there were fewer rearrests of ATV graduates than of those not attending ATV (Chandler and Yu 1994: 2).

The Later Years: Psychotherapeutic Feminism

In the mid 1990s, the ATV program changed substantially for a variety of reasons, which eroded its privileged status within the judiciary, its major funding source. It had expanded into a large and complex organization with two shelters and two batterer intervention programs and an annual budget of well over one million dollars. The Executive Director continued to hire staff without professional degrees for the shelters, which some members of the board and staff thought was a mistake, claiming that some of these people were incompetent. The early egalitarian feminist organization was gradually replaced by a more hierarchical structure. A series of incidents in the early 1990s, involving accusations of civil rights violations by some staff and findings of "fiscal improprieties" and charges of theft against the Executive Director, led to her resignation in 1993 and to her replacement by a professional Executive Director, with a Master's degree (*Hawaii Tribune-Herald*, 26 Mar. 1995, 1). Several of the experienced facilitators and the original ATV Director also left, some setting up competing programs, with the claim that the new ATV was no longer feminist. By that time, there were about six alternative batterer intervention programs in town, as well as private therapists offering anger management programs. Although ATV still received judiciary funding, it was no longer the only option for batterer intervention, and lawyers were becoming skilled in helping their clients avoid ATV. The shift from feminist activism to service delivery is common for domestic violence programs (see Schechter 1982 ...)

In 1998, the program for men was substantially redirected toward a new model, called Healthy Realization. It was first introduced to the staff by a psychotherapist from Honolulu, who provided a day of training at a staff retreat. This is a more supportive approach to batterer retraining, which encourages men to build self-esteem. It draws heavily on conceptions of being mentally healthy and focuses on improving a person's level of psychological functioning. Men are no longer challenged and told they are criminals but are asked how they feel and what they think is good about themselves. Facilitators try to emphasize positive features. Discussions are less didactic. Participants are far less often required to fill out anger and control logs, a teaching technique that asks men to write down incidents in which they have been angry and examine why they behaved that way, what their underlying beliefs were, and how they could have acted differently. Facilitators report that the men dislike this task. Instead, they encourage the men to think about themselves in positive ways while they teach them to recognize and avoid their violence.

Charting the Change

... Since the late 1990s, ATV has shifted from seeing gender violence largely as the result of oppression to viewing it as a characteristic of individual psychological functioning. In place of a theory that battering is the product of patriarchy, the program sees battering as the result of low self-esteem and an inability to understand feelings in a society that allows men to express their self-doubt violently. The new approach is part of a broader psychotherapeutic theory of human behavior, widespread on the US mainland as well as globally. Program strategies focus on building men's self-esteem and looking for their strengths as well as communicating that battering is wrong and that men and women are equal. The analysis of structures of domination has become far less prominent...

This examination of changes in the ideology and practices of this batterer intervention program reveals the importance of ideas imported from the US mainland and, more broadly, those such as the Duluth model and psychotherapeutic approaches to change. Because it was pressured to change, ATV has lost some of its critical edge. Now, its strategies increasingly focus on feelings: on feeling good about oneself, on deciding how to act, and on learning how to get along. Patriarchy has moved to the background and has been replaced by theories about how children need to be protected from the violence of their mothers as well as their fathers so that they do not grow up to be violent adults.

Religion: The New Hope Christian Fellowship

Pentecostal Beginnings

Religion is one of the major alternatives to the feminist, rights-based approach to gender violence. The New Hope Christian Fellowship in Hilo belongs to the Foursquare Gospel Church, one of the rapidly growing churches in the burgeoning Christian Pentecostal movement. New Hope is part of a global Pentecostal movement that has expanded enormously since its origins in the early 20th century. Pentecostalism emphasizes direct experience of the Spirit through ecstatic forms such as speaking in tongues, trance, vision, healing, dreams, and dance and offers the millennial hope of a Second Coming and new age (Cox 1995: 82). Spiritual and physical healing is very important. Cox attributes Pentecostalism's success to its promise of racial equality and a deeper form of religious experience. It has prospered by criticizing the materialism of modern society and suggesting an alternative, a message that appeals to the poor and disenfranchised, those who could imagine a radically new order only through the actions of a loving God. Pentecostals resist organization and spurn the Protestant denominations, claiming a spiritual space outside conventional society (Blumhofer 1993b: 12–14, 88, 160)...

Healing Gender Violence

... New Hope does not put a major emphasis on gender violence, but it has expressed more interest than many similar churches. In 1994, New Hope Hilo was regularly providing counseling for men sent by the court and was working with the county to set up an anger management program, with court referrals...

New Hope blends Pentecostal ideas of ritual healing and driving out demonic forces with the burgeoning field of Christian family counseling. This is a national movement that blends fundamentalist Christian beliefs and psychotherapy. Most of the books on marriage and family life for sale at New Hope and used in pastoral and marriage counseling courses at the Foursquare college in Los Angeles, the Life Bible College, are written by counselors, psychotherapists, psychologists, and doctors who are also conservative Christians...

New Hope shares the view of other Pentecostal churches that healing is a battle between the power of God and Satan. I interviewed several pastoral counselors at New Hope who told me that they often deal with violence in marital relationships and usually use both Christian ideas of demonic influence and psychotherapy to help couples. They see anger as the result of demons in a person's body and the devil, residing in the flesh, as the ultimate source of sin....

It is sometimes necessary to expel the demons. This process, called "deliverance," requires prayer, reading Scripture, and renewing the mind, as well as commanding the demons to leave (see Csordas 1994). In extreme cases, exorcism is necessary. Deliverance requires eliminating the stronghold where a demon lives and opening the space to the Holy Spirit to prevent the demons from returning. Bitterness and unforgiveness create strongholds for evil spirits. If a person is not repentant and able to remove these strongholds, even demons that are rebuked and driven away will come back....

Thus, the Pentecostal spiritual war against demons lodged in the flesh has joined with imported psychotherapeutic concepts of self-esteem, learning about feelings, and making choices. In general, anger is understood as the result of strongholds of demons rather than as the product of patriarchy or inequality and oppression. The Native Hawaiian pastor has taken a different path, drawing on ideas from the Hawaiian sovereignty movement.

Community: The Ho'oponopono Process

Indigenous Beginnings to the 1970s

An indigenous Hawaiian problem-solving process seems as if it should be quite distinct. And, indeed, much of its underlying philosophy and understanding of human behavior and the importance of the community is very different from ATV or New Hope. On the other hand, it also has moved toward incorporating more-psychotherapeutic forms of constituting the self, just as ATV and New Hope have done. Ho'oponopono is a Native Hawaiian process for resolving family problems through repentance and forgiveness. It is a deeply spiritual process that has been used for a long time in Hawaiian communities. It cures or prevents physical illness, depression, or anxiety by discovering the cause of the person's trouble, resolving interpersonal problems, and untangling or freeing agents from transgressions by apology and forgiveness (Boggs and Chun 1990: 125–6)....

The Development of Ho'oponopono in the 1980s and the 1990s

The major impetus behind the revival of ho'oponopono in the 1980s and 1990s was the work of a psychiatrist, a psychologist, several social workers, and Mary Kawena Pukui, as the Culture Committee of the Queen Lili'uokalani Children's Center (QLCC), a social service agency for Native Hawaiian children established by the Queen. This committee met weekly from 1963 until at least 1970 to discuss ways of building bridges between "Western" ideas of mental health and Hawaiian ones (Pukui et al. 1972). Although the project was an effort to reinterpret Hawaiian beliefs in psychological terms, it was also a way to validate Hawaiian beliefs rather than to dismiss them....

During the 1980s and 1990s, there were also efforts to develop ho'oponopono as an alternative to the criminal justice system. In the 1980s, the Neighborhood Justice Center in Honolulu suggested ho'oponopono as an alternative to mediation (Shook 1985). However, it is different from mediation, which focuses more on compart-mentalizing problems and less on a holistic approach (Meyer and Davis 1994). In 1994, the Native Hawaiian Bar Association (NHBA), concerned with the rising population of incarcerated Native Hawaiians, set up a program to divert some family court cases out of the judicial system (Meyer and Davis 1994: 5). Encouraged by an enthusiastic group of family court judges, the NHBA sponsored the training of a cadre of ho'oponopono practitioners for court and Neighborhood Justice Center referrals by experts taught originally by Pukui. This included attorneys, people from the Neighborhood Justice Center, and from the community. One radical group protesting prison construction in 2000 suggested ho'oponopono as an alternative to incarceration for Native Hawaiians.

Ho'oponopono is now being incorporated into a burgeoning global movement to promote forms of restorative justice, many of which are based on indigenous peoples' judicial mechanisms...

Confronting Gender Violence Through Ho'oponopono

Ho'oponopono works by gathering the family together to pray and ask the help of the Akua, or Gods, to try to get to the heart of the problem and to move the discussion through recognizing the problem, repentance, forgiveness, and reconcili-ation. It is basically a family process, under the leadership of a family elder or leader. If a person refuses to repent or go along with the group's views, he will be evicted from the family....

This haku's philosophy is that everyone has the capacity to make choices and make changes. God has given every person wisdom, intelligence, knowledge, and compassion, and it is up to the person what he or she does with it. Childhood stresses, deprivations, and foster homes are certainly difficult, but regardless of how people grow up, they can make something of themselves. They are all children of God. The haku assists God rather than making changes happen herself; she helps the person to discover herself. Clearly, there are parallels between ho'oponopono and the understanding of personal transformation within New Hope. Both are spiritual processes that rely on the power of God and will wait until the person is ready. Neither expects transformation in six months.

Courts and probation officers sometimes referred Native Hawaiians in battering situations to ho'oponopono, either along with the issuance of restraining orders or after some form of punishment.

This haku admonishes men to love and care for, not abuse, women. She will confront a man about his violence against his wife. If a person is holding a grudge, she will tell him/her he has to let it go. If a person is being violent, she will point out the risk that the other person will leave. She does not stress keeping marriages together at all costs but recommends that a woman take a violent man back only with conditions. But she emphasizes that the woman has to be ready to stop fighting as well. Change has to come from the people themselves, and may take several months. This haku feels that she works through God, not by herself, and that God gives her the insight and wisdom. At the same time, she clearly makes people responsible for their own actions and lets the consequences of their actions encourage them to change.

Thus, ho'oponopono has developed and changed dramatically over the past 25 years, moving into new areas of social services and political movements for indigenous peoples. It is rooted in Native Hawaiian conceptions of healing and spirituality, but has also contributed significantly to the transnational movement toward restorative justice. It retains its core features of process and naming, but has incorporated ideas from psychotherapy and dispute resolution. Although ho'oponopono grounds its legitimacy in early Hawaiian practices and ideas of the family and community, much of its current form represents a joining of ideas from mental health, dispute resolution, and restorative justice, many of which have mainland United States or transnational origins. . . .

There are also tensions between courts and ho' oponopono. Mandating defendants to ho'oponopono violates the principle that a person seeks out the process when he/she is ready. Handling the problem as a dispute resolution case referred from the court means reading case files and dealing with people who are strangers rather than family members. There may be pressure to seek a resolution in a limited period of time rather than waiting until the parties are ready. Reporting back to the court is antithetical to the spirit of ho' oponopono. The unwillingness to hold clients legally accountable makes some judges reluctant to use it. But in ho' oponopono, a violent person who cannot change will be 'oki, or cut from the family, a serious penalty. Feminist leaders of the battered women's movement worry about using ho' oponopono in violence cases because they think men are not held morally accountable for their violence, a view also expressed by a prosecutor in Hilo who said that she never allows defendants to use ho'oponopono.

[. . .]

Conclusion

This comparison shows that the three approaches to violence against women based on rights, religion, and community start from very different cultural places. They began from sharply different conceptions of gender and marriage and ideas about personal transformation. The rights-based approach grew out of a feminist critique of patriarchy and the role of violence in maintaining that system of power. It relies extensively on criminalization to protect women and to show that society considers violence unacceptable. Rational participatory discussions of batterers' beliefs about male privilege are used to teach new values and emphasize that violence does not pay. The religious approach began from a critique of secular society and its lack of attention to spiritual meanings and delineated an alternative social order articulated in the Bible and based on religious experience and a hierarchical family order. Transformation comes through spiritual experiences and the power of God. The community approach resituates the individual within a caring community of family members who work toward reconciliation and forgiveness, with the understanding that genuine repentance should be accepted but failure to repent can mean exile. Thus, there is a fundamental divide between spiritual and secular approaches. Both New Hope and ho' oponopono rely heavily on the power of spirituality to effect change, while ATV depends on the law and its conceptions of rights. Each of these programs deals with relatively marginal people, typically economically vulnerable and relatively uneducated. Although not all Native Hawaiians fit into this category, this is a population that, overall, stands at the bottom of the state's statistics on health, education, and well-being.

Despite these different beginnings, each of these programs has adopted a similar set of technologies of self-formation. As we have seen, all have drawn on psycho-therapeutic approaches that rely on understanding feelings, making choices, and building self-esteem. There are differences in how this is done, of course. All three seek to build self-esteem on the basis of seeing one's identity as special, but the particular identities – survivor, born-again Christian, Native Hawaiian – are quite disparate. Moreover, while all three approaches are fundamental to the making of the modern subject, with its emphasis on self-management and selfrestraint, they are also compatible with older ideas in these traditions. Christianity has long empha-sized self-restraint, particularly in the domain of sexuality, and Native Hawaiian society has always strongly valued controlling negative feelings that might injure others. Mutual assistance, hospitality, and other forms of reciprocity were funda-mental parts of the ordering of local Native Hawaiian communities, and those who failed to abide by these principles were excluded (Handy and Pukui [1958] 1972: 49–51). Rules of morality traditionally focused on the quality of interpersonal relationships and feelings and controlling feelings toward others (Malo [1898] 1951: 72–4). Thus, the globalizing technology of the self appears even in domains that assert their distinctiveness; there is homogeneity in the midst of difference.

Ironically, these are domains founded on radical critiques of modern society. Each of the approaches discussed here began with grassroots initiatives that criticized modern society. The feminist approach argued that modern society was inherently patriarchal in its fundamental organization and endeavored to create an alternative social order that was egalitarian and collaborative. Protecting women from violence was another way of creating a new kind of society. Pentecostal religious groups have long emphasized their separation from the secular world and their antipathy to its ways. They have frequently sought to withdraw as much as possible (Blumhofer 1993b: 88, 160). New Hope members also see themselves as set apart, as members of the saved. And proponents of ho' oponopono are engaged in recreating a Hawaiian social order that is more interpersonally engaged, generous, and connected than modern society. Both of the latter two groups desire a more spiritual life. Thus, each of these three groups began from a critique of modern society and an effort to contribute to its reformation. They established separate communities within which they could construct a different kind of society and personhood.

Yet, over time, each group gradually changed, moving away from its radical origins and assimilating a more mainstream perspective. There are signs of resistance to this change in all three. The feminist approach has become less confrontational but still emphasizes safety for women. The religious approach has downplayed its focus on demons and healing through spiritual gifts but retains these beliefs in more private places. The Native Hawaiian approach is becoming less family centered, more secular, and more structured, but some haku insist that this is a fundamentally Hawaiian process in which the haku's connection to his/her genealogy and the land is essential. Although there is clearly colonization of these disparate discourses by modern technologies of the self, the colonization is never complete: Its effect is not uniformity but similarities within distinct cultural spaces.

The moving force in each case was the pressure to maintain the organization. Although ATV felt the funding pressure most strongly, all three needed to attract clients, members, or participants in order to generate the funds to keep going. Each moved away from its initial radical vision and adopted a more mainstream approach to personal transformation in order to survive and grow. ATV changed from a grassroots feminist program run by women who had been battered to a more professional organization under the management of people with college and advanced degrees. Hilo's crises were unique, but the general shift from a collective feminist organization to a service delivery bureaucracy is common. The new Healthy Realization model probably serves to keep men in the program longer, thus diminishing the dropout rate and improving participation statistics. Although staff members regret the move away from a militant feminism, the new approach is less antagonistic to the men and less likely to drive them away. New Hope, in contrast, needs members rather than funding. The church tones down the emotional intensity of its Sunday programs in order to attract newcomers while saving the more charismatic and emotional features for Wednesday night services. New Hope aspires to become a mega-church on the pattern of several huge churches in the United States; so, it puts top priority on attracting members. Offering self-esteem and God's love along with a critique of materialism and hierarchy has proven effective. Those who treasure the more spiritual engagement with signs and wonders and speaking in tongues find the space for such activities restricted.

Ho'oponopono practitioners who work in government programs sometimes experience pressures to abandon the spirituality of the process, to keep records and monitor caseloads, and to finish cases rather than simply working through problems. Those who are considering providing the service for a fee confront even more difficult questions about abandoning the Hawaiian terminology, the emphasis on Hawaiian cultural knowledge, and the spiritual basis of the process. Thus, all three approaches are pressured by funding and survival demands to moderate their critiques of modern society and adopt techniques of personal transformation that are more compatible with modern ways of managing the self and less distinctive from the surrounding society. Funders, converts, and clients find them more accessible.

Each of these approaches has changed over the years in response to external influences. Each transformation has been promoted by connections to larger movements, both United States and international. The feminist movement is now worldwide, fully incorporated into the human rights system and committed to promoting shelters and the criminalization of batterers around the world. The power/control wheel appears from New Zealand to Israel and in many countries in between. The Healthy Realization model is, of course, an imported psychological theory. The Foursquare Church, like other Pentecostal Churches, is part of a booming global movement with missions around the world. The extensive collection of Christian guides to love, marriage, and parenting for sale in the church, as well as the content of sermons and viewpoints of pastors, suggest that mainland ideas of Christian counseling and healing are at least as strong as those of demonic possession or local culture. Ho'oponopono's rebirth is part of a global movement to revive indigenous cultural practices and sovereignty. As the international restorative justice movement expands, there are pressures to transplant versions of the process that strip away some of its Hawaiian cultural framework and spirituality.

Despite these very different and anti-modern beginnings, each of these programs was, in a different way, colonized by modern technologies of self. Much as Rose has argued, they reveal the growing centrality of self-management and self-reflection as technologies of governance at the end of the 20th century (1999). It is of course possible that their convergence simply reflects the greater effectiveness of this approach and that my worries about homogenization grow out of anthropological commitments to diversity. Nevertheless, this expansion reflects and promotes the growing global influence of a neoliberal vision of the person as responsible for making him/herself through consumption and autonomous choice. As the global movement against violence against women expands and activists from around the world seek consensus on how the problem should be defined and what kinds of solutions it requires, the debates roiling Hilo are being replayed with new intensity, particularly between those who advocate secular approaches and those who advocate spiritual ones. My observations of important human rights discussions on violence against women at the Beijing Plus Five UN General Assembly Special Session in 2000, the Commission on the Status of Women meeting in 2001, and the Commission on Human Rights in 2001 indicated major divisions between those who advocated secular approaches to women's rights and those who advocated religious ones. The former place greater stress on protecting women from violence; the latter on preserving a religiously strong social fabric with intact marriages. In these forums, culture appears as a hindrance to human rights; discussions of cultural relativism are virtually nonexistent. As these debates are raging, the homogenization of modern subjectivity is colonizing differences even within the relatively autonomous domains of religion and culture.

REFERENCES

Abraham, Ken (1997) *Who Are the Promise Keepers? Understanding the Christian Men's Movement*. New York: Doubleday.

Blumhofer, Edith L. (1993a) *Aimee Semple McPherson: Everybody's Sister*. Grand Rapids, MI: William B. Eerdmans Publishing.

——(1993b) *Restoring the Faith: The Assemblies of God, Pentecostalism, and American Culture*. Urbana and Chicago: Univ. of Illinois Press.

Boggs, Stephen T., and Malcolm Naea Chun (1990) "Ho' oponopono: A Hawaiian Method of Solving Interpersonal Problems," in K. A. Watson-Gegeo and G. M. White, eds. *Disentangling: Conflict Discourse in Pacific Societies*. Stanford, CA: Stanford Univ. Press.

Carbonatto, Helene (1999) "Expanding Intervention Options for Spousal Abuse: The Use of Restorative Justice," Occasional Papers in Criminology, New Series: no. 4, Institute of Criminology. Wellington, New Zealand: Victoria University of Wellington.

Chandler, David B., and Mary K. Yu (1994) *An Evaluation of the Domestic Violence Programs in the State of Hawaii*. Program on Conflict Resolution. Honolulu, HI: Univ. of Hawaii at Manoa.

Collier, Jane F., Bill Maurer and Liliana Suarez-Navaz (1995) "Sanctioned Identities: Legal Constructions of Modern Personhood," 2 *Identities: Global Studies in Culture and Power* 1–27.

Cordeiro, Wayne (n.d.) *Anger and How to Resolve It*. Hilo, HI: New Hope Christian Fellowship.

Cox, Harvey (1995) *Fire from Heaven: The Rise of Pentecostal Spirituality and the Reshaping of Religion in the Twenty-First Century*. Reading, MA: Addison-Wesley.

Crabb, Larry (1975) *Basic Principles of Biblical Counseling*. Grand Rapids, MI: Zondervan Publishing House.

——(1991) *Men and Women: Enjoying the Difference*. Grand Rapids, MI: Zondervan Publishing House.

Csordas, Thomas J. (1994). *The Sacred Self: A Cultural Phenomenology of Charismatic Healing*. Berkeley and Los Angeles: Univ. of California Press.

Dalbey, Gordon (1995) *Fight Like a Man: Redeeming Manhood for Kingdom Warfare*. Wheaton, IL: Tyndale House Publishers.

Dobson, James (1975) *What Wives Wish Their Husbands Knew about Women*. Wheaton, IL: Tyndale Books.

Evans, Tony (1994) "Spiritual Purity," in A. Janssen and L. K. Weeden, eds. *Seven Promises of a Promise Keeper*. Colorado Springs, CO: Focus on the Family Publishing.

Field, Martha H., and Henry F. Field (1973) "Marital Violence and the Criminal Process: Neither Justice Nor Peace," 47 *Social Science Rev.* 221–40.

Foucault, Michel (1980a) "Two Lectures," in C. Gordon, ed., *Power/Knowledge: Selected Interviews and Other Writings, 1972–1977*. New York: Pantheon.

Foucault, Michel. (1980b) "Truth and Power," in C. Gordon, ed., *Power/Knowledge: Selected Interviews and Other Writings, 1972–1977*. New York: Pantheon.

Galaway, Burt, and Joe Hudson, eds. (1996) *Restorative Justice: International Perspectives*. Monsey, NY: Criminal Justice Press.

Gutmanis, Jane, Theodore Kelsey and Susan G. Monden (1976) *Kahuna La'au Lapa'au* (The Practice of Hawaiian Herbal Medicine): The Island Heritage Collection.

Handy, E. S. Craighill and Mary Kawena Pukui (1972) *The Polynesian Family System in Ka'u, Hawai'i*. Rutland, VT: Charles E. Tuttle.

Hanna, Cheryl (1998) "The Paradox of Hope: The Crime and Punishment of Domestic Violence," 39 *William & Mary Law Rev.* 39 1505–84.

Healy, Kerry, Christine Smith, with Chris O'Sullivan (1998) *Batterer Intervention: Program Approaches and Criminal Justice Strategies*. Series: Issues and Practices. U.S. Department of Justice, Office of Justice Programs, National Institute of Justice. <http://www.ncjrs.org/textfiles/168638.txt>.

Ito, Karen L. (1985a) "*Ho'oponopono*, 'To Make Right': Hawaiian Conflict Resolution and Metaphor in the Construction of a Family Therapy," 9 *Culture, Medicine, and Psychiatry* 201–17.

——(1985b) "Affective Bonds: Hawaiian Interrelationships of Self," in G. White and J. Kirkpatrick, eds., *Person, Self, and Experience: Exploring Pacific Ethnopsychologies*. Berkeley and Los Angeles: Univ. of Calif. Press.

——(1999) *Lady Friends: Hawaiian Ways and the Ties that Define*. Ithaca: Cornell Univ. Press.

Lewis, Gregg (1995) *The Power of a Promise Kept*. Colorado Springs, CO: Focus on the Family Publishing.

Longclaws, Lyle, Burt Galaway, and Lawrence Barkwell (1996) "Piloting Family Group Conferences for Young Aboriginal Offenders in Winnipeg, Canada," in J. Hudson, A. Morris, G. Maxwell, and B. Galaway, eds., *Family Group Conferences: Perspectives on Policy and Practice*. New South Wales, Australia: Federation Press, Criminal Justice Press.

Ma, Nalani Thomas, and Dassar Palama (1980) "The Young and the Old: A Study of Ho'oponopono," Masters in Social Work thesis, School of Social Work, Univ. of Hawai'i, typescript.

Malo, David [1898] (1951) *Hawaiian Antiquities (Moolelo Hawaii)*, 2d edn. Trans. by Nathaniel B. Emerson. Bernice P. Bishop Museum, Special Publication 2. Honolulu, HI: Bishop Museum Press.

Merry, Sally Engle (1995) "Gender Violence and Legally Engendered Selves," 2 *Identities: Global Studies in Culture and Power* 49–73.

——(1998) "Global Human Rights and Local Social Movements in a Legally Plural World," 12 *Canadian J. of Law & Society* 247–71.

——(2000) *Colonizing Hawai'i: The Cultural Power of Law*. Princeton: Princeton Univ. Press.

Meyer, Manu (1995) "To Set Right: Ho'oponopono, A Native Hawaiian Way of Peacemaking," *The Compleat Lawyer* (fall) 30–35.

Meyer, Manu Aluli, and Albie Davis (1994) "Talking Story: Mediation, Peacemaking, and Culture," *American Bar Association Dispute Resolution Magazine* (fall) 5–9.

O'Malley, Pat (1992) "Risk, Power, and Crime Prevention," 21 *Economy & Society* 252–75.

——(1993) "Containing Our Excitement: Commodity Culture and the Crisis of Discipline," 13 *Research in Law, Politics, & Society* 151–72.

——(1996) "Indigenous Governance," 25 *Economy & Society* 310–26.

——(1999a) "Governmentality and the Risk Society," 28 *Economy & Society* 138–48.

——(1999b) "Consuming Risks: Harm Minimization and the Government of 'Drug-Users,'" Russell Smandych, ed. in *Governable Places: Readings on Governmentality and Crime Control*. Aldershot, England: Dartmouth Publishing Company.

O'Malley, Pat, and Darren Palmer (1996) "Post-Keynsian Policing," 25 *Economy & Society* 137–55.

Paglinawan, Lynette K. (1972), *Ho'oponopono Project Number II:* "Development and Implementation of Ho'oponopono Practice in a Social Work Agency," Hawaiian Culture Committee, Queen Lili'uokalani Children's Center, Honolulu. Sponsored by the Progressive Neighborhood Task Force, July. Typescript. Hilo, HI: Univ. of Hawai'i Library, Hawaiian Collection.

Pence, Ellen, and Michael Paymar (1993) *Education Groups for Men Who Batter: The Duluth Model*. New York: Springer Publishing.

Pleck, Elizabeth Hafkin (1987) *Domestic Tyranny: The Making of Social Policy Against Family Violence from Colonial Times to the Present.* New York: Oxford Univ. Press.

Ptacek, James (1988) "Why Do Men Batter Their Wives?" in K. Yllo & M. Bograd, eds., *Feminist Perspectives on Wife Abuse.* Newbury Park, CA: Sage.

——(1999) *Battered Women in the Courtroom: The Power of Judicial Responses.* Boston: Northeastern Univ. Press.

Pukui, Mary Kawena, E. W. Haertig & Catherine A. Lee (1972) *Nana I Ke Kumu* (Look to the Source). Vol. 1. Honolulu: Queen Lili'uokalani Children's Center.

——(1979) *Nana I Ke Kumu* (Look to the Source). Vol. 2. Honolulu: Queen Lili'uokalani Children's Center.

Robertson, Jeremy (1996) "Research on Family Group Conferences in Child Welfare in New Zealand." in J. Hudson, A. Morris, G. Maxwell and B. Gallaway, eds., *Family Group Conferences: Perspectives on Policy and Practice*, Leichardt, New South Wales, Australia: Federation Press, Criminal Justice Press.

Rodriguez, Noelie Maria (1988) "A Successful Feminist Shelter: A Case Study of the Family Crisis Shelter in Hawaii," 24 *J. of Applied Behavioral Science* 235–50.

Rose, Nikolas (1989) *Governing the Soul: The Shaping of the Private Self.* London: Routledge.

——(1996) "The Death of the Social? Re-Figuring the Territory of Government," 25 *Economy & Society* 327–56.

Rose, Nikolas (1999) *Predicaments of Freedom.* Cambridge: Cambridge Univ. Press.

Rose, Nikolas, & Peter Miller (1992) "Political Power Beyond the State: Problematics of Government," 43 *British J. of Sociology* 173–205.

Rose, Nikolas, and Mariana Valverde (1998) "Governed by Law?" 7 *Social & Legal Studies* 541–51.

Rosenbaum, Michael D. (1998) "To Break the Shell without Scrambling the Egg: An Empirical Analysis of the Impact of Intervention into Violent Families." 9 *Stanford Law & Policy Rev.* 409–27.

Schechter, Susan (1982) *Women and Male Violence: The Visions and Struggles of the Battered Women's Movement.* Boston: South End Press.

Schneider, Elizabeth (1994) "The Violence of Privacy," in Martha Albertson Fineman and Roxane Mykitiuk, eds., *The Public Nature of Private Violence: The Discovery of Domestic Abuse.* New York: Routledge.

Shook, E. Victoria (1985) *Ho'oponopono.* Honolulu, HI: East-West Center, Univ. of Hawaii Press.

22

Relational Practices and the Marginalization of Law: Informal Financial Practices of Small Businesses in Taiwan

Jane Kaufman Winn

Introduction: Economic Development, the "Informal Sector," and Law in Taiwan

This study examines extra-legal techniques used by small and medium-size businesses in Taiwan to conduct their affairs. The question Jane Kaufman Winn asks is whether regulatory systems based on Western law have been a significant factor in the rapid economic development of Taiwan. Her contention is that what she calls "relational practices," those based on networks of personal connections rather than on formal legal institutions, have been and continue to be central to Taiwan's economic success. She uses the phrase "the marginalization of law" to refer to the systematic by-passing of formal legal institutions. Her paper is a criticism of the notion that economic development means "modernization" and that "modernization" means the Westernization of all institutions and practices, including, of course, legal institutions. She emphasizes the personal networks and social underpinning of the Taiwanese economy, and describes the particularities of the way they function.

This is a study by a lawyer, but it involves the use of anthropological field techniques in the collection of information. When she studied the means by which small businesses obtained financing, she quickly realized that the formal regulated financial system was not available to them, and that such people relied on personal networks and extra-legal techniques to obtain the financial

From Jane Kaufman Winn, "Relational Practices and the Marginalization of Law: Informal Financial Practices of Small Businesses in Taiwan," *Law and Society Review* 28(2) (1994), pp. 193–8, 200–1, 203–5, 208–15, 219–22, 227–8, 330–2.

resources they needed. How were the rules in such a system enforced? Winn explains that instead of going to court, one technique was to rely on gangs and their thugs. To collect a debt, all that needed to be done was for the debtor to be told that such a criminal gang was on its way to enforce collection, and to keep himself from being beaten up, or his business disrupted, the debtor would quickly mobilize all of his contacts to pay the debt. The same gangs collected protection money from legitimate businesses.

Some of the assets that could be mobilized by small-scale entrepreneurs were funds from rotating credit associations. Attempts were made to regulate these, but by and large the credit associations have avoided such interventions. Another device was the use of post-dated checks, an activity once guaranteed by the existence of criminal penalties for bounced checks. But even since the criminal penalties have been abolished, both regulated financial institutions such as banks, and informal lenders continue to make use of post-dated checks as a part of loan agreements. Apparently it was easier to get someone prosecuted for a bounced check than to sue in the event of a default. The shame, loss of face, and erosion of business reputation was a major factor in the threat posed by a failure to pay a post-dated check in the hands of a creditor. A third resource in the informal economy were the moneylenders. Their connections with organized crime gave them the capacity to collect debts on short term loans offered at high interest rates.

What Winn concludes is that the informal sector of the Taiwanese economy is large, continuing, and basically unregulatable. This moves her to infer that it is an analytic error to judge the basis of development in a non-Western country in terms of Western ideas of modernization. Relational practices and the marginalization of formal law are clearly no bar to economic prosperity. The small businesses that produced the "Taiwan miracle" could rely on rules and institutions generated outside the formal legal structure.

For an anthropologist, this case study confirms the fact that the formal legal system is in many countries no bar to alternative structures of norms, credit and debt collection. This writer would contend, of course, that one need not go as far as Taiwan to make such a point. The informal sector of the American economy is substantial. One has only to think of the drug trade let alone other businesses, and that they, too, do not conform to the system of legal norms. It is probably not helpful to analyze societal differences of this kind in terms of the duality of more modern or less modern, meaning more like the supposed formal Western model or less like it.

Differences between societal locales exist in the nature of the local extra-legal activities, and in the social relationships that underpin them, as well as in what falls within the purview of the formal system and what does not. Winn objects to any effort to slot the Taiwan example into one of the prevailing theoretical rubrics, either as a system of "legal centralism" or "legal pluralism." She argues that it is much more useful to stick close to the empirical observations cited here. Clearly the informal economy has multiple ways of generating legal rules, credit, and modes of enforcement, many of which could be said to have contributed to Taiwan's economic development. Heretofore, the partial marginalization of law has worked well for them and may continue to do so. Winn leaves unanswered the question whether legal typologies are good to think with even though no actual society fits any of them perfectly.

S.F.M.

Winn, *Taiwan Business*

This study examines routine and wide-spread economic activities in which the impact of modern legal institutions is limited or indirect at best: those in the "informal sector" or "underground economy...."

Studying the practices of small and medium-sized businesses is a crucial step in understanding the origins of Taiwan's "economic miracle," because such firms have played a greater role in Taiwan's economic development than they have in other East Asian newly industrialized countries (Orrù et al. 1991:368). Until the mid-to late 1980s, small and medium-sized enterprises in Taiwan relied heavily on financial resources from outside the formal financial system because of a shortage of credit from regulated sources (Wade 1990:161). While limited access to bank financing clearly contributed to the growth of Taiwan's informal financial system, certain features of Taiwanese society also contributed to that growth, among them the maintenance of networks of personal connections, the availability of informal surrogates for legal enforcement, and the marginalization of formal legal institutions.

The findings of this study point to an apparent paradox. The development of a modern formal legal system may belie the social realities in Taiwan, obscuring the propensity of legal institutions to foster relational practices rather than displace them. The very commitment of many legal practitioners and government officials to the maintenance of a modern legal system based on foreign models seems to contribute to the marginalization of modern formal ROC legal institutions in a manner reminiscent of the marginalization of formal legal institutions in the traditional Chinese polity (Ch'ü 1961). In addition, the formalism of Taiwan's transplanted version of the Western legal tradition seems to limit the law's flexibility in adapting to contemporary Taiwanese social practices, thereby increasing the dependence of businesses on relational practices outside the law...

I Marginalization of Law in Taiwan

A The Paradox of Modern Legality in Taiwan

... Among the most well-known and successful legal initiatives taken by the ROC government are the Statute for Encouragement of Investment and related changes in tax, land use, and labor and company laws facilitating direct foreign investment in Taiwan and export-oriented growth through the establishment of export-processing zones (Hsu 1985:283). These laws were introduced or amended as part of a broad program of economic reforms in the early 1960s. These reforms laid part of the foundation for Taiwan's subsequent "economic miracle" and its transformation from an underdeveloped agricultural country to a highly industrialized country. Today, Taiwan's per capita GNP is equivalent to that of some European countries.

While the success of these governmental initiatives is well known, they are not representative of the general role played by the modern ROC legal system in Taiwanese society. Indeed, focusing on government led programs that helped nurture Taiwan's successful export-oriented industrialization obscures the role more commonly played by the ROC legal system in regulating economic activity. Much of

Taiwan's industrialization has taken place outside the relatively highly regulated environments of the export-processing zones and through domestic rather than foreign investment (Haggard & Chen 1987:93). Thus, the visibility of such initiatives can easily lead to overestimating the importance of state-sponsored regulation and underestimating the importance of alternative ordering mechanisms[5] ...

2. Legal Pluralism, Legal Marginalism, and Chinese Society

One attempt to capture the salient elements of the role of law in traditional Chinese society is expressed by the idea of the "Confucianization of law" (Ch'ū 1961:267). This refers to the development and maintenance of a formal legal system not as the core of a universal, state-centered normative order but rather as a device to reinforce and stabilize networks of human relationships. According to Confucian precepts, these relationships constitute the basis of a virtuous and harmonious society. In the traditional Chinese polity, the administration of law (fa) was understood to be punitive, coercive, and morally debased in comparison with the uplifting spiritual influence of ritual practices and human relationships (li) (Bodde and Morris 1971:13).

Although Confucian teachings may have limited vitality in modern Taiwanese society, participation in relationships remains the primary factor both in determining the sense of self and in constituting the social order in the contemporary Taiwanese world view and social psychology (Bond & Hwang 1986:221) ...

Legal institutions in Taiwan are marginalized not only by the propensity of members of society to seek their objectives through networks of relationships but also by a distinctive sense of what legal institutions can and should accomplish. One of the fundamental premises of the "legal centralist" idea of modern law is that law, together with individual expressions of free will within the framework of a social order demarcated by law, should constitute the normative structure of liberal society. The traditional Chinese sense of the relationship between law (fa) and the social order is very different. In terms of Confucian ideology, li (often translated as "ritual" or propriety) is regarded as the morally superior wellspring of social order, while positive law is merely a tool of the state, to be invoked as necessary to censure antisocial behavior.

It would be simplistic and inaccurate to assume that these Confucian ideas operate in modern Taiwanese society in the same form they once had in traditional Chinese society. However, some semblance of these ideas is still visible under the veneer of modern legality in Taiwan, like a pentimento reappearing through the image that has been painted over it. Many Taiwanese people interviewed for this study, including legal professionals steeped in modern Western traditions of legality, routinely presumed that the invocation of law involved suppression and punishment and often dismissed the idea that law could empower participants in realizing their objectives. The unstated assumption that law is best suited to reprimand misconduct and that nonlegal forms of social intercourse were better suited to enabling or facilitating voluntary interactions often underlay the distinctive manner in which local participants interpreted laws and decided whether to avail themselves of legal institutions in Taiwan ...

Unofficially, ROC authorities often tolerate gross and notorious violations of the law for extended periods of time, as was the case with underground investment companies. From 1982 until the collapse of most of these firms in 1989, Taiwanese people invested the equivalent of U.S.$8.5 billion in underground investment companies, most of which were little more than Ponzi schemes (Chen 1992:127). In addition, ROC authorities have been known to selectively enforce highly restrictive regulations in order to achieve unofficial, unstated objectives such as the harassment of political dissidents (Arrigo 1994)...

Another significant factor limiting the autonomy of the legal system from political and relational influences is the relatively small number of legal professionals in Taiwan and the large numbers of "back doors" to the legal profession. This is important because the number of practicing lawyers in Taiwan has historically been very restricted. In 1991, the ROC Ministry of Justice estimated that there were only 2,254 members of the private bar.[8] Until very recently, the tiny number of successful candidates passing the regular bar exam[9] was never adequate to meet even the limited demand for lawyers recognized by the ROC authorities. Before the recent relaxation in standards applied to candidates sitting the bar exam, the number of lawyers in Taiwan was supplemented by admissions to the bar under other criteria. These "back doors" to admission are often open to lawyers who pass no formal qualifying examination, or pass a less rigorous qualifying exam, but who have been screened according to informal, often political, criteria[10]...

Discussions with government officials charged with enforcing business registration and licensing laws indicated that while the official posture was one of rigorous and uniform enforcement of the law, in fact, given the magnitude of noncompliance, the official practice in most instances was one of tolerance. Official investigations and prosecutions were only commenced in response to complaints, and in the absence of any complaints, any enforcement action was unlikely against even quite obvious violations.

The administration of law in Taiwan is thus a highly complex and nuanced process, reflecting the limitations imposed on legal institutions by the structure of legislation, political constraints, cultural predispositions, and other variables. While the ROC legal system may function with a high degree of efficacy in some contexts, that degree of effectiveness is clearly not uniform. The restrictions on the effectiveness of the ROC legal system are so substantial, however, that the ROC legal system cannot be said to stand in the relation of hierarchic control over other normative systems in Taiwanese society that conformity with the ideal of legal centralism would require. Given the diminished scope of state-centered law in Taiwanese society, a theory of the role of law and development in Taiwan must identify alternative sources of normative ordering outside the state and then determine what factors account for the displacement of formal law in some situations and not others. The primary alternatives in Taiwanese society seem to be networks of relationships and informal surrogates for the legal system.

C   Relational Practices and Other Alternatives
to Legal Regulation

[...]

2   Organized Crime as a Surrogate for Law

If the ROC legal system is unable fully to provide the necessary backstop for a relationship in modern Taiwan, the parties have the option of turning to substitutes. Organized crime plays a significant role in policing transactions in the informal sector in Taiwan. While the term *liumang* is used in ordinary conversation to denote either a hooligan/delinquent or a member of an organized gang, the discussion that follows focuses on the activities of the latter, more formally known as *bangliufenzi*.

Gang members may own and operate businesses themselves, they may demand protection money from other businesses, or they may provide various services to other businesses. Operating barbershops (i.e., massage parlors/brothels) or nightclubs, gambling, moneylending, and smuggling are among the illicit activities organized gangs undertake in Taiwan, although in recent years they have become more active in otherwise legitimate businesses such as real estate development and stock brokerages (Sheu 1990).

Gangs also derive substantial revenues by demanding protection money from legitimate businesses such as restaurants and other retail establishments. Informants described the following process: a man (presumed to be associated with the organized gang with jurisdiction over the location of the store) offers for sale a container of cheap tea for 10 or 20 times its fair value. The merchant or restauranteur then pays the sum demanded rather than risk a disruption of business.

According to informants who claimed to have first-hand experience dealing with gang members in commercial contexts, gangsters also offer such services as providing bodyguards, offering to represent interested parties in negotiations, collecting debts, or other dispute resolution services. Members of organized gangs perceive themselves as providing valuable services and operating a business with a view to its long-term growth and continued operations, and thus avoid unnecessary violence in the discharge of their duties (Sheu 1990). They sometimes even have business cards printed showing themselves as officers of enterprises offering, for example, dispute resolution and debt collection services.

While recourse to gang members was mentioned repeatedly by informants as one element of doing business in the underground economy in Taiwan, very few informants would admit to having personally dealt with gang members, making it difficult to know if the practice is really as widespread as informants seemed to think it is. For example, in response to "How can you tell you are dealing with a gangster rather than an ordinary business person?" one businessman who claimed to have dealt with gangsters stated that they can be identified from among a group of businessmen because although they have no apparent qualifications or ability, they act in an arrogant and overbearing manner. Another businessman stated that gang members can be identified because they stand to the side of negotiations with their hands in their pockets, suggesting they are carrying guns. Short of overt acts of violence, the criteria informants used for distinguishing gang members from legitimate businessmen is apparently fairly vague and situation-specific.

Informants variously reported that gangsters work for flat fees payable in advance and on a contingency fee basis, suggesting that gangsters may negotiate different forms of compensation for different matters. There was a striking consistency, however, in the descriptions of how a party learns that the other side of a commercial dispute has hired gang members to assist in resolving the dispute. The gang members might be hired, for example, to settle a dispute about whether allegedly nonconforming goods should be paid for in full, or whether work under a lucrative contract should be subcontracted to a particular party. The party being threatened arrives at work to find several strange men sitting around, perhaps in the reception area. The men say nothing, sitting patiently all day or playing cards to pass the time. The threatened party can infer from this that the other party to the dispute has hired gang members and that if the dispute is not brought to a speedy resolution, the level of intimidation will soon increase. Increased sanctions include threats to kidnap family members or of bodily harm to the threatened person.

Gangsters can also be more effective than courts in collecting debts acknowledged to be due. Courts are often perceived as unhelpful to litigants because, in the words of several informants, the standard of proof is "too high," although this may just be another way of saying the court expects formal documentation of transactions that most parties cannot provide. Assuming a party can obtain a favorable judgment, he or she may still not be able to locate any assets to attach. Debtors' assets in Taiwan are difficult to locate because of a lack of public access to records of ownership of company assets, unreliable accounting practices, and the ease and regularity with which assets can be transferred or held in the name of family members. Thus the relational system of relying on family and friends and not on formal, public recordkeeping can frustrate legitimate attempts at debt collection. By hiring gang members to collect debts, however, the relational system that obscures the location of assets from formal collection attempts is mobilized in reverse to generate assets. If a debtor or a debtor's family members are threatened with physical harm, then the debtor will mobilize assets by calling on relational ties to pay the obligation, thus permitting a creditor to recover in excess of the debtor's personal assets. . . .

II Informal Financial Practices of Small Businesses in Taiwan

. . . In this article, "informal" will denote activities that should be registered or licensed by the authorities but are not, or that give rise to a tax liability but no taxes are paid. Business enterprises in Taiwan are required to register with the appropriate administrative agency in order to receive permission to engage in economic activities (ROC Business Registration Law, art. 3). Small-scale businesses apply to local or municipal authorities, while larger businesses apply to the Ministry of Economic Affairs. The dividing line is whether a business has paid-in capital of over New Taiwan ("N.T.") $40 million and assets of over N.T. $120 million. According to official statistics compiled in 1989, 98% of all registered businesses in Taiwan are small and only 2% are large, whereas 60% of GNP is contributed by small businesses and 40% by large (ROC SMMB 1989). A business may engage only in those activities for which it has applied and been granted permission by the relevant authority – blanket authorizations to engage in "any lawful business" are not granted. Informal activities in Taiwan are conducted not only by companies that fail to register but also by companies that exceed the scope of activities authorized by their business registration.

Business enterprises are also required to register with tax authorities. Local tax authorities collect the business tax – a value-added tax ("VAT") introduced in 1986 – and the land value increment tax,[16] while central authorities collect the income tax levied on profit-seeking enterprises. Informal activities are carried on by businesses that fail to pay any tax, as well as those that pay some tax but take deliberate steps to understate the level of taxable activities they have undertaken...

Small businesses in Taiwan typically have relied more heavily on debt finance than on equity capital and have been forced to look to the informal financial sector to provide that debt finance (Wade 1990:160–61). Until the significant liberalization of banking in Taiwan beginning in the late 1980s (Winn 1991), commercial banks and other regulated financial institutions in Taiwan catered primarily to the needs of large and medium-sized businesses, leaving small businesses to secure financing through whatever channels they could. This bifurcation in credit allocation was due to a variety of factors: until the mid-1980s, there was a chronic shortage of credit generally in Taiwan; small businesses did not usually maintain the kind of accounting records that commercial lenders required; and commercial banks allocated credit to large and medium-sized businesses in accordance with policies established by the government, which not only regulated the banks but also owned them.

Some of the financing of small businesses is provided by family and friends in the form of capital contributions not rigorously styled as either equity or debt. Other financing is acquired through the use of rotating credit lotteries, known as *biaohui*; discounting postdated checks; borrowing from underground moneylenders who usually operate with at least the protection of organized gangs; and real estate loans arranged by scriveners, known as *daishu*...

Biaohui, Mutual Savings & Loan Societies, and Small & Medium Business Banks

1 The Structure of Biaohui

Rotating credit associations, known as *biaohui* in Chinese, have been found in cultures and regions as diverse as sub-Saharan Africa, Southeast Asia, Korea, and the West Indies (Geertz 1962). The basic structure (subject to countless variations) is that a group of people agree to meet at regular intervals, each making contributions of an agreed amount, creating a pool of savings that is then given in turn to the highest bidder. The right to bid is reserved to members who have not yet received the collected pool until finally each member of the group has received the pool once. This form of savings lottery is common in societies that possess a monetized economy yet do not have well-established modern financial institutions. Rotating credit lotteries reinforce community bonds while mobilizing savings. In so doing, they facilitate investment and the accumulation of capital.

Biaohui have existed in China for hundreds of years and are still very popular in Taiwan today. According to a recent Ministry of Justice study (1985:302–4), 68% of adults in Taiwan had participated in biaohui, while 95% thought they were a very popular and widespread activity. In 1985, many informants declared that biaohui were not as popular as they once were because they rely on the strength of such traditional Chinese values as face and the importance of relationships, and those values were being eroded in contemporary Taiwanese society by the process of rapid economic development. In 1990, however, informants acknowledged that biaohui seemed as popular as ever but still predicted their imminent demise because of the general decline in moral standards. It is therefore difficult to determine whether biaohui are actually losing popularity. It is possible that the frequent assertion that biaohui are losing popularity should be interpreted as an expression of disquiet at the rapid pace of social transformation in Taiwanese society rather than as a factual observation.

According to various informants, biaohui may be organized by friends, such as co-workers or neighbors, on a noncompetitive basis so that the collected pool of funds is received by each member in turn without bidding. They may also be organized on a very large scale by entrepreneurs raising the equivalent of venture capital by drawing together a large group whose only common interest is some connection to the organizer of the biaohui. Individuals may participate in biaohui to generate personal savings, to participate in a social activity with friends, to raise money to meet unexpected expenses such as uninsured medical expenses, to ease sudden cash-flow problems in a business, to make a major purchase such as an automobile, or to make a down payment on property (ROC Ministry of Justice 1985:95).

Among the reasons given in response to the Ministry of Justice survey for the popularity of biaohui were interest rates for investors that were higher than regulated financial institutions could offer; instant availability of funds; no parallel to the requirement usually imposed by regulated lenders that borrowers furnish either collateral or a surety; no troublesome procedures involved in launching a biaohui; and the lack of alternative sources of funds (ibid., p. 55). Another factor enhancing of the appeal of biaohui is that participants do not generally pay taxes on their earnings[19] ...

B   Postdated Checks

A large component of Taiwan's informal financial sector is comprised of postdated check ("PDC") transactions (Winn 1986). The popularity of the PDC as a financing vehicle stems from the fact that from 1960 to 1987 the ROC Negotiable Instruments Law ("NIL") provided criminal penalties for bouncing checks. The holder of a dishonored check could therefore initiate criminal proceedings against the drawer of the check, in effect sentencing him or her to debtors' prison, with the costs of prosecution paid by the state rather than creditor.

The intent of legislators in adding criminal penalties to checks but not to other negotiable instruments was to safeguard the security of Taiwan's then-nascent modern payment system. The unintended consequence of adding criminal penalties was that the ROC legal system provided a cheap and effective tool creditors could use to reinforce otherwise precarious business relationships. Parties interacting through networks of relationships assumed they could verify the other party's good faith by simply asking for a PDC to document any extension of credit. The fear of criminal prosecution was used to supplement the more traditional fear of loss of face that would follow any default on the debt. Using PDCs to document commercial transactions thus helped maintain the viability of attenuated relationships without forcing the parties to assume the expense and inconvenience of completely converting the transaction from a relational to a legal basis by drawing up a contract that fully expressed the parties' agreement.

According to several informants interviewed in 1990, PDCs are still commonly issued by businesses needing short-term credit to purchase goods and services, even after the repeal of criminal penalties for bouncing checks. PDCs are either held by businesses that can afford to wait until they become due or, if the party receiving a PDC in payment cannot afford to wait several weeks or months for payment, they are sold at a discount to banks or moneylenders. Regulated financial institutions such as banks regularly purchase PDCs at a discount, so these transactions are also significant in the formal financial system, but the ease of documentation associated with PDC transactions and ready transferability of PDCs makes them a popular form of finance in the informal sector as well.

Banks restricted access to checking accounts due to the specter of criminal penalties looming as a consequence of miscalculating the balance in one's checking account, thus preventing checks from gaining widespread use as a cash equivalent. According to bankers, checking accounts were only made available to people in business and persons with substantial assets, while the average consumer in Taiwan paid cash for all purchases. Even after a customer agreed to open a checking account, banks rationed the number of checks a customer could have at one time, waiting until one set of checks cleared before giving the customer a few more.

Notwithstanding the restrictive posture adopted by banks in opening checking accounts, PDCs became very popular as a financing vehicle. As the economy of Taiwan grew rapidly during the 1970s and 1980s, and it became more difficult to do business exclusively with family and close friends, PDCs were used to bolster increasingly tenuous networks of connections. The assumption that few people would willingly risk incarceration as a cost of doing business gave people in business the confidence to do business with people outside or only tangentially connected to their networks of personal relations.

PDCs, however, were an imperfect substitute for the personal connections they supplemented or even replaced because deceitful borrowers devised various ruses to avoid suffering criminal penalties. Informants reported that people willing to engage in deliberately fraudulent practices such as *exin daobi* (bad faith business failures) would usually abscond long before criminal prosecution could begin, leaving those guilty of nothing more than bad business judgment to go to jail.[22] In 1983, in the midst of a recession in the local economy, ROC officials estimated that up to 40% of the inmates in Taiwan's overcrowded prisons were serving sentences for writing bad checks (U.S. Department of State 1985:752).

In spite of these shortcomings, PDCs became popular with informal lenders and borrowers as well as with regulated financial institutions. Bankers even acknowledged requiring borrowers or lessees signing loan agreements or leases to provide the bank with a PDC for every payment due under the agreement at the time it was signed. A banker explained that they did this because prosecuting a bounced check was easier than suing in the event of default...

C Moneylenders and Daishu

A significant segment of the informal financial system in Taiwan is comprised of *dixia qianzhuang* or underground moneylenders. These moneylenders often have connections to organized crime (Sheu 1990) and provide very short-term credit at high interest rates. This credit is not provided within the context of relationships but is based on strictly calculated, self-interested short-term transactions between the parties involved. Thus, while not legal, the structure of these transactions is highly legalistic, and sanctions are imposed by legal surrogates such as the gangsters who provide these moneylending services or provide protection to moneylenders....

IV   Conclusion

There is a significant relationship between Taiwan's rapid economic development and indigenous Taiwanese social practices and ideas about law. This relationship has generally been misconstrued or overlooked by much of the academic literature discussing Taiwan's economic "miracle." Networks of interpersonal relationships have played a significant role in promoting economic development, while the ROC legal system has often been reduced to a role of enabling those relationships rather than establishing the kind of universal normative order often associated with the idea of a modern legal system. A substantial component of Taiwan's economic development has taken place in the informal sector, outside the purview of the ROC legal system. This study is the first attempt to develop a systematic account of the marginalization of Taiwan's modern legal system and the concomitant heightened significance of alternatives, such as networks of personal connections or informal surrogates for legal regulation, in contributing to Taiwan's rapid economic development....

If, however, Taiwan's system is not so much moving toward convergence with Western models as developing along alternative lines, then analyzing how formal legal institutions in Taiwan are marginalized may better explain processes of economic development and democratization in many nations outside the Western legal and political tradition.

REFERENCES

Arrigo, Linda Gail (1994) "From Democratic Movement to Bourgeois Democracy: The Internal Politics of the Taiwan Democratic Progressive Party in 1991," in Rubinstein 1993.
Becker, Gary (1964) *Human Capital*. New York: National Bureau of Economic Research.
Bond, Michael Harris, and K. K. Hwang (1986) "The Social Psychology of the Chinese People," in M. H. Bond, ed., *The Psychology of the Chinese People*. Hong Kong: Oxford Univ. Press.
Bourdieu, Pierre (1977) *Outline of a Theory of Practice*. Cambridge: Cambridge Univ. Press.
Cheng, Tun-Jen (1989) "Democratizing the Quasi-Leninist Regime in Taiwan," 41 *World Politics* 471.
Ch'ü, Tung-tsu (1961) *Law and Society in Traditional China*. Paris: Mouton.
Coase, R. H. (1937) "The Nature of the Firm," 4 *Economica*, n.s., 4, 386.
Galanter, Marc (1992) "Pick a Number, Any Number," *American Lawyer*, p. 82 (May).
Galanter, Marc, and David Luban (1993) "Poetic Justice: Punitive Damages and Legal Pluralism," 42 *American Univ. Law Rev.* 1393.
Geertz, Clifford (1962) "The Rotating Credit Association: A 'Middle Rung' in Development," 11 *Economic Development & Cultural Change* 241. George, Henry (1879) *Progress and Poverty*. San Francisco: W. M. Hinton & Co.

Haggard, Stephan, and Tun-jen Cheng (1987) "State and Foreign Capital in the East Asian NICs," in F. C. Deyo, ed., *The Political Economy of the New Asian Industrialism*. Ithaca, NY: Cornell Univ. Press.

Huq, Muzammel, and Maheen Sultan (1991) "'Informality' in Development: The Poor as Entrepreneurs in Bangladesh," in A. L. Chickering and M. Salahdine, eds., *The Silent Revolution: The Informal Sector in Five Asian and Near Eastern Countries*. San Francisco: ICS Press.

Hwang, Kwang-Kuo (1987) "Face and Favor: The Chinese Power Game," 92 *American J. of Sociology* 944.

Jones, William C. (1974) "Studying the Ch'ing Code—The Ta Ch'ing Lü Li," 22 *American J. of Comparative Law* 330.

Kenney, Roy W., and Benjamin Klein (1983) "The Economics of Block Booking," 26 *J. of Law & Economics* 497.

Liu, Lawrence S. (1990) "Brave New World of Financial Reform in Taiwan, Republic of China – Three Waves of Internationalization and Liberalization and Beyond," 8 (1988–89) *Chinese Yearbook of International Law & Affairs* 134.

McElderry, Andrea (1976) *Shanghai Old-Style Banks (Ch'ien-Chuang), 1800–1935: A Traditional Institution in a Changing Society*. Ann Arbor: Center for Chinese Studies, Univ. of Michigan.

Meany, Constance Squires (1992) "Liberalization, Democratization and the Role of the KMT," in T-J. Cheng and S. Haggard, eds., *Political Change in Taiwan*. Boulder, CO: Lynne Rienner Publishers.

Ocasal, Christopher (1992) "Pick Again, Professor," *Texas Lawyer*, p. 14 (20 April).

Orrù, Marco, Nicole Woolsey Biggart, and Gary G. Hamilton (1991) "Organizational Isomorphism in East Asia," in W. W. Powell and P. J. DiMaggio, eds., *The New Institutionalism in Organizational Analysis*. Chicago: Univ. of Chicago Press.

Redding, S. Gordon (1990) *The Spirit of Chinese Capitalism*. New York: W. de Gruyter.

ROC Ministry of Finance, Small and Medium Business Bureau ("ROC SMBB") (1989) *Zhonghua Minguo Taiwan Diqu Zhongxiao Qiye Jingji Huodong Baogao (1989)* [ROC Small and Medium Business Statistics, Taiwan Region]. Taipei: Small and Medium Business Bureau, ROC Ministry of Finance.

ROC Ministry of Justice (1985) *Taiwan Diqu Minjian Hehui Xiankuang zhi Yenjiu* [Research on Contemporary Popular Cooperative Associations in the Taiwan Region]. Taipei: ROC Department of Justice.

Rubinstein, Murray, ed. (1994) *The Other Taiwan 1945–1991*. Armonk, NY: M. E. Sharpe.

US Dept. of State (1987) *Country Reports on Human Rights Practices for 1986*. Washington: GPO.

Wade, Robert (1990) *Governing the Market: Economic Theory and the Role of Government in East Asian Industrialization*. Princeton, NJ: Princeton Univ. Press.

Winn, Jane Kaufman (1986) "Decriminalizing Bad Checks Should Help to Rationalize Taiwan's Financial System," 8 (8) *East Asian Executive Reports*. 9.

——(1991) "Banking and Finance in Taiwan: The Prospects for Internationalization in the 1990s," 25 *International Lawyer* 907.

23

Enacting Law through Social Practice: Sanctuary as a Form of Resistance

Susan Bibler Coutin

Introduction: The Sanctuary Movement of the 1980s

A religious network formed in the 1980s to help undocumented Salvadoran and Guatemalan refugees is described by Susan Bibler Coutin. In its interaction with the American legal system it disputed official interpretations of the illegal status of immigrants. While the law, embodied in statutes and in the acts of the Immigration and Naturalization Service, defined the persons they were helping as illegal aliens, the church groups insisted that those official categorizing agencies and the courts had been misinterpreting the law. They invoked, not only moral and humane considerations, but the United Nations protocol on refugees, international law, and the wording of the 1980 Refugee Act. The Sanctuary activists contended that their interpretation was not only in keeping with the letter of the law, but was much more congruent with constitutional rights and the spirit of the law. They argued that deportation of these persecuted aliens would expose them to further persecution, and that this was plainly illegal. The government disagreed. In fact, fourteen movement men were indicted on felony charges of conspiracy and alien smuggling, and eight of them were convicted. Thus the attempt of ordinary Americans to reinterpret the law failed. But it is of no small interest that they tried to mount such a revision and that they got as far as they did with it.

Here we see that in this instance direct confrontation of the government by citizens to force a reinterpretation of the law was not effective. They were challenging what they saw as a discretionary decision by officials that could

From Susan Bibler Coutin, "Enacting Law through Social Practice: Sanctuary as a Form of Resistance," in Mindie Lazarus-Black and Susan F. Hirsch (eds.) *Contested States, Law, Hegemony and Resistance* (New York and London: Routledge, 1994), pp. 282–91, 299–303.

have been decided another way. Was the result a feature of the political climate of the time? Could citizen action of this kind ever succeed? Civil rights groups in the US are bringing analogous actions with respect to detainees not charged with anything specific, but held under the various legislative acts and executive decisions dealing with terrorists. These issues bring out questions concerning the scope of state sovereignty in the shadow of the overarching and increasingly cogent reach of international law. But these are not only abstract issues about law itself. They are also issues about people, which people do what, which officials and official bodies are making what rulings, and which citizens are ready to challenge them. It is at this level that observations that anthropology can provide become illuminating. In the instance of the Sanctuary Movement, the anthropologist was able to observe what went on in the citizen group and to come to understand their vision of their mission, and to note the difference between their interpretations of the law and those of the government. It is significant that the Sanctuary Movement saw its activities as acts of "civil initiative" not as acts of "civil disobedience," putting their activities in a constructive light. The government did not agree.

S.F.M.

Coutin, *Sanctuary and Resistance*

One Sunday afternoon in April 1987, representatives of twenty-six congregations that had declared themselves sanctuaries for Central American refugees gathered in a Protestant church in Berkeley, California, for their monthly steering committee meeting. Among the agenda items was an announcement about an upcoming event: a "Journey to Central America." Instead of its regular business meeting in May, the Northern California Sanctuary Covenant – a group of eighty sanctuary congregations, to which the twenty-six that were meeting in Berkeley belonged – would hold "a smorgasbord of events" designed to renew participants' enthusiasm for sanctuary work. According to a flyer that was distributed to representatives, the Journey would have "something for everyone!... New people may hear their first testimonies, and ask those first difficult questions. Experienced workers may be refreshed in a workshop on Christian base communities, or get the latest information on Human Rights violations." The journey took place, and, at the June steering committee meeting, a local minister declared that it had been a success. There had been delicious Salvadoran food, informative updates on the situation in Central America, and "some people there heard their first testimonies!"

The testimonies featured during the journey to Central America were among the oppositional legal practices created by members of the Sanctuary movement: a grassroots religious-based network that formed in the early 1980s to aid undocumented Salvadoran and Guatemalan refugees. The Central Americans assisted by the movement were in a *contested state of being*. Because these immigrants had entered the country without the knowledge or authorization of the US government, the US legal system defined them as illegal aliens. Religious workers who encountered these immigrants and heard their stories of persecution concluded that they met the legal definition of "refugee" and therefore deserved asylum in the United States.

After attempts to secure asylum for these immigrants proved futile, volunteers resorted to granting Central Americans the refuge to which they felt they were entitled. Drawing on their knowledge of US immigration law, volunteers began screening Central Americans who were still south of the border, bringing those deemed refugees into the United States, sheltering Central Americans in volunteers' homes and religious institutions, and publicizing these immigrants "testimonies" – their accounts of flight and persecution. Paradoxically, these practices, which derived from law, also *redefined* law by authorizing private citizens to determine immigrants' legal statuses.

The fact that a dissident movement used the law to challenge the deportation of torture victims would appear to settle a much-debated question: Does law legitimize or limit repression? To Sanctuary workers, US and international refugee law seemed an indictment of authorities' treatment of Central American immigrants. Participants' knowledge of the law fueled their shared sense of injustice, became a basis for movement practices, and enabled volunteers to construct persuasive public arguments. By grounding their actions in law, Sanctuary workers made the community, rather than the government, the ultimate legal authority, and thus created a form of popular justice. However, the political implications of movement practices were more complex than this analysis suggests. By assuming the authority to interpret law, Sanctuary workers created hierarchies between themselves and Central Americans. For example, although the testimonies performed during the journey to Central America drew listeners into the discourse of the movement, these tales of torture subjected Central Americans to the scrutiny of Sanctuary workers who would define these immigrants' legal identities and use this knowledge to fuel volunteers' own activism. The Sanctuary movement's oppositional legal practices thus demonstrate the difficulty of drawing on the law's potential for resistance without simultaneously invoking its capacity to oppress (see, e.g., Foucault 1980; Abu-Lughod 1990; see also Hirsch and Lazarus-Black this volume). Fully understanding how the movement's use of law was simultaneously hegemonic and resistant requires a deeper exploration of the ways that Sanctuary practices both shaped and were shaped by US immigration law.

US Immigration Law

US immigration law consists not only of legal codes, juridical procedures, and institutional structures, but also of meanings and practices that pervade everyday social relations. These meanings and practices form a discourse that both derives from and produces written law. The assumptions that make it possible to divide the US populace into citizens, legal residents, illegal aliens, and so forth have become so culturally ingrained that these categories shape individuals' perceptions of social reality. Moreover, just as police surveillance and court hearings judge individuals' legal statuses, daily activities, such as going to the bank or applying for a job, continually objectify, identify, and classify individuals within legal categories. These classifications *materially constitute* individuals as legal beings, making people's privileges, rights, and actions dependent on their juridical statuses. As law creates social reality, social reality reproduces the law. When individuals are defined within particular legal categories, these categories are reauthorized and recreated on an ongoing basis. The fact that law shapes and is reconstructed through social life makes everyday social practices an arena in which juridical notions (and ultimately, the formal legal statutes) can be contested and reshaped. It was this dialectic between legal notions and social action that enabled religious volunteers to create the Sanctuary movement.

The legal category that most deeply affected the social reality that Sanctuary workers sought to change was "illegal alien." In the United States, this category derives from forms of juridical identity that emerged with constitutional government and that distinguish sharply between citizens and aliens. Citizenship, which replaced the monarch-subject relationship when the American colonies became a nation, is an abstract linkage between an individual and the law. The legal nature of citizenship is demonstrated by the fact that, to become U.S. citizens, individuals swear allegiance to the Constitution, and even those who are citizens by birth are assumed to have accepted the law's authority (Foucault 1979). Their relationship to the law grants citizens a *jural* existence in addition to their *physical* existence – a form of legal personhood that is attested to through birth certificates, death certificates, and the like. The creation of citizenship also produced this category's antithesis: alienage. All those who are not party to the law of a given nation are aliens. Unlike citizens, aliens do not intrinsically possess a jural existence.

If citizens remained within their country's borders and aliens remained without, then physical and juridical reality would coincide. However, individuals do cross international boundaries, therefore states have assumed the authority to grant partial or temporary legal statuses (such as "resident alien") to aliens whose presences are authorized, and to define those whose presences are *not* authorized as *illegal* aliens: beings who, paradoxically, are physically present but legally nonexistent. In the United States, the days of open immigration, when "aliens simply arrived on our shores, found lodging and jobs, and were assimilated by degrees into the society" (Harwood 1986:2), ended in 1882 with the Chinese Exclusion Act. Over the years, the United States established quotas to regulate the immigration of different nationalities and criteria to exclude such people as homosexuals, communists, and criminals. By 1986, the federal prosecutor who tried eleven Sanctuary workers on alien-smuggling charges could proclaim, "Every nation has the absolute power to control its borders, to determine who comes in their country, when they come in, where they come in, how long they are going to be here, what they are going to do, how they are going to support themselves and when they are going to leave" (Official Trial Transcripts 1986:14191). When being present in the United States without governmental permission became a crime, actions such as overstaying one's visa or clandestinely crossing the border became *states of being* (see, e.g., Asad 1983) – though, these might be better termed states of *non*being, since illegal aliens are in, but not of, society.

The jural notions out of which the construct "illegal alien" was formed authorize and derive from institutional structures that situate individuals within this and other legal categories. These structures include law enforcement authorities who scrutinize the population, extracting knowledge that can be used to categorize individuals. Along the US Mexico border, over four thousand border patrol agents use motion detectors, surveillance cameras, helicopters, and spotter aircraft to identify unauthorized border crossers. In the interior, Immigration officials observe bus and train stations, check the highways for suspicious-looking travelers, raid workplaces, and inspect employee records (Harwood 1986). Immigration discourse is institutionalized not only in the form of law enforcement officials but also in detention centers that hold apprehended illegal aliens pending deportation or a redefinition of their legal statuses. By separating "illegal aliens" from the rest of the population, detention centers restore the alignment between physical and juridical reality. Finally, immigration discourse is embodied in Immigration courts and Immigration judges; institutions that further scrutinize immigrants by eliciting statements and documents that are then measured against legal categories in order to properly classify individuals. Those judged to be illegal aliens are returned to their sites of legal existence, not as a punishment, but rather as a means of restoring order.

The structures that locate individuals within particular immigration categories – and thus reproduce these categories – are not limited to the formal legal apparatus. US immigration law and policy hold individuals accountable for the legal statuses of those whom they harbor, transport, and hire. As a result, private individuals as well as government officials scrutinize the populace and judge immigration statuses. Identity documents, social security numbers, and proofs of citizenship are sometimes required by hospitals, college admissions officers, landlords, employers, social service agencies, religious charities, banks, and granting agencies, usually by individuals with no connection to the US Immigration and Naturalization Service (INS). To give but a few examples, one community college denied admission to an otherwise qualified undocumented Salvadoran immigrant, social workers screened Arizona welfare applicants by tapping into INS computers (Fischer 1986), and, as of 1988, the Tucson Salvation Army not only required proof of legal status from aid recipients, but also detained undocumented women and children arrested by the border patrol (personal communication). Because those who are defined as illegal immigrants are usually denied services, daily social life separates the undocumented and the documented as surely as the bars of detention centers. Thus, the classifications performed by private citizens, like the judgments rendered by Immigration officials, recreate the legal discourse that defines individuals as juridical (or nonjuridical) beings.

The mutually influencing relationship between immigration law and daily social life creates a potential for resistance that Sanctuary workers exploited. By acting according to *their own* rather than the state's, interpretation of US immigration and refugee law, movement members sought to produce a different legal and social reality than is usually created by interaction between the documented and the undocumented.

Devising Oppositional Legal Practices

It was in the early 1980s, when they encountered undocumented Central American immigrants, that the religious volunteers who eventually would become Sanctuary workers first realized that their actions were being defined by US immigration law. Until then, most of these middle-class, white, more often than not middle-aged members of mainline congregations had had little contact with the legal system, and even less with immigration law. Soon, however, they found themselves preparing asylum applications, attending deportation hearings, raising bail bond for detained Central Americans, and serving as legal guardians for Salvadoran and Guatemalan minors apprehended by the INS. These experiences gave volunteers the legal expertise – what Merry (1990) terms the "legal consciousness" – that enabled them to formulate their own interpretations of US refugee and immigration law. Volunteers discovered that it could be illegal to act on these interpretations by aiding Central Americans who had not been detained by Immigration officials and who therefore lacked even a temporary legal status. Volunteers also realized that if they did *not* aid undocumented Central Americans, they would be allowing their own actions to define Central Americans as illegal aliens who could be detained and deported. This awareness led volunteers to devise practices that would prevent deportations, define Central Americans as refugees rather than as illegal aliens, and promote their own understanding of US immigration law.

The first contact between undocumented Central Americans and religious volunteers in Tucson, Arizona, and the San Francisco East Bay in California – the two communities where I did fieldwork – occurred during the summer of 1980, when a group of Salvadorans was found in an Arizona desert where they had been abandoned by their *coyote*, an individual who, for a fee, smuggles undocumented people into the United States. Half had perished. Several church groups in Arizona set out to aid the survivors, only to find the INS preparing to deport them to El Salvador. This shocked church workers who had resettled Cuban, Southeast Asian, Indonesian, and Chilean refugees with the *support* of the US government. One volunteer reported that such governmental actions taught her "the difference between a 'refugee' and a 'refugee.' Before, I'd thought of a refugee as someone who is seeking shelter, but after working with the Central Americans, I became aware that it's a legal status." Shortly after the Salvadorans were abandoned in the desert, the Manzo Area Council, a local community organization, informed Tucson church groups that undocumented Salvadorans had begun requesting legal assistance. Outraged over the INS's treatment of the abandoned Salvadorans and galvanized by the growing publicity about human rights abuses in Central America, the churches readily agreed to help. Manzo, Tucson church groups, and the INS developed the following arrangement: Manzo prepared and submitted asylum applications for Central Americans, churches agreed to meet asylum applicants' material needs, and the INS accepted applications without detaining applicants.

Church groups' outrage over INS treatment of Central Americans deepened when INS policy changed and religious volunteers learned that, all along, the INS had been detaining Salvadoran and Guatemalan immigrants who were not associated with church groups. In the spring of 1981, shortly after former president Ronald Reagan's inauguration, a Manzo client who had voluntarily entered an INS office to apply for political asylum was taken into custody rather than released. A Manzo representative traced the client to the El Centro detention center only to discover some two hundred Central Americans imprisoned in deplorable conditions. Reportedly, it was common for the INS to expose prisoners to the Arizona sun in order to coerce them into signing deportation papers. Inmates lacked medical attention, attorneys, and the ability to receive phone calls. Members of Manzo and the Tucson Ecumenical Council of churches met to address this situation. A minister present at the meeting related: "[We] decided to mount an enormous effort to bond out the people who were in detention. Within a short period of time, we had raised something like $30,000 for bond money, and folks put up their homes for the bonds.... I think that we bonded out fourteen people in one day.... We found that we were responsible for a legal aid project, for raising bonds, and for social services for people who were bonded out."

As they prepared asylum applications and raised money for bail bond, Tucson church workers became convinced that Salvadorans and Guatemalans were entitled to refugee status, but that the political asylum process was stacked against them. Tucson volunteers reported that the INS pressured detained Salvadorans and Guatemalans to sign deportation papers by separating families and telling each member that the others had already signed. Government officials raised bond fees from $500 to $1,000 to $5,000, draining volunteers' sources of bond money. The immigrants that were bailed out by Tucson church groups were almost immediately replaced by newly detained Central Americans. The asylum applications prepared with congregation members' assistance were consistently denied. Tucson volunteers soon discovered that their experiences were not unique. At a fall 1981 meeting, church and legal groups from Tucson, Los Angeles, San Francisco, Texas, and elsewhere compared notes and concluded that INS harassment of Central American asylum applicants and their advocates was widespread and systematic. A minister who attended this meeting commented, "We thought at first that what we were experiencing was a strange, isolated situation of some rednecked administrator, but we discovered that everyone had had the same experiences."

As they began to conclude that helping Central Americans apply for political asylum was futile, religious workers in Tucson resorted to what they then considered illegal actions. Volunteers continued to submit asylum applications for detainees, since this was the only way to secure their release. However, rather than bringing undetained Central Americans to the attention of INS officials by way of an asylum application, volunteers began helping unapprehended Salvadorans and Guatemalans evade detection. The pastor of one of the churches involved in this effort explained that his congregation had refused to let immigration law determine its response to the persecuted: "We decided that we had always helped people before on the basis of human need, and that we'd never asked anyone for their IDs, or green cards." When the INS warned participating church groups that they would be indicted if they continued to aid undocumented Central Americans, Tucson religious workers decided to seek public support. On March 24, 1982, Southside Presbyterian Church in Tucson, five East Bay congregations, and a handful of churches around the United States publicly declared themselves sanctuaries for Central American refugees. At the time, participants believed that the declarations broke the law. A March 23, 1982, letter from Southside's pastor to the US attorney general stated, "We are writing to inform you that Southside United Presbyterian Church will publicly violate the Immigration and Nationality Act, Section 274(A)" (Corbett 1986:36). The letter justified the church's actions by noting that the US government was violating both international law and the 1980 Refugee Act by detaining Central Americans and deporting them to places of persecution.

As, during the coming months and years, the original Sanctuary congregations were joined by others, members of what was fast becoming a movement redefined the legal significance of their actions. After consulting their attorneys and further studying US and international refugee law, church groups concluded that, far from breaking the law, offering sanctuary to undocumented Salvadorans and Guatemalans *obeyed* US and international laws guaranteeing refuge to victims of persecution. As early as sixteen months after the original declarations, attorneys began to advise Sanctuary workers that their actions could be considered legal under the very laws they accused the government of breaking. For example, in July 1983, Ira Gollobin, the immigration law consultant for Church World Service, informed Sanctuary workers that the United Nations protocol on refugees, which was made part of US law in 1968, prohibited returning individuals with a well-founded fear of persecution to their countries of origin, even if they had entered another country illegally. Gollobin concluded, "In granting sanctuary to the Salvadoreans seeking asylum here, the Churches act in conformity with the letter, as well as the spirit, of constitutional rights and statutory law" (Corbett 1986:64).

Sanctuary workers had an opportunity to test their claim that sanctuary was legal (and to develop additional legal expertise) when, in January 1985, a Tucson grand jury indicted fourteen movement members on felony charges of conspiracy and alien smuggling. These were not the first charges filed against Sanctuary workers, since, during the previous year, four volunteers had been arrested in Arizona and Texas in separate incidents. However, the extent of the indictments and the discovery that the government had resorted to infiltrating the movement led many Sanctuary workers to regard this legal contest as the deciding battle in their struggle on behalf of Central Americans. Sanctuary communities around the United States contributed to the defense effort, while, in Tucson, the indicted and their attorneys further elaborated their legal arguments in preparation for the courtroom confrontation. However, Sanctuary workers' initial enthusiasm for having their day in court faded when, at the trial's outset, the judge ruled most of their legal arguments inadmissible. When the trial ended with convictions for eight of the eleven defendants who actually stood trial, movement members renewed their determination to continue sanctuary work.

When I began doing fieldwork in Tucson and East Bay Sanctuary communities some six months after the trial's conclusion, I learned how Sanctuary workers' interpretations of the law had shaped movement practices. In Tucson, Sanctuary activists sought to define Central Americans as refugees through a legal philosophy and praxis that participants called "civil initiative." Civil initiative is grounded in the notion that communities have a sense of law that is more fundamental than the formal legal codes.[4] According to the Sanctuary workers who devised civil initiative, this fundamental sense of law concerns basic human rights which, because they are universally valid, are codified in international and religious law. Tucson Sanctuary workers argued that in the case of US immigration law, the problem was not that US legal codes conflicted with basic human rights, but rather that the US government had *interpreted* its immigration statutes in ways that violated the community's consensus that the persecuted should not be deported to face further persecution. To correct this misinterpretation, Sanctuary workers decided to act as they felt the government ought to have been doing. They reasoned that this would force the US government to comply with community legal norms in one of two ways. Either the government would fail to prosecute Sanctuary workers, thus tacitly legitimizing their claims, or authorities would issue indictments, thus giving Sanctuary workers the opportunity to state their position before a jury of peers who, presumably, would share their interpretation of the law. (Movement members did not consider the Tucson Sanctuary trial a true test of this theory, since defendants had not been permitted to present their legal arguments.) Participants called their legal strategy civil initiative rather than civil disobedience because they believed that it enforced, rather than violated, federal and international law.

Although sharing Tucson volunteers' belief in the legality of their work, East Bay Sanctuary activists' use of the law was not as complex as that of their Tucson counterparts. East Bay Sanctuary workers did not differentiate between communities' understanding of the law and the formal legal codes, but rather argued simply that sanctuary was legally justified on the basis of federal and international law. Legal arguments were less important to East Bay Sanctuary workers than to Tucsonans for several reasons. East Bay Sanctuary workers devoted a greater portion of their time to stopping US military aid to El Salvador, while their Tucson colleagues focused more on establishing refugee rights. Due to their distance from the US-Mexico border, East Bay activists were not involved in the legally risky work of border crossings, nor had any East Bay Sanctuary worker been arrested for participating in the movement. However, there were parallels between Tucson and East Bay activists' legal philosophies. Both groups declared that their work was legal, that Salvadorans and Guatemalans were refugees rather than economic immigrants, and that the US government's refugee policy violated US and international law. Both also incorporated immigration law into movement practices in order to establish the validity of these contentions. The political implications of the movement's use of law can be assessed by examining movement practices that both derived from and sought to influence U.S. immigration law. There were three such practices: screening potential immigrants; giving sanctuary to undocumented Central Americans within the United States; and publicizing refugees' testimonies.

[...]

Conclusion

US immigration law creates interconnected potentials for power and for resistance. For example, holding individuals accountable for the immigration statuses of their peers makes private citizens agents of surveillance but also implies that individuals are capable of interpreting and enforcing the law. When Sanctuary workers used their knowledge of the immigration system to devise practices that would promote their own legal notions, they inevitably both resisted and furthered repression. On the one hand, screening, sheltering, and publicizing the stories of undocumented Salvadoran and Guatemalan immigrants challenged US Central American and refugee policy, contested the exclusivity of the state's control of international travel, declared that individuals could be legal refugees without having been so designated by government officials, made the community, rather than the state, the ultimate legal authority, and overcame some of the divisions between the documented and the undocumented. On the other hand, these practices reinforced distinctions between legal and illegal immigration, criminalized the presence of the immigrants denied movement assistance, subjected Central Americans to the scrutiny of movement members, objectified Central Americans by measuring their lives against legal defin-itions, and created a hierarchy between the Sanctuary workers who defined and the refugees who were defined. The movement's effort to define Central Americans as refugees in some ways reinforced the system that constituted these immigrants as illegal aliens...

The political complexity of Sanctuary practices suggests that, because immigra-tion law and social life shape one another, other forms of interaction between the documented and the undocumented are equally contradictory. In creating movement practices, Sanctuary workers did not intend to reinforce the subjugation of undocu-mented people or to create hierarchical relations between themselves and Central Americans. Rather, movement members sought only to compel government officials to recognize Salvadorans' and Guatemalans' status as political refugees. However, the political implications of social practices derive not only from their ultimate goals, but also from the practices themselves. When Tucson Sanctuary workers concluded that a Salvadoran met the legal definition of "refugee" and deserved to be brought into the United States, these activists asserted that citizens were em-powered to interpret and apply US immigration law. This assertion challenged the US government's claim to be the sole legitimate arbiter of immigration status, but placed Sanctuary workers in positions of authority vis-à-vis the Salvadoran in question. Similarly, when a Sanctuary congregation invited an undocumented Gua-temalan refugee to give her testimony during Sunday morning services, the congre-gation publicized the voice of one whose very presence was forbidden but also subjected the Guatemalan to an invasive if well-meaning examination by congre-gation members. If such legally inspired social actions could deconstruct and re-inforce power relations, so too can a nurse's decision to treat an undocumented patient, or an employer's refusal to hire a day laborer who lacks papers. The power and resistance that inhere in Sanctuary practices are intrinsic to the relationship between law and social life.

REFERENCES

Abu-Lughod, Lila. 1990. "The Romance of Resistance: Tracing Transformations of Power through Bedouin Women." *American Ethnologist* 17(1): 41–55.

Asad, Talal. 1983. "Notes on Body Pain and Truth in Medieval Christian Ritual." *Economy and Society* 12:287–327.

Corbett, Jim. 1986. *Borders and Crossings. Vol. I: Some Sanctuary Papers, 1981–86.* April ed. Tucson: Tucson Refugee Support Group.

Coutin, Susan, 1993. *The Culture of Protest: Religious Activism and the U.S. Sanctuary Movement.* Denver: Westview Press.

Fischer, Howard. 1986. "Panel OKs INS Trace for Welfare." *Arizona Daily Republic,* 2 April:1C.

Foucault, Michel. 1979. *Discipline and Punish: The Birth of the Prison.* Alan Sheridan, trans. New York: Vintage Books.

Greenhouse, Carol. 1989. "Interpreting American Litigiousness." In *History and Power in the Study of Law: New Directions in Legal Anthropology.* June Starr and Jane F. Collier, eds. Ithaca: Cornell University Press. 252–76.

Harwood, Edwin. 1986. *In Liberty's Shadow: Illegal Aliens and Immigration Law Enforcement*. Stanford: Stanford University Press.

Merry, Sally. 1990. *Getting Justice and Getting Even: Legal Consciousness among Working-Class Americans*. Chicago: University of Chicago Press.

Official Trial Transcripts. 1986. *U.S. v. Aguilar*. No. CR–85–008–PHX–EHC (D. Ariz.).

24

Deciding Who Gets In: Decisionmaking by Immigration Inspectors

Janet A. Gilboy

Introduction: Decisionmaking by Immigration Inspectors

This article by Janet A. Gilboy gives one a glimpse of the kind of rapid assessment that lower level decision-makers produce on a daily basis. It is a straightforward description of observations of inspectors at work made in an international airport. There were two levels of inspection. The job of the primary inspectors was to look over the travel documents of foreign nationals who wanted to get into the USA, to question them rapidly about their reasons for visiting, and then, in a matter of minutes, to decide whether they should be admitted or whether the case should be referred to a secondary inspector for further questioning and possibly for a baggage check. If the decision is that a person is not admissible, then the individual is given the choice of deportation, going home on the next plane, or of having a determination made before a Department of Justice immigration judge.

Anyone who has seen the lines that form in airports when planes arrive will understand the time pressure involved, and will be impressed by the discretionary powers exercised by the inspectors after a very small investigation. What is of sociological and anthropological interest is the way the inspectors make their job into a practically realizable task. The federal law iterates certain "exclusion categories," but it is up to the inspectors to decide which people are, for example, security risks, or are likely to become public charges because they are entering without sufficient funds and no ascertainable means of support. There are various types of training for the job of inspector, but the most important part is the experience of watching a seasoned inspector at work. The training

---

From Janet A. Gilboy, "Deciding Who gets In: Decisionmaking by Immigration Inspectors," *Law and Society Review* 25(3) (1991), pp. 574–8, 580–99.

provides guidelines, but it is the conversation among inspectors, primary and secondary, comparing notes about what is involved in a particular day's work that ultimately determines the standards they apply. They consider nationals of certain countries suspect, and of other countries "safe." Thus in quite an informal way, a socially defined set of standards evolves. One wonders how much the key pieces of negative information about nationality, ethnic group, and the like have changed since the alarms have sounded about terrorism.

Clearly an issue of importance in this kind of review is the numbers processed. There is a limit to the number of persons involved, whether of inspectors, or Department of Justice hearing agents. The primary task of giving or withholding the legal status of admissibility is initially in the discretion of non-judicial personnel. This is the operation of bureaucratic legal decision-making by lay persons who, to some extent, collectively and individually generate their own standards of operation.

S.F.M.

Gilboy, *Immigration Inspectors*

I Introduction

...This article contributes to this emerging "organizationally grounded" approach to social control decisionmaking by examining the nature of categorization in an area rarely examined – immigration primary inspection. Immigration primary inspection consists of officers' questioning of foreign nationals at ports of entry to the United States. Decisions are made regarding individuals' admissibility to the country. There is little research on current admission-exclusion processing...

My data are drawn largely from a study at an international airport ("Metropolitan Port") in the United States. Every day thousands of individuals fly into this airport seeking to be admitted to the United States. Many are US citizens returning from vacations or business trips. Others are foreign nationals seeking to enter or reenter the United States.

Every traveler is inspected by a primary inspector. Prior to collecting their baggage, each arriving passenger's entry documents (passports, permanent resident cards, etc.) are reviewed by an inspector. Should the inspector suspect that a person is ineligible to enter, the person will be referred to a secondary inspector for further questioning and a possible baggage search. At the port studied, about 2 percent of the foreign nationals seeking to enter as nonimmigrants are referred for secondary inspection (see table 1). If the secondary inspector concludes that the individual entering with a visa is not admissible, that person typically is given the choice of going home on the next plane or being detained and having admissibility determined in exclusion proceedings before a Department of Justice immigration judge.

Primary inspectors theoretically possess extensive discretion stemming from broad delegations of legal authority and from the organizational characteristics of enforcement. Legally, the federal law contains nine exclusion categories (including health, criminal, and security reasons). Broad discretionary power lies in the fact-

Table 1   Overview of Disposition of Inspected Foreign Nationals ("Metropolitan Port")

	Total Foreign Nationals (Nonimmigrants) Inspected		Admitted After Primary Inspection		Admitted After Secondary Inspection		Paroled into U.S.		Inspection Deferred		Not Admitted	
	No.	%	No.	%	No.	%	No.	%	No.	%	No.	%
1986	329,619	100.0	321,761	97.6	6,674	2.0	250	0.1	313	0.1	621	0.2
1987	416,014	100.0	406,039	97.6	8,343	2.0	768	0.2	319	0.1	545	0.1
1988	527,505	100.1	513,724	97.4	11,374	2.2	1,370	0.3	337	0.1	700	0.1
1989	598,195	100.0	585,062	97.8	11,555	1.9	481	0.1	336	0.1	761	0.1

Source: Developed from Immigration and Naturalization Service ("Metropolitan Port") District Office, Monthly Office Workload Summary, G22.1 forms.

finding process for establishing these grounds for exclusion. Moreover, given the social organization of immigration enforcement, inspectors potentially have considerable scope within which to exercise their discretion. Organizationally, this is a policing activity insulated to a considerable extent from outside demands or complaints for enforcement, thus giving the agency much leeway in the development and implementation of enforcement strategies that ultimately affect the identification and processing of suspected excludable foreign nationals (see generally Hutter 1986:117; Black 1971:1095; Waegel 1981:270). Then, too, primary inspectors are operating in a relatively low-visibility decisionmaking position (by themselves in glass booths), in a one-to-one private interaction with passengers, in which superiors have little means to know if they are making mistakes or doing the job properly. This is not to say there are no limits on the discretion of primary inspectors. As discussed later, national and port policy require some types of travelers to be automatically sent by inspectors for further secondary inspection.

To collect data for this study, I traveled to Metropolitan Port and observed inspections for 102 days. Fieldwork began early in March 1988; the last trip to the port took place in December 1990. The selection of Metropolitan Port was partly a practical choice relating to matters of travel and access. But, more importantly, the port of entry is one of the largest US international airports and one at which the Immigration and Naturalization Service (INS) annually processes hundreds of thousands of applications for admission by foreign nationals, US citizens, and permanent residents, thus providing an excellent opportunity to look at how national exclusion laws and procedures are implemented...

II "Working the Line": Primary Inspection

"Flights in! Flights in!" The shout filters back to the small lunchroom as inspectors quickly move to the passenger arrival area and take their seats in the glass-partitioned booths stretched across a wide room. Another afternoon of inspecting international air travelers has begun.

The port of entry is a large and busy place with thousands of international travelers arriving within a few hours. At peak times, such as the summer, travelers almost continuously spill into the port and join other weary travelers standing in line for inspection. As each traveler completes inspection, tens of others are also beginning or completing their inspections in front of other primary inspectors.

Although full-time permanent primary inspectors receive several months of formal inspection instruction and language training, they chiefly learn how to make decisions by "working the line." Inspection work is informed not only by inspectors' experience on the primary line but also by secondary inspection work. The dead time between flights regularly allows inspectors to share stories and knowledge about passengers as well as to check up on cases they referred to secondary – thus learning from one another as well as reinforcing shared notions about travelers. More experienced inspectors also do secondary inspections, which helps them see what kinds of cases can be developed from bits of information generated on the primary line. Finally, inspectors share information in occasional staff meetings, discussing problem groups of travelers and hearing announcements regarding policies for inspections...

Indeed, like other decisionmakers faced with the need to make decisions on the spot, inspectors organize and make sense of their world using two major techniques: (1) focused data collection and (2) categorization.

1   Focused Data Collection

Primary inspection is focused. Inspectors tend to work with a few standard questions. Their task usually is not one of streamlining existing mounds of data, as it is for some decisionmakers (e.g., parole officers, Hawkins 1983:114–16) but rather one of generating kernels of useful information.

When time permits, the more experienced inspectors scan the lines of waiting passengers to learn more about individuals. For the most part, though, inspections are confined to information gathered at the inspection booth. The initial key pieces of data sought from questioning and document examination include the purpose of the trip (business or pleasure), length of stay, and who or what (family, friends, company, or trade show) the person is visiting...

In inspection work there are few features of cases (e.g., "nervousness," "a request to stay in US for many months," "touring without a destination," "no plane tickets" or "tickets without a return date") that by themselves trigger a secondary inspection referral. The salience and interpretation of bits of information are understood through the filter of understandings from categories of cases that inspectors learn while working at the port.

These categories provide a starting point for the direction of more developed questioning when items of information from the standard question tip off the inspector that something may be wrong. The conception of the normal tourist/ business traveler and the *unfolding nature* of the inspection in the face of discrepancies is described by one inspector.

> If they say they're going to be here for two to three weeks, to me that's a bona fide entry. If they're going to stay six months, then I have to know how much money they have in order to support themselves. Have they abandoned their residence? I tend to think that they may be taking up residence here in the US If they just came here for two or three

months and then go and return, I want to question that, and we'll send them to secondary. Most of those people are just living here, and they went back for a short visit, and are returning here again. (Inspector 1) . . .

While inspectors can and do reformulate their pictures of travelers, they can never completely ignore the fact that their task is to quickly move the line while still looking for the bad ones. Most inspectors frequently wonder whether they have asked enough questions of a traveler they just admitted to the country. Indeed, a striking feature of work is the degree of uncertainty about many completed inspections.

2 Normal Case Categories: "High-Risk" and "Low-Risk" Travelers

Categorization of events and people abounds in inspection work. The entire world of the inspector is one of well-honed understandings and occupational typifications of events and people. For instance, some flights come to be described by all inspectors as "dirty flights" – flights perceived as having an unusual concentration of morally repugnant travelers (e.g., fraudulent passport users). Other flights are labeled as "bad flights" – flights requiring inspectors to deal with matters viewed as unrelated and inferior to their occupational skills (e.g., filling out travelers' uncompleted entry documents) (Hughes 1958:70–2; Emerson and Pollner 1976:244). Flights not marked by such problems are labeled "clean flights." Moreover, inspectors take great pride in their knowledge of their setting – for instance, in identifying the nationality of passengers by the height of the men, by the straightness of the inspection queue, or the existence of pushing in it.

Inspectors hold a set of notions about the problems they are likely to find on various flights and with various types of individuals. These preconceptions tend to be organized into a number of unwritten "normal cases," that is, "locally recognized, recurrently encountered types of case[s], usually comprised of a series . . . of more specific typifications" and formulated to deal with certain organizational situations or problems (Emerson 1988:7).

Inspectors describe passengers in terms of "high-risk" or "low-risk" groups of travelers . . .

In the immigration setting, the bifurcated case set of high- and low-risk travelers reflects the binary nature of the decision task of primary inspectors – deciding who to let through and who to secondary. The categorization reflects and assists inspectors' thinking about the allocation of the port's secondary resources under general working conditions of uncertainty about the nature of cases being inspected. The high-risk travelers are ones on whom the port is willing to expend its secondary inspection resources. Indeed, the categorization contains a specific decision type (type II error) – a willingness to err in the direction of overinclusiveness or erroneous referrals to secondary inspection of travelers subsequently found admissible. The opposite decision error is embedded in perceived low-risk categories. Nonindividualized sorting sometimes occurs, and generally an approach of "we'll get you the next time" (rather than a secondary referral) exists on the primary line when an officer is suspicious but unable to put his finger on anything concrete.

There are good reasons why inspectors are willing to err on the side of admission with low-risk cases. The occasional admission of an otherwise inadmissible alien is not viewed as serious or dangerous to the nation – at the worst, the admitted alien may be an intending immigrant or worker, not a terrorist, smuggler, or criminal. If inspectors mistakenly admit an inadmissible foreign national, there is no review of the decision and no one is likely to know of the mistake. In contrast, their judgment is likely to be called into question if they refer a series of perceived "nothing" cases to secondary inspectors. Different settings have different costs for different types of decision errors; for example, the parole board that erroneously releases an offender can be criticized. In this setting, individual inspectors, and the port in general, are far more open to complaints and criticisms for slowing down the primary line with lots of questioning or for referring travelers while digging too deeply for the needles in the haystack.

3   Types of Travelers – Negative and Positive Categories

A number of unwritten specific types of high-risk and low-risk travelers are used in inspection work. These types are derived primarily from organizational knowledge rather than from general cultural or common-sense knowledge. The types discussed are images of travelers shared by primary inspectors,[17] and inspectors themselves typically reported them in the course of describing particular inspections. Their knowledge about these types emerges largely from local port experience, but port awareness of problem travelers seen at other ports (from agency intelligence reports) informs that local experience to some extent. These types are learned on the job, and although inspectors are aware that they contain generalities that "prejudice" the individual traveler in the primary inspection, use of the categories is viewed as crucial to competent inspection . . .

Each specific type is a picture providing a fairly detailed description of the social and demographic features of the individuals, a prediction as to their likely intentions, and a "handling recipe" (Waegel 1981:272–3) that defines the appropriate response to individuals so categorized. In addition, categories in this setting typically are associated with a broader conception of the social organization of applications for admission (legal and illegal) and a formulation of the problems of policing (if any) they present – an assessment reflecting the port's own organizational interests and concerns that are both enforcement oriented and at times political in nature. In inspectors' descriptions of specific types of high-risk and low-risk travelers are often embedded judgments of credibility, that is, assessments of the likely trustworthiness or validity of statements and documents of individuals seeking admission to the United States.

> [*Commenting on one Asian country*] They're the best, we have very little fraud, visa or passport problems. They are legit. . . . *What they claim to be is the truth; they are not trying to pass themselves off as something that they are not.* (Inspector 16)
>
> Any male [from one specific Asian country] you secondary. You don't waste your breath. They're not going to tell you anything. They're going to give you a sing-song language, or *they are going to lie to you anyway.* (Inspector 14)
>
> What you're asking is mainly, "*does that person appear to be what he says he is.*" Quite often the national background makes a difference. Let's say he's from [a specific European country]. Now [they] come, and they say they backpack. . . . In most cases, that is just what they are going to do. (Inspector 23)

The imagery of how credibility assessments are made often plays down or ignores this larger categorization that embodies and influences initial assessments and their revisability. Credibility judgments are seen as the product of reactions to discrete characteristics of individuals, the outgrowth of decisionmakers' reactions to the way an individual speaks or acts. Implicit is a focus on the individual as the unit for analysis of how decisionmakers make assessments of credibility. Yet, in a variety of organizational circumstances, including the setting studied here, assessments of credibility are sometimes so shaped by decisionmakers' prior work experience or the local work culture that to view them as simply reactions to the behavior of the particular individual being judged is to misunderstand the nature of judgments...

a) Negative category – nationality

Many of the prominent types of high-risk travelers are based on nationality. These named types sometimes are not more precise than the country name (although sometimes age and gender are mentioned), since more refined distinctions are not relevant for the primary inspector's task. The importance of nationality is discussed by several inspectors...

Any inspector will describe one high-risk nationality category involving an Asian country – as typically young men coming with $1,000, going to "any hotel" and carrying no baggage but a briefcase. Such high-risk nationality categories are usually associated with routine processing and disposition practices that reflect the organization's priorities, concerns, incentives, and at times, political assessments.

At the port studied, the perception that the incidence of photograph substitutions on passports and visa fraud is very high for a number of countries has led to a port policy of automatically sending for secondary inspection all individuals presenting passports from those countries.

Little or no individualized inspection occurs; presentation of the country passport suffices to judge what type of individual is requesting admission. This handling implicitly reflects inspectors' notions about the individual's limited credibility, that is, lack of trustworthiness of statements or documents. "Judgments of credibility" thus are fundamentally shaped by the distinctive organizational task of the primary inspector – a quick sifting and referral of cases, with more individualized assessments left to the secondary officer. In short, judgments of credibility are embodied in the nationality categorization and are shaped as much, if not more, by decisionmakers' knowledge and experience with other cases than by specific features of the individual being assessed in the primary inspection. The reverse dispositional situation also exists. Individuals from some nations (described later) receive relatively limited primary questioning; their credibility is presumed, and their cases are rarely pursued in a secondary inspection.

Primary inspectors are aware that certain individual attributes (age, gender, economic status) are likely to be relevant in whether suspicions and assessments are eventually confirmed or discounted in these high-risk and low-trust cases. But these more refined classifications of travelers or individualized credibility assessments are not relevant for primary inspectors' specific practical decisionmaking task. The categorization, however, does not create blinders that prevent a later broader view of the case. In the secondary inspection, these initial preconceptions can be modified as additional information is gained from further questioning, baggage search, and technical document analysis.

In this setting, the "preformed decision" of an automatic referal is not unlike that used in other agency settings where administrators use this organizational strategy to provide control over low-visibility decisionmaking.... At the port studied, the preformed decision of automatic referral for certain countries is rooted in practical organizational concerns – the agency's high enforcement priority of identifying document fraud and smuggling, the port's interest in detecting as many serious immigration violators as possible for good port statistics, and the presence of inexperienced and busy inspectors on the primary lines whose technical equipment is less sophisticated than that in secondary inspection.

A developed conception of the organization of immigration fraud also underlies the port's extraordinary efforts to detect illegal entries in high-risk cases by limiting the discretion of primary inspectors. The problems in high-risk cases are viewed as fundamentally different from immigration troubles with most other travelers. High-risk cases, such as those in which document fraud appears, are viewed as involving highly organized crime rings. It is thought that if travelers using such documents get through one port, the crime rings will send more individuals to the port. Sending someone with a fraudulent entry document home from the airport is viewed as "getting a message back" that they are not going to get through this port, thus stemming future attempts. Finally, like the police in Skolnick's classic study (1975:45, 218–19), immigration inspectors place some immigration violations on a different moral level from others. The greater importance attached to serious criminal law violations (e.g., document fraud) than to relatively minor rule violations (child-care helpers or fiancées arriving without proper visas) may help explain the zealous efforts taken and the perceived reasonableness of these actions, even though some innocent travelers may be caught in the broad net of automatic secondary referrals.

The use of automatic referrals for high-risk nations, however, is also partly shaped by political assessments. For instance, early in the research, I observed that inspectors perceived that travelers from one European country routinely claiming to be tourists were coming to the United States to work temporarily. The Service could have made a concerted effort (as it does with some countries) to show that some of these travelers were not tourists, by automatic secondaries and routine searches of the luggage for physical evidence that they are planning to work. This was not done in part because experience suggested it was extremely difficult to find evidence to establish work intentions (e.g., letters from employers). But also inspectors perceived that introduction of such tactics was likely to provoke an outcry from a politically powerful local constituency and their local and national politicians. Moreover, they perceived that Department of State foreign policy interests in the preferred positive treatment of these nationals would make officials responsive to the anticipated intervention by political representatives.

Finally, nationality case categories resist extinction. While there may be cognitive reasons for this, there are also reasons grounded in inspectors' understanding of these cases. Long periods when there are no port problems for a particular nation do not necessarily signal a lack of need for the port's close scrutiny of a nation through automatic secondaries, but merely suggest that the individuals are not coming to the

United States or are going to other ports. Thus the very conception of the organization and nature of illegal activity diminishes the likelihood that these normal case categories will be readily extinguished.

b) Negative category – nannies

Another prominent working category of problem travelers is the "nanny," understood to be a young woman typically coming from certain specific European countries, in the early weeks of summer, for a so-called visit of several months with friends of her family who have small children. As an inspector explained in one case: "When I saw her, I knew she was bad. She was coming here for six months and she didn't know the family. She was typical. She fit a pattern" (Inspector 8).

Claims by young girls – that the visits are to see friends of the family who happen to have young children and that she will travel and holiday for several months – are "stories" that inspectors have heard many times and routinely result in referral to secondary inspection. The primary inspections are quickly terminated after "items of information" suggest commonalities between the particular case and the known nanny type – the remaining digging to confirm or disconfirm the initial suspicions is left to in-depth inquiry at the secondary stage. This response to such "stories" reflects the perceived similarity of the particular case to a whole set of other previously detected nanny cases that inspectors become aware of through follow-up of their primary referrals and (for some officers) from doing secondary inspections themselves...

Importantly, the bits of information that make up often-told stories by young girls do not provoke the same response when told by elderly men and women. Inspectors respond to these older travelers in very different ways since their stories are viewed as credible within the working knowledge of inspector.

Moreover, just as there is a developed conception of the world of immigration fraud, there is also a picture of the world of what some call nanny "smugglers." Hiring women to come to the United States to care for children would not be illegal had the family gone through the proper agencies and paperwork. But the conception is that families choose not to follow the law since the paperwork is too much trouble, the terms of employment limit the girl's working hours below those desired, and legal procedures require them to pay higher wages and benefits than they prefer. General knowledge about the category type of nanny also includes awareness of the unpleasant problems of dealing with wealthy, powerful, and often politically well-connected families when enforcing the law against illegal employment. These latter attributes usually are not attended to by primary inspectors, although they are not oblivious to them. These nanny attributes do concern the secondary inspectors and supervisors who must decide the lengths to which the port will go to remove a suspected nanny (e.g., whether there will be a concerted effort to "break" the girl), if no "foolproof" evidence, such as a letter from the employer, is found.

c) Positive category – nationality

Positive nationality types also guide decisionmaking. Business and tourist travelers from one Asian country have reputations for honesty and integrity in immigration matters and receive relatively little screening. There is a tendency where inaccessible airline interpreters prevent good communication to admit the individual despite these impediments to a full inspection. As one inspector described business travelers from this country: "[Their] businessmen are what they say they are. They have money and they have credit cards. They are here for what they say they are. They are low risk" (Inspector 8).

Country origin does not, however, exercise a consistent direct influence on categorization. Rather, national origin takes on a positive or negative image as it is filtered through the prototypical conceptions held by inspectors screening individuals with different organizational purposes in mind. At the port of entry the US Customs Service seeks to identify travelers involved in drug and merchandise smuggling or possible money-laundering schemes. Although immigration inspectors categorize the above-described Asian travelers as low risk for immigration purposes, when considering Customs concerns, they have doubts about their honesty. It is not uncommon for travelers from this nation to fail to declare that they are carrying more than $10,000 in cash, thus leading inspectors to screen them closely for possible further Customs questioning and baggage search.

d) Positive category – business travelers

Who a traveler is visiting also shapes processing. As in some other regulatory contexts, whether an enforcer is dealing with a large or small company leads him to have certain expectations about the kind of company and people he is dealing with and their willingness to comply with the law. These general understandings affect the way any particular case is handled (Hawkins 1984:114–15; Knapp 1981:550).

In the immigration area, people visiting large, so-called respectable companies (companies seen as unlikely to hire illegal aliens, such as big accounting firms or major corporations) are seldom queried at length except to establish that they are from the company. Once that is established, further examination is suspended, since the type of individual is understood to be low risk. In these cases, there is a tendency for inspectors to rely on the company's own screening of job candidates. This is essentially "surrogate screening," in which an earlier institution's decisionmaking is substituted for a fresh screening. Thus, decisions by other institutions, not within the legal system, come to affect legal decision-making. This shifting of screening to other institutions also is augmented by the additional weight given to the State Department's consular visa issuance process . . .

4   Short-Term Categories

Decisionmakers work not only with long-term normal case types but also with more short-term, temporary, or transitory categories developed through daily inspections. Inspectors learn of public or business events (trade shows, athletic events, biker's rallies) from other inspected passengers, and they draw on what they have learned about the intended length of visit and destination of these other visitors in decision-making. This information forms a valuable background for determining the scope and line of questioning, comparing the applicant's story to that of others before him, and filtering certain potentially "troubling" information as not relevant to the admission decision since these concerns have already been considered and discounted in other earlier inspections. For instance, as one inspector describes the inspection of several farmers traveling as a group, "They are farmers, and you don't ask them about money because they have little.... It's very obvious after the second one, they had the same ticket, and they're going to Sacramento to the show there. I have been seeing that all week. I know what it was."...

The mere presence of a group tour in the inspection line does not trigger a batch processing routine unless the nationality of the group is acceptable. For instance, during the processing of a tour from one Asian country I asked the inspector whether the fact that it was a tour affected the processing of these passengers? He volunteered: "It makes it faster.... Now, if it's a [negative category country] tour group, you do not approach it in the same way. You thoroughly check each one. There is a high degree of fraud. It sounds like prejudice, but it's just experience talking." Thus, implicit in the use (or nonuse) of batch processing is a conception about the type of travelers being inspected. When batch processing is employed, inspectors expect these groups to contain low-risk travelers whose more individualized inspection can be suspended because they are credible – the group contains neither travelers attempting to enter the country with fraudulent documents nor travelers whose stated intentions to tour are likely to conceal a different agenda.

5 Justifications for Secondary Referrals and Implications

Table 2 shows the justifications given by primary inspectors for their referrals to secondary inspection. Several points are worth mentioning. First, at the port studied decisions are heavily skewed to one outcome – admission (see table 1). The study has described the shared categories, decision rules, and practical procedures primary inspectors employ in sorting among passengers. Table 2 suggests that a significant portion (about half) of the secondaries occur because passengers fit an INS or port-designated category for mandatory or automatic secondary referral. The bulk of these referrals are due to port concerns and related categorization of certain nationalities as high risk for which a port policy of mandatory referral has emerged. In other words, for these and several other sorts of travelers (table 2 (b)-(d)), primary inspectors exercise little discretion in handling procedures once the case is categorized.

Second, the relatively large proportion of referrals accounted for by mandatory referrals and another prominent negative case type (the "nanny") raises the question whether reliance by decisionmakers on known categories operates to the detriment of seeing other opportunities for action. Particularly in this striking setting of day-in and day-out repetitive, routinized, brief, and pressured encounters, are inspectors' preconceptions and work routines open to revision as new problem travelers appear on the scene? While it is hard to answer this question given the focus and scope of the study, my data do indicate that categorization is not static. During the research, a new category of high-risk traveler arose. Passengers arriving on a newly scheduled South American flight began to be labeled as problem travelers after several altered passports were identified. The flight was viewed as bringing in an "element" from the nation that differed from previous travelers from the country.

Various ports in the United States (including the one studied) have an intelligence officer whose role is to identify categories of problem travelers and disseminate information to inspectors at the port and elsewhere in the agency. To the extent that

Table 2 Justifications for Secondary Inspection of Foreign Nationals

Basis of Referrals	No.	%
Mandatory/automatic:		
a) Designated nations	80	32.0
b) Asylum requested	7	2.8
c) INS/Customs "hit"	8	3.2
d) Lost permanent resident card	19	7.6
Total	114	45.6
Other:		
e) Possible "nanny"	13	5.2
f) Permanent resident illegally living outside U.S.	13	5.2
g) Fraudulent/altered documents	25	10.0
h) Missing or improper visa/documents	28	11.2
i) Verification of seaman status	7	2.8
j) Coming to live/work/insufficient funds	43	17.2
k) Assorted reasons	7	2.8
Total	136	54.4
Grand total	250	100.0

Source: Developed from oral and written data collected on 10 randomly sampled days during June, July, and August 1990 at "Metropolitan Port."

intelligence officers rely on patterns gleaned from secondary referrals, will the "normal" case profile types relied on by primary inspectors suppress (except in extraordinary cases such as blatantly tampered-with documents) the emergence of new or fresh assessments of travelers? The influence of organizational arrangements (e.g., existence and location of "trouble-spotter" positions) on the emergence of new categories and perhaps even persistence of old ones is a further fertile area for future research.

REFERENCES

Anker, Deborah E. (1990) "Determining Asylum Claims in the United States: An Empirical Study of the Adjudication of Asylum Claims Before the Immigration Court" (Executive Summary), 2 *International Journal of Refugee Law* 252.

Black, Donald J. (1971) "The Social Organization of Arrest," 23 *Stanford Law Review* 1087.

Diamond, Shari Seidman (1990) "Revising Images of Public Punitiveness: Sentencing by Lay and Professional English Magistrates," 15 *Law and Social Inquiry* 191.

Dingwall, Robert, and Topsy MURRAY (1983) "Categorization in Accident Departments: 'Good' Patients, 'Bad' Patients and 'Children'," 5 *Sociology of Health and Illness* 127.

Emerson, Robert M. (1988) "Discrepant Models of Categorization in Social Control Decision-making" (draft, September 1988).

Emerson, Robert M., and Melvin POLLNER (1976) "Dirty Work Designations: Their Features and Consequences in a Psychiatric Setting," 23 *Social Problems* 243.

Galanter, Marc (1974) "Why the 'Haves' Come Out Ahead: Speculations on the Limits of Legal Change," 9 *Law & Society Review* 95.

Hawkins, Keith (1983) "Assessing Evil," 23 *British Journal of Criminology* 101.

Hughes, Everett C. (1958) *Men and Their Work*. Glencoe, IL: Free Press.

Hutter, Bridget M. (1986) "An Inspector Calls: The Importance of Proactive Enforcement in the Regulatory Context," 26 *British Journal of Criminology* 114.

Knapp, Will S. (1981) "On the Validity of Accounts About Everyday Life," 29 (N.S.) *Sociological Review* 543.

Skolnick, Jerome H. (1975) *Justice Without Trial: Law Enforcement in Democratic Society*. New York: John Wiley & Sons.

Waegel, William B. (1981) "Case Routinization in Investigative Police Work," 28 *Social Problems* 263.

D. The Large Scale: Pluralism, Globalism, and the Negotiation of International Disputes

General Introduction

Anthropological perspectives on law at the transnational and national levels have become as de-localized as the topics themselves. Gone is the exclusive commitment to fieldwork. Anthropologists are as apt to examine the regulation of a scattered multinational network of private business dealings as to describe the workings of the constitution of a multicultural state. Or they may comment on the content of treaties and agreements among nations. Institutional statements of policy and regulatory frameworks such as emanate from the European Union, the World Bank, and the International Monetary Fund also become part of their large library of documentary resources. Because it is too dangerous, they are less likely to examine illegal transnational transactions in drugs and weapons and the trafficking in other forbidden objects. But they are very aware that such lie in the background of the safe-to-study respectable exchanges.

Such investigators of large-scale matters have left the classical preoccupations of an earlier type of ethnography, and have moved into the domain of supra-local affairs. What has happened to the fieldwork aspects of ethnography, the close personal contact with the site of observation and the persons involved? Of course, global activities have their local effects on particular people and places, and the ethnography of such locales can be accomplished in the classic vein treating the transnational aspects as background. But some studies focus on the transnational itself. These explorations necessarily involve methodological shifts of attention and the rethinking of theoretical questions.

Political issues also present themselves for Western anthropologists. One question that arises repeatedly is how to think about the fact that the conceptions and practices of the West are spreading globally along with its economic power. Some see this as a beneficial development, others as pernicious domination. The legal aspects of Westernization are sometimes conceived of in a positive light as steps toward greater justice, toward economic/technical modernization political democratization and the reduction of corruption. Western legal concerns may also be interpreted as carrying with them an ever-greater awareness of, and respect for, human rights. But just as often a negative assessment is offered. The whole phenomenon is sometimes described as an extension of Western dominance and political power whose principal aim is to achieve ever-greater profits for the West, with little regard for the needs and concerns of local people in the rest of the world. Some argue that it remains to be seen whether Western business practices and Western law will remain dominant (Snyder, 1999: conclusions, fifth item). The transnational law that is the object of study includes the practices of contracting parties, the laws and policies of governments, international treaties and the policies of international bodies such as the UN, the WTO, the African Union, the EU, and other regional policy-making bodies.

A very lively and related discussion took place at an EASA conference in the mid-1990s that points the way for future research in anthropology. In the course of that meeting, the study of policy was proposed as a new field for anthropological work. The general scope of the field was to be the investigation of "the connections between policy, power, subjectivity and changing forms of government" (Shore and Wright, 1997: xiii). It was conceived as taking up and extending "debates about "the impact of policy by exploring its mechanisms, disguises, and its implications for cultural practices in different societies" (p. xiii). There are echoes of Michel Foucault (1977) in the assertion by the organizers that "individuals constitute themselves in terms of the norms through which they are governed so that although 'imposed' on individuals, once internalized, [these norms] influence them to think feel and act in certain ways" (Lukes 1973:15). There is no better domain than the study of transnational law and its surrounding institutions for the exploration of the process of norm-setting, the standardization of practices, the rationalizing claims that are attached as part of the discourse, the intersection of multiple power structures, and the impact of these. Anthropologists interested in law and politics have only begun to step into the oceans of relevant material, but there is no doubt that this topic will be pursued by many more scholars in the future. It heralds a major change in anthropological techniques and preoccupations. Micro-social observations of particular locales used to be turned into socially significant knowledge by extension, by presuming that they represented the cultural normativity of a larger territory, the workings of a society. This new turn in the anthropology of law assumes that many facts of social order emanate from large regulatory organizations, and widespread networks of interaction, not from the village or neighborhood up, but from the large scale down. The small scale will certainly feel the impact of operations on the large scale, though not necessarily those which were intended. This broadening of the anthropological field to include the large scale is a growing methodological sea change and a salutory one.

S.F.M.

REFERENCES

Foucault, Michel, 1977 *Discipline and Punish*. Harmondsworth: Penguin.

Lukes, Stephen, 1973 *Emile Durkheim, His Life and Work*. Harmondsworth: Penguin.

Shore, Cris, and Susan Wright, (eds.,) 1997 *Anthropology of Policy*. London and New York: Routledge.

Snyder, Francis, 1999 Governing Economic Globalization: Global Legal pluralism and European Union Law. *In Economic Globalization and Law*. Special issue. *European Law Journal* 5(3).

25

Multiculturalism, Individualism, and Human Rights: Romanticism, The Enlightenment, and Lessons from Mauritius

Thomas Hylland Eriksen

Introduction: Divided Loyalties in Mauritius

The fact that ethnic groups are at war with each other in many parts of the world is one of the discouraging facts of current political life. Thomas Hylland Eriksen asks how that violence has been avoided in Mauritius. There, about a million inhabitants live together in peace though their cultural loyalties are very much divided. Hindus, "Creoles" of African descent, Indian Muslims, Tamils and Telugus, and a few Chinese and French live together peacefully on this small island in the Indian Ocean. Mauritius became fully independent in 1968, and has contended with the problem of accommodating multiculturalism for a long while, from its beginnings in the colonial period to its modern form in the independent state.

Much has been written about nationalism, about the full development of statehood in circumstances where cultural homogeneity and political boundaries are identical. The most succinct statement of this in recent times is that of Ernest Gellner (1983). He saw nationalism as an evolutionary development, as the latest in a historical series of modes of geographical/political integration. Perhaps one of the most eloquent illustrations of this thesis of the unity between blood and citizenship can be found in the former German constitution. Membership in the German polity was treated as a hereditary trait. The biological foundations and the cultural heritage were considered to be carried by the same population.

From Thomas Hylland Eriksen, "Multiculturalism, Individualism and Human Rights: Romanticism, the Enlightenment and Lessons from Mauritius," in Richard A. Wilson (ed.) *Human Rights, Culture and Context* (London and Chicago : Pluto Press, 1997), pp. 49, 51–2, 55–8, 62–4, 66–9.

The curious thing about the applicability of the Gellner thesis is that most states today find themselves in the midst of ethnic or religious or other categorical fragmentation. Far from moving in the 19th-century direction in which the fiction of a common ancestry for all citizens was developed in the European nation-states, the effects of contemporary migration, the realities of ancestral divisions, and the creation of new bases of cleavage lead in the opposite direction. What we are witnessing today are powerful micro-nationalisms, in which sub-groups within the state assert their distinctiveness. These sub-groups are in a vigorous competition for recognition, and for control over some part of the polity (Taylor 1992). At the same time, states are trying to restrict the number of migrants they will admit, trying to protect their national boundaries.

Often these matters are hardened into law, in constitutions defining citizenship, voting rights, access to education and other benefits, rights to own property, conduct businesses, and the like. Eriksen's paper devotes limited attention to the officialization of this state of affairs in legal frameworks, but emphasizes the underlying social/cultural conditions, and what he calls "similar, Western derived notions of justice" (p. 63). What Eriksen's paper describes is a small polity in which the various ethnic and religious sectors tolerate each other, interact with each other, and manage their areas of competition and difference in a peaceful manner. It is interesting that he attributes this capacity to shared premises, a shared political culture, common modes of communication and access to the labor market as a matter of individual skills rather than ethnic membership. He builds his essay around the tension between liberal principles of individual equality and what he calls "political multiculturalism" (p. 63). The preoccupation of his essay is in the political philosophical realm in which multiculturalist thought and human rights thinking are at odds. But his ethnographic presentation makes it clear that the political/philosophical controversy is not what matters in Mauritius, that peace is the result of the general commonalities of practice and the dominant style of mutual respect.

S.F.M.

REFERENCES

Gellner, Ernest 1983 *Nations and Nationalism*. Ithaca and London: Cornell University Press.
Taylor, Charles 1992 *Multiculturalism and the Politics of Recognition*. Princeton: Princeton University Press.

Eriksen, *Multiculturalism*

This chapter is restricted to a discussion of one particular political aspect of multiculturalism, and investigates under which circumstances multiculturalist ideas may be at odds with individual human rights (as depicted in the original UN charter). As a consequence, it is necessary to review the concept of 'culture' invoked in multiculturalist thought. This conceptual discussion (which has practical ramifications) forms the head and tail of the article, the main body of which is devoted to a critical presentation of multiculturalist practices and debates in Mauritius, which is used here as an exemplar of multiculturalist dilemmas and opportunities.[1]

Cultural Variation as a Political Challenge

... The basic dilemma of polyethnic societies can be phrased like this: on the one hand all members of a liberal democracy are (in principle if not in practice) entitled to the same rights and opportunities. On the other hand, they also have the right to be different – and in the 1990s, the rights of minorities to maintain and promote their cultural specificity, and to be visible in the public sphere, including the media, school curricula and so on, are increasingly insisted on. A crucial challenge for multi-ethnic societies therefore consists in allowing cultural differences without violating common, societally defined rights...

The contradiction between the demands for equal rights and for the right to be different is accentuated at present by two main tendencies. First, it has finally become clear in public discourse – nearly 80 years after Woodrow Wilson famously announced the right to self-determination of peoples – that hardly any ethnic group has its territory by itself. States are polyethnic, and any ideology stating that only people 'of the same kind' should live in a country is potentially dangerous. This problem was recognised already by Renan (1992 [1882]), but it has acquired unprecedented importance since the 1960s. Second, the current processes of cultural globalisation break down cultural boundaries and make it difficult to defend the idea that a 'people' is culturally homogeneous and unique. Cultural creolisation (or 'hybridisation', or again 'bastardisation' if one prefers), migration and increased transnational communication are important keywords here.

A widespread counter-reaction against the perceived threat of boundary dissolution through globalisation consists in ideological emphases on 'cultural uniqueness'. In this sense, cultural homogenisation and ethnic fragmentation take place simultaneously; they are consequences of each other and feed on each other in dynamic interplay (cf. Friedman 1990)...

The position to be defended below argues that culture is not a legitimating basis for political claims, and that cultural singularities among minorities and majorities in modern societies can only be defended to the extent that they do not interfere with individual human rights....

In order to illustrate and further develop the preceding points, I shall now turn to an extended empirical example, which brings out many of the tensions and contradictions inherent in ideas of multiculturalism.

Ethnicity in Mauritius

Since Mauritius was permanently settled by French planters and their African and Malagasy slaves in 1715, this island in the south-western Indian Ocean has been a polyethnic society, and still is very much so, as witnessed in official symbolism as well as many aspects of everyday life (Eriksen 1988; Bowman 1990). The currency is the rupee, and the text on the bank notes is in English, Hindi and Tamil. However, Mauritian newspapers tend to be in French, but the video shops offer mostly Indian and East Asian films. A leisurely walk through the capital, Port-Louis, may bring one past, within half an hour or so, a Buddhist pagoda, a Sunni mosque, an Anglican church and a Catholic one, and two Hindu temples – one North Indian, one Tamil. And it is by no means uncommon that Mauritians have names like Françoise Yaw Tang Mootoosamy.

Contemporary Mauritius, with a surface of some 2,000 square kilometres, has about a million inhabitants. Their ancestors came from four continents, and they belong to four different 'world religions'. According to official categories, the largest ethnic groups are Hindus from North India ('Hindi-speaking', 42%), 'Creoles' of largely African descent (27%), Muslims of Indian origin (16%), Tamils and Telugus of South Indian descent (9%), Chinese (3%), *gens de couleur* (2%) and Mauritians of French descent (2%). Mauritius, independent since 1968 and a republic since 1992, is a liberal multi-party democracy and a capitalist society (meaning, in this context, that both labour and consumption are mediated by money) which was impoverished, relatively overpopulated and dilapidated, with a vulnerable single export economy (sugar cane) and a high level of unemployment during the first decades after the Second World War. Mauritius has undergone an astonishing economic transformation since the early 1980s, and is now a relatively prosperous society with a dynamic economy based on sugar, textiles and tourism.

Mauritius is one among many peaceful polyethnic societies in the world. Although many of the country's inhabitants are concerned with their cultural identity, their 'roots' and the maintenance of local ethnic boundaries, compromise and tolerance are important ingredients in the shared Mauritian political culture. Notions which form part of a shared cultural repertoire include the admission that it would have been impossible to win a civil war, that secessionism would have been absurd, and that the country's political stability rests on a precarious balance between ethnic group interests. Therefore Mauritians have developed many more or less formalised methods for the maintenance of this balance (see Eriksen 1992 for details)...

During the twentieth century, and particularly since the extension of the franchise after the Second World War and the accession to full independence in 1968, policies relating to inter-ethnic tolerance have been extended so as to include the entire population. There is a continuous search for *common denominators* (Eriksen 1988) in legislation and in everyday social life, which are necessary for societal and national integration to be at all possible ('multicultural' or not, people need to have something in common if they are to have a society), and those universalist principles are balanced against the alleged conventions and culturally specific rights claimed by certain members of each constituent group.

Modes of Inter-ethnic Compromise

The electoral system in Mauritius is more or less a carbon copy of the British Westminster system, with simple majorities rather than proportional representation. The parties are largely organised along ethnic lines, and very many Mauritians vote for politicians who they feel represent their ethnic (sectional) interests. Attempts at creating inter-ethnic alliances or supra-ethnic alternatives (based on, for example, class) have generally been short-lived.

Although ethnic competition is in this way thematised in politics, there is nevertheless wide agreement over the political rules, and electoral results are respected . . .

An important element in the Mauritian political system is the so-called *Best Loser* arrangement, which guarantees the representation of all ethnic groups through allotting a limited number of parliamentary seats to runners-up at General Elections. The 'best losers' are selected so as to ensure the representation of all ethnic groups in the Legislative Assembly. In this way, the importance of ethnic differences is made an integral part of the electoral system.

As in many other multi-ethnic societies, questions concerning schooling, religion and language are among the most complicated and controversial ones in Mauritius. It is perhaps here that the dilemma of equal rights and cultural differences is most evident. In all three fields, compromises of various kinds have been developed.

Regarding religion, the popular idiom *Sakenn pé prié dan so fason* ('Everyone prays in his/her own way') has nearly achieved legal status. As mentioned, four 'world religions' are represented in the island, and three of them (Christianity, Islam and Hinduism) are divided into a large number of sects and congregations. Religious groups receive state funding according to the size of their membership. In this field, a consistent compromise has been established, where no religion is given priority by the state.

The Mauritian schooling system represents a different kind of compromise. Here, equality is emphasised rather than differences. Thus core curricula are uniform island-wide, as are exams. However, classes in 'ancestral languages' are offered as optional subjects. As a matter of fact, a growing majority of Mauritians speak *Kreol*, a French-lexicon Creole, as their first language, and scarcely know the language of their ancestors, but Kreol is rarely written. It could be said, therefore, that Mauritian schooling stresses equal opportunities yet allows for the expression of symbolic differences. It represents a compromise not only between ethnic groups, but also between a Romantic and an Enlightenment view of society.

A third kind of compromise is expressed in language policies. Officially, as many as fifteen languages are spoken in Mauritius; in practice, at least four or five are the mother-tongues of various groups. When Mauritius was to become independent from Britain in the late 1960s, in practice the new government faced four possibilities. First, it could have opted for Hindi, which is the ancestral language of the largest ethnic group (although many Mauritian Hindus do not understand it). Second, it could have chosen Kreol, which, in spite of its being held in low esteem, is by far the most widely spoken language. Third, French could have been an alternative, having been the dominant written language throughout the history of Mauritius.

In the end it was the fourth alternative, English, which was to win. English is an international language, and is learnt by Mauritians in the same way as non-native speakers elsewhere in the world learn English as a foreign language. This means that most Mauritians master it only partially. More importantly, perhaps, English was nobody's ethnic language, the few Anglo-Mauritians (most of them colonial civil servants) having either returned or become assimilated into the Franco-Mauritian group. By choosing English, an ethnically neutral language, as the language of the state, Mauritians avoided turning nation-building into a particularistic ethnic project at the beginning.

The other languages are nevertheless also supported through the state and its agencies. Public radio and TV broadcasting alternates between the major languages of Mauritius, and French still dominates in the written mass media. North American films are dubbed in French. There is in other words a clear, but negotiable division of labour between the non-ethnic language English, the supra-ethnic languages Kreol and, to some extent, French, and the ethnic languages, chiefly Bhojpuri/Hindi, Urdu, Tamil, Mandarin and Telegu.

[…]

Individualism as a Key Factor

It has often been asked why Mauritius is such a stable democracy, incorporating, as it does, a vast number of religious groupings and people originating from different continents. The question is wrongly asked, and it reveals an inadequate understanding of culture. At the level of everyday representations and practices, Mauritian culture can actually be described as quite uniform in the sense that there is a wide field of shared premises for communication encompassing most of the population: there is a shared political culture and a standardised and standardising educational system, there is considerable linguistic uniformity, and recruitment to the labour market is increasingly based on individual skills. It is generally not difficult to argue the virtues of individual human rights among Mauritians; they tend to share similar, Western-derived notions of justice. It is, in other words, only superficially (if noisily) multicultural even if it may be profoundly multi-ethnic.[2]

It should be noted that the 'multiculturalist' model of coexistence, as practised in Mauritius and elsewhere, collapses unless the constituent groups share basic values of individualism and, in all likelihood, a shared *lingua franca*. For instance, it is widely believed, not least in that country itself, that the US has been capable of absorbing a great number of different nationalities without homogenising them culturally. This is wrong, and generally, migrants to the US have changed their language within two generations. One could perhaps say that the descendants of late nineteenth/early twentieth-century immigrants to the US have been assimilated to a degree of 99%, and have been allowed to use the remaining 1% to advertise their cultural uniqueness, which exists largely as a set of symbolic identity markers. As a Norwegian from Norway, I have often met Americans who identify themselves as 'Norwegians' but who unfailingly seem to betray, in their verbal and non-verbal language, lifestyle and values, a strong attachment to the moral discourses of US society.

If political multiculturalists favour equal individual rights, the 'culture' in their rhetoric is but a thin cosmetic film. If, on the other hand, they seriously defend the right of ethnic minorities to run their own political affairs according to a cultural logic of their own, they run the risk of defending practices which conflict with the human rights of individual group members.

The solution, or rather, the 'good multiculturalism', must arrive at a blend of sharing and difference. It requires common denominators in key sectors, including politics, education and the labour market, and it must institutionalise a dialogic principle (see Giddens 1994 on 'dialogic democracy') enabling a variety of voices to be heard on an equal footing. This is not relativism, but rather the recognition and democratisation of different value orientations in society, in the manner acknowledged as necessary and non-relativistic by Bauman (1993) when he notes the ill effects of the attempts at extending the Western 'ethical code over populations which abide by different codes . . . in the name of one all-human ethics bound to evict and supplant all local *distortions*' (Bauman 1993: 12, italics in the original). It is a question of striking a proper balance between the demands for formal equality and the demands for justice in a more general sense, including the equivalence of cultural heritages *as well as* the right not to acknowledge a heritage. The keyword is dialogue, which, it should again be noted, presupposes the existence of common denominators or shared meaning at the outset.

NOTES

1   Fieldwork in Mauritius was carried out in 1986 and 1991–92. Thanks are due to Richard Wilson for his perceptive and useful comments on an early version of the chapter.
2   This recalls a memorable passage by V.S. Naipaul, where he writes, bitterly: 'Superficially, because of the multitude of races, Trinidad may seem complex, but to anyone who knows it, it is a simple colonial philistine society' (Naipaul 1979 [1958]).

REFERENCES

Bauman, Zygmunt. 1993. *Postmodern Ethics*. Oxford: Blackwell.
Bowman, Larry. 1990. *Mauritius: Democracy and Development in the Indian Ocean*. Boulder, CO. Westview Press.
Eriksen, Thomas Hylland. 1988. *Communicating Cultural Difference and Identity. Ethnicity and Nationalism in Mauritius*. Oslo: Department of Social Anthropology, Occasional Papers in Social Anthropology, 16.
—— 1992. 'Containing Conflict and Transcending Ethnicity in Mauritius', in Kumar Rupesinghe (ed.) *Internal Conflicts and Governance*. London: Macmillan.
Friedman, Jonathan. 1990. 'Being in the World: Globalization and Localization', in Mike Featherstone (ed.) *Global Culture. Nationalism, Globalization and Modernity*. London: Sage.
Gellner, Ethest 1994. Personal communication.
Giddens, Anthony. 1994. *Beyond Left and Right*. Cambridge: Polity.
Renan, Ernest. 1992 [1882] *Qu'est-ce qu'une nation?* Paris: Presses Pocket.
Turner, Terence. 1994. 'Anthropology and Multiculturalism: What is Anthropology that Multiculturalists Should be Mindful of It?' in Theo Goldberg (ed.) *Multiculturalism: A Critical Reader*. Oxford: Blackwell.

26

Governing Economic Globalization: Global Legal Pluralism and European Law

Francis Snyder

Introduction: Global Barbie and the Pertinent Law

There are many categories of law being invoked on the global scene. Some look deceptively simple, imbedded in claims of universality such as human rights law, and some are quite obviously inordinately complex. One complex type outlined in Francis Snyder's paper includes the kind of composite that results from many international agreements (conventions ratified by nations), and many contracts (made by private companies and private persons either among themselves or with governments and their agencies). In some instances a series of contracts are dovetailed, each contract an agreement to manufacture and sell materials that will later be combined to make up a saleable product. The contracts may be made in different countries, by parties anchored in separate national systems having different laws. The law described in Francis Snyder's article is of this complex kind, and it pertains to the production of the Barbie doll, and the conditions that govern the sales of the Barbie doll. She may look like a dumb dolly, but her parts come from more places than one might imagine, and the laws that impinge on her conditions of existence are myriad. She was launched in 1959, making her forty-something years old, but she takes care not to show her age.

Snyder says, ''The Barbie doll's label says 'made in China' . . . China provides the factory space, labour, and electricity, as well as cotton cloth for the dress . . . Japan supplies the nylon hair, Saudi Arabia provides oil. Taiwan refines oil into ethylene for plastic pellets for the body, Japan, the US and Europe supply almost all the machinery and tools, most of the molds . . . come from the US, Japan, or

---

From Francis Snyder, "Governing Economic Globalization: Global Legal Pluralism and European Union Law," *European Law Journal* 5 (3) (1999), pp. 334–9, 342–3, 345–6, 351–74.

Hong Kong, etc." The technical complexity of gathering together the material elements that make up this highly profitable doll is mind-boggling. The "global" law which governs these matters is, to say the least, "decentered and non-hierarchical" (Teubner, ed., 1997, cited by Snyder.) Among others, it involves powerful toy buyers, trade associations, conventions of the International Labor Organization, conventions of the World Customs Organization and the like. The members of the WCO are states, and it had a membership of 150 states in 1995. The WCO is concerned with the harmonization of technical customs, rules, and practices. Many of the countries which have ratified the basic agreement on which the organization is founded have ratified it in full. Others pick and choose what they agree to, and what they refuse to agree to. This is a thicket for the specialists.

Particularly significant for anthropologists is an awareness of the many players in this international game, and of the many sites of regulation and sources of ideas and standards that are in play. It also matters to know who really dominates particular business negotiations. Much of the talk about "globalism" in the literature today, though it alludes to the large scale, is highly selective about the aspects it connects with the field site. It is of the utmost importance to be aware of the complexity and breadth of the scene, of the flow of investments and profits involved, and of the stakeholders in that process, and of what ideas and actions are dominant. There have been highly successful UN sponsored international meetings on the environment, on women, and on a number of other topics of broad concern. However it is not sufficient for anthropologists to link the themes of discourse on those occasions with local fieldwork scenes as trends in global thinking without taking into account a wider conception of international activity. This paper by Snyder provides a glimpse of what would be involved.

Eve Darian-Smith's review essay on "Structural Inequalities in the Global Legal System" is another indication of the scope of the issues, and the kinds of debates that are emerging. In a critique of Saskia Sassen's *Globalization and Its Discontents: Essays on the New Mobility of People and Money*, she protests that, "Sassen's argument that the global political economy and the international human rights regime are emerging as two new sites for institutional normativity, alongside that of the nation-state, does not adequately engage with the current weight of Western legal hegemony and its impact on ordinary people," (Darian-Smith, 2000:826). "Alternative spaces and spheres of power may indeed be emerging, notwithstanding the overwhelming weight of Western legal norms, which is precisely what Sassen points out. In my opinion, however, she falls short by not fully examining the asymmetrical power relations between regional economies and political philosophies" (p. 826). These are indeed weighty matters.

S.F.M.

REFERENCES

Darian-Smith, Eve, 2000 Structural Inequalities in the Global Legal System. *Law and Society Review*, 34(3): 809–828.
Sassen, Saskia, 1998 *Globalization and Its Discontents: Essays on the New Mobility of People and Money*. New York: New Press.

Snyder, *Global Legal Pluralism*

B   The Meaning of Globalisation

Thinking about how global economic networks are governed requires a concept of globalisation. By globalisation, I refer to an aggregate of multifaceted, uneven, often contradictory, economic, political, social and cultural processes which are characteristic of our time. This paper concentrates primarily on the economic aspects, but these need to be set within a more general framework.

In economic terms, the most salient features of globalisation, driven by multinational firms, are, for the present purposes, the development of international production networks (IPNs), the dispersion of production facilities among different countries, the technical and functional fragmentation of production, the fragmentation of ownership, the flexibility of the production process, worldwide sourcing, an increase in intra-firm trade, the interpenetration of international financial markets, the possibility of virtually instantaneous worldwide flows of information, changes in the nature of employment, and the emergence of new forms of work.

Viewed from a political standpoint, globalisation has witnessed the rise of new political actors such as multinational firms, non-governmental organisations and social movements. It has tended to weaken, fragment, and sometimes even restructure the state, but has not by any means destroyed or replaced it. Globalisation has also radically altered the relationship to which we have become accustomed in recent history between governance and territory. It has thus blurred and splintered the boundaries between the domestic and external spheres of nation-states and of regional integration organisations, fostered the articulation of systems of multi-level governance, interlocking politics and policy networks, and helped to render universal the discourse of, and claims for, human rights. In many political and legal settings, such as the European Union, it has raised serious questions about the nature and appropriate form of contemporary governance.

Among the manifold social processes involved in globalisation are the spread of certain models of production and patterns of consumption from specific geographic/political/national contexts to others. Contradictory tendencies have developed towards internationalisation and localisation within, as well as among, different regions and countries. We have also witnessed the uneven development of new social movements based on different, if not alternative, forms of community.

Seen as a cultural phenomenon, globalisation has implied the emergence of a new global culture, which is shared, to some extent, by virtually all élite groups. This has enhanced the globalisation of the imagination and of the imaginable. At the same time, it has contributed both to the transformation of many local cultures, sometimes strengthening them, sometimes marginalising them, sometimes having both consequences simultaneously. Consequently, it has sometimes increased the range and depth of international and infranational cultural conflicts, as well as the resistance to new forms of cultural imperialism.

C   An Analytical Strategy

The remainder of the paper is divided into four main parts. The next part (Part II) introduces the global commodity chain in toys, an empirical anchor for my theoretical argument. Part III then sketches what I consider to be the basic elements of global legal pluralism. Part IV presents in more detail the shape of global legal pluralism, bringing together examples of institutional, normative, and processual sites and the segments of the global commodity chain in toys, which they govern. The conclusion briefly summarises the argument and proposes hypotheses for further research.

II   A Global Economic Network: The Global Commodity Chain in Toys

Global economic networks take various forms. I focus here on the international toy industry. The toy industry's global reach and domestic impact can be illustrated clearly by the Barbie doll. In European countries, imports of toys from Asia have sometimes provoked reactions bordering on xenophobia. In the United States, they have triggered outrage against cheap Chinese labour and trade deficits with China, which, in the case of the toy trade between China and the USA, was claimed by the US to amount to US $5.4 billion. This has not, however, been true by and large of the Barbie doll, which is usually viewed as a United States or even global product.

The Barbie doll's label says 'made in China'. This suggests, correctly, that, in the production of Barbie, China provides the factory space, labour, and electricity, as well as cotton cloth for the dress. It conceals, however, the facts that Japan supplies the nylon hair, Saudi Arabia provides oil, Taiwan refines oil into ethylene for plastic pellets for the body, Japan, the US, and Europe supply almost all the machinery and tools, most of the moulds (the most expensive item) come from the US, Japan, or Hong Kong, the United States supplies cardboard packaging and paint pigments, and Hong Kong supplies the banking and insurance and carries out the delivery of the raw materials to factories in Guangdong Province in south China, together with the collection of the finished products and shipping. Two Barbie dolls are marketed every second in 140 countries around the world by Mattel Inc. of El Segundo, California. There is a Barbie doll museum in Palo Alto, California. Barbie celebrated her 40th birthday on March 9, 1999, and the US Post Office released a commemorative US postage stamp in June in her honour. The Barbie doll is quintessentially American in origin, style and culture, and is, of course, the result of a global commodity chain powered by a US buyer. But Barbie is a global product, if by 'global' we refer to the fragmentation of the production process, the dispersion of production facilities among different countries, and the organisation of production within international production networks...

The international toy industry is a prime example of an international commodity chain dominated by the buyers. It is hierarchically organised. At the top of the hierarchy are large buyers as well as large retailers. The buyers include several US manufacturers, two Japanese manufacturers, and one European company. The most important buyers are two American companies, Mattel and Hasbro. The key elements in the power of buyers are designs and brands. The large buyers are the node in various networks of inventors and creators of toys. Through contract, they control the access of inventors, intermediaries, and factories to the market. The most important retailers include large specialist stores such as Toys 'R' Us, discount houses such as Wal-Mart in the US, and hypermarkets or catalogue stores in the EU. Taking buyers and retailers together, the power of this group lies in its control of design, brands, and marketing.

Buyers and retailers compete, however, with regard to access to retail markets. The powerful buyers are dependent, to some degree, on large retailers, such as Toys 'R' Us and discount stores such as Wal-Mart. As economic downturns reveal, however, the two groups have conflicting interests with regard to the retail market. To maintain market share, and to enhance their dominant position in the global commodity chain, buyers have recently tried to lessen their dependence on retailers. Their strategies for doing so include increased direct-to-consumer sales, including catalogues and Internet sales, either from their own website or from online retailers.

The US firms have regional headquarters and a significant share of the toy market in Europe. The European Union toy market is supplied mainly through importer-wholesalers. Each country has its own distinctive retail sector, varying from catalogue stores through hypermarkets to independent retailers. Except for Lego, established in Denmark in 1932 and now one of the world's ten largest toy manufacturers, there are no large manufacturers or specialist retailers based in Europe similar to those based in the USA. Together with LEGO and the Japanese firm Bandai, the US firms dominated the first main peak trade association, Toy Manufacturers of Europe, formed in the early 1990s, and are now the principal players in the current EU peak association, Toy Industries of Europe (TIE).

Further down the hierarchy come the Hong Kong companies which act as intermediaries between these multinationals and the toy factories. In East Asia, Hong Kong has been of signal importance in the development of the toy industry. Its role first started in the 1940s as an export platform, then developed in the 1980s as original equipment manufacturers (OEM) for overseas importers or as intermediaries between local manufacturers and overseas buyers until, starting in the 1990s, Hong Kong became a re-exporter of toys made in China. In 1998, licensing and contract manufacturing for overseas manufacturers, usually to production specifications and product designs provided by the buyers, accounted for an estimated 70% of total domestic toy exports. US buyers accounted for 51% of Hong Kong's toy exports in the first ten months of 1995. Today, Hong Kong is the location of management, design, R&D, marketing, quality control, finance and, usually, shipping.

At the bottom of the hierarchy are the factories, most of which are located in China. By 1995, toy production in China involved about 3,000 factories employing more than 1.3 million people. Such factories usually occupy the structural position of original equipment manufacturer (OEM) producing to other companies' specifications with machinery provided by the buyer. However, some now operate on the basis of original design manufacturer (ODM), producing to designs supplied by the buyer but sharing the cost of machinery and investment as well as markets according to an agreement with the buyer. Today, China and Hong Kong account for nearly 60% of world's toy trade.

III   Elements of Global Legal Pluralism

...Global legal pluralism, as I use the term, comprises two different aspects. The first is structural, the second relational.

First, global legal pluralism involves a variety of institutions, norms, and dispute resolution processes located, and produced, at different structured sites around the world. Legal scholarship has traditionally paid most attention to understanding state, regional, and international legal institutions, legally binding norms, and dispute resolution processes involving law. Much of the most interesting recent work concerns the 'constitutionalisation' of international trade regulation. In addition, international lawyers and related specialists in international relations have also studied international negotiations, norms that, at least in principle, are not legally binding, global regulatory networks, and intergovernmental networks. The analysis of international regimes, multi-level governance, and other types of institutional arrangements, such as credit rating agencies, has largely been the province of political scientists and specialists in international relations. Examples in the field of EU legal and political science scholarship concern multi-level governance, committees, and different types of settings, whether highly institutionalised with specified norms, rules and procedures or non-hierarchical and decentralised. While it is possible to generalise to some extent from this previous work, no one has tried to unite these different elements. Some basic questions remain, therefore, to be answered. What is a site? States and regional and international organisations are included, but so are a diversity of other institutional, normative, and processual sites, such as commercial arbitration, trade associations, and so on. How are sites created, and how do they grow, survive or die? How are they structured? What does it mean to say that different structured sites are the anchors of contemporary legal pluralism?

Second, the relations among these sites are of many different types, in terms of both structure and process...

IV   The Shape of Global Legal Pluralism

...Several sites of global legal pluralism play a role in shaping or determining the number of component units in any given box in the international commodity chain in toys. Consider some examples.

First, with regard to invention, production, and marketing of toys, United States intellectual property law is of crucial significance in determining the number of buyers and maintaining their market power. The highest barriers to entry in buyer-driven commodity chains typically concern product conception, design and marketing. Intellectual property law creates or consolidates barriers to entry.

Second, antitrust law has an important impact on production, marketing, and distribution. In the United States, Europe, or Japan, it helps to define the number of key buyers or manufacturers in the international toy industry. American antitrust law in particular affects the possibility of mergers among buyers. When market leader Mattel Inc acquired the third largest toy manufacturer, Tyco Toys Inc., in

1996, Mattel was quoted in the American media as expressing confidence that the deal would not be blocked by US antitrust law, even though the companies' combined sales represented 19% of the US toy market.

Third, the lack of binding legal regulation of Internet retailing lowers barriers to entry into the retail market in toys. Consequently, when buyers are squeezed by traditional retailers, they turn without great difficulty to the Internet in order to enter the retail sector themselves, either through specialist Internet retailers or by means of the buyers' own websites.

A fourth example, explored in more detail here, concerns EC international trade and customs law concerning the access of importers to the EU toy market. It illustrates clearly the role played by EU legislation and the European Court of Justice in restructuring the EU toy industry. In 1994, the Council of the European Union adopted two major complementary legislative reforms. The first was Council Regulation 519/94 on common rules for imports from certain third countries. It was the general regulation governing imports from non-market economy countries, except for textile products. The second was Council Regulation 520/94 establishing a Community procedure for administrative quantitative quotas. It established a new way of administering quotas, based on a system of licences issued by the Member States according to quantitative criteria established at Community level. Both were part of a package deal, designed to secure acceptance of the Uruguay Round of multilateral trade negotiations, to reinforce existing trade policy instruments and to complete the EC's Common Commercial Policy.

Both the new quota regime and provisions for administering it exemplified the Europeanisation of law. They involved the total or partial replacement of the law of the Member States by EC law...

This final step in our saga of legislative reform occurred in the context of – and contributed to – the transformation of the EU toy industry. By definition, therefore, it also affected the gradual restructuring of the global toy commodity chain, including factories in China. By 1996, the EU toy industry had already adapted its production structures and improved production quality to such an extent that, at least from the standpoint of the Commission and most, if not all, national governments, import quotas were no longer necessary. The EU's restructured toy enterprises imported items that were no longer produced in Europe. As the Commission noted, '[m]ost manufacturers in Europe are also becoming importers of some items which may be necessary for them to keep their market share both in the EU and on export markets.' EU producers were able to compete in foreign markets: exports of European toys outside the EU grew by a record 16.8% in 1996 while imports in the same year rose by only 3%. The European Commission ascribed this successful adaptation to law. In its view, the temporary protection assured to EU industry by Community quotas permitted the necessary restructuring. It thus also facilitated the redefinition of the role of these EU firms in the global commodity chain.

Changes in the organisation of political representation in the EU toy sector reflected these changes in the organisation of production and marketing. The first major peak association in the EU toy sector was the European Federation of Toy Industries founded in 1967. It comprised the national associations of the UK, France, the Netherlands, Germany, Italy, Greece, and Spain. In the early 1990s, the UK association, together with the major multinational toy companies (Hasbro,

Mattel, Lego, Tomy, Bandai, etc.) founded the Toy Manufacturers of Europe (TME). Greece and Italy also joined the TME, as did the German national association composed of larger companies. German producers of plastic toys, France, and Spain remained in a separate association, now known as the Fédération Européenne des Industries du Jouet (FEIJ). The French and Spanish associations, however, began negotiations with the TME to form a single peak association. These negotiations culminated in 1997 with the merger of the TME and the FEIJ to form a new peak association, Toy Industry in Europe (TIE). It had essentially the same structure as the TME, with large firms having a major role, but also with representation of industrial unions, except for those of Germany which remained divided. Subsequently, the Greek association and the small associations of the Nordic countries also joined the TIE. As of February 1999, the co-presidency of TIE was held by the United Kingdom and Spain. The economic changes in the EU toy sector viewed as part of the global commodity chain were thus mirrored, more or less directly, in terms of industrial associations and political representation.

Since its formation, TIE strongly supported the immediate and total abolition of quotas on toys. In its view, quotas represented an administrative burden, especially for small businesses, and in any event failed to restrict toy imports from China. Rephrasing this view, one might say that quotas were an obstacle to EU firms which sourced partly finished products from abroad, and thus prevented the successful operation of newly articulated global networks. In summary, both the European Commission and the main European trade association agreed by 1997 that toys from China should not be subject any longer to quotas. Instead, they should be subjected merely to surveillance, requiring only an import licence...

C   Geographic Concentration or Dispersal

...We have already seen that invention, finance, marketing, and retailing in the international toy industry are concentrated: the first in the USA, the second and third in the USA and Hong Kong, and the last, so far as control is concerned, in the USA and, to lesser extent, Europe and Japan. Production has, until recently, tended to be concentrated mainly in Asia, though it could potentially be much more dispersed. The geographical separation of production from finance, marketing, and retailing is encouraged by international norms concerning the customs operations known in the EU as inward processing and outward processing. It is no exaggeration to describe the existence and increased use of these customs rules as the legal basis for what has been called 'the new international division of labour'.

The overarching international legal framework is provided by the International Convention on the Simplification and Harmonisation of Customs Procedures, a veritable international customs code. It was first signed at Kyoto on 18 May 1973 and entered in force on 25 September 1974. An updated version was adopted on 25 June 1999 but has not yet been ratified by all parties. The Kyoto Convention is the fruit of the Customs Co-operation Council (CCC), founded in 1952. Since 1994, the CCC has been known as the World Customs Organisation (WCO). The WCO now oversees the implementation of the Kyoto Convention. Its supervisory functions began with the establishment of the CCC, whose initial *raison d'etre* was partly to supervise the application and interpretation of the customs classification system known as either the Brussels Tariff Nomenclature (BTN) or the Customs Co-operation Council Nomenclature.

The WCO, as of 1999, has 150 members. The EC Member States have participated since the beginning. However, membership is limited to states, and as a customs union, the EC formally has only observer status, even though the European Court of Justice has taken the view that the Community has replaced the Member States in commitments arising from the Convention. The US joined the CCC in 1970. Hong Kong and China are also members.

The WCO, which is based in Brussels, is virtually the sole international body concerned with the harmonisation of technical customs rules and practices. As currently constituted, its highest body is a Council, composed of the Directors-General of Customs from all Members. The Council is assisted by a Finance Committee of 17 Members and a Policy Commission of 24 Members. In addition, Technical Committees work in the areas of nomenclature and classification, valuation, customs technique, and origin. Council bodies at all levels are helped by a General Secretariat, headed by a Secretary-General, assisted by a Deputy Secretary-General and three Directors.

The tasks of the WCO are four-fold. First, it drafts and promotes new agreements, mainly concerning customs techniques. Second, it makes recommendations to ensure uniform interpretation and application of its existing conventions, notably with regard to the Convention establishing a Customs Co-operation Council, the Nomenclature Convention, and the Valuation Convention. The legal status of these recommendations is ambiguous, and probably not very important from the practical standpoint, but it has been suggested that their acceptance by contracting parties 'carries with it an obligation not to arbitrarily resile from the recommendations'. Third, the WCO acts as a conciliator in disputes between contracting parties. Fourth, it provides information and advice to governments in its fields of activity...

The 1973 Kyoto Convention on the Simplification and Harmonisation of Customs Procedures had approximately [sic] contracting parties; the number has increased to 114 for the 1999 revised Convention. For the present purposes, let us focus on the EC, its Member States, the USA, and China in relation to the 1973 Convention, Annex E.6, on inward processing, Annex E.8, on outward processing, and Annex F.1, on free zones. As of 1 January 1993, all fifteen EC Member States had ratified the Convention, but not all have accepted all of these three annexes. The EC was a contracting party, since a customs union was entitled to be a contracting party if its member states were also parties. The EC had taken advantage of this provision; but it does not have the right to vote. The EC had accepted Annexes E.6, E.8, and F.1, which entered into force for the EC on 26 September 1974. The United States had ratified the Convention and had accepted Annex E.8, on outward processing, and Annex F.1, on free zones, but not Annex E.6, on inward processing. China had ratified the Convention but had not accepted any of these three annexes. Chinese specialists considered Chinese legislation concerning the SEZs, Special Economic Zones, as not recognised under international law, and the European Commission considered it to be incompatible with the GATT. It remains to be seen how the 1999 revised Convention will develop after it has been fully ratified.

These legal provisions have encouraged and facilitated the geographical separation from production, invention, distribution, and marketing in the international commodity chain in toys. Since the early 1980s, however, Chinese legislation, both central and local, on Special Economic Zones has also had a direct influence on the concentration of production facilities. Chinese laws on foreign direct investment (FDI) and labour are of special importance. Most toy factories in China are located in the Shenzhen SEZ. Shenzhen rules on foreign direct investment (FDI) provide for Chinese-foreign joint ventures, Chinese-foreign contractual joint ventures, wholly foreign-owned enterprises, international leasing, compensation trade, and processing and assembling with materials and parts from foreign suppliers. Recently, however, the fact that labour costs in Shenzhen are higher than in the rest of Guandong Province, due partly to law, has encouraged toy companies to establish outside the SEZ, though still in Guandong.

In fact, however, to this part of south China belongs a wider economic area which includes Hong Kong. Toy factories enjoy very close links with enterpreneurs in Hong Kong and are often part of Hong Kong companies. Production, distribution, quasi-political activities such as participation in trade associations, and often personal or family relations are closely intertwined. Chinese companies, such as Early Light in the Shenzhen Special Economic Zone, produce toys on out-sourcing contracts for the world's biggest toy companies, not only Mattel but also Hasbro, Fisher-Price, Ertl from the United States, and Bandai and Tomy from Japan. These contracts are often arranged and managed by Hong Kong-based entrepreneurs, who, in addition to their role as middlemen, sometimes run their own toy manufacturing company in China and are also prominent in the main Hong Kong sectoral trade association, the Hong Kong Toys Council. More than half of China's toy production is re-exported through Hong Kong. To the extent that power in the toy chain lies in Asia, it is based in Hong Kong. For this reason, as well as to preserve maximum flexibility in a highly innovative and rapidly changing market, the production of toys for the export market usually takes place in wholly owned subsidiaries rather than joint ventures . . .

E Property

Fourth, *property arrangements*. What property-like arrangements (such as use, ownership, management, control) are associated with the units of a specific box? Which sites of global legal pluralism are the most relevant to these arrangements? Which specific institutions, norms, and processes are determinative with regard to the arrangements in a particular site? Why? If different property-like arrangements prevail among the various units in a box, what institutions, norms, and processes encourage or tolerate diversity? How is such diversity managed?

Intellectual property is crucial to the international toy industry . . .

It is not surprising, therefore, that a number of intellectual property cases have been brought by international buyers in Hong Kong courts. For example, Mattel, the manufacturer of Barbie dolls, sued the Tonka Corporation in the Hong Kong High Court in 1991 for infringement of copyright. It alleged that the defendant's Miss America dolls copied the Barbie dolls' head sculpture and that its packaging infringed registered trade-marks by stating that the Miss America doll's clothes also fit the Barbie doll. Lego brought an action in 1995 against a small Hong Kong company that used the word 'Lego' in its business of publishing entertainment and football magazines. The defendant deleted the word 'Lego' from its name during the course of the court hearing. On the whole, the Hong Kong courts have been favourable to such claims.

F Labour

... The codes of conduct elaborated under the aegis of multinational companies and sector-specific trade associations may be much more important in practice than formal national or local legislation. The large toy companies, retailers, and trade associations have all adopted sector-specific codes of conduct which are imposed upon, or recommended to, their factories. Such codes of conduct have been described as 'typically book-sized documents that specify working conditions down to the dimensions of the medical boxes on the wall', and as 'changing China's toy industry more than anything else'.

One example is the Code of Business Practices of the International Council of Toy Industries (ICTI). ICTI was established in 1974 and incorporated under the law of New York. It is an association of toy associations, embracing manufacturers and marketers. Its members, as of February 1999, comprised the toy associations of Hong Kong, China, the United States, Japan, Denmark, France, Italy, Spain, Sweden, and the United Kingdom, as well as Argentina, Australia, Brazil, Canada, Hungary, Korea, Mexico, Philippines, Taiwan, and Thailand. The general management functions of ICTI are performed by a president and a secretary, both currently held by Toy Manufacturers of America. English is ICTI's official language.

The ICTI Code of Business Practices, which was revised and approved on 1 June 1998, is a voluntary code of conduct containing specific operating conditions which members are expected to meet, for which members are expected to obtain contractor adherence in advance, and to which supply agreements with firms manufacturing on behalf of ICTI members are expected to provide for adherence. The operating conditions refer to labour practices and the workplace...

These codes have been adopted mainly as a result of pressure from non-governmental organisations (NGOs). For example, the Coalition for the Safe Production of Toys (Toy Coalition) has been instrumental in getting codes of conduct on labour practices adopted by associations of toy manufacturers and companies. The Toy Coalition was started by several Thai and Hong Kong groups in 1994. It was established in response to fires at a Kader toy factory in Thailand and at a doll factory in Zhili, China, and three other factory accidents in Shenzhen and the nearby area in 1993: 188 people died in the Kader fire, 87 people died and 51 were injured in the Zhili fire, and a total of 71 people died in the Shenzhen accidents. Various officials were sent to prison, and following an inspection tour by President Jiang Zemin and Foreign Minister Qian Qichen measures were taken to improve working conditions, such as monitoring the payment of the minimum wage. This concerned mainly small- and medium-sized Japanese, Taiwanese, Hong Kong, and South Korean factories. The workers in Western joint-ventures are reported to have had better conditions. In its campaign the Toy Coalition was joined by other such groups, including the World Development Movement (UK), ICFTU, AFL-CIO (US), Trocaire (Ireland), Italian organisations, the Workers Party (France), Asia Pacific Workers Solidarity Links, PSPD (Korea), the Japan Citizens'

Liaison Committee for the Safe Production of Toys (Japan), Indonesian groups, and the Maquila Solidarity Network (Canada). These NGOs thus constitute worldwide networks linking NGOs in Europe, the United States, Asia and other parts of the world, thus mirroring, to some extent, multinational corporations and affecting, conditioning, and helping to create the norms which are imposed on and by them.

Despite their political origins, these codes of conduct reflect the organisation of power in the global toy commodity chain in three different respects. First, precisely because the dominant buyers are few in number, they are unusually susceptible to political pressure. Non-governmental organisations from various countries have successfully put pressure on the small number of powerful American buyers and on the national and international trade associations they control, to elaborate codes of conduct with regard to their mainly Asian workforce. Second, the dominant buyers, whose power rests on their control of brands and marketing, are able, in effect, to determine the content of industry-wide codes of conduct and then to impose them on their suppliers, at least contractually if not always in practice. Codes of conduct thus are analogous to multilaterally negotiated treaties which are then applied as standard-form contracts laid down by the leading firms in a particular market. Third, power struggles within the chain occur latently and sometimes overtly between buyers and original equipment manufacturers. The main US buyers use soft law codes, essentially outside the legal system, as a way of ensuring their dominance over Hong Kong OEM and Chinese producers, while the latter struggle to develop their own ideas and designs in order to break out of their dependence on foreign buyers and foreign market niches.

Based partly on the ICTI example, the Hong Kong Toys Council (HKTC) introduced a Code of Practice for the Toy Industry in July 1997. Although not legally binding, it serves as a reference, and as an educational and promotional device for its members. In fact, however, it is not clear whether it (or another such code) is widely adopted; if adopted, whether it is enforced; or even what enforcement and compliance might mean given that the Code is not legally binding and sanctions for non-compliance are inadequate...

Even if a factory has a code of conduct, effective implementation and monitoring thus remain crucial issues. At least in certain industries, pressure from critics and labour rights groups for effective enforcement of codes of conduct can prove effective. The Nike case is instructive. A Vietnam factory of Nike Inc. was criticised in 1997 for unsafe working conditions. By 1998, the company had improved its working conditions, and its earlier critic issued a report noting substantial improvements. In March 1999, the chairman of Nike announced that the company, based in Beaverton, Oregon, USA, would disclose the location of all its foreign factories and open them to independent monitors if competitors would agree to do the same. He also sent letters to universities with Nike contracts to enlist them to 'ensure that licensed products bearing the names and logos of schools are manufactured under fair conditions'. Although the structure of the athletic footwear industry differs somewhat from that of the toy sector, both are buyer-driven commodity chains, so this example may be instructive in demonstrating that action by independent researchers or labour rights groups can have an effect...

H   Connections Between Economic Relations and Specific Sites

... The lack of congruence between governance, economic processes, and territory can be illustrated by two examples. The first concerns EC environmental and health legislation. Greenpeace put pressure on EU institutions and national governments to ban all toys containing phthalates, an additive used to soften PVC products. As yet, however, no such EU legislation has been enacted. Nevertheless, the risk that such legislation might be enacted in the future has already changed the practices of some toy factories in China. Some factories consider it the major issue confronting Chinese exports of toys to the EU. Their international buyers instructed them to substitute hard plastic for PVC. Some individual EU Member States have already banned imports of toys containing PVC or certain other substances, and these measures have affected toy production in Hong Kong and China. In the United States, the main buyers stopped using phthalates in certain baby products in early 1999, even though, as in the EU, there is no legislation prohibiting it; these business decisions will inevitably affect toy production in China.

A second example refers to toy safety. It exemplifies the interaction and potential incompatibility of norms, institutions and processes from two geographically discrete sites. The EC 'toys directive' provides that all toys sold in the EU must meet essential safety requirements and bear a 'CE' mark indicating conformity. It was revised in 1996 to be similar to current US requirements, perhaps indicating progress towards mutual recognition and standardisation on toy safety requirements. Such requirements condition Chinese production of toys for export to Europe and the conduct of inspections in Hong Kong. But EU and US safety standards are not the only ones which apply to the marketing of toys produced in Hong Kong and China. In May 1998, the Swedish company, Ikea, was reported to be facing prosecution in Hong Kong for selling in Hong Kong a toy that caused the death of a boy in Europe; the toy met EU safety requirements but did not meet the more stringent specifications of the Hong Kong Toys and Children's Products Safety Ordinance.

A third example concerns the European Court of Justice. In 1998, the European Court of Justice decided the cases brought by the UK and Spain in 1994 against quotas on imports of toys from China. I focus here on the United Kingdom case. The point of departure of the ECJ's analysis was the principle of liberalisation of trade; the introduction of quotas was in its view an exception. The ECJ noted, however, that the abolition of quotas on imports was 'not a rule of law which the Council is required in principle to observe, but rather the result of a decision made by that institution in the exercise of its discretion'. It remarked that more than 98% of the imports in question were liberalised before the contested Regulation was adopted, and that the quotas introduced by the Regulation reduced the level of Community trade by almost 50% for some of the toys in question. It followed its previous case law, however, in concluding that, when assessing complex economic situations, the Council enjoyed substantial discretion, including making findings of fact, and that the exercise of this discretion was subject only to limited judicial review. Similarly, in adopting new Community rules, the Council was required to take account only of the general interests of the Community as a whole. The Court also held, following its Advocate-General on this point also, that the Council was entitled to do so by basing its evaluation on 'the mere risk of disturbance', and this could be deduced from the increase in Chinese toy imports. In other words, the judiciary will not substitute its evaluation of the facts for that of the legislator unless the legislator's assessment appears manifestly incorrect in the light of the information available to it at the time of the adoption of the rules. The ECJ, therefore, dismissed the UK's application for annulment.

This decision and that in the case brought by Spain were taken more than four years after the cases were brought, and more than two years after the Advocate-General's opinion in both cases. In accordance with ECJ practice, the judgment was unanimous, but the length of time taken to reach it suggests that the form of unanimity masked the substance of deep disagreement. The ECJ judgment, just like the Council regulation that had provoked the litigation, was a delicate compromise.

The judgment represented a judicial compromise, articulated in the form of a unanimous judgment, which protected the integrity of a prior legislative compromise that was expressed in the form of a complex regulation. The compromise in this second-order sense, achieved by judicial deliberation, served to ensure the discreteness and integrity of the EC political process and to insulate it, to some extent, from the judicial process. A Member State, or other strategic actor, could not use litigation to upset or revise a complex political compromise.

This double-order compromise was intimately bound up with the definition of EU rules for the globalisation game. These rules potentially concerned relations between market actors, relations between market actors and governance structures, and relations between different governance structures. But the ECJ did not address these issues directly. Instead, its judgment dealt with them indirectly, by emphasising the importance of judicial restraint in the face of politically sensitive Council legislation. Nevertheless, it had wider consequences. It ensured, to some extent, the integrity of the EU political process, insulating it from collateral attack by means of judicial review. It maintained a political space, structured, to some extent, by objective interests, populated by conflicts among subjective interests, and involving Member States, firms, trade associations, and EU institutions. This space was a political market, in which the EU economic market for toys, structured by the global toy commodity chain, was interpenetrated with the EU political market, with a supply of, and demand for, economic regulation and regulatory law. Both of these markets, at least in the United Kingdom case, were characterised by what Weber called the factual 'autonomy' of the propertied classes, that is, an asymmetry of property, information, power, and influence upon the Member States and thus the EU legislator. The double-order compromise of the ECJ judgment tended to insulate and enhance the integrity of this political space and strengthen its market-oriented normative order.

The ECJ judgment thus occurred in a highly political context, and was in fact highly political. Its main importance did not lie in a short-term economic impact. A judgment either way would probably have had only marginal financial effects on the distribution of resources among EU importers, producers, retailers or others that lost or gained as a result of the existence of quotas between the adoption of the Regulation and the date of the judgment. The primary significance of the judgment lay in articulating legal principles for the future and in its broader implications for the relationship between EU law and other institutional, normative, and processual sites. . . .

I Relations Between Sites and the Chain as a Whole

... Certain sites concern several parts of the chain or the chain as a whole. The most well-known example is the Uruguay Round agreements associated with the World Trade Organisation (WTO). This includes the General Agreement on Tariffs and Trade (GATT), the General Agreement on Trade in Services (GATS), and the Agreement on Trade-Related Aspects of Intellectual Property (TRIPS). For some time, they have been important in regard to the international commodity chain in toys, even though the main producer, China, is not yet a WTO member.

The GATT/WTO was a crucial conditioning element in the negotiation of the EU quota on toys from China in 1993–4 and the related litigation between 1994–8. It also cast a long shadow with regard to future disputes, notably by holding out, to China and multinational companies 'located' there, the promise of new institutions, norms, and processes, which would be available on eventual Chinese accession. When China joins the GATT, the firms located there will benefit from Article XI GATT concerning the general elimination of quantitative restrictions. The provision of services and the protection of intellectual property in brand names are likely to be affected by the eventual application of GATS and TRIPS. It may also be argued that the impact of the GATT on China is already real, even if China has not yet acceded to the WTO. Companies are already positioning themselves in anticipation of further opening up of China's domestic market to imported toys and foreign toy retailers. One has only to note that in 1997, the same year it purchased a major competitor, Tyco, Mattel launched Barbie in China.

These examples do not, of course, mean that the WTO is the only site governing international trade. Nor does it necessarily mean that, from a sociological, as distinct from a positivist law, standpoint, international trade law norms are arranged in a hierarchical fashion, or that the WTO stands at the apex of an institutional and normative hierarchy. The examples do indicate, however, that the WTO affects many aspects of the global commodity chain in toys, perhaps more aspects than any other site. This, in turn, provides a social, economic, political, and cultural basis for the WTO's claim *qua* institution to have a dominant position in international trade law, though not necessarily global law generally. It also tends to aliment institutional, and often individual, support for the argument that international trade law is hierarchical in nature, with the WTO site at the top. Seen sociologically, such developments are processes, not yet acquired positions or states of affairs.

VI Conclusion

I have argued here that global economic networks are governed by the totality of strategically determined, situationally specific, and often episodic conjunctions of a multiplicity of institutional, normative, and processual sites throughout the world. The totality of such sites represents a new global form of legal pluralism.

The development of the global economic relations involved in the international toy industry owes much to corporate strategies. Such a view is consistent with the approach taken here, which privileges the perspective of strategic actors. But these strategies themselves have been pursued taking account of the framework of the law and other normative frameworks and have been elaborated by using them. They take place, are conditioned by, and have contributed to, the development of global legal pluralism. To put it more accurately, the development of global networks in the toy industry has occurred in conjunction with the development of a variety of structural sites throughout the world, each of which comprises institutions, norms, and dispute resolution processes...

First, global legal pluralism is a way of describing the structure of the sites taken as a whole. Seen from the perspective of a specific global commodity chain, global legal pluralism may be described as a network, even if some segments of the network may be occupied alternatively by two or more possible sites.

Second, the sites of global legal pluralism may be classified provisionally into two rough categories. Some sites are market-based, being generated by economic actors as part of economic processes. Some are polity-based, in that they form a part of established political structures; this includes sites which are convention-based, deriving from agreements between governments. This classification scheme distinguishes between different types of sites according to their mode of creation.

Third, the various sites differ in decision-making structure, that is, in their institutions, norms and processes. They vary in the extent to which their institutions, norms, and processes are inserted in a hierarchy. They may differ in their reliance on case law, the use of precedent, and the binding force of norms and decisions: in other words, in respect of those characteristics which are often associated with law. These factors affect the outcomes of the various sites, including the different ways in which they allocate risk. At the same time, however, it is important not to overlook the extent to which sites are interrelated, for example, in relation to institutional arrangements such as jurisdiction, copying or borrowing of norms, and the interconnection of their dispute-resolution processes.

Fourth, the sites are not all equally vulnerable to economic or political pressures. It is going too far to say that the network of global legal pluralism which is put into play by the economic processes of any specific global commodity chain reflects the structure of authority and power in the global commodity chain in question. Some types of institutions, some types of processes, and some types of norms are more permeable to economic processes than others. It should also be noted that in cases of political conflict, for example, between NGOs and multinational buyers in the international commodity chain in toys, the struggle between the competing groups is not limited to a single site. Each of the groups may invoke institutions, norms, and processes of different sites. This may lead to a wider conflict between different sites, including conflicts of effectiveness and even of legitimacy...

These broad hypotheses need to be tested. In addition, numerous questions remain to be addressed by future research. For example, how are sites created? How are they constituted, developed, and legitimated as sites? Which sites have a specific geographical location, and if so, why? What determines the modes and organisation of dispute resolution? What decision processes are involved? Do sites vary in their resemblance to state law (insertion in a hierarchy, reliance on case law, binding decisions, use of precedent, etc.), and why? To what extent do the norms of a particular site combine hard law and soft law? To what extent are sites interconnected, and how are they connected? How are groups, hierarchies and networks of sites created, and how, if at all, are such processes connected to economic and political relations? Do certain sites tend to converge or become more uniform in their institutional characteristics, norms, or dispute settlement processes, and why? How do conflicts between sites arise, what are the consequences of such competition, and how are conflicting institutional, normative, and processual claims handled? The answers to these questions will help us to understand further how economic globalisation is governed.

NOTE

See: Francis Snyder, "Governing Economic Globalization: Global Legal Pluralism and European Law," *European Law Journal* 5(3) (1999), 334–9, 342–3, 345–6, 351–74, for complete notes.

27

Civilization and Its Negotiations

Laura Nader

Introduction: Nader on Negotiations

A number of legal studies in anthropology during the 1960s were occupied with the difference between adjudication and negotiation as alternative modes of dispute management. At that time, the contrast between these two approaches was treated as pivotal to understanding the variety of ways a satisfactory resolution could be reached in instances of dispute. The protagonists who presented these two approaches were Max Gluckman and Philip Gulliver.

Max Gluckman, having produced "The Judicial Process among the Barotse" in 1955 could be said to have unwittingly initiated the controversy. His book used an ethnographic description of cases in an "indigenous" court in Africa to illustrate what he saw as the universal principles of the logic of judging. In fact, these "indigenous" courts, though staffed by Africans, were part of the colonial system of native courts. Neither their procedure nor their substantive rules were by any means entirely African (Moore 1992). He wanted to show that the mode of reasoning of the judges in Africa could be seen to be like that of judges in the courts of the industrial world. The facts in the cases were different because of differences in the societies in which they arose, but the logic of the judges in reasoning from general principles to particular instances seemed to him to be the same. As a result of publishing that book, Gluckman became identified with a particular way of looking at judicial procedures for settling disputes. In contrast, Philip Gulliver's "Social Control in an African Society" (1963) presented a detailed description of the way the Arusha approached the disputing process. The Arusha mounted negotiations that took place between the principals, and between the lineage supporters of the principals. The Arusha avoided the courts.

From Laura Nader, "Civilization and Its Negotiations," in Pat Caplan (ed.) *Understanding Disputes* (Oxford and Providence: Berg Publishers, 1995), pp. 39–40, 42–63.

After Gulliver's work received major attention, the two approaches to dispute "settlement," judicial and negotiated, became fixed points of comparison in many academic discussions. What seemed plain from some of Gulliver's examples was that the party that prevailed in a negotiated settlement was likely to be the more politically powerful one. Thus the salient difference between judicial and negotiated settlements of dispute came to be conceived as the contrast between judicial and political outcomes, the judicial being a decision in accordance with a system of rules and the negotiated being decided in accordance with the distribution of power.

There were further developments from the emphasis on negotiated settlements that Gulliver initiated. These emerged in the later work of Sally Merry (1990) and Laura Nader (1989). Both anthropologists became interested in the way American courts diverted some cases from the courts into informal channels. This helped them deal with their overloaded calendars. These alternative sites of dispute settlement were often run by lay people. They did not adjudicate cases according to rules of law, but mediated and negotiated settlements out of court. This was part of the movement for Alternative Dispute Resolution.

In the abbreviated article which follows here, Laura Nader continues to develop these themes, but this time does so on the international plane. She explores international river disputes. If a carefully conducted judicial proceeding was once considered the mark of civilization, while negotiation was a more "primitive" mode of dispute settlement, what is the situation today in international conflict over water control? Is there an evolutionary trend to be seen? Nader asks whether adjudication in such an adversarial process is generally considered less "civilized" than a process of arbitrating, negotiating, or mediating. She argues that indeed the trend has been away from adjudication/arbitration toward negotiation. And she makes a political point, that powerful nations are not primarily interested in problem-solving techniques as such, but are pushing for control in whatever forum they think they are likely to get what they want. She illustrates her thesis with accounts of specific international water disputes. How relevant are earlier opinions about procedural evolution? Is evolution the issue, or is this simply a historical sequence? Is it time to abandon such evolutionary models?

S.F.M.

REFERENCES

Gluckman, Max, 1955 *The Judicial Process Among the Barotse of Northern Rhodesia*. Manchester: Manchester University Press.

Gulliver, Philip, 1963 *Social Control in an African Society*. London: Routledge.

Merry, Sally Engle, 1990 *Getting Justice and Getting Even*. Chicago and London: University of Chicago Press.

Moore, Sally Falk, 1992 Treating Law as Knowledge: Telling Colonial Officers What to Say to Africans about Running "Their Own" Native Courts. *Law and Society Review* 26(1).

Nader, Laura, 1989 The ADR Explosion: The Implications of Rhetoric in Legal Reform. *Windsor Yearbook of Access to Justice*, pp. 269–291.

Nader, *Civilization and Its Negotiations*

Introduction

Writings on the anthropology of law often rest on notions of social evolution. These works often place dispute-resolution forums on a scale, so that self-help and negotiation are commonly placed at the starting-point on an evolutionary continuum towards civilization. Then, with development, societies are shown to move along from these bilateral means, to mediation, arbitration, and adjudication (see Hobhouse, Wheeler and Ginsburg 1930). These same works consider the presence of courts as a sign of societal complexity, or evolution, or development, or all of these, while the simplest societies lack mediation (see Hoebel 1954).

In this paper, I argue that preferences for ranking dispute-resolution forums change with the 'civilizing mission' of major power-holders. Indeed, from a preliminary sampling of international negotiation in water disputes, it appears as if the ranking preference for dispute-handling forums changes to mirror the distribution of international power. The interests of power-holders (in this paper dominant nation-states) are furthered by an entrepreneurial spirit among interested professionals such as negotiators.

A number of writers, including myself, have documented the ideological shift (Nader 1989) from adversarial forums (courts) to alternative forums (arbitration, mediation, negotiation) within the United States. In this preliminary paper I move the discussion to the international arena, where the scene is striking in its similarity to that of the US Alternative Dispute Resolution (ADR) movement of the 1970s and 1980s – a move which requires an understanding of the elastic nature of definitions of 'civilized' behaviour...

In the present context, it appears that a new standard of international negotiations is being promoted as the older standard of adjudication/arbitration in the World Court has become less useful to the more powerful nations of the world. The older standard lost its utility since the emergence in the 1960s of new nations, many of them 'Third World' nations ready to use the International Court of Justice to represent new interests. It is even more interesting that the pendulum swing from adjudication and the rule of law to a valorizing of negotiation and harmony coincided with the development of ADR in the United States and its export abroad, often in the guise of expanding democracy through law.

What follows are: (1) introductory notes on the World Court, illustrating *why* it no longer appears to be useful to stronger nations; (2) a description of the professional culture of international negotiators, whose activity illustrates *how* the negotiating standard has been promoted; and (3) key points of a series of international water disputes to show how the alleged positional superiority of harmony practice plays itself out for the benefit of the stronger disputant. The concluding remarks (4) suggest that valorizing negotiation and harmony above the rule of law is part of the radiation of ADR. It functions to hold the line on power redistribution, and is reminiscent of other neo-colonialist attempts to maintain and increase hegemony by means of civilizing (or development) missions.

From the World Court to International Negotiating Teams

The International Court of Justice is the supreme court for international law. The Court is situated at the Hague, having inherited the precedents of the Permanent Court of International Justice, which was a part of the League of Nations. At present, the Court operates under statute as part of the United Nations Charter organized after the Second World War. The Court consists of fifteen independent judges elected by the Security Council and the General Assembly of the United Nations. Although a series of US presidents supported US membership in both courts, others (including members of the US Congress) voiced concern that national sovereignty would be threatened. The US joined in 1946. Since that time, there have been important changes in the Court's composition and in the types of cases it considers. For example, in 1946, two-thirds of the judges were either Americans or West Europeans. With the addition of over one hundred states (many of them post-colonial 'Third World' states), the World Court now consists of judges who are often sympathetic to the causes of the newer 'Third World' nations (Franck 1986:36) . . .

In 1985, the Reagan administration withdrew the US's 1946 agreement voluntarily to comply with the compulsory jurisdiction of the World Court, which effectively ended any serious US commitment to its viability. This was perhaps the most visible continuation of a wider United Nations tendency: for a decreasing percentage of member states to submit to compulsory jurisdiction (ibid.: 49). This phenomenon has been described by one legal scholar as 'the Court's vanishing clientele' (ibid.: 47). A gradual diminishment of jurisdiction, coupled with an inability meaningfully to enforce its decisions, clearly have limited the Court's role in adjudicating international disputes. Furthermore, the Soviet Union in the mid-1960s and the US in the mid-1980s, both charter members of the World Court, have both withheld dues, thereby abdicating their financial responsibility and evincing a mood of indifference to international law.

The instrument which Calvin Coolidge described as 'a convenient instrument to which we could go, but to which we could not be brought' (ibid.) was no longer convenient, possibly because of its role in several major controversies such as the Iran-hostage issue, the use of the CIA to attack Nicaragua, the Iran–Iraq conflict, the Afghanistan war, the Vietnam–Kampuchea war (Yoder 1989:116–19). In sum, the US commitment to international law and the International Court of Justice has, for the most part, been declining. The Third World presence in the Court has made it generally less beholden to 'developed' nations since the late 1960s, and as a result there has been a gradual divergence between the Court's decisions and the national interests of the developed countries. As the interests of the 'developed' world are at stake, fewer countries are willing to recognize the jurisdiction of the World Court. Thus the US shift in 1986 was away from compulsory jurisdiction. Interestingly, this new trivialization of international adjudication came about at the height of the 'ADR explosion' in the United States and its attacks on domestic adjudication. In addition, a number of 'Third World' countries have also refused to recognize the court's jurisdiction because they are unwilling to surrender their newly gained national sovereignty.

The recent stimulus for international negotiation teams sprang from a different source than did the International Court of Justice, although negotiation is part of the work of the United Nations. During the Reagan years and the decade before Reagan, there was a movement in the United States away from adversarial processes for dispute settlement and towards dispute management by the use of 'alternative dispute resolution' (ADR). It was an attempt to stem the 'rights movements' of the 1960s – a pacification scheme in part. In the 1970s, the role of the Chief Justice of the US Supreme Court Warren Burger was pivotal in highlighting the rhetoric about what is civilized behaviour in dispute processing: 'Our distant forebears moved slowly from trial by battle and other barbaric means of resolving conflicts and disputes and we must move away from total reliance on the adversary contest for resolving all disputes...' (Burger 1984). His remedy was privatization, to move toward taking a large volume of private conflicts out of the courts. An ADR profession was born and institutionalized. The prime focus was on organizational expansion, with implications for profitable new jobs for professionals, and a new source of repression for American citizens (Grillo 1991).

International Negotiators

Who were these new professionals, and what was new about them anyway? ADR professionals come from a variety of fields – law, economics, psychology, political science, therapy – very few from anthropology. What was new was not so much that they were practising mediation, arbitration or negotiation – after all, such modes of dispute-processing had been around for a long time, and in the US as well. What some had in common was a distaste for a confrontational adversarial process, for courts as a way to handle the problems of the masses (or we might say the uncivilized), for justice by win–lose methods.

At the time I thought I was witnessing a forum fetish – the non-rational preference of one forum over another for purposes of dispute-processing. Gradually, I began to interpret such preference as part of a moving escalator in the civilizing mission, activity commonly associated with assertions of superiority. What had been thought to characterize a primitive level of development – negotiation – was now civilized, and what had been thought to be civilized – litigation – was not.

Probably the most well-known international negotiator of recent US history is former President Jimmy Carter. Carter published an address on negotiation in a book entitled *Negotiation: The Alternative to Hostility* (1984) in which he states his position. Basically he agrees with and echoes Chief Justice Burger's publicly proclaimed position: litigation is an 'unnatural process'; negotiation is the absence of litigation or war. In summarizing the number and diversity of negotiations that he was personally involved in, he observes that negotiations have become increasingly more prevalent as a means of conflict-resolution than in previous decades. He refers to the most well-known issues: the Panama Canal Treaty, Salt II, majority rule in South Africa, securing the release of hostages in Iran, peace in the Middle East, relations with China. Carter is practised in his advice and clearly indicates a flexible framework. He concludes in a manner that recognizes power differentials:

'Although military, economic and political strength certainly favours the more powerful side, the matter of simple justice is a counterbalancing factor. Once the talks begin, there is at least some presumption that a final agreement will be fair to all affected people.' Jimmy Carter was speaking from practice, experience, and an inclination towards peace that may have been based more on his religious beliefs than on his notions of justice in a civil society...

In sum, the programmatic social science literature on negotiation is a conglomeration of disciplinary styles, concepts, and content, the total of which sometimes appears both confused and confusing. However, it is somewhat interesting as an example of interdisciplinary borrowings with an absence of the standards of any particular discipline. For example, negotiation and mediation are sometimes conflated, negotiation is equated with bargaining, power differentials are often ignored, culture is confused with social structure, ethnocentrisms are common, and there is little consideration given to the possibility that the dispute may necessarily lead to zero-sum outcomes (especially where material resources are concerned). The overall implication in much of the literature is that anything can be negotiated, and the concepts of anthropologists such as Gulliver are being used as controlling processes.

The literature gets truly interesting when the analyst deals with the detail of empirical instances. It is in these specific cases that all mention of 'civilized' conduct drops away, and is replaced by phrases like 'mutual learning', 'information-sharing', 'harmonizing', and 'co-operation'. Zero-sum settlements become 'hostile', and information, analysis and solution get in the way of 'constructive dialogue'. Under such conditions, mind-games become a central component of the negotiation process, and toxic poisoning is transformed into a 'perception of toxic poisoning'.

In the following section, some of the water-resource disputes surveyed are indicative of the transition of dispute-resolution forums that was suggested earlier, away from adjudication/arbitration and towards negotiation. The progression is best reported in the case of the Danube River Basin, and moves from (1) procedures of international adjudication/arbitration, to (2) basin-wide planning where river basin commissions deal co-operatively, to (3) bilateral agreements resulting from international bargaining, to (4) non-governmental organizations operating across political and bureaucratic boundaries and working towards the institutionalization of international co-operation (Linnerooth 1990). The transition found in these Danube cases illustrates the progression from third-party adjudication/arbitration, to informal bilateral arrangements, to 'institutionalized' co-operation through negotiation. Such a transition mirrors the 'privatization' of justice through ADR centres in the United States in a genuinely striking manner (see Nader 1989: 282–5).

In the next section, on international river disputes, the progressions noted above become apparent. As we see, many of the authors writing on international negotiation imply that there exists a 'universal diplomatic culture' of negotiators, a common culture of national governmental administrators, the international 'scientific community', and environmental groups (Linnerooth 1990: 637; see also Zartman and Berman 1982: 226). What is claimed to be universal is, I claim, a hegemonic perspective on disputing, one developed in the United States during the seventies and exported world-wide, a hegemony that I refer to as 'harmony ideology', and whose primary function is pacification (Nader 1990).

International River Disputes

...Only a very few international water disputes have been settled by adjudication. The *Lake Lanoux* case between France and Spain is the classic example from the late 1950s. When John Laylin and Rinaldo Bianchi wrote about 'The Role of Adjudication in International River Disputes' (1959), both authors were engaged in resolving two international river disputes by negotiation. At the same time, they believed that adjudication could play a useful role in finding solutions for such disputes. They point out what is peculiar to sharing waters of an international river. Firstly,

> the geographical position of one riparian often is such that it can adversely affect the rights of others without acting outside its own boundaries. A lower riparian has for instance, certain advantages, not enjoyed on the high seas, over the shipping interests of an upper riparian or non-riparian; similarly an upper riparian has an advantage over, say, the irrigation interests of a lower riparian.

Although their paper was written over forty years ago, it addresses the issue being raised in this paper – that without the possibility of third-party decision-makers, the more powerful disputants can use ADP negotiations to greater advantage...

Laylin and Bianchi make their case for the usefulness of adjudication in reference to the *Lake Lanoux* case. Lake Lanoux lies within French territory and is fed by waters rising in France. It empties into a tributary which crosses into Spain. France contemplated utilizing the waters of Lake Lanoux in projects that would affect the flow of water to Spain. From 1917 to 1929 France and Spain were unable to come to agreement over French development plans. In 1929, 12 years after the beginning of the dispute, both countries signed an agreement under which they agreed to submit unresolved disputes either to arbitration or to adjudication by the World Court, an agreement which they have since utilized. Laylin and Bianchi's description of the conflicting rights of upstream vs. downstream nations, as well as the more obvious right of a downstream nation to enjoy an adequate supply of water, seems to point to a disagreement that was framed in terms of rights. After being cast in these terms, the dispute was successfully adjudicated by a regional tribunal consisting of judges from several European nations. As Lon Fuller (1978) has noted, adjudicated disputes frequently become either issues of violated rights or accusations of guilt. In the *Lake Lanoux* case, the dispute was presented as a question of infringed rights, and consequently lent itself to settlement by adjudication.

When cases that should be adjudicated are negotiated, as illustrated in Laylin and Bianchi's vignette (ibid., pp. 39–41) about a 1940s dispute between the US and Mexico over the Colorado River, the explicit connections between international law and the World Court, water rights, and the advantages of negotiation become obvious. The authors indicate that many US Senators, in a debate over whether or not to act unilaterally, were emphatic about the desirability of negotiating a rapid settlement: one senator states, 'I say that we should be advised thereby and not lose one day in stopping Mexico from building up any future right [to Colorado River water]' (ibid., p. 40). Here we see that 'efficiency' in negotiation can really mean minimizing losses. Interestingly enough, Senator Tom Connally (an active participant in the US Senate debate on the World Court) instructs the stenographer to keep *this* debate off the record: 'Lift your pen, Mr. Reporter' (ibid., p. 40). Connally must have realized how cynical the process of friendly negotiations might appear in the *Congressional Record*.

The tone of the Danube River Basin case as synthesized by Joanne Linnerooth (1990) is in complete contrast to Laylin and Bianchi's reasoning. Her article links the issues of negotiation (using the formulaic language common to contemporary writings on negotiation) to international water rights, with special reference to pollution in the Danube. Linnerooth recognizes the power imbalances between upper- and lower-riparian countries, but takes the view that the more powerful upstream nations are at a disadvantage if they agree to negotiate 'cooperative [water quality] policies', while weaker nations are at an advantage. Linnerooth does not acknowledge the possibility that the opposite may be true – namely, bilateral negotiation may put the stronger nation at a bargaining advantage *vis-à-vis* the weaker nation. Indeed, she argues that 'some compensating advantage or incentive for the upper riparian states is a prerequisite for co-operation' (p. 643). She seems unaware of other cases where no enticements to negotiate were necessary. In these kinds of cases upstream nations often simply wish to minimize their losses by avoiding a trial (or third-party involvement) that would prove them to be in the wrong, as was for example the cases of India in 1977 (Begum 1988) and the US in the 1940s Colorado River dispute with Mexico (Laylin and Bianchi 1959).

Linnerooth, like many other international negotiating 'professionals,' implies that there is a 'universal negotiating culture' or what she calls a 'common culture' composed of national government administrators, international scientific communities, and emerging environmental groups (ibid., p. 637). The language Linnerooth uses in describing how conflicting, adversarial interests might be negotiated is revealing: 'mutual learning' and 'information-sharing', as my research assistant notes, sounds more like marriage counselling, not unravelling conflicts over river pollution. Therapy talk is a strong influence in ADR. Her 'negotiating culture' gives little consideration to disputes that *are* in fact zero-sum. Linnerooth does not seem to be looking for the limits of negotiation, because in her view anything can be negotiated, even if 'perceptions' must first be moulded: '...among groups with different perceptions of the problem...a fundamental shift will be necessary to orient negotiation support away from "information, analysis, and solution" to providing the very mechanisms necessary for a constructive dialogue' (ibid., pp. 658–9). The literature on dispute resolution in fact gives us little reason to believe that the stronger nation is going to exert the patience or consideration to 'learn' or 'share' without the force of law, the threat of litigation, or the presence of mutually recognized authority.

The Danube River Basin is an interesting example because it is one of the most international river basins in the world. The Danube is Europe's second largest river, with eight riparian countries bordering (including Germany, Austria, Czechoslovakia, Hungary, the former Yugoslavia, Romania, Bulgaria, and the former Soviet Union). The Danube also transfers water from the non-riparian countries of Albania, Italy, Switzerland, and Poland. Eight countries spanning Eastern and Western Europe have declared the need to co-operate on confronting the mounting problems of water pollution. The Danube Declaration is non-binding, a step towards a more co-operative ecosystem approach to the management of the river. The contemporary central issues are the deteriorating quality of the water and demands for exploitation of the river for the generation of electrical energy. The Danube River Basin is home to over 70 million people, people of different cultures and economic prosperity who have different standards on water quality. The rich upper riparian countries use the Danube primarily for industrial and waste disposal and energy purposes. The lesser-developed lower riparian countries use the river for drinking water, irrigation, fisheries, and tourism (ibid., p. 636). As Linnerooth notes, there is a 'mismatch between countries which would benefit from pollution control and those with the resources for providing this control' (ibid., p. 636).

Recognizing the power asymmetry between upstream and downstream nations and recognizing also the poorly defined issue of water pollution, Linnerooth nevertheless proposes co-operation through bilateral, stepwise negotiations. She believes that it is 'unlikely that mini-governments with the power to legislate and implement river basin policies across national boundaries will emerge. The role of transboundary commissions in defining negotiating agendas, linking issues, and facilitating the negotiating process may, on the other hand, have considerable potential promise' (ibid., p. 648). Yet forums do not just 'work' or 'emerge' naturally. They work because forces behind them want them to work. Nevertheless, she continues to argue that in the absence of an international river basin authority, mechanisms for collaboration are most likely to be mainly bilateral agreements and international bargaining, which are increasingly influenced by non-governmental organizations operating across political and bureaucratic lines. 'Win–win' bargaining is to be accomplished by those who share 'a certain professional rationality and thus a common overall frame of the issue' (ibid., p. 657), or what she calls 'limited-authority committees' (ibid.). Negotiating participants may 'translate the border' – its imagery, social expectations, jurisdictional responsibilities and processes, as well as the differences in resources (ibid., p. 659, note 108). In short, what Linnerooth proposes is the transition from third-party litigation/arbitration and enforcement, through informal bilateral arrangements, to the non-governmental institutionalization of international co-operation (in other words the 'privatization' of international justice), arguing that expanding the authority of the Danube Commission will not work in the absence of an international river basin authority.

Within Spain and Portugal, the allocation of water is a less involved case than the Danube, but nevertheless raises some of the same questions regarding asymmetry of power and upstream–downstream issues. In the *Lake Lanoux* decision, France was the stronger nation, yet Spain succeeded in the arbitration. In the current situation between Spain and Portugal, Spain is stronger than Portugal, and has the advantage of having learned a lesson (as the weaker party) from the *Lake Lanoux* case: if you are an upstream nation, do not agree to adjudicate a water dispute.

According to Joseph Dellapenna (1992) the surface water in the Iberian peninsula may be an opportunity for co-operation or a source of conflict. Basically the situation is this: approximately 70 per cent of Portugal's surface fresh water comes from rivers that arise in Spain, while Spain receives virtually none of its surface fresh water from Portugal (Dellapenna 1992: 807). Thus, Portugal is at a severe disadvantage *vis-à-vis* Spain, with limited means of persuading Spain to take its interests into account. Exacerbating the problem are the increased pollution of waters coming from Spain and the Spanish plan to place their only nuclear waste disposal site along the Duero/Douro river just above the Spanish–Portuguese border. The proposed nuclear waste facility at Aldeadávila will be less than one kilometre from Portugal, and any contamination of the river will end up in Portugal. Given that Spain has the worst record of non-compliance with European Community environmental directives of any nation in the Community, Portugal has a right to ask why they must share the risk of disposing of another country's nuclear wastes. Furthermore, the Portuguese construction of the Algueva Dam on the Guadiana River to provide irrigation, hydroelectric generation, and urban and industrial water-supply is threatened by Spanish activities upstream. The Guadiana River rises in Spain, where the Spanish have developed their own irrigation project. Spanish plans would undoubtedly deplete the waters before they reach the reservoir for the Algueva Dam. Portugal has been unwilling to challenge Spain, although the 1927 convention provides for recourse to the International Court of Justice should the parties fail to agree. However, thus far, there has been no implementation of a judicial award.

The profile from Dellapenna's writing emerges as follows: the European Community (of which both Portugal and Spain are members) seems reluctant to get involved, and advises bilateral negotiation (ibid., pp. 806, 823). But Portugal's weak approach in dealing with Spain would not bode well for a fair bilateral settlement, literally because of the freshwater power differential between the two nations (ibid., pp. 806, 812, 822). Although a 1927 convention signed between Portugal and Spain provides for recourse to the World Court, this has not been a considered option. In fact, Dellapenna does not advocate the World Court as a solution, because he sees for a fact that Spain is in clear violation of customary international law; rather, he believes that a legal regime should be created to manage the common waterways (ibid., pp. 813–25). It is law rather than negotiation that he recommends...

The second author, J. Roman Calleros, a researcher from Mexico's El Colegio de la Frontera Norte, wants to pursue the problem by advocating the equity issue. He does not take a procedural approach, and he does not advocate litigation. He is simply insistent on Mexico's right to its share of the water...

In an article to which reference has already been made Dellapenna (1992) points out that even clearly dominant states hold back in taking all the water needed for fear of retaliation against the state's own water facilities, and he cites the instance of the Jordan Valley. Even in the midst of various phases of Middle East conflicts and wars over the last fifty years 'tacit cooperation has been the almost unbroken rule between Israel and its neighbours, particularly Jordan' (ibid., p. 805). Israel and Jordan are the primary users of the waters of the Jordan, which satisfies one-half of their combined demands (Neff and Matson 1984). The other riparian states are Lebanon and Syria, whose use of the Jordan waters is minor in comparison to that of the others, satisfying about 5 per cent of their total water demand. Conflict over the Jordan River results from a complex hydrological structure shared by four states, and from the hostilities between these four states. The Arab-Israeli conflict has overshadowed efforts to reach agreement on joint utilization of the waters.

The Jordan River is a complex system: the Dan River, which originates in pre-1967 Israel, discharges into the upper Jordan; the Hasbani River, which originates in south Lebanon, discharges into the upper Jordan; the Banias River, which originates in the Syrian Golan Heights, discharges into the upper Jordan; the Yarmouk river, which forms the border between Syria and Jordan, discharges into the lower Jordan. In the first half of the 1950s a number of water allocation plans were devised with the active involvement of a third party, US ambassador Eric Johnston, leading to the Unified Plan. The Plan was accepted by the technical committees from both Israel and the Arab League, although neither of the groups was able formally to commit itself to the Plan for domestic political reasons. In the absence of 'impartial monitoring' these water allocation plans deteriorated.

A series of unilateral actions followed. Both countries began development projects, and Israel completed the National Water Carrier project in the mid-1960s. In 1967 and by means of war Israel occupied the Golan Heights and the West Bank, which effectively gave them control of the Jordan headwaters and the Yarmouk River. Thus the situation went from mediated negotiations to unilateral action to violent conflict, without any consideration of an adjudicated settlement – this in spite of the success of the *Lake Lanoux* case during this time-period. Neff and Matson (ibid., p. 45) discuss 'secret negotiations' mediated again by the US between Jordan and Israel. Apparently a series of such meetings took place in the early 1970s as well.

The statistics that Neff and Matson present (ibid., pp. 45, 47–8) indicate the gross inequities present in the consumption of water by Israel and by the settlers on the West Bank. As the authors indicate, these inequities border on the infringement of human rights. According to one source, the Palestinian average in some areas of the West Bank has gone down since the beginning of the *Intifada* to less than 44 litres per caput per day – 'less than the United Nations reckons is necessary for maintaining minimal health standards' (Lowi 1992: 43). Like the *Lake Lanoux* case, this issue can be presented in terms of violated rights, specifically of human rights. For this reason, the Jordan River dispute would seem to be an appropriate case for adjudication.

A final case (see Begum 1988) refers to the long-standing Ganges River dispute between East Bengal/Bangladesh and India, and gives a clear example of the politics of international negotiation, and the advantages of bilateral negotiation for the stronger party...

Each nation has its own preferred solution to the problem. Bangladesh's solution would involve Nepal's participation, while India would like to keep the issues of water strictly between itself and a weaker Bangladesh. As described by Khurshida Begum (ibid., pp. 204–14), 'peaceful' negotiations, strictly bilateral, are a hegemonic tool for India. Over the course of the negotiations a series of 'discrepancies' between the facts reported by India and Bangladesh reveals exactly the purpose for which court trials are used – disagreements of fact. As Laylin and Bianchi have noted (1959) these could be resolved through a third party, or experts independent of the disputants. Also, the serious effects of water shortage claimed by Bangladesh would seem to put this case on the level of human rights violation rather than merely a political tug-of-war in the process of hammering out these agreements. Once again, we are reminded of Laylin and Bianchi's arguments for 'The Role of Adjudication in International River Disputes' (1959) as a means of balancing power discrepancies, while recognizing that adjudication cannot be simply equated with a better outcome for weaker parties.

Concluding Comments

In 1991 the *American Journal of International Law* published an editorial titled 'The Peace Palace Heats Up: The World Court in Business Again?'. The author, Keith Highet, announces that the Hague is busier than ever. Its docket is jammed. Nobody forecast such activity. The voices against the Court have been strident, particularly amongst those supporting the policies of the United States in Central America in the 1980s. The author lists nine new cases brought before the full court in the previous two years, only about half of which are clearly between unequal powers. Furthermore, even 'unpopular' states like Libya and Iran are resorting to World Court adjudication, since this is probably one of the few ways of settling an international dispute without the risks of power play.

In the same editorial the author notes that the United Nations Law of the Sea has a provision for the formation of a specialized tribunal – the so-called Hamburg Court. Such a duplicative tribunal, the author continues, might not be necessary in the light of the fact that the World Court will be undertaking a large number of these cases soon and setting precedents for future Law of the Sea cases. However, the Hamburg Court has strong proponents – the five permanent members of the Security Council – who support this 'alternative solution to existing litigation before the full tribunal' of the World Court (ibid., pp. 653–4). These powerful states are, according to Highet, 'as ever uncomfortable with the [World] Court's activities' (ibid.).

The editorial concludes with the idea that perhaps the developed nations are in support of The Hamburg Court because they would have a stronger hand in it. He believes that the real work of the World Court over the next decade 'will be the reconciliation of the interests of developing countries with those of the developed countries ... however, in the nine recent cases, the litigants have represented a wide range of middle-level powers, not the greater powers' (ibid.). Thus the piece is hardly reassuring on the role of the World Court as power-equalizer.

In a recent journalistic piece W. T. Anderson (1993) speaks about 'Governing the World without Governments', noting that there is a 'demand for a new system of governance', as national governments, inter-governmental organizations and the United Nations fail. 'Global governance' he calls it. The strong interest in alternative systems suffers from a lack of introspection about the alternative experiments to date, experiments biased towards the powerful. Words like 'global civilization' sound grand; but, as I have indicated in this paper, the 'civilized' – the network of global intellectuals, businessmen, and activists that Anderson speaks about – have a way of diminishing institutions that may function as power-equalizers.

What is so powerful about professional cultures is their built-in protection against participating professionals examining the underlying assumptions of their trade. In the literature on 'modern negotiation' there is little to indicate that 'modern negotiators' are critically examining their trajectories or assessing the broader significance of their work. They write more like 'true believers', avoiding controversy even at the cost of self-reflection, which would necessarily involve understanding the historical and socio-cultural context in which a newly re-civilized negotiation serves as hegemonic power. P. Gulliver could afford to focus on the process of negotiation to the exclusion of broad cultural contexts and social situations as long as the subject-matter was intra-societal and micro in scope. However, in the arena of international power-brokers the purpose of negotiation may not be problem-solving, but control.

REFERENCES

Anderson, W. T. (1993). 'Governing the World without Governments', *Pacific News Service*, June 21–5

Begum, K. (1988). *Tension over the Farraka Barrage: A Techno-political Tangle in South Asia*. Stuttgart – Wiesbaden: Steiner Verlag

Burger, W. (1984). 'Annual Message on the Administration of Justice', Warren E. Burger, Chief Justice of the United States at the Mid-year Meeting, American Bar Association, February 12, 1984

Dellapenna, J. (1992). 'Surface Water in the Iberian Peninsula: An Opportunity for Co-operation or a Source for Conflict?', *Tennessee Law Review* 59(4), 803–25

Franck, T. (1986). *Judging the World Court*. New York: Priority Press Publications

Fuller, L. (1978). 'The Forms and Limits of Adjudication', *Harvard Law Review* 92(2), 353–409

Grillo, T. (1991). 'The Mediation Alternative: Process Dangers for Women' *Yale Law Review* 100, 1545–610

Gulliver, P. H. (1979). *Disputes and Negotiations: A Cross-Cultural Perspective*. New York: Academic Press

Hobhouse, L. T., Wheeler G. C., and Ginsberg M. (1930). *The Material Culture and Social Institutions of the Simpler Peoples*. London: Chapman and Hall

Hoebel, E. A. (1954). *The Law of Primitive Man*, Cambridge, Massachusetts: Harvard University Press

Laylin, J. G. and Bianchi, R. L. (1959). 'The Role of Adjudication in International River Disputes: The Lake Lanoux Case', *American Journal of International Law* 53(1), 30–49

Linnerooth, J. (1990). 'The Danube River Basin: Negotiating Settlements to Transboundary Environmental Issues', *Natural Resources Journal* 30(3), 629–60

Lowi, M.R. (1992). 'West Bank Water Resources and the Resolution of Conflict in the Middle East', Occasional Paper Series of the University of Toronto Project on Environmental Change and Acute Conflict, Number 1, 29–60

Nader, L. (1979). 'Disputing without the Force of Law', *Yale Law Journal* 88, No. 5 (Special Issue on Dispute Resolution), 998–1021

Nader, L. (1989). 'The ADR Explosion: The Implications of Rhetoric in Legal Reform', *Windsor Yearbook of Access to Justice* 269–91

Nader, L. (1990). *Harmony Ideology: Justice and Control in a Mountain Zapotec Village*. Stanford, California: Stanford University Press

Neff, T. and Matson, R. C. (1984). *Water in the Middle East: Conflict or Cooperation?* Boulder, Colorado: Westview Press

Yoder, A. (1989). *The Evolution of the United Nations System*. New York: Crane Russak

Zartman, I. W. and Berman, M. R. (1982). *The Practical Negotiator*. New Haven, Connecticut and London: Yale University Press

E.   Law and the Future

General Introduction

The design of legal interventions that reshape society, or parts of it, are a major practical problem in our world today. The evolving development of such measures raises questions that need to be answered about law and context, about efficacy and failure and about comparative situations. From this perspective, legislation, the work of administrative agencies, and many court cases can be seen to be oriented toward forming the future. So, indeed, are many of the rule-making and organizing directives of non-governmental corporate organizations.

The theoretical problems at issue not only include the work of governments but extend to other organized attempts to create durable forms of regularized social order. Some anthropologists writing about legal matters have begun to turn their attention to this processual aspect of law and society studies. It is an important theoretical development.

Laws, inserted into ongoing social contexts undergo transformations. Both law and the socio-cultural context into which they have been inserted are moving entities. It is no small task to use fieldwork methods to trace their ongoing double histories, even for a short period. While some studies have begun to address this topic, law and anthropology scholars have not focussed as much attention on this in-tandem process as they might.

One of the constraints on anthropological investigations has been the time-limited nature of the work. A year or two of intensive fieldwork seldom does justice to the full length of a historical process, absorbed as it is in reporting what has been witnessed at the particular period of investigation. But if ethnography is treated as a slice of current history, the perspective on the fieldwork period is changed. In addition to producing detailed, time-bound, locally preoccupied studies, the fieldwork analysis attempts to place the immediately visible present in a larger scale and longer term framework.

Looking at the recent literature, one can see that a number of anthropological studies have already attempted this, using law as their point of departure. One example is Darian-Smith's account of the construction of the Chunnel that links England to Europe, and the evolution of its far-reaching repercussions (1999). Another is Borneman's study of constrasting legislative attempts to reform the family in East and West Germany before the fall of the Wall (1992). Lazarus-Black's legal history of the Caribbean islands of Antigua and Barbuda traces in detail the continuous reworking of the uses of laws and courts which came to be used to new purposes by different sectors of the population (1994:260). A collection on land laws and land use in colonial and post-colonial societies compares changes in property practices in those situations (de Moor and Rothermund 1994). A contrasting circumstance, the de-collectivization of property in post-socialist countries, is explored by Verdery (1998) and by Stark (1992). The cultural context of human rights is taken up in a variety of case studies (Wilson 1997; Cowan, Dembour and Wilson 2001; An-n Na'im 2002). Legal measures intersecting with international development add another dimension (Cooper and Packard 1997). Something analogous to the process of imbedding social changes in law is often found in studies of directed development where laws and law-like rules are made and implementing organizations are constructed (Ferguson 1990). Burawoy has collected work that uses ethnographic techniques to address the global scale (Burawoy 2000).

Of course, since law and society is a multi-disciplinary concern, by no means are all the studies along these lines are by anthropologists. There are numerous studies by lawyers that track just such changes, and the changing climate of judicial and public opinion in which they are found. For example see Griffiths on the gradual, case by case, development of legalized euthanasia in the Netherlands (1998), Galanter on on the emergence of law in modern India (1989). Likosky on a variety of current transnational legal processes (2002).

The legal measures introduced by governments are often more similar to each other than the social contexts in which they are placed, and more similar that the local outcomes. For example, in the constitutions of the non-Western world there are myriad legislative pieties about democracy and equality that indicate intentions, but implementation is another matter. In Africa, for example, the local context of constitutions is highly variable (Zoet hout, Pietermaat-Kros and Akkermans 1996).

One of the boldest attempts to define a large comparative question is the work of a historian, D.A. Low (1996). He has written about the widespread attempts from 1950 to 1980, to abolish large landed estates in Asia and Africa. He says that all these plans ended in failure. He summarizes the situation in more than a dozen countries to show that existing rural regimes outlasted the reforming attempts, despite the very different ideologies and states that legislated the changes.

It goes without saying that the slice of time described in a fieldwork study occurs in the course of a longer historical trajectory. But how much can fieldwork illuminate that trajectory? What I am arguing here is demonstrated by some of the ongoing work that has been cited. Even though the fieldwork period is limited, the orientation of field work can be consciously directed to understanding the way people involved conceived of the future and used legal measures to try to shape it. The complex entanglements of the legal in the socio-cultural context that follow are bound to emerge as a sequence is tracked.

The different approaches in law and anthropology in the 1950–99 period are described in the text of the Huxley Lecture which follows here. That period saw major shifts in subject matter, and concomitant changes in method and theoretical preoccupation. Today one sees that the increasing presence of globalization and the domination of transnational economies have worked further changes in the questions addressed, that localized systems appear in a new light, and that active attempts to design new norms and institutions loom large. Clearly another major shift in the field of law and anthropology is under way. The processual study of legally instituted transformations will be a significant part of it.

S.F.M.

REFERENCES

A An-Na'im, Abdullah, 2002 Cultural Transformations and *Human Rights in Africa*. London and New York: Zed Books.

Borneman, John, 1992 *Belonging in the Two Berlins*. Cambridge: Cambridge University Press.

Burawoy, Michael, 2000 *Global Ethnography*. Berkeley and London: University of California Press.

Cooper, Frederick and Randall Packard, eds., 1997 *International Development and the Social Sciences* Berkeley and London: University of California Press.

Cowan, Jane K., Marie-Benedicte Dembour, and Richard A. Wilson, eds. 2001 *Culture and Rights*. Cambridge: Cambridge University Press.

Darian-Smith, Eve, 1999 *Bridging Divides*. Berkeley and London: University of California Press.

De Moor, Jap and Dietmar Rothermund, eds., 1994 *Our Laws, Their Lands*. Munster, Hamburg: Lit Verlag.

Ferguson, James, 1990 *The Anti-Politics Machine: "Development," Depoliticization and Bureaucratic Power in Lesotho*. Cambridge: Cambridge University Press.

Galanter, Marc, 1989 *Law and Society in Modern India*. Delhi, Bombay, Calcutta, and Madras: Oxford University Press.

Lazarus-Black, Mindie, 1994 *Legimate Acts and Illegal Encounters*. Washington and London: Smithsonian Institution Press.

Wilson, Richard, 1997 *Human Rights, Culture and Context*. London, Chicago, and Illinois: Pluto Press.

Low, D. A., 1996 *The Egalitarian Moment*. Cambridge: Cambridge University Press.

Stark, D., 1992 'Recombinant Property in East European Capitalism.' *American Journal of Sociology* 101 (4): 993–1027.

Verdery, Katherine, 1998 Property and Power in Transylvania's Decollectivization. In *Property Relations*. C. M. Hahh, ed. pp. 160–180. Cambridge: Cambridge University Press.

Zoethout, Carla M., Marlies E. Pietermaat-Kros, and Piet W. C. Akkermans, eds., 1996 *Constitutionalism in Africa*. Rotterdam: Sanders Institut, Erasmus University.

28

Certainties Undone: Fifty Turbulent Years of Legal Anthropology, 1949–1999

Sally Falk Moore

What legal domains have anthropologists examined in the fifty years we are considering? How much have their topics changed? How much do the changes in topic reflect the shifting political background of the period? The big picture is simple enough. What was once a sub-field of anthropology largely concerned with law in non-Western society has evolved to encompass a much larger legal geography. Not only does legal anthropology now study industrial countries, but it has expanded from the local to national and transnational legal matters. Its scope includes international treaties, the legal underpinnings of transnational commerce, the field of human rights, diasporas and migrants, refugees and prisoners, and other situations not easily captured in the earlier community-grounded conception of anthropology, though the rich tradition of local studies continues along a separate and parallel track.

This expansion and change has involved a shift in methodology and theoretical emphasis. For a long while, dispute-processing was the centre of the field, with insight into local norms and practices as an essential adjunct. Now, though looking at disputes remains a favoured way of entering a contested arena, the ultimate objects of study are immense fields of action not amenable to direct observation. The nature of the state today, and the transnational and supra-local economic and political fields that intersect with states, are the intellectually captivating entities now. Here, we will be looking at the issues legal anthropology addressed fifty years ago and will trace its gradual progress towards these new questions. Of necessity this will be a selective account, one which, where it can, takes note of the resonance of background political events.

From Sally Falk Moore, "Certainties undone: Fifty Turbulent years of Legal Anthropology, 1949–1999," Huxley Memorial Lecture, *Journal of the Royal Anthropological Institute* 7(1) (2001), pp. 95–116.

Changes in the empirical focus of legal anthropology have been accompanied by disagreement about how to approach and answer the question of how and why the legal acquires a particular form in a particular social setting. To simplify, one could say that three general interpretations have prevailed.

Law as Culture

The first suggests that law is tradition-driven, particularly outside the West but sometimes within it. Culture is all. However, culture is simply a label denoting durable customs, ideas, values, habits, and practices. Those who treat law as culture mean that law is a particular part of that package, and that the combined totality has internal systemic connections.

The stress on the constraining power of 'the traditional' can be found in colonial conceptions of the 'customary law' of subject peoples, and is deeply embedded in Durkheim's (1961) vision of what I might call 'the elementary forms of social unanimity'. It is also found in Weber's (1978: 226–40) conception of 'traditional authority'. This view is reiterated in some of Habermas's (1979: 78–84, 157) evolutionary writings about law and society. A powerful version of the cultural argument is found in Geertz's (1983: 232–3) commentary on law. Tradition also looms large in Rouland's (1988) textbook overview.

Cultural context once supplied some anthropologists with an apparently innocent descriptive explanation of variations in values and styles of life (see Hoebel 1954). But culture has lost its political innocence. Today, when cultural difference is offered as a legitimation for and explanation of legal difference, cultural context often comes up as an aspect of a consciously mobilized collective identity in the midst of a political struggle, and it arises in relation to constitutions, collective inequalities, insiders and outsiders, and other aspects of national and ethnic politics.

Law as Domination

The second common explanation of legal form is that everything in law can be understood to be a mask for elite interests, both in the West and elsewhere. Thus, law purports to be about furthering the general interest, but really serves the cause of the powerful, generally capitalists and capitalism. (The conservative counterpart, the law and economics argument about efficiency, has not entered the anthropological literature.)

The 'elite interests' argument is Marxisant in style. A version of it is found in Bourdieu (1987: 842), in the work of the Critical Legal Studies Movement (Fitzpatrick 1987; Fitzpatrick and Hunt 1992; Kelman 1987), and elsewhere. For example, consider Snyder's (1981a: 76) comment concerning Senegal: 'Produced in particular historical circumstances, the notion of "customary law" was an ideology of colonial domination'.

Law as Problem-Solver

The third explanation offered by some anthropologists (and many lawyers) is a technical, functional one. Law is a rational response to social problems. That is the explanation enshrined in many appellate opinions as well as in sociological writings. In this explanation, law is a problem-solving, conflict-minimizing device, consciously arrived at through rational thought in the West and elsewhere. Ann Marie Slaughter, Professor of International Law at Harvard Law School, was recently heard to express succinctly what is a commonplace in law schools, 'I see law as a problem-solving tool' (pers. comm.).

This rationalist framework is widely used in the legal profession, and appears as one of the keys to modernity in Weber's sociology. Conceptions of law as essentially problem-solving were also embedded in the essays of the well-known legal realist, Karl Llewellyn, who was interested in anthropology and wrote a book on the Cheyenne (Llewellyn and Hoebel 1941; for a brief critique, see Moore 1999). Importantly, however, Llewellyn did not make the Weberian assumption that Western society (and modernity in general) had a monopoly on sophisticated juridical thought. In fact, he attributed this mode of thinking to the Cheyenne.

These three scholarly explanations of law – as culture, as domination, as problem-solving – recur throughout the fifty years we will review, frequently mixed together. My review will emphasize fieldwork studies and the general political background of legal anthropology. Anglophone contributions will be given most attention, but they are by no means the whole story. Reasons of space limit what I can discuss. Not only must I omit the contribution of French, Dutch, and other writers, but much anglophone material also must be excluded.[1]

My approach is partly chronological, partly conceptual. Themes will be cited as they emerged historically, but subsequent traces of the same ideas will sometimes be tracked forwards as they reappear. That messes up the chronology, but illuminates continuities in the sub-discipline.

Gluckman and the rationales of judges: reasoning, reasonableness and rules

Gluckman was the dominant personality in law and anthropology studies at the half-century and beyond (for assessments, see Gulliver 1978; Werbner 1984), and he stood astride the divide between the colonial and the postcolonial in Africa. He did fieldwork in Africa in the colonial period, but went on publishing influential work on a variety of topics well into the first decades of independence.

In the classical manner of British social anthropology of the time, he was interested in discovering what had been the shape of pre-colonial society, the 'true' Africa. Yet no one was more aware than Gluckman that what actually surrounded him were African societies that had experienced decades of colonial rule, labour migration, Christian influence, alterations of economy and organization, and more. He tried to understand the two Africas at once, the historical past and the living present. Furthermore, he was the first anthropologist systematically to study a colonial African court in action, to listen carefully to the stories of complaint and the arguments as they unfolded.

Hitherto, law in Africa had generally been reported as a set of customary rule-statements elicited from chiefs and other authorities. These so-called customary rules were then supposed to be used as guidelines in the colonial courts (see e.g. Gluckman 1969). But customary law was, in fact, so altered a version of indigenous practice that it must be recognized as a composite colonial construction. That began to be acknowledged in Fallers's (1969) discussion of Soga law, and in Colson's (1971) writings on land rights, and was made unmistakably explicit by Snyder (1981a, 1981b), Chanock (1985 [1998]), and Moore (1986b).

In Gluckman's time, customary law was assumed to be largely an expression of indigenous tradition, and when Gluckman listened to disputes and heard decisions, he focused on rules and reasoning. He tried to figure out what rule the judges were applying, what standard of reasonable behaviour was being used. This was not always easy or straightforward since the several judges in the highest Lozi court often disagreed with each other.

Gluckman distinguished Lozi norms from the logical principles used by judges to decide which norm to apply, and how and when to apply it. His argument was that, while Lozi norms were special to their society, Lozi juridical reasoning relied on logical principles found in all systems of law. Some subsequent commentators saw this as a falsifying Westernization of Lozi law. However, critics did not see that this universalist interpretation embodied a political position (Gluckman 1955: 362). Gluckman wanted to show that indigenous African legal systems and practices were as rational in the Weberian sense as Western ones. Their premises were different because the social milieu was different, but the logic and the process of reasoning were the same. To demonstrate that Africans were in every way the intellectual equal of Europeans, he showed at tedious length (e.g. 1955: 279–80) what he saw as the comparabilities between African and Western juridical thought. Embedded in his gloss on Lozi ideas was a splendid message about racial equality.

Ten years later, in a series of lectures, Gluckman (1965) commented on Barotse constitutional conceptions, ideas of property, notions of wrongdoing and liability, and conceptions of contract, obligation, and debt. However, again he had a distinct preoccupation, comparison. He argued that certain Barotse concepts were characteristic of societies with a simple political economy: simple economy, low levels of technology, rudimentary political-social order. His comparative orientation merits more exploration but, until recently, work of this sort had all but disappeared, partly because of serious methodological problems.[2] However, before these problems were recognized, Nader pursued the possibility that comparing the techniques of dispute management of different societies could lead to fruitful insights (see Nader 1969; Nader with Todd 1978). In time, legal anthropologists finally decided that they could not resolve the issues of form, function, and context that these sorts of comparisons raised. However, such questions are again being asked.

What strikes one today is the extent to which Gluckman (esp. 1955; 1965) was preoccupied with a racially egalitarian interpretation of African logic, and an evolutionary interpretation of African political economy. These preoccupations display the reasoning of an anthropologist who was politically on the side of Africans, yet who interpreted their social systems and legal concepts as containing a substantial residue of an earlier, pre-capitalist economy. It seems not insignificant that, between the date of the first book and of the second, the colonial era had ended in most African countries. In his opinions, Gluckman had managed to identify simultaneously with Marx and Maine.

The main point about my hasty summary of a few of Gluckman's arguments about law is that he began a revolution in field method with his attention to cases in court. Ever since, local dispute-watching has been the principal form of social voyeurism in legal anthropology (for a recent illustration, see Caplan 1995). What has been said here may suggest why Gluckman not only was the founder of the Manchester department but was also the initiator of many durable controversies, which was very good for academic business.

Law as an expression of basic, and often unique, cultural premises

One of the major criticisms immediately levelled against Gluckman's universalist notions about legal logic was Bohannan's (1957) counter-contention that in law, as in everything else, every culture is unique, and that, for anthropology, its uniqueness is what is important about it. Bohannan contended that even translating the legal concepts of another society into English terms was a distortion. His is one of the more extreme versions of the non-political 'law as culture' argument. His contentions were the object of a heated debate with Gluckman at a conference in the 1960s (see Bohannan in Nader 1969: 401–18).

Many years later, a similar argument was offered by Geertz, in which he took 'his distance' from Gluckman (Geertz 1983: 169). Geertz contended that three major cultural traditions – the Islamic, the Indic, the Malaysian – each had different legal 'sensibilities'. He sought to demonstrate this by choosing two central concepts in each tradition and comparing them. He chose to translate all of these paired concepts as 'fact and law'. But of course, in each of the three traditions the scope of reference of these concepts was not identical. The result was a *tour de force* in part because Geertz used 'fact and law' as the translation for all three, and because he defined 'fact' as 'what is true' and 'law' as about 'what is right'. That is not what the distinction between fact and law means in Anglo-American law, but Geertz's recasting of these terms into philosophical and moral ones is not accidental. He was not taking up conventional questions of comparative law, he wanted to place these terms in a grand scheme of cultural thought. He argued (1983: 232), in a now much-repeated phrase, that law is 'a species of social imagination' and that comparisons should be drawn in those terms. He says (1983: 232) that 'law is about meaning not about machinery'. He saw comparative law as an opportunity to shed light on cultural difference, and he identified the analysis of cultural difference as the central purpose of anthropological work (1983: 233). So much for Gluckman's universals.

The emphasis Bohannan and Geertz put on the importance of cultural difference preceded today's full-blown politics of identity, but their approach certainly resonates with many current forms of multiculturalism, as well as with Taylor's (1992) ideas about the importance of a politics of recognition. Today, cultural difference is a sectoral political cause in many parts of the world. No wonder that culture as the source of legal form remains a live proposition (see Greenhouse and Kheshti 1998).

It serves those who have their own political reasons to emphasize collective boundaries, and to distinguish themselves from others.

Rosen has generated another version of the 'law as culture' thesis. A lawyer-anthropologist, he was at one time a student of Geertz, and has adopted much of the Geertzian package in his work. He has written on an Islamic village court in Morocco that deals largely with family law, the court he studied being restricted by statute to such matters. He is concerned to show that, despite its lack of precedents and records, the court does not make arbitrary decisions, that it does *not* dispense what Weber called 'kadi justice', even though the judge has a great deal of discretion (Rosen 1980–1). Rosen (1989:18) says: 'the regularity lies... in the fit between the decisions of the Muslim judge and the cultural concepts and social relations to which they are inextricably tied'.

Another instance of 'legal form as cultural product' is French's sketch of Tibetan law as it was in the period from 1940 to 1959, a project of historical reconstruction. She calls her work a 'study in the cosmology of law in Buddhist Tibet in the first half of the twentieth century as reconstructed', characterizing her effort as 'an exercise in historical perspective and imagination' (1995: 17). She concludes that in dealing with dispute cases, Tibetan jurists did not make decisions according to a prescribed set of rules, but made complex discretionary judgements. They approached each case as a unique combination of features, a perception which she attributes to Buddhist philosophy, to a way of thinking about 'radical particularity' (1995: 343).

The link between a system of case-by-case rulings and the Buddhist background seems less certain when one looks at comparative materials. After all, there are many societies and institutional settings in which hearing agencies that are not Buddhist make decisions case by case and emphasize situational uniqueness, such as the Islamic court described by Rosen. Decentralized institutional arrangements seem to be the crux of the matter. Are these the consequence of religio-philosophical conceptions, or social-structural history?

That brings us to questions derived from the Weberian construction of legal rationality in the modern West. To what extent are Western judges' decisions in fact governed by mandatory rules, and how much is left to judicial discretion? Posner has provided some marvellously candid American answers. Posner is the eminent founder of the law and economics movement, Professor of Law at the University of Chicago, and sometime commentator on legal anthropology, who now sits as a judge on the Court of Appeals of the Seventh Circuit in the US. Though not all judges would admit, as Posner (1998: 235) does (and Justice Holmes did), to using a 'puke' test of disgust as a way of deciding when to use discretion rather than to apply existing rules, his acknowledgement of his own reactions and the importance of judicial discretion is neither new nor revolutionary in American law.

However, with the exception of Rosen (1980–1) anthropologists of law have usually paid little attention to judicial discretion in both Western and non-Western systems. Of course, discretion can be difficult to detect if it is masked by an allusion to rules. Equally, acknowledging the importance of discretion undermines a purely culture-driven analysis. The problem-solving rationale of legal form is congruent with the use of discretion, but invites a question: in whose interest are decisions made? Where is the rule of law when judges can decide as they see fit? Here we have an example of the way all three of the modes of accounting for legal form mentioned at the outset of this article can become entwined in contradictory ways in the project of explaining juridical thought.

Ways of using law: litigant interests and strategies

Since the 1960s and 1970s, anthropologists became less and less likely to see behaviour as being overwhelmingly driven by pre-existing cultural patterns and social rules. Even in Bourdieu's Marxisant conception of social reproduction, the idea of the 'habitus' (1977: 78) had to take improvisation and invention into account.

The connection between the emerging anthropological interest in choice and change and the socio-political background of the 1960s and 1970s is difficult to prove but impossible to ignore. Challenges to authority were prominent features of public life, with substantial repercussions in universities. With the end of colonial rule in the 1960s, the ex-colonized peoples were, at least formally and legally, in charge of themselves. Retrospective complaints about the colonial period were actively voiced. In the US the Vietnam War elicited enormous popular resistance, with legal repercussions for the protesters. The civil rights movement was launched. Legislative and social changes were demanded and a lengthy struggle ensued. The women's movement started its task of consciousness-raising in a milieu in which a new technology of contraception altered sexual behaviour, moral consciousness, and many gender-oriented laws. There were analogous social hurricanes in Europe.

In view of all of this contemporary political activity, there was not much place for an anthropology of law focused on conformity. Agency came into its own. Cases were heard and read in terms of litigants' motives. Law was seen as a representation of social order, but it was understood to be usable in a great variety of ways by people acting in their own interest. The strong and powerful could, of course, further their interests more effectively than the weak.

Early examples of ethnographic work that intimated some of these changes in analytic attitude towards normative justice appeared in Gulliver's (1963; 1969) writings. In his fieldwork among the Arusha, in colonial Tanganyika, he observed that they often managed their legal disputes, not by going to existing (colonial) Native Courts, but through a system of 'informal', non-official, negotiated settlements. Lineage representatives of the contending parties assembled and bargained solutions on behalf of the principals. He concluded that the winners of these negotiated settlements were always the more politically powerful parties. The discourse involved in these negotiations referred to norms, but he contended that norms did not determine the outcome. He contrasted this negotiation process with judicial decisions, in which he assumed that the outcome was normatively determined. Thus he was still assuming not only that a normative system existed, but that it was systematically enforced in formal tribunals.

The analytic scenario changed even further in the direction of agency a few years later. Law began to be treated as a set of ideas, materials, and institutions that were being used as a resource by people pursuing their own interests. For example, Collier's ethnographic work among Maya-speaking Mexicans treated Zinacanteco legal categories and concepts 'as a set of acceptable rationalizations for justifying behavior' (Collier 1973: 13). Her central objective was to identify the Zinacantecos' way of conceiving the world and their handling of transactions and disputes in the light of these ideas. However, Collier also made it clear that the Zinacanteco world was far from completely autonomous, far from impervious to the interventions of Mexican state institutions. Collier showed that the Zinacanteco legal system was neither static nor insulated from the outside world.

The early Gulliver challenge to Gluckman about whether power or norms determined the outcome of disputes remained lively in England for a time. A conference of the Association of Social Anthropologists even carried this as its theme (Hamnett 1977). Definitively putting the lid on that ASA discussion, and supporting their argument with convincing empirical materials, Comaroff and Roberts (1981) produced a well-known and widely read book that made the point that, even in judicial tribunals, rules did not always rule. Using case material collected among the Tswana of southern Africa, they showed that many types of dispute-processing could exist in the same system. Rules and the social relations of litigants, as well as their interests, appeared within the same universe of litigation. The cases demonstrated that Tswana often took the opportunity to use arenas of litigation to renegotiate personal standing, to obtain recognition of social relations that were being contested (1981: 115). This kind of confrontation occurred as if it were an argument about norms: the language in which the arguments were presented was 'culturally inscribed and normatively encoded' (1981: 201). They speak of 'dualism in the Tswana conception of their world, according to which social life is described as rule-governed yet highly negotiable, normatively regulated yet pragmatically individualistic' (1981: 215). 'Disputes range between what are ostensibly norm-governed "legal" cases and others that appear to be interest-motivated "political" confrontations . . . The point, however, is not simply that these different modes co-exist in one context . . . but that they are systematically related . . . transformations of a single logic' (1981: 244).

Is this accommodation of contradictory ideas special to the Tswana, or more general? I would argue that this situation is commonplace. In keeping with this view, on a number of occasions in the 1970s I argued that the sociology of causality was ill served by a conformity-deviance model of the place of rules of law in societies, as if there were a single set of rules, clearly defined, totally discrete, and without contradictions or ambiguities (Moore 1970, 1973, 1975a, 1975b, 1978). 'The social reality is a peculiar mix of action congruent with rules (and there may be numerous conflicting or competing rule-orders) and other action that is choice-making, discretionary, manipulative' (1978: 3). What also matters is that the choices and manipulations are not only made by the litigants in dispute situations, they are also made by the authorities who decide what the outcome shall be, and who make reference to norms and normative ideologies in other contexts.

Allusions to rules or ideologies with normative implications often characterize the behaviour of authorities in and out of dispute contexts. The place of moralizing statements by authorities and leaders is an issue as important to the analysis of the relationship between legal rules and behaviour as is the understanding of litigant manipulations. The organization of authority and its relation to the representation of normative ideas is a major piece of the framing, presentation, and implementation (or non-implementation) of law. By focusing on dispute, anthropologists have gained some access to the status of that putatively normative body of ideas, but what the authorities and others actually do with them is something else again.

Questioning authority: issues of class and domination in the interpretation of law

Given their lack of doctrinal and technical legal expertise, it is often assumed that anthropologists studying industrial societies are best off observing 'informal' legal processes analogous to those found in small-scale village communities: negotiation and mediation, informal institutions such as small claims courts, internally generated neighbourhood arrangements, family law, and the like. A number of anthropologists have done successful fieldwork and case analysis in just such settings. They contribute to our understanding of social and cultural issues other than those which would turn up in more formal settings: popular attitudes towards litigation and towards legal institutions, conceptions of law as part of the culture of community, the actual practices of officials in interaction with lay people, and the like (Abel 1982; Conley and O'Barr 1990; Greenhouse 1986; Greenhouse, Yngvesson and Engel 1994; Merry 1990; Yngvesson 1993; Yngvesson and Hennessey 1974).

However, in the 1970s a curious test of the anthropological taste for informal institutions appeared when informality was officially embraced by the American judicial system. When the courts added Alternative Dispute Resolution (ADR) to options open to litigants, anthropologists were not pleased. ADR was publicized as a response to the needs of the poor and of those who had minor claims that would otherwise have gone unheeded.[3] However, the judiciary embraced the programme because their court calendars were overloaded. Less felicitously, some judges remarked that they wanted to get 'garbage cases' out of their courts (Nader 1992: 468).

Nader, being passionately public-interest minded (see Nader 1999), argued that, in fact, the courts themselves should be made more accessible to the poor. She (1980: 101) asserted that the legitimacy of a legal system in a democracy depends on providing access to the courts for all. This resonated with her earlier work on dispute settlement in two rural Zapotec villages in Mexico, work which began in the 1950s (see Nader 1990). When Nader first started this project there were no lawyers in these villages, and the position of judge rotated among the senior men, each one serving a fixed term. The judges evidently saw themselves as mediators, trying to work out compromise solutions between persons in conflict. Nader described her experience in Mexico when she lectured at American law schools, and she reproached her audiences for not trying to provide less expensive, more accessible compromise solutions to the everyday problems that were commonplace in the United States. From the start, she used her ethnographic work to comment on what she saw as the shortcomings of American society.

But when many jurisdictions actually established ADR, Nader's reaction was negative. She contended that the question was what was just and what was unjust under the rule of law, not whether people could be forced to compromise in mediatory settings as if it were some kind of therapy. Nader (1993: 4) asked what this coercive 'harmony ideology' signified in relation to the inequalities in American life. Here we have one of the three recurrent themes about legal form mentioned earlier, the representation of the law as serving elite interests when it should be solving problems for rich and poor alike. Nader (1992: 468) is clear about what she sees as the connection with the politics of the period. 'Trading justice for harmony is one of the unrecognized fall-outs of the 1960s... In an effort to quell the rights movements (civil rights, women's rights, consumer rights, environmental rights) and to cool out the Vietnam protestors, harmony became a virtue extolled over complaining or disputing or conflict'.

Other critics of the ADR movement also argued that such mediatory measures reduced social conflict that might reform society (e.g. Abel 1982). That seems to me a big and not altogether warranted interpretative leap, but for some it seemed a certainty. Thus, Merry (1990: 9) also speaks of mediation as 'a process of cultural domination exercised by the law over people who bring their personal problems to the lower courts'. But in her fieldwork, the many individual troubles brought to mediation seem to be only tangentially connected with social class, and indeed seem to be the sort of personal grievances between individuals who know each other well which might appear in any class, disputes between neighbours, husbands and wives, parents and children.

What is plainly attributable to social class is the fact that Merry's people find themselves in a public mediation process, rather than using private lawyers to negotiate for them. In mediatory settings they subject themselves to a considerable dose of patronizing advice, often psychological. But the question that remains is whether what transpires has much to do with a 'harmony ideology' that keeps major social confrontations in check.

Nader also applies her 'harmony ideology' thesis to her history of disputing in a Mexican-Zapotec mountain village. Her current vision of the village's history is that the people presented themselves as resolving all disputes harmoniously as part of a political strategy to keep colonial authorities from meddling in village affairs (1990: 310). She says that harmony ideology was the price of village 'autonomy and self-determination' (1990: 321).

The work of Nader, Merry, and Abel illustrates how some people drew an analogy between the situation of colonial people and the poor in industrial countries. Obliquely drawn into the same model in other works is the predicament of women in asymmetrically gendered situations, often in ex-colonial settings. What motivates these writers is the idea that law should mean equal rights and treatment for everyone. Obviously, it often does not, either because of lack of access, judicial bias, or other obstacles (Griffiths 1997; Hirsch 1998).

Thus, for some anthropologists the theme of domination and resistance emerges as the principal aspect of their interpretation of law, and their writing implies that latent, unrealized major social protests and revolts are just waiting to happen. But that is probably a great exaggeration, and has little to do with domestic disputes, fights between neighbours, landlord-tenant arguments, and consumer complaints. There may well be a lot of resentment embedded in these disputes, but does it represent potential mobilization for social reform? It seems plain that an unnuanced domination-resistance model is too simple a framework to capture the diversity of sites of control and the sources of social movements. Hirsch (1994, 1998) and Griffiths (1997), concerned with gender, illustrate the complexities revealed by detailed studies, and show the considerable difference between using the idea of resistance on the one hand and, on the other, imputing resistance in more generalized critiques of domination.

The complexities involved in analysing how law, economy, and sociopolitical change are interconnected are particularly evident in longitudinal, historical studies. A few anthropological works have combined detailed legal-historical material with ethnographic fieldwork. In the 1980s, Snyder (1981b) wrote a Marxist account of capitalism and legal change among the Diola of Senegal, and Gordon and Meggitt (1985) traced changes in government authority in New Guinea from colonial times. In the first wave of ethnographic-historical studies of law, I wrote an ethnography-cum-history of the people of Kilimanjaro from 1880 to 1980 (Moore 1986b). This interweaves the story of the lives and legal disputes of living individuals (and that of their lineage ancestors) who gave accounts of their own experiences with the documented record of economic, demographic, and institutional change on the large scale.

A few years after Nader published her historical Zapotec study, Lazarus-Black (1994) followed the uses of the courts in Antigua and Barbuda that bore on slavery. She shows how the law was used to restrict slaves and protect slave-owners, but also how slaves were, at times, able to use the courts for their own advantage. Most recently, the Comaroffs have included some remarks about law in their history of missionary and colonial activities in southern and central Africa. Their general approach to history is encapsulated in the idea that 'the European colonization of Africa was often less a directly coercive conquest than a persuasive attempt to colonize consciousness, to remake people by redefining the taken-for-granted surfaces of their everyday worlds' (Comaroff and Comaroff 1991: 313). Some ideas basic to English law are inconsistent with the indigenous life world and become instruments in the colonization of consciousness. They remark on the way ideas of private property and possessive individualism, lawful wedlock, and other legal conceptions, fit into the project of revising the way Africans thought about the world they lived in (Comaroff and Comaroff 1997: 366–404; see also Comaroff 1995).

The historical particulars of each of the colonial experiences studied in the works mentioned above differed greatly. Each area was involved in (or made peripheral by) the world economy in a distinctive way, colonized in a different way. Each had a distinctive social and cultural formation, which shifted over time, both before and after colonization. That the common European background of the colonizers gave the colonized a stock of similar legal ideas is no surprise. What is striking is the remarkable variation in the way these ideas were received and used by the dominated populations (for a reconsideration of some legal-historical issues, see Moore 1989a; Roberts and Mann 1991; Starr and Collier 1989).

Legal pluralism: disassembling the moving parts of the state

The concept of the state as a unified entity has been more than slightly revised in the past half-century. Cultural pluralism and political divisions have long been recognized as basic and durable features of many polities (Furnivall 1948; Smith 1965); governments dealing with culturally distinct collectivities have often acknowledged such differences in legal terms (Hooker 1975). In the 1960s, the early period of independence, the legacy of colonial pluralism loomed large in intellectual debate (e.g. Kuper and Smith 1969; Moore 1989b).[4] There was much contention about whether the newly independent states of Africa would succeed in becoming unified nations, given that they were internally divided and had a history of being ruled by colonial governments that often reinforced the boundaries between ethnic groups.

That ethnic and racial pluralism posed profound political, constitutional, and other legal issues was evident not only in Africa but elsewhere (Kuper and Smith 1969: 438–40). These issues spelled trouble ahead, and Maybury-Lewis (1984) addressed this by asking what might be the political consequences of official policies based on ethnicity.[5] Recent events in the Balkans provide a gloomy answer. In this kind of political literature the term 'pluralism' is repeatedly used to refer to societies which incorporate a diversity of institutionally distinct collectivities. It is, for example, used in that sense by Tambiah (1996) in his book on ethnic violence in Asia.

But in legal anthropology these days, 'pluralism,' or more precisely 'legal pluralism', is often used in an entirely different sense. One relatively new use dates from an article by Griffiths (1986: 3), who attacks 'legal centralism', the idea that law is 'an exclusive, systematic and unified hierarchical ordering of normative propositions' emanating from the state. One is hard put to imagine what social scientist supports such a contention today, but it makes a nice springboard for his further argument. Griffiths asserts that the legal reality anywhere is a collage of obligatory practices and norms emanating both from governmental and non-governmental sources alike. He says 'that...all social control is more or less legal (1986: 39). The whole normative package, of whatever provenance, is what he calls 'legal pluralism'.

Shortly after Griffiths's article was published, a symposium was held on 'Legal pluralism in industrialized societies', in 1988, and Griffiths's paper was reviewed and publicized by Merry (1988: 879) in a much-cited article summarizing the literature (see Greenhouse and Strijbosch 1993; Teubner 1992). Following Griffiths, some writers now take legal pluralism to refer to the whole aggregate of governmental and non-governmental norms of social control, without any distinctions drawn as to their source.

However, for many purposes this agglomeration has to be disaggregated. For reasons of both analysis and policy, distinctions must be made that identify the provenance of rules and controls (Moore 1973, 1978, 1998, 1999, 2000). To deny that the state can and should be distinguished from other rule-making entities for many practical purposes is to turn away from the obvious. And if one wants to initiate or track change, it is not only analytically useful but a practical necessity to emphasize the particular sites from which norms and mandatory rules emanate. To make such distinctions is not necessarily to adopt a 'legal centralist' view.[6]

It is clear that much of the debate that surrounds legal pluralism is not just an argument about words, but is often a debate about the state of the state today, one that asks where power actually resides. The discourse on this topic gets mixed with arguments about current transformations of the state through the empowerment of sub-national collective entities, through transnational phenomena, and 'globalism'. Today, 'pluralism' can refer to: (1) the way the state acknowledges diverse social fields within society and represents itself ideologically and organizationally in relation to them; (2) the internal diversity of state administration, the multiple directions in which its official subparts struggle and compete for legal authority; (3) the ways in which the state itself competes with other states in larger arenas (the EU, for one instance), and with the world beyond that; (4) the way in which the state is interdigitated (internally and externally) with non-governmental, semi-autonomous social fields which generate their own (non-legal) obligatory norms to which they can induce or coerce compliance (see note 6); (5) the ways in which law may depend on the collaboration of non-state social fields for its implementation; and so on.

Wilson (2000) has made a persuasive ethnographic case for the appropriateness of such an intricate view of legal pluralism in his discussion of human rights in South Africa. He shows the simultaneity of diverse ideas of justice, as well as the procedures and performances through which these contradictory ideas, emanating from different sources, are given practical form, from reconciliation to public beatings. His is a subtle, complex, historically and ethnographically grounded, picture of the struggles implied when one talks about legal pluralism.

Asking about obstacles to democracy: three very recent works

Anthropologists presently are using their interest in the legal to engage with political questions, addressing them more directly than ever. And no wonder: the 1980s and 1990s have seen as much political upheaval as the previous twenty years. We live now in a post-socialist, post-Cold War, post-apartheid period in which many governments have been overturned and replaced. Questions are raised about the new regimes and whether they are or will be 'democracies', and about what 'democracy' means. Building new regimes and reforming old ones occur in many parts of the world. The legal dimensions of these processes are beginning to attract new kinds of anthropological attention. However, the construction of national governments is not a process that can be divorced from transnational matters. Global concerns inevitably enter the discussion.

The academic debate that surrounds these issues is uneasy, but it has begun to consider large-scale context in novel ways. This can be illustrated by three strikingly different anthropological approaches to the legal domain, all published in the past two years and all concerned with civil rights. I shall describe the books very briefly to give a sense of the way the field of legal anthropology is now giving voice to new forms of direct political commentary. Theoretically, all three have to do with the idea of democracy and what to make of it. All three analyse legal events framed in the context of mass communication in a world conceived globally.

I begin with Coombe (1998), concerned with trademark law. Coombe is both a lawyer and an anthropologist, and in her hands 'trademarks, protected indicia of celebrity personas, and marks of governmental authority' (1998: 286) become the occasion for a remarkably interesting and often funny set of essays on emblems in the mass media and the cultural life of intellectual properties. The insignia of Coca Cola, the image of Marilyn Monroe, and certain badges of governmental office are recognizable to everyone, but they cannot be used freely by all.

Coombe argues that our environment is filled with these manufactured symbols. The production of demand through the advertising of commodities and the publicizing of celebrities fills our environment and stuffs our consciousness. She says that 'such images so pervasively permeate all dimensions of our daily lives that they are constitutive of the "cultures" in which most people in Western societies now live' (1998: 52). She is right. They furnish our native thought and our natural world. And this inventory of images and names is being extended through mass communication to the rest of the world. Batman lives in New York, Hong Kong, and Dakar.

Coombe's heart is obviously with those who use these symbols illegally to satirize them (1998: 271). She contends that, because the symbols are ubiquitous, the 'practices of appropriation or "recoding" cultural forms are the essence of popular culture' (1998: 57, see also 285). In effect, she is asking us to pay more attention to our commercially constructed symbolic environment and to who owns it and controls its content and deployment. Expressive activity, she argues (1998: 186, 194), should generally be unfettered, to permit the construction of a dialogic democracy. I question whether restrictions on the freedom to copy MacDonald's Golden Arches trademark directly interferes with democratic dialogue, but that does not detract from Coombe's many other insights into our trademark-infested symbolic environment and its commercial control. Plainly, communication is not altogether free, when our symbolic vocabulary is supplied under these conditions.

The second book is a collection of essays edited by Wilson, which presents a number of studies of human rights situations, some of extreme persecution. But the orientation of the book is not only on what happened, but also on discourse, on the way these situations have been reported and discussed. Wilson (1997: 13) describes the collection of essays as 'an exploration of how rights-based normative discourses are produced, translated and materialised in a variety of contexts'. Each chapter confronts 'the tension between global and local formulations of human rights' (1997: 23). What interests the contributors is the way that struggles in a local field of action are 'structured by transnational discourses and practices' (1997: 24). These are, of course, very diverse, as are the situations described.

Fieldwork concerned with human rights is by definition carried out in an arena of conflicting reports and representations, often at terrible moments of crisis. What can anthropology add to what other disciplines have to say about such matters? Wilson's collection candidly addresses what anthropologists can and cannot do, and that is one of its distinctions. Contributors willingly acknowledge the limits of anthropological competence. The problematic that contributors address has obviously broadened beyond the accumulated knowledge of one profession, beyond one locale, and often beyond one moment in time. Now anthropologists are tangling with international law, with transnational political relations, with the aftermath of national political persecution, and with the way events in these arenas are being reported.

The third book, by Borneman (1997), embodies just such material. He describes the public demands for justice that were heard after the fall of the Berlin Wall and the beginning of German unification. East Germans who had been denounced or suffered in other ways under the socialist government were demanding that wrongs be set right, that some means be found to restore their lost dignity, names, or reputations. There also were demands that members of the East German elite be prosecuted and that property be returned or redistributed. Various institutional forms were invented to satisfy these demands, and Borneman did fieldwork in some of them.

Borneman describes the prosecution of an important lawyer who was an intermediary between East and West Germany in the days of the Wall, a case that raises the issue of the retrospective criminalization of acts which were legitimate when carried out. He also tells us about the hearings set up within the radio and television industry to deal with social injuries experienced there. Borneman (1997: 99) argues that all of these proceedings were (and are, for they are not over) efforts to establish the state as a moral agent. The new state tried to dissociate itself from the crimes of the past. For the state, recognizing injustices was both a practical act of redress and a symbolic act of ritual purification. Within this framework, Borneman affirms the importance of official recognition of suffering. He argues that such recognition points to a reassessment of the nature of the citizen. Suffering is reincorporated 'into the identity of the national subject' (1997: 134).

He ends with summaries of data from other East and Central European countries in the first four years after regime changes. At its broadest his argument throughout the book is that failure to engage in retributive justice leads to cycles of retributive violence and, most importantly, that there can be no democracy without political and personal accountability realized through law (1997: 3, 145, 165).

All three of these books depart from an earlier, narrower anthropology. All deal with contested political principles, with law in action, and with transnational questions. All take explicit positions on the issues they address. All are concerned, not with charming native customs, but with tragic possibilities glimpsed in the fieldwork scene.

Conclusion

It is obvious that legal anthropology has been saturated with political messages in the past fifty years. At mid-century, the anthropological project was to elaborate on the rationality of the 'indigenous' legal practices of non-Western peoples, most of them under colonial domination. Law was addressed as a technique for managing disputes, as a local problem-solving method, its style the product of culture and history. For obvious reasons, at the time there was little direct critique of colonial rule.

In the post-colonial world, the practices of colonial governments were attacked as never before. Attention also turned to Western legal institutions and governments, and law both in former colonies and in the West was seen as a rule imposed by some on others, often with systematic distortions (Abel 1982; Burman and Harrell-Bond 1979; Chanock 1985 [1998]; Fallers 1969; Galanter 1989; Moore 1986a, 1986b; Nader 1980). For some, domination and resistance were the analytic preoccupation. But at the same time, the culture-minded continued with their own form of legal analysis, attending to the variety of ways that people conceived the world, themselves, and their situations, and continued to presume that these cultural conceptions were causative.

In the United States this was the period of the Vietnam War, with its accompanying protests, of the civil rights movement, the women's movement, and overshadowing all, the Cold War. It is not surprising that there should have been an accompanying anthropological critique of legal authority. And on the theoretical plane, with the attribution of agency to the anthropological subject, the importance of action and choice modified the earlier dominant vision of normative rules as the central concern of cultural and legal analysis.

A broadened definition of reglementary control emerged. Control came to be seen as exercised in and by multiple social fields. The perception that many sites of control existed simultaneously redefined the state as only one among many sources of mandatory obligation. Debating the concept of semi-autonomous social fields and the idea of legal pluralism, legal anthropology redefined its object and itself.

Could one identify the newest concern in legal anthropology today? As I see it exemplified in the three studies I have just described, that concern is with a very much wider vision of the political milieu in which law is imbricated. They inspect the legal data for inputs and events in the global political turbulence of the day. Whether it is the law-related control of intellectual property, the definition of human rights, or the accountability of persons for the policies of regimes, it is evident that nothing is merely local in its formation or in its repercussions.

As I see it, their commentary, direct and indirect, on the possibility of realizing democracy is profoundly important and innovative. They are using their fieldwork to show the negative political implications of actions they have witnessed. They are saying that if what they have described continues, open democratic discourse is unachievable, human rights will be trodden underfoot, cycles of violence may well repeat themselves.

This approach is important because it involves a newly selective use of fieldwork data to comment on the large cultural and political entities which the fieldwork describes. Within the mixed and miscellaneous aggregations that are the state and that compose the global scene, this approach focuses on the elements that are willed legal creations. It is the potential future of that intentionally constructed dimension that these three works address.[7] They involve small-scale fieldwork, but comment on large-scale issues. The two levels are harnessed when the writer asks whether the field work data show that there are major obstacles that stand in the way of realizing the freedoms and accountabilities that are part of the ideal of a liberal democracy.

These works ask, 'What kind of a world is it in which these particular events are actually happening? Is democracy possible?' They use fieldwork on legal issues to identify legal and non-legal practices that stand in the way. In the process they redefine the scope and direction of anthropological inference. They ask what kind of a political totality could accommodate what they describe.[8] Coombe, Wilson, and Borneman directly confront the legal production of political consequences. That is the way they have framed their analyses.

They are not just talking about what is going on. They also are talking about what could go on. They are willing to consider the democratic ideal, while pointing out how far short people are of realizing it. They are treating their own critical commentary as a form of social action. They are moved to question the damaging effects of many laws and legal institutions. But they are also mindful that in some countries and in some international institutions, law is being used for reconstructive purposes. It can make social disasters, but in some situations it can help to prevent and repair them.

When anthropologists are moved to ask under what conditions legal institutions can contribute to democratic practice, they are inadvertently showing some small signs of optimism about the possibilities for intentional action. Such enquiries demonstrate that even a habitually sceptical profession can acknowledge that perhaps things could be better. At the very least, situations could be better understood.

To this end, anthropology has expanded the scope of its own scholarly analysis by contextualizing legal field materials more extensively and more deeply. It has always known that law is a major political instrument, and it has always had something to say about the way law has been used. But in recent decades it has gone further, it has aspired to alter the way law is conceived.

NOTES

This was originally presented as the Huxley Memorial Lecture at the University of Manchester in 1999 at the opening session of a symposium celebrating the fiftieth anniversary of the founding of Manchester's department of anthropology.

1   There are two domains that I do not have space to discuss, but which are so important that they must at least be mentioned here. One is the study of property, the other is the sociolinguistics of law.

   Property. There is a vast body of rich material dealing with the idea of property, not amenable to brief characterization. It touches on everything from kinship to inheritance, from collective to individual 'ownership' of land, from the redistribution of land to economic development, and beyond (see Low 1996 on worldwide attempts to redistribute land; Peters 1994 on dividing the commons).

   In the context of economic development, systems of land tenure have often received attention from anthropologists. Four institutions in particular are associated with this work. The Laboratoire d'anthropologie juridique in Paris, directed by M. Alliot and E. Le Roy, and the Centre Droit et Cultures at the University of Paris X-Nanterre, founded by R. Verdier, have produced studies on African property systems. The Land Tenure Center at the University of Wisconsin is concerned with the comparative study of land tenure systems all over the world. At the Agricultural University of Wageningen in the Netherlands, F. von Benda Beckmann focuses on property in Indonesia. Together with K. von Benda Beckmann, he has produced an important series of publications (1979; 1985; 1994; & with H. Spiertz 1996).

   Sociolinguistic approaches to law. A number of illuminating, relatively recent publications use sociolinguistic techniques to analyse legal materials (e.g., Conley & O'Barr 1990; 1998; Mertz 1994; O'Barr 1982). The analysis of the form of legal texts, attention to the verbal disciplines used in legal proceedings, and the treatment of speech as text have been significant methodological additions to the tool kit of legal anthropology.

   A particularly clear and subtle recent work that shows what can be done is Hirsch (1998). She uses detailed linguistic analysis to show the effect of gendered speech in litigation in East Africa. She shows that the language used by women to describe their situation, to make claims, and to carry on legal disputes, at once describes and illustrates their predicament and how they feel about it.

   Attention to the linguistic dimension of the legal will doubtless grow. After all, it is the law that gives many performative statements and written acts their ultimate authoritative efficacy.

2   There are a few exceptions to the abandonment of comparison. For example, Newman (1983) uses a Marxisant approach combined with Murdock-like quantitative comparisons. For new kinds of comparison, see Greenhouse (1996) and Bowen and Petersen (1999). Of course, comparative law continues as a specialty within the legal profession and involves some of the same theoretical problems relating to what is being compared that anthropologists have addressed (see Moore 1986b; Riles 1999).

3 In the same period, a major international survey was undertaken to inspect the general problem of access to legal institutions (Cappelletti & Garth 1978–9; Cappelletti & Tallon 1973). Alternatives to the courts were sought in many countries.

4 There was an earlier, non-ethnic conception within anthropology of the multiple sites where law could be generated, Pospisil's theory of legal levels. He postulated that every social sub-group had its own internal 'law', and he alluded to groups such as families, clans, and communities. He (1971: 273) said: 'We have to ask whether a given society has only one consistent legal system . . . or whether there are several such systems'.

5 See Moore (1989b) on the production of pluralism as a process; Greenhouse (1996) on democracy and ethnography.

6 See Moore (1973) on semi-autonomous social fields, a paper from which Griffiths drew inspiration and which he cites with approval.

7 I have tried to address this issue in various ways in my own recent writings (e.g. Moore 1998; 1999; forthcoming).

8 These questions that revolve around 'What kind of a world is this?' are paraphrasing the tragic, sardonic cry of Ken Saro Wiwa when he was brought to the gallows to be hanged and the mechanism failed, and he was brought back again, and again, and he said 'What kind of a country is this?' Packed in those words is a commentary not only on the incompetence of the hangmen, but on the judges and the prosecutors and the Nigerian state, the whole apparatus that condemned him to death (see Soyinka 1996).

REFERENCES

Abel, R. (ed.) 1982. *The politics of informal justice*. (2 vols.) New York: Academic Press.

Benda Beckmann, F. von 1979. *Property in social continuity*. The Hague: Martinus Nijhoff.

——with K. von Benda Beckmann 1985. Transformation and change in Minangkabau. In *Change and continuity in Minangkabau: local, regional, and historical perspectives on West Sumatra* (eds) L. Thomas and F. von Benda Beckmann, 235–78. Athens, Ohio: Ohio University Center for International Studies, Center for Southeast Asian Studies.

——with—— 1994. Property, politics and conflict: Ambon and Minangkabau compared. *Law and Society Review* 28, 589–607.

——with——and H. Spiertz 1996. Water rights and policy. In *The role of law in natural resource management* (eds) J. Spiertz and M. Wiber, 77–99. The Hague: Vuga.

Bohannan, P. 1957. *Justice and judgment among the Tiv*. London: Oxford University Press.

Borneman, J. 1997. *Settling accounts*. Princeton: University Press.

Bourdieu, P. 1977. *Outline of a theory of practice*. Cambridge: University Press.

——1987. The force of law: toward a sociology of the juridical field. *Hastings Law Journal* 38, 814–53.

Bowen, J. and R. Petersen (eds.) 1999. *Critical comparisons in politics and culture*. Cambridge: University Press.

Burman, S. and B. Harrell-Bond (eds.) 1979. *The imposition of law*. New York: Academic Press.

Caplan, P. (ed.) 1995. *Understanding disputes*. Oxford: Berg.

Cappelletti, M. and B. Garth (eds.) 1978–9. *A world survey* (2 vols.), *Access to justice* (gen. ed.) M. Cappelletti, vol. 1. Alphen aan den Rijn: Sijthoff and Nordhoff; Milan: A Giuffre.

——and——(eds.) 1981. *Access to justice and the welfare state*. Alphen aan den Rijn: Sijthoff.

—— and D. Tallon 1973. *Fundamental guarantees of the parties in civil litigation*. Dobbs Ferry, N.Y.: Oceana.

Chanock, M. 1985 (1998). *Law, custom and social order*. Cambridge: University Press.

Collier, J. 1973. *Law and social change in Zinacantan*. Stanford: University Press.

—— 1975. Legal processes. *Annual Review of Anthropology* 4, 121–44.

Colson, E. 1971. The impact of the colonial period on the definition of land rights. In *Profiles of change: African society and colonial rule* (ed.) V. Turner, 193–215, *Colonialism in Africa* (comp.) L.H. Gann, vol. 3. Cambridge: University Press.

Comaroff, J. 1995. The discourse of rights in colonial South Africa: subjectivity, sovereignty, modernity. In *Identity, politics and rights* (eds.) A. Sarat and T. Kearns, 193–236. Ann Arbor: University of Michigan Press.

—— and J. Comaroff 1991. *Of revelation and revolution*. Chicago: University Press.

—— and —— 1997. *Of revelation and revolution*, vol. 2. Chicago: University Press.

—— and S. Roberts 1981. *Rules and processes: The cultural logic of dispute in an African context*. Chicago: University Press.

Conley, J. and W. O'Barr 1990. *Rules versus relationships*. Chicago: University Press.

—— and —— 1998. *Just words: law, language and power*. Chicago: University Press.

Coombe, R. 1998. *The cultural life of intellectual properties*. Durham, N.C.: Duke University Press.

Durkheim, E. 1961. *The elementary forms of the religious life*. New York: Collier.

Fallers, L. 1969. *Law without precedent*. Chicago: Aldine.

Fitzpatrick, P. 1992. *The mythology of modern law*. London: Routledge & Chapman Hall.

—— and A. Hunt (eds.) 1987. *Critical legal studies*. Oxford: Blackwell.

French, R. 1995. *The golden yoke: the legal cosmology of Buddhist Tibet*. Ithaca: Cornell University Press.

Furnivall, J. 1948. *Colonial policy and practice*. London: Cambridge University Press.

Galanter, M. 1989. *Law and society in modern India*. Delhi: Oxford University Press.

Geertz, C. 1983. *Local knowledge: further essays in interpretive anthropology*. New York: Basic Books.

Gluckman, M. 1955. *The judicial process among the Barotse of Northern Rhodesia*. Manchester: University Press for the Rhodes Livingston Institute.

—— 1965. *The ideas in Barotse jurisprudence*. New Haven: Yale University Press.

—— (ed.) 1969. *Ideas and procedures in African customary law*. Oxford: University Press for the International African Institute.

Gordon, R. and M. Meggitt 1985. *Law and order in the New Guinea Highlands*. Hanover, N.H.: University Press of New England.

Greenhouse, C. 1986. *Praying for justice*. Ithaca: Cornell University Press.

—— 1996. *A moment's notice*. Ithaca: Cornell University Press.

—— (ed.) with F. Strijbosch. 1993. *Legal pluralism in industrialized societies* (*Journal of Legal Pluralism* 33, special issue).

—— and R. Kheshti (eds.) 1998. *Democracy and ethnography*. Albany: State University of New York Press.

——, B. Yngvesson and D.M. Engel (eds.) 1994. *Law and community in three American towns*. Ithaca: Cornell University Press.

Griffiths, A. 1997. *In the shadow of marriage: gender and justice in an African community*. Chicago: University Press.

Griffiths, J. 1986. What is legal pluralism? *Journal of Legal Pluralism and Unofficial Law* 24, 1–55.

Gulliver, P. 1963. *Social control in an African society*. Boston: University Press.

—— 1969. Introduction. In *Law in culture and society* (ed.) L. Nader, 11–23. Chicago: Aldine.

——(ed.) 1978. *Cross-examinations: essays in memory of Max Gluckman*. Leiden: E. J. Brill.

Habermas, J. 1979. *Communication and the evolution of society*. Boston: Beacon Press.

Hamnett, I. (ed.) 1977. *Social anthropology and law* (ASA Monograph 14). London: Academic Press.

Hirsch, S. 1994. Kadhi's courts as complex sites of resistance: the state, Islam, and gender in post-colonial Kenya. In *Contested states* (eds.) S. Hirsch and M. Lazarus-Black, 207–30. London: Routledge.

——1998. *Pronouncing and persevering: gender and the discourse of disputing in an African Islamic court*. Chicago: University Press.

Hoebel, E. 1954. *The law of primitive man*. Cambridge, Mass: Harvard University Press.

Hooker, M. 1975. *Legal pluralism*. Oxford: University Press.

Kelman, M. 1987. *A guide to critical legal studies*. Cambridge, Mass: Harvard University Press.

Kuper, L. and M.G. Smith (eds.) 1969. *Pluralism in Africa*. Berkeley: University of California Press.

Lazarus-Black, M. 1994. *Legitimate acts and illegal encounters: law and society in Antigua and Barbuda*. Washington: Smithsonian Institution Press.

Llewellyn, K. and E. Hoebel 1941. *The Cheyenne way*. Norman, Ok.: University of Oklahoma Press.

Low, D. 1996. *The egalitarian moment: Asia and Africa, 1950–1980*. Cambridge: University Press.

Maybury-Lewis, D. (ed.) 1984. *The prospects for plural societies* (Proceedings of the American Ethnological Society, 1982) Washington, D.C.: American Ethnological Society.

Merry, S. 1988. Legal pluralism. *Law and Society Review* 22, 869–96.

——1990. *Getting justice and getting even: legal consciousness among working-class Americans*. Chicago: University Press.

Mertz, E. 1994. Legal language: pragmatics, poetics and social power. *Annual Review of Anthropology* 23, 435–55.

Moore, S. F. 1969. Law and anthropology. In *Biennial Review of Anthropology* (ed.) B. Siegel, 52–300. Stanford: University Press.

——1970. Politics, procedures and norms in changing Chagga law. **Africa** (October), 321–44.

——1973. Law and social change: the semi-autonomous social field as an appropriate subject of study. *Law and Society Review* 7, 719–46.

——1975a. Selection for failure in a small social field: Kilimanjaro, 1968–69. In *Symbol and politics in communal ideaology* (eds.) S. F. Moore and B. Myerhoff, 109–43. Ithaca: Cornell University Press.

——1975b. Epilogue: uncertainties in situations: indeterminacies in culture. In *Symbol and politics in communal ideaology* (eds.) S. F. Moore and B. Myerhoff, 210–39. Ithaca: Cornell University Press.

——1978. *Law as process*. London: Routledge & Kegan Paul.

——1986a. Legal systems of the world: an introductory guide to classification, typological interpretations, and bibliographical resources. In *Law and the social sciences* (eds) L. Lipson and S. Wheeler, 11–62. New York: Russell Sage Foundation for the Social Science Research Council.

——1986b. *Social facts and fabrications: 'customary' law on Kilimanjaro 1880–1980*. Cambridge: University Press.

——1989a. History and the redefinition of custom on Kilimanjaro. In *History and power in the study of law* (eds.) J. Starr and J. Collier, 277–301. Ithaca: Cornell University Press.

——1989b. The production of cultural pluralism as a process. *Public Culture* 1: 2, 26–48.

——1998. Changing African land tenure: reflections on the incapacities of the state. *European Journal of Development Research* 10: 2, 33–49.

—— 1999. Systematic judicial and extra-judicial injustice: preparations for future account-ability. In *Memory and the postcolony: African anthropology and the critique of power* (ed.) R. Werbner, 126–51. London: Zed Books.

—— forthcoming. An international legal regime and the context of conditionality. In *Trans-national legal process* (ed.) M. Likosky. Oxford: University Press.

Nader, L. (ed.) 1969. *Law in culture and society.* Chicago: Aldine Press.

—— (ed.) 1980. *No access to law: alternatives to the American judicial system.* New York: Academic Press.

—— 1990. *Harmony ideology: justice and control in a Zapotec mountain village.* Stanford: University Press.

—— 1992. From legal processing to mind processing. *Family and Conciliation Courts Review* 30, 468–73.

—— 1993. Controlling processes in the practice of law: hierarchy and pacification in the movement to re-form dispute ideology. *The Ohio State Journal on Dispute Resolution 9,* 1–25.

—— 1999. Pushing the limits: eclecticism on purpose. *Political and Legal Anthropology Review* 22, 106–10.

—— (ed.) with H. Todd 1978. *The disputing process: disputing in ten societies.* New York: Columbia University Press.

Newman, K. 1983. *Law and economic organization: a comparative study of preindustrial societies.* Cambridge: University Press.

O'Barr, W. 1982. *Linguistic evidence: language, power and strategy in the courtroom.* New York: Academic Press.

Peters, P. 1994. *Dividing the commons; politics, policy and culture in Botswana.* Charlottes-ville: University Press of Virginia.

Posner, R. 1998. Pragmatic adjudication. In *The revival of pragmatism* (ed.) M. Dickstein, 235–53. Durham, N.C.: Duke University Press.

Pospisil, L. 1971. *Anthropology of law: a comparative theory.* New York: Harper & Row.

Riles, A. 1999. Wigmore's treasure box: comparative law in the era of information. *Harvard International Law Journal* 40, 221–83.

Roberts, R. and K. Mann (eds.) 1991. *Law in colonial Africa.* Portsmouth, N.H.: Heinemann Educational.

Rosen, L. 1980–1. Equity and discretion in a modern Islamic legal system. *Law and Society Review* 15, 217–45.

—— 1989. *The anthropology of justice: law as culture in Islamic society.* Cambridge: Univer-sity Press.

Rouland, N. 1988. *Anthropologie juridique.* Paris: Presses universitaires de France.

Smith, M.G. 1965. *The plural society in the British West Indies.* Berkeley: University of California Press.

Snyder, F. 1981*a.* Colonialism and legal form: the creation of customary law in Senegal. *Journal of Legal Pluralism* 19, 49–90.

—— 1981*b. Capitalism and legal change.* New York: Academic Press.

Soyinka, W. 1996. *The open sore of a continent.* Oxford: University Press.

Starr, J. and J. Collier 1989. *History and power in the study of law.* Ithaca: Cornell University Press.

Tambiah, S.J. 1996. *Leveling crowds.* Berkeley: University of California Press.

Taylor, C. 1992. *Multiculturalism and the politics of recognition.* Princeton: University Press.

Teubner, G. 1992. The two faces of Janus: rethinking legal pluralism. *Cardozo Law Review* 13, 1443–62.

Weber, M. 1978. *Economy and society.* Berkeley: University of California Press.

Werbner, R. 1984. The Manchester School in South Central Africa. *Annual Review of Anthropology* 13, 157–85.

Wilson, R. (ed.) 1997. *Human rights: culture and context*. London: Pluto Press.

——— 2000. Reconciliation and revenge in post-apartheid South Africa. *Current Anthropology* 41, 75–98.

Yngvesson, B. 1993. *Virtuous citizens, disruptive subjects*. London: Routledge.

——— and P. Hennessey 1974–5. Small claims, complex disputes. *Law and Society Review* 9, 219–74.

Index

Printed and bound by CPI Group (UK) Ltd, Croydon, CR0 4YY

24/10/2021

03088600-0001